A·N·N·U·A·L E·D·I·T·I·O·N·S

DEVIANT BEHAVIOR 00/01
Fourth Edition

Editor

Lawrence M. Salinger
Arkansas State University

Dr. Lawrence M. Salinger is associate professor of criminology and sociology in the Department of Criminology, Sociology, Social Work, and Geography at Arkansas State University in Jonesboro, Arkansas. He received his Ph.D. from Washington State University in 1992. Dr. Salinger is also a coeditor of *White-Collar Crime: Classic and Contemporary Views*, 3rd edition. In his courses, he emphasizes critical thinking, application of knowledge and theory to policy making, and humor.

Dushkin/McGraw-Hill
Sluice Dock, Guilford, Connecticut 06437

Visit us on the Internet
http://www.dushkin.com/annualeditions/

D1247439

Credits

1. Deviance
Unit photo—United Nations photo by John Isaac.
2. Crime
Unit photo—Courtesy of U.S. Drug Enforcement Agency.
3. Family Deviance
Unit photo—New York Times photo by Bill Aller.
4. Organizational Deviance
Unit photo—United Nations photo.
5. Drugs
Unit photo—United Nations photo by Jane Schreibman.
6. Sexual Deviance
Unit photo—Courtesy of EPA/Documerica.
7. Mental Illness
Unit photo—WHO photo by Jean Mohr.
8. Societal Deviance and Social Inequality
Unit photo—United Nations photo by Shelley Rother.
9. International Perspectives on Deviance
Unit photo—AP photo by David Brauchli.

Cataloging in Publication Data
Main entry under title: Annual Editions: Deviant Behavior 2000/2001.
    1. Deviant behavior—Periodicals. I. Salinger, Lawrence M., *comp.* II. Title: Deviant behavior.
ISBN 0-07-236536-6   302.542'.05   ISSN 1091-9953

Fourth Edition

Cover image © 2000 PhotoDisc, Inc.

Printed in the United States of America   1234567890BAHBAH543210   Printed on Recycled Paper

Copyright

iii

In publishing ANNUAL EDITIONS we recognize the enormous role played by the magazines, newspapers, and journals of the public press in providing current, first-rate educational information in a broad spectrum of interest areas. Many of these articles are appropriate for students, researchers, and professionals seeking accurate, current material to help bridge the gap between principles and theories and the real world. These articles, however, become more useful for study when those of lasting value are carefully collected, organized, indexed, and reproduced in a low-cost format, which provides easy and permanent access when the material is needed. That is the role played by ANNUAL EDITIONS.

New to ANNUAL EDITIONS is the inclusion of related World Wide Web sites. These sites have been selected by our editorial staff to represent some of the best resources found on the World Wide Web today. Through our carefully developed topic guide, we have linked these Web resources to the articles covered in this ANNUAL EDITIONS reader. We think that you will find this volume useful, and we hope that you will take a moment to visit us on the Web at *http://www.dushkin.com* to tell us what you think.

Deviant behavior exists throughout our society. We come into contact with many common forms of deviance on a daily basis. One cannot pick up the morning paper or watch the evening news without being exposed to murder, rape, and other types of crimes. It is common to read about homosexuality, prostitution, and mental illness. Our exposure to the topic of drugs has reached the point that it is hard to watch a television program without drugs as the subject of the show and also the topic of a commercial between its episodes. At the same time, less common forms of deviance exist. Some, such as naked people "streaking" down the road, exist as short-time fads, while others, such as "body art," appear to have established a strong foothold in our society.

Deviance is socially defined, and thus is relative to the changing social context of the society. For example, if a woman has her ears pierced for the purpose of wearing earrings, she is considered nondeviant. However, if she chooses to have her nose, lip, or navel pierced for the purpose of wearing a ring, her behavior may be considered deviant by some segments of society. Since deviance and its social definition are subject to change, texts are often out of date by the time they are published. Furthermore, the articles found in traditional readers tend to place a greater emphasis on theories of deviance and less emphasis on behaviors. *Annual Editions: Deviant Behavior 00/01* attempts to maintain currency by providing the most up-to-date materials available on a wide range of topics.

This anthology contains units concerning general deviance, crime, family deviance, occupational deviance, organizational deviance, drugs, sexual deviance, mental illness, social inequality as deviance, and international deviance. The articles were selected because they are current and informative. Also, each article was chosen on the assumption that I would want to read it if I were a student. The ordering of units and articles follows no particular deviant-behavior textbook, but rather allows for the use of this volume as a useful supplement for any textbook.

Included in this volume are several features designed to be useful to students and professors alike. These include a *topic guide* for finding articles dealing with a specific subject; the *table of contents* abstracts, which summarize each article and feature key concepts in bold italics; and, preceding each unit, an *overview* that provides a background for informed reading of the articles, emphasizes critical issues, and presents challenge questions.

I would like to thank my graduate assistant Arlene Barsness for her gracious assistance in helping me complete this edition.

We would like to know what you think of the selections contained in this edition, so we would like you to fill out the *article rating form* on the last page. Many of the articles will be changed or retained based on your comments. If you wish, please feel free to send e-mail to me at lars@shoshoni.astate.edu.

Lawrence M. Salinger

Lawrence M. Salinger
Editor

Contents

UNIT 1

Deviance

Five articles discuss what deviance is and review some of the current behaviors considered deviant.

UNIT 2

Crime

Criminal deviance in today's society is examined in the five unit articles.

The concepts in bold italics are developed in the article. For further expansion please refer to the Topic Guide and the Index.

UNIT 3

Family Deviance

Five articles address deviance in the context of family relationships.

The concepts in bold italics are developed in the article. For further expansion please refer to the Topic Guide and the Index.

UNIT 4

Organizational Deviance

The five unit selections discuss how people in working situations abuse their roles and how organizations work to cause social disruption.

The concepts in bold italics are developed in the article. For further expansion please refer to the Topic Guide and the Index.

UNIT 5

Drugs

The unit's five articles address the impact of illegal and legal drugs on the social order.

The concepts in bold italics are developed in the article. For further expansion please refer to the Topic Guide and the Index.

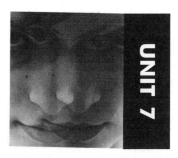

Sexual Deviance

Five unit articles review some of the
current forms of sexual deviance.

Mental Illness

The unit's five selections address
various forms of deviant behavior
as reflected by mental differences.

The concepts in bold italics are developed in the article. For further expansion please refer to the Topic Guide and the Index.

UNIT 8

Societal Deviance and Social Inequality

The seven selections in this section review some of the inequalities in today's social structure.

The concepts in bold italics are developed in the article. For further expansion please refer to the Topic Guide and the Index.

UNIT 9

International Perspectives on Deviance

Five unit selections examine several
international forms of deviance.

The concepts in bold italics are developed in the article. For further expansion please refer to the Topic Guide and the Index.

This topic guide suggests how the selections and World Wide Web sites found in the next section of this book relate to topics likely to be of interest to students and professionals involved with the study of deviant behavior. It is useful for locating interrelated articles and Web sites for reading and research. The guide is arranged alphabetically according to topic.

The relevant Web sites, which are numbered and annotated on pages 4 and 5, are easily identified by the Web icon (◉) under the topic articles. By linking the articles and the Web sites by topic, this ANNUAL EDITIONS reader becomes a powerful learning and research tool.

TOPIC AREA	TREATED IN	TOPIC AREA	TREATED IN
Child Abuse	14. Perils of Polygamy 15. Consequences of Violence 45. Bitter Harvest 47. State Abandons Kidnapped Kids ◉ *11, 13, 18, 34, 36*	**Ethics**	2. Darwin's Truth, Jefferson's Vision 4. Mortality around the World 5. Marks of Mystery 7. We Are Training Our Kids to Kill 8. Stopping Abuse in Prison 11. Problem with Marriage 13. How Are We Doing with *Loving?* 16. American Sweatshop 18. It's What's for Dinner 19. What Doctors Don't Know 35. Mental Health Reform 39. Does Silencio = Muerte? 40. Hunger in America 41. Q: Should Juries Nullify Laws? ◉ *3, 5, 16, 17, 18, 20*
Children	2. Darwin's Truth, Jefferson's Vision 7. We Are Training Our Kids to Kill 8. Stopping Abuse in Prison 11. Problem with Marriage 12. I'm O.K. You're O.K. 13. How Are We Doing with *Loving?* 14. Perils of Polygamy 15. Consequences of Violence 26. Where'd You Learn *That?* 36. Where Bias Begins 37. Corporate Welfare 43. Crimes of War 45. Bitter Harvest 46. Is AIDS Forever? 54. State Abandons Kidnapped Kids ◉ *11, 12, 13, 15, 34, 36*		
		Family Violence	4. Mortality around the World 6. Men, Honor and Murder 14. Perils of Polygamy 15. Consequences of Violence 45. Bitter Harvest ◉ *6, 8, 11, 12, 13, 15*
Cover-Ups	8. Stopping Abuse in Prison 16. American Sweatshop 18. It's What's for Dinner 19. What Doctor's Don't Know 38. Plucking Workers 42. Wrong Men on Death Row 43. Crimes of War 45. Bitter Harvest 46. Is AIDS Forever? 47. State Abandons Kidnapped Kids ◉ *6, 16, 17, 18*	**Governmental Misconduct**	8. Stopping Abuse in Prison 9. Can Hackers Be Stopped? 16. American Sweatshop 17. Razing Appalachia 18. It's What's for Dinner 19. What Doctors Don't Know 20. Sex @ Work: What Are the Rules? 35. Mental Health Reform 37. Corporate Welfare 38. Plucking Workers 40. Hunger in America 41. Q: Should Juries Nullify Laws? 43. Crimes of War 45. Bitter Harvest 46. Is AIDS Forever? 47. State Abandons Kidnapped Kids ◉ *6, 10, 17, 20, 21*
Crime	6. Men, Honor and Murder 7. We Are Training Our Kids to Kill 8. Stopping Abuse in Prison 9. Can Hackers Be Stopped? 10. Stolen Identity 14. Perils of Polygamy 15. Consequences of Violence 23. Crank 24. More Reefer Madness 25. Beyond Legalization 27. Sex Industry 28. Who Owns Prostitution? 41. Q: Should Juries Nullify Laws? 42. Wrong Men on Death Row 43. Crimes of War 44. Yakuza Inc. 45. Bitter Harvest 47. State Abandons Kidnapped Kids ◉ *6, 8, 9, 16, 17, 18, 20, 21, 26*	**Heterosexual Deviance/ Homosexuality**	3. Taboo: Don't Even Think about It! 13. How Are We Doing with *Loving?* 14. Perils of Polygamy 20. Sex @ Work: What Are the Rules? 21. Addicted 22. Passion Pills 26. Where'd You Learn *That?* 27. Sex Industry 28. Who Owns Prostitution? 29. Pleasure of the Pain 30. Gay No More? 45. Bitter Harvest 46. Is AIDS Forever? ◉ *11, 14, 20, 24, 25, 26, 27, 30*
Crime Rates	6. Men, Honor and Murder 7. We Are Training Our Kids to Kill 25. Beyond Legalization 41. Q: Should Juries Nullify Laws? ◉ *11, 20, 21*	**Illegal Drugs**	21. Addicted 23. Crank 24. More Reefer Madness 25. Beyond Legislation ◉ *19, 20, 21, 23*
Divorce	11. Problem with Marriage 12. I'm O.K. You're O.K. 13. How Are We Doing with *Loving?* 14. Perils of Polygamy 15. Consequences of Violence 37. Corporate Welfare 47. State Abandons Kidnapped Kids ◉ *12, 15*	**Illegal Sex**	8. Stopping Abuse in Prison 20. Sex @ Work: What Are the Rules? 27. Sex Industry 28. Who Owns Prostitution? 29. Pleasure of the Pain 45. Bitter Harvest 46. Is AIDs Forever? ◉ *11, 24, 26, 27, 30*

● AE: Deviant Behavior

The following World Wide Web sites have been carefully researched and selected to support the articles found in this reader. If you are interested in learning more about specific topics found in this book, these Web sites are a good place to start. The sites are cross-referenced by number and appear in the topic guide on the previous two pages. Also, you can link to these Web sites through our DUSHKIN ONLINE support site at *http://www.dushkin.com/online/*.

The following sites were available at the time of publication. Visit our Web site—we update DUSHKIN ONLINE regularly to reflect any changes.

General Sources: Deviance

1. Behavior OnLine: The Mental Health and Behavioral Science Meeting Place
http://www.behavior.net
This site is unusual in that it provides meeting rooms with ongoing, real-time discussions of behavioral and psychological issues, as well as behavior-related sources.

2. Clinical Psychology Resources
http://www.psychologie.uni-bonn.de/kap/links_20.htm
This page contains Internet resources for clinical and abnormal psychology, behavioral medicine, and mental health.

3. Euthanasia and Physician Assisted Suicide: All Sides
http://www.religioustolerance.org/euthanas.htm
Many topics related to euthanasia are discussed at this simply arranged site, including definitions, historical beliefs, ethical questions, and euthanasia in different countries.

4. Psychology Research on the Net
http://psych.hanover.edu/APS/exponnet.html
Psychologically related experiments on the Internet can be found at this site. Biological psychology/neuropsychology, clinical psychology, developmental psychology, emotions, health psychology, personality, sensation/perception, and social psychology are just some of the areas addressed.

5. Yahoo! Full Coverage—Assisted Suicide Debate
http://headlines.yahoo.com/Full_Coverage/US/Assisted_Suicide/
This page is a compilation of links relating to assisted suicide and euthanasia. The site is constantly updated and offers links to the newest information on the subject.

Crime

6. Center for the Study and Prevention of Violence
http://www.colorado.edu/cspv/
The CSPV site is simple in layout, easy to navigate, and yet provides numerous valuable links and resources.

7. Death Penalty; Capital Punishment; Ethics; Punishment
http://ethics.acusd.edu/death_penalty.html
Covering many topics related to capital punishment, this site offers articles written from numerous viewpoints, including pieces written both about and by death row inmates.

8. Explanations of Criminal Behavior
http://www.uaa.alaska.edu/just/just110/crime2.html
Here is an excellent outline of the causes of crime, including major theories, which was prepared by Darryl Wood at the University of Alaska–Anchorage

9. National Fraud Information Center
http://www.fraud.org
This site features links to pages providing information on fraud, a searchable database, and links to other online resources.

10. Terrorism Research Center
http://www.terrorism.com/terrorism/index.html
The Terrorism Research Center features original research, counterterrorism documents, a comprehensive list of Web links, and monthly profiles of terrorist groups.

Family Deviance

11. Child Abuse: Statistics, Research, and Resources
http://www.jimhopper.com/abstats
This site, compiled by Jim Hopper of the Trauma Center of HRI Hospital in Brookline, Massachusetts, provides an extremely thorough insight into various aspects of child abuse.

12. Divorce Source: Family Law , Custody, Alimony, Support, and Visitation
http://www.divorcesource.com
Divorce Source provides divorce information pertaining to child custody, child support, alimony (spousal support), counseling, visitation, individual rights, taxes, the legal process, mediation, and property appraisals.

13. National Data Archive on Child Abuse and Neglect
http://www.ndacan.cornell.edu
This site is a convenient starting point for research on child abuse subjects. NDACAN's mission is to facilitate secondary analysis of relevant research data on child maltreatment.

14. Polygamy Page
http://www.familyman.u-net.com/polygamy.html
This site presents a pro-polygamy viewpoint and provides counterarguments to traditional religious objections to the practice of polygamy. It also provides links to Web sites.

15. Single Parent Resource: Articles
http://www.parentsplace.com/family/singleparent/
This site contains articles intended to help the single parent; topics range from budgetary concerns to psychological issues of raising children single-handedly.

Organizational Deviance

16. Institute for Business and Professional Ethics
http://www.depaul.edu/ethics/
The Institute site represents an attempt to pioneer a hypertext-linked ethics network throughout the Internet. Pages provide links to other ethics-related sites, as well as research articles on business ethics–related subjects.

17. Legalethics.com: The Internet Ethics Site
http://www.legalethics.com
The Legalethics site offers the legal profession links and references to ethics rules, regulations, and articles relating to the integration of the Internet into the practice of law.

18. National Labor Committee Homepage
http://www.nlcnet.org
This site, which provides articles and links relating to United States and international labor abuses, is maintained by the National Labor Committee, a human rights advocacy group, whose focus is the promotion and defense of worker's rights.

Drugs

19. The Center for Alcohol & Addiction Studies
http://center.butler.brown.edu
The Center for Alcohol & Addiction Studies, established by Brown University in 1982, promotes the identification, prevention, and effective treatment of alcohol and other drug-use problems through research, publications, education, and training. The site provides information related to drug addiction and links to medical resources online.

20. DEA—Home Page
http://www.usdoj.gov/dea/index.htm
The home page of the Drug Enforcement Administration provides articles and statistics on illegal-drug issues, information on DEA programs, and links to other Internet sources of drug-related material.

21. Indiana PRC—Drug Statistics Master Page
http://www.drugs.indiana.edu/drug_stats/home.html
This master source of statistics on the use of alcohol, tobacco, and other drugs includes the latest national survey results from the Indiana Prevention Resource Center and other servers.

22. The Institute of Alcohol Studies
http://www.ias.org.uk
The aim of the Institute of Alcohol Studies is to increase knowledge of alcohol and the social and health consequences of its misuse. This easy-to-navigate site offers fact sheets and a search engine.

23. Yahoo!—Substance Abuse Search Index
http://www.yahoo.com/Health/Mental_Health/ Diseases_and_Conditions/Substance_Abuse/
This is a good starting point for all topics related to substance addiction, with numerous links to research and programs available on the Internet.

Sexual Deviance

24. Kinsey Institute for Research in Sex, Gender, and Reproduction
http://www.indiana.edu/~kinsey/
The purpose of the Kinsey Institute's Web site is to support interdisciplinary research and the study of human sexuality. The site provides an online library of research articles from the Institute's 50 years of analyzing sex and social issues in the United States.

25. PlanetOut
http://www.planetout.com
PlanetOut is one of the major gay male and lesbian Web sites, featuring pages dedicated to legal, social, and political issues relating to this community.

26. Prostitution Issues: PENet—Prostitutes Education Network
http://www.bayswan.org/penet.html
This site provides a wide variety of articles related to prostitution. Legal aspects are covered, as well as statistics on prostitution in general and links to other online resources.

27. Sex Laws
http://www.geocities.com/CapitolHill/2269/
This site is based on a simple index of laws concerning sexual practices, organized by country and state. Links to related information are also provided.

Mental Illness

28. Ask NOAH About: Mental Health
http://www.noah.cuny.edu/illness/mentalhealth/mental.html
This enormous resource contains information about child and adolescent family problems, mental conditions and disorders, suicide prevention, and much more.

29. Mental Health Infosource: Disorders
http://www.mhsource.com/disorders/
This no-nonsense page lists hotlinks to psychological disorders pages, including anxiety, panic, phobic disorders, schizophrenia, and violent/self-destructive behaviors.

30. Sexual Recovery Institute
http://www.sexualrecovery.com
This site provides coverage of many issues related to sexual addiction and recovery, including online articles, self-tests, recovery resources, and treatments.

31. Sigmund Freud and the Freud Archives
http://plaza.interport.net/nypsan/freudarc.html
Internet resources related to Sigmund Freud can be accessed through this site. A collection of biographical materials and the Brill Library archives can be found here.

Societal Deviance and Social Inequality

32. Corporate Accountability Project
http://www.corporations.org/index.html
Full of information about corporate power and corporate welfare, this site will lead you to the fascinating underbelly of corporations, 51 of whom are counted in the 100 largest economies, rather than countries!

33. Stereotypes and Prejudices
http://remember.org/guide/History.root.stereotypes.html
The subjects of genocide, stereotypes, scapegoats, prejudices, and discrimination are explored are explored here in detail.

International Perspectives on Deviance

34. Coalition against Trafficking in Women
http://www.uri.edu/artsci/wms/hughes/catw/catw.htm
From this site there is access to personal testimony on global sexual exploitation of women and girls worldwide and a study of prostitution as a contemporary form of slavery.

35. Frontline: The Crime of Genocide
http://www.pbs.org/wgbh/pages/frontline/ shows/rwanda/reports/dsetexhe.html
This chapter from *Rwanda and Genocide in the Twentieth Century* by Alain Destexhe is an excellent discussion of genocide and its criminal intention.

36. Initiatives against Sexual Exploitation of Children: The Issues
http://www.crin.org/iasc/sekiss.htm
This site contains the full text of policy and briefing papers on initiatives against the sexual exploitation of children around the world, and contains many links to other sites.

We highly recommend that you review our Web site for expanded information and our other product lines. We are continually updating and adding links to our Web site in order to offer you the most usable and useful information that will support and expand the value of your Annual Editions. You can reach us at: *http://www.dushkin.com/annualeditions/.*

www.dushkin.com/online/

Unit Selections

1. **On the Sociology of Deviance,** Kai T. Erikson
2. **Darwin's Truth, Jefferson's Vision: Sociobiology and the Politics of Human Nature,** Melvin Konner
3. **Taboo: Don't Even Think about It!** Michael Ventura
4. **Mortality around the World,** Lawrence E. Sullivan
5. **Marks of Mystery,** Elizabeth Austin

Key Points to Consider

❖ Why is deviant behavior important to societies?

❖ Give examples of deviant behavior from the four perspectives outlined by Marshall Clinard and Robert Meier: statistical, absolutist, reactivist, and normative, in their book *Sociology of Behavior* (1995).

❖ How is deviant behavior socially defined?

❖ How would you define deviance?

 **Links**   **www.dushkin.com/online/**

1. **Behavior OnLine: The Mental Health and Behavioral Science Meeting Place**
   http://www.behavior.net
2. **Clinical Psychology Resources**
   http://www.psychologie.uni-bonn.de/kap/links_20.htm
3. **Euthanasia and Physician Assisted Suicide: All Sides**
   http://www.religioustolerance.org/euthanas.htm
4. **Psychology Research on the Net**
   http://psych.hanover.edu/APS/exponnet.html
5. **Yahoo! Full Coverage—Assisted Suicide Debate**
   http://headlines.yahoo.com/Full_Coverage/US/Assisted_Suicide/

These sites are annotated on pages 4 and 5.

Deviance exists wherever human beings coexist with one another. Émile Durkheim, in his book *The Rules of Sociological Method* (1982), discussed the importance of deviance in maintaining the existence of a society. He argued that deviance was necessary to the survival of a healthy society for three reasons. First, deviance socially defines the moral boundaries of acceptable behavior and unacceptable behavior within the society. Second, deviance promotes group solidarity among those persons whose behavior is socially defined as being acceptable. Third, deviance promotes socially change in a healthy society. Likewise, the term *deviance* and the conditions under which behaviors are labeled as deviant are also socially defined.

Marshall Clinard and Robert Meier, in their book *Sociology of Deviant Behavior* (1995:9), suggest that behaviors can be socially defined as deviant from four perspectives. The *statistical* perspective views behaviors that are statistically in the minority as deviance. For example, a person who is obese exceeds statistical weight limits for the general population. Therefore, obesity may be considered deviance. Likewise, the poverty-line index is a statistical measure of whether a family unit lives in poverty or not. Thus, a family living below the poverty-line index is engaging in deviance from this perspective. From the *absolutist* perspective, behaviors that are morally wrong and perceived as sin are necessarily deviant. For example, murder is a violation of the biblical Ten Commandments, and, therefore, it is deviance. In the same spirit, pro-life advocates view abortion as deviant. The *reactivist* perspective assumes that a behavior is deviant only if people react to it. For example, from the reactivist perspective, speeding is deviant only to the extent to which it is observed and reacted to by a police officer. The most common perspective for socially defining deviance is the *normative*. From the normative perspective, behavior is deviant if it violates societal norms. Norms may be defined as expectations for behavior (Clinard and Meier, 1995:9). Norms can be prescriptive or proscriptive (Clinard and Meier, 1995:11). Prescriptive norms tell us how we should act. For example, generally one should be joyful at a wedding. To act sad and somber may be considered deviant. Proscriptive norms tell us what we should not do. For example, shoplifting is deviant because it violates the proscriptive norm that one should not steal property that belongs to others. Norms can also be classified based on the severity of the behavior. Mores are strict norms, violations of which are considered extremely deviant. An example of such a norm is the proscription against murder. Violations of folkway norms, on the other hand, are considered minor violations of societal customs and traditions. For example, while a certain behavior may be considered to be disgusting, such as a child picking his nose, it is a violation of a folkway norm, rather than a morality-based norm, because it is a minor violation.

In addition to the various perspectives from which deviance can be socially defined, it is also the case that, in terms of behaviors, what is defined as deviant or not is relative. There are five factors associated with the "relativity of deviance" (Clinard and Meier, 1995:17). When a behavior occurred can determine whether it is defined as deviant. For example, in Texas up until September 1987 it was legal to drink alcoholic beverages while driving a vehicle. However, it was illegal to be drunk while driving a vehicle. Currently, it is illegal, and therefore deviant, to drink while driving a vehicle in Texas. Where the behavior occurs may also be useful in determining whether or not an act is deviant. Someone could, for example, live in a dry county, which means that alcohol cannot be purchased in the county. However, the county directly to the south is a wet county, which means that alcohol can be purchased in that county. The context, or situation, within which the behavior occurs may determine whether or not it is deviant. For example, if a professional boxer knocks out another boxer during a televised match, he wins a lot of money. If, on the other hand, he knocks out someone in a tavern, he has committed a violent crime. The person engaged in the action can determine whether or not a behavior is deviant. Consider this scenario: if a murder victim's mother kills the murderer in court, then the mother has committed murder. However, if the state executes the murderer under a legal mandate, its behavior may not be defined as deviant. Finally, who observes the behavior may determine whether or not an act comes to be socially defined as deviance. A punk rocker, for example, whose friend is wearing a ring through the navel may consider the act nondeviant. However, the ring-wearer's mother may view the behavior as deviant. These factors have an influence on the social definition of a particular behavior as deviance.

The readings in this unit provide examples of how different phenomena can become defined as deviance. For example, Michael Ventura discusses different taboos that exist in our culture and how they compare to taboos in other cultures. Taboos, to some extent, themselves define which behaviors are deviant and which are not. Likewise, there may be behaviors that we would normally agree on as being deviant, but not always. For example, scarring and scarification can be viewed differently, depending on how society views them. How different societies deal with death, in part, gives us a deeper understanding of the meanings that different cultures apply to a natural phenomenon. The articles in the remaining units of this anthology will deal with behaviors that are socially defined as well.

Deviance

On the Sociology of Deviance

Kai T. Erikson

Department of Psychiatry
Emory University

IN 1895 Emile Durkheim wrote a book called *The Rules of Sociological Method* which was intended as a working manual for persons interested in the systematic study of society. One of the most important themes of Durkheim's work was that sociologists should formulate a new set of criteria for distinguishing between "normal" and "pathological" elements in the life of a society. Behavior which looks abnormal to the psychiatrist or the judge, he suggested, does not always look abnormal when viewed through the special lens of the sociologist; and thus students of the new science should be careful to understand that even the most aberrant forms of individual behavior may still be considered normal from this broader point of view. To illustrate his argument, Durkheim made the surprising observation that crime was really a natural kind of social activity, "an integral part of all healthy societies."[1]

Durkheim's interest in this subject had been expressed several years before when *The Division of Labor in Society* was first published.[2] In that important book, he had suggested that crime (and by extension other forms of deviation) may actually perform a needed service to society by drawing people together in a common posture of anger and indignation. The deviant individual violates rules of conduct which the rest of the community holds in high respect; and when these people come together to express their outrage over the offense and to bear witness against the offender, they develop a tighter bond of solidarity than existed earlier. The excitement generated by the crime, in other words, quickens the tempo of interaction in the group and creates a climate in which the private sentiments of many separate persons are fused together into a common sense of morality.

Crime brings together upright consciences and concentrates them. We have only to notice what happens, particularly in a small town, when some moral scandal has just been committed. They stop each other on the street, they visit each other, they seek to come together to talk of the event and to wax indignant in common. From all the similar impressions which are exchanged, for all the temper that gets itself expressed, there emerges a unique temper... which is everybody's without being anybody's in particular. This the the public temper.[3]

The deviant act, then, creates a sense of mutuality among the people of a community by supplying a focus for group feeling. Like a war, a flood, or some other emergency, deviance makes people more alert to the interests they share in common and draws attention to those values which constitute the "collective conscience" of the community. Unless the rhythm of group life is punctuated by occasional moments of deviant behavior, presumably, social organization would be impossible.[4] ...

One of the earliest problems the sociologist encounters in his search for a meaningful approach to deviant behavior is that the subject itself does not seem to have any natural boundaries. Like people in any field, sociologists find it convenient to assume that the deviant person is somehow "different" from those of his fellows who manage to conform, but years of research into the problem have not yielded any important evidence as to what, if anything, this difference might be. Investigators have studied the character of the deviant's background, the content of his dreams, the shape of his skull, the substance of his thoughts—yet none of this information has enabled us to draw a clear line between the kind of person who commits deviant acts and the kind of person who does not. Nor can we gain a better perspective on the matter by shifting our attention away from the individual deviant and looking instead at the behavior he enacts. Definitions of deviance vary widely as we range over the various classes found in a single society or across the various cultures into which mankind is divided, and it soon becomes apparent that there are no objective properties which all deviant acts can be said to share in common—even within the confines of a given group. Behavior which qualifies one man for prison may qualify another for sainthood, since the quality

From *Wayward Puritans: A Study in the Sociology of Deviance* by Kai T. Erikson, pp. 3–8. © 1966. Reprinted by permission of Allyn and Bacon.

of the act itself depends so much on the circumstances under which it was performed and the temper of the audience which witnessed it.

This being the case, many sociologists employ a far simpler tactic in their approach to the problem—namely, to let each social group in question provide its own definitions of deviant behavior. In this study, as in others dealing with the same general subject,[5] the term "deviance" refers to conduct which the people of a group consider so dangerous or embarrassing or irritating that they bring special sanctions to bear against the persons who exhibit it. Deviance is not a property *inherent in* any particular kind of behavior; it is a property *conferred upon* that behavior by the people who come into direct or indirect contact with it. The only way an observer can tell whether or not a given style of behavior is deviant, then, is to learn something about the standards of the audience which responds to it.

This definition may seem a little awkward in practice, but it has the advantage of bringing a neglected issue into proper focus. When the people of a community decide that it is time to "do something" about the conduct of one of their number, they are involved in a highly intricate process. After all, even the worse miscreant in society conforms most of the time, if only in the sense that he uses the correct silver at dinner, stops obediently at traffic lights, or in a hundred other ways respects the ordinary conventions of his group. And if his fellows elect to bring sanctions against him for the occasions when he does misbehave, they are responding to a few deviant details scattered among a vast array of entirely acceptable conduct. The person who appears in a criminal court and is stamped a "thief" may have spent no more than a passing moment engaged in that activity, and the same can be said for many of the people who pass in review before some agency of control and return from the experience with a deviant label of one sort or another. When the community nominates someone to the deviant class, then, it is sifting a few important details out of the stream of behavior he has emitted and is in effect declaring that these details reflect the kind of person he "really" is. In law as well as in public opinion, the fact that someone has committed a felony or has been known to use narcotics can become the major identifying badge of his person: the very expression "he is a thief" or "he is an addict" seems to provide at once a description of his position in society and a profile of his character.

The manner in which a community sifts these telling details out of a person's overall performance, then, is an important part of its social control apparatus. And it is important to notice that the people of a community take a number of factors into account when they pass judgment on one another which are not immediately related to the deviant act itself: whether or not a person will be considered deviant, for instance, has something to do with his social class, his past record as an offender, the amount of remorse he manages to convey, and many similar concerns which take hold in the shifting mood of the community. Perhaps this is not so apparent in cases of serious crime or desperate illness, where the offending act looms so darkly that it obscures most of the other details of the person's life; but in the day-by-day sifting processes which take place throughout society this feature is always present. Some men who drink heavily are called alcoholics and others are not, some men who behave oddly are committed to hospitals and others are not, some men with no visible means of support are charged with vagrancy and others are not—and the difference between those who earn a deviant title in society and those who go their own way in peace is largely determined by the way in which the community filters out and codes the many details of behavior which come to its attention.

Once the problem is phrased in this manner we can ask: how does a community decide which of these behavioral details are important enough to merit special attention? And why, having made this decision, does it build institutions like prisons and asylums to detain the persons who perform them? The conventional answer to that question, of course, is that a society creates the machinery of control in order to protect itself against the "harmful" effects of deviation, in much the same way that an organism mobilizes its resources to combat an invasion of germs. Yet this simple view of the matter is apt to pose many more problems than it actually settles. As both Emile Durkheim and George Herbert Mead pointed out long ago, it is by no means evidence that all acts considered deviant in society are in fact (or even in principle) harmful to group life. It is undoubtedly true that no culture would last long if its members engaged in murder or arson among themselves on any large scale, but there is no real evidence that many other of the activities considered deviant throughout the world (certain dietary prohibitions are a prominent example) have any relationship to the group's survival. In our own day, for instance, we might well ask why prostitution or marihuana smoking or homosexuality are thought to endanger the health of the social order. Perhaps these activities *are* dangerous, but to accept this conclusion without a thoughtful review of the situation is apt to blind us to the important fact that people in every corner of the world manage to survive handsomely while engaged in practices which their neighbors regard as extremely abhorrent. . . .

Notes

1. Emile Durkheim, *The Rules of Sociological Method,* trans. S. A. Solovay and J. H. Mueller (Glencoe, Ill.: The Free Press, 1958), p. 67.
2. Emile Durkheim, *The Division of Labor in Society,* trans. George Simpson (Glencoe, Ill.: The Free Press, 1960).
3. *Ibid.,* p. 102.
4. A similar point was later made by George Herbert Mead in his very important paper "The Psychology of Punitive Justice," *American Journal of Sociology,* XXIII (March 1918), pp. 577–602.
5. See particularly the words of Edwin M. Lemert, Howard S. Becker, and John I. Kitsuse.

DARWIN'S TRUTH, JEFFERSON'S VISION

SOCIOBIOLOGY AND THE POLITICS OF HUMAN NATURE

BY MELVIN KONNER

As the new field of sociobiology has emerged during the past quarter century, it has met with firm and unrelenting opposition from prominent liberal critics. Sociobiology—also known as evolutionary psychology or neo-Darwinian theory—holds that many patterns of human behavior have a basis in evolution. Because this approach often suggests biological explanations of gender roles, it affronts many feminists. It has also drawn opposition from a group of biologists on the left who have raised general scientific and philosophical objections and have had great influence in shaping liberal opinion. The scientific critics have included highly respected figures in biology: Ruth Hubbard, Stephen Jay Gould, Richard Lewontin, and Jonathan Beckwith, among others. None in this group had done direct research on human behavior when sociobiology first emerged in the 1970s. Nonetheless, they immediately perceived a grave threat to liberal values, and their opposition has persisted ever since.

However respected the source, the criticism from this group has had little effect on the direction of scientific research: sociobiology is now firmly established as an accepted branch of normal science. As a result, liberal opinion about sociobiology has increasingly diverged from scientific opinion. If liberals are to understand why this has happened, they need to consider the possibility that Gould, Lewontin, and other prominent scientific critics were wrong in their attack on sociobiology in the first place.

Liberal uneasiness about sociobiology is understandable. A bad odor hangs about any social application of Darwinian ideas. Right-wing intellectuals in the past have abused Darwin's legacy in efforts to justify colonialism, imperialism, racism, and even mass murder. But the old ideological associations of scientific ideas are sometimes a poor guide to their present incarnations. To be sure, some conservative intellectuals infer from sociobiology that liberal reforms are doomed by human nature. But sociobiology today is not nineteenth-century social Darwinism reborn. As I intend to show, there is no conflict between liberal political philosophy and sociobiology. Indeed, quite the contrary is true. A deep understanding of the foundations of liberalism and the fundamental processes of Darwinian reasoning will readily show that the opposition to sociobiology has been based on a superficial view of both. The across-the-board attack on sociobiology was ill-conceived to begin with, and it is time to put it to rest.

THE ALTRUISM PUZZLE

Current intrusions of Darwin's theory into our awareness stem from the mid-1960s, when the British geneticist W. D. Hamilton proposed a solution to the problem of altruism. For traditional social scientists who see societies as functioning organisms, the existence of altruism does not pose a problem. In this view, without altruism societies would not work; groups that lacked it would not survive.

But this is no comfort to strict Darwinians, who see natural selection as operating at the level of individuals, even to the extent of disrupting the cohesiveness of societies. In their view, natural selection should have long since erased altruism. Hamilton's solution was that evolution selects for altruism if it is directed at relatives in proportion to their relatedness, for then the altruist's kin are more likely to survive to pass on the contributing genes. Thus kindnesses are instances of universal nepotism. Reciprocal altruism, proposed by Robert Trivers in the early 1970s, was a you-scratch-my-back-and-later-I'll-scratch-yours model. Like kin selection, it required no real genetic generosity, only delayed self-interest. With these ideas, biologists seemed to have little further need for the metaphor of society as organism.

These and related ideas were organized and popularized in the late 1970s by two scientists in particular. Edward O. Wilson, a Harvard zoologist previously known for meticulous research on insect behavior, published *Sociobiology,* a sweeping, voluminous summary of the new field, and *On Human Nature,* which, like the infamous last chapter of the earlier work, suggested some implications for humans. Richard Dawkins, a young British zoologist, wrote *The Selfish Gene,* which proposed that in evolution properly understood, only replicators matter; that genes are the fundamental biological replicators; and that an organism is basically a gene's way of making another gene.

This postulate leads to a key conclusion: evolution is not mainly about survival, but about

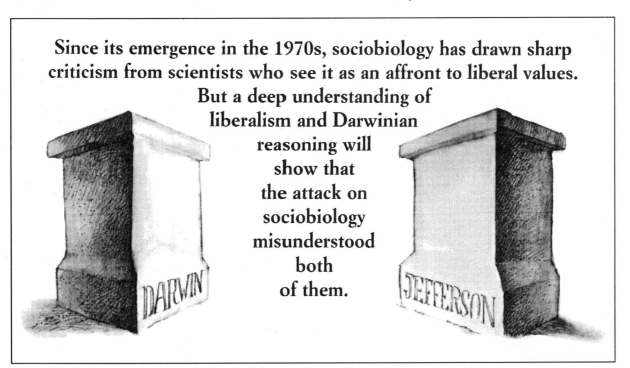

Since its emergence in the 1970s, sociobiology has drawn sharp criticism from scientists who see it as an affront to liberal values. But a deep understanding of liberalism and Darwinian reasoning will show that the attack on sociobiology misunderstood both of them.

reproduction. It is about keeping some genes in the stream of hereditary material—or as Dawkins aptly calls it, the "river out of Eden"—while culling others. Survival is dandy—when it serves reproduction. But if the two are at odds, reproductive demands will win every time. This conclusion in turn bears heavily on the question of gender differences. Males should in theory be less committed, more restless, and more aggressive than females. Females should be more careful in choosing their mates and less risk-prone in their lifelong reproductive strategies. This is basically because females—in mammals, at least—have much more to lose.

These and other claims of neo-Darwinian theory were scarcely ignored in the wider culture. *Sociobiology* was heralded on the front page of the *New York Times,* an extraordinary coup for what was basically a technical treatise, and *On Human Nature* won the Pulitzer Prize. *The Selfish Gene* became immediately popular and has stayed in print as a staple of undergraduate courses ever since. And a long excerpt from Robert Wright's fiercely Darwinian 1994 book *The Moral Animal* made a rare literary cover story at *Time.*

Wilson, Dawkins, and Wright are prose stylists of rare excellence, which contributed to the popularity of their work—and the concern it evoked among liberal biologists. Although *Sociobiology* was favorably reviewed in the *New York Review of Books* in 1975—by the respected British geneticist C. H. Waddington—a more common view was expressed in those pages later that year, in a long letter from 16 scientists, teachers, and physicians, including Steven Jay Gould, Ruth Hubbard, and Richard Lewontin, all colleagues of Wilson's at Harvard. It was titled "Against 'Sociobiology,' " and they were very much against it.

"What we are left with," they concluded, "is a particular theory about human nature, which has no scientific support, and which upholds the concept of a world with social arrangements remarkably similar to the world which E. O. Wilson inhabits. . . . Wilson joins the long parade of biological determinists whose work has served to buttress the institutions of their society by exonerating them from responsibility for social problems." Whether Wilson had done any such thing, inadvertently or otherwise, is debatable; a fair perusal of the book supports no such claim. But the letter set the tone for avowedly left-wing criticism of sociobiology ever since.

> Sociobiology has turned out to be neither the nefarious evil its critics feared, nor the complete scientific revolution its proponents hoped.

Writing a decade later in the mid-1980s, Lewontin, Steven Rose, and Leon Kamin had no doubt that sociobiology was popular because it helped to justify the economic policies of the Thatcher-Reagan era. In their book *Not In Our Genes,* they renounced the claim of objectivity for any sort of science and declared, "We share a commitment to the prospect of the creation of a more socially just—a socialist—society." They called for a "radical science movement" dedicated to "the possibility of a critical and liberatory science." Of course, this hoary rhetoric did not necessarily make them wrong, but their book was naive at best. They tendentiously attacked long outdated research on intelligence testing and struck out wildly against psychiatric and even neurological medications. Guilt by juxtaposition served in place of evidence and argument to make modern behavioral biologists of all kinds seem as much as possible like nineteenth-century racists.

Hardly anyone today would try to defend the positions on intelligence testing or psychiatry that those authors took then. Yet Lewontin, Gould, and other biologists with admittedly left-wing goals have continued to criticize sociobiology in only somewhat more muted terms. Criticism is welcome, of course. But because these scientists are so well respected—deservedly so, in the cases of Lewontin and Gould—their influence may extend beyond the power of their arguments. Neither has ever engaged in primary research in the human sciences, but both often proclaim sociobiology inapplicable to them. Gould has a well-earned major public platform in the form of a monthly column in Natural History, and he and Lewontin write regularly for the New York Review, which to its credit has also published the views of evolutionists such as John Maynard Smith.

The danger, though, is that the "anti" position may become so congenial for liberals that they ignore the almost universal acceptance of neo-Darwinian or sociobiological theory among researchers in natural history and animal behavior and among many psychologists and social scientists. Studies motivated by such theory and apparently confirming components of it have routinely been published in leading refereed journals in all these fields for many years. Indeed, one need only read regularly the rest of the magazine for which Gould writes his column to see that this body of theory is now routinely accepted.

OBNOXIOUS BUT USEFUL

Contrary to predictions made by opponents in the 1970s and 1980s, sociobiology was not a nefarious plot to give scientific credence to a right-wing policy agenda. It was not nearly that important. And contrary to early predictions of its greatest enthusiasts, sociobiology has not pushed aside the rest of the behavioral and social sciences, nor has it folded them all neatly into its wide theoretical embrace. What has happened instead is something neither side wanted to believe, but that was expected by open-minded people with no direct stake in the controversy: sociobiology has become a small but significant part of the spectrum of behavioral and social science.

Like all good theories, it is sometimes unsuccessful in particular situations. Even in the nonhuman world, nepotism is imperfect and inexplicable acts of altruism occur. It may be in the interest of males to control uteruses as theory predicts, but females of many species, including allegedly monogamous ones, cheat. Thus males, with the best will in the world, often get flummoxed out of reproductive success. But such is evolution—females have their interests too, and pursue them very nicely, thank you. This is not a failure of neo-Darwinian theory, but a legitimate adjustment of it.

That the theory is obnoxious I freely concede. That it often leads to oversimplification there can be no doubt. But whatever we may wish, the former cannot make it wrong, and the latter is in the nature of theory. Proponents push it as far as they can, and let others sweep up the failures after them—or, in the worst case, sweep up the broken pieces of their theory. They are willing to stumble, fall, look silly, get up and brush themselves off, and push some more. So much the better for the rest of us, who may eventually benefit in gained understanding without having had to risk ridicule.

The theory's failures have been local; it has proven uninformative in many instances, and specific hypotheses arising from it have often failed empirical tests. As an overarching viewpoint, though, it successfully organizes much of the behavior and social organization of animals—including, to some extent, us. For example, kin selection predicts that if males take over a group in which females are caring for infants, they might benefit from doing away with the infants and reimpregnating the females. This has been seen in lions, langur monkeys, and many other species. In other circumstances, however, males transferring into a group might not be able to take over, but instead have to sue for acceptance by the powers that be. In such instances these relatively weak newcomers might have to befriend females by being gentle and caring toward their infants, even though the infants have been sired by other males. This has been seen in baboons, among other species.

Needless to say, the theory sometimes seems eerily able to handle any facts on the ground, a tendency Lewontin and Gould have aptly labeled "Panglossian adaptationism," after Voltaire's character who found everything for the best in this best of all possible worlds. Neo-Darwinian theorists would like nothing better, however, than to find ways to predict which species will turn out like lions and which like baboons, rather than offering post hoc explanations. In fact, they are working like beavers on this and similar problems, which is what theories are supposed to make scientists do. That is called heuristic value. This theory has heuristic value in abundance.

Still, it is difficult to see what theory other than this one would predict so costly and nasty a natural phenomenon as competitive infanticide. That is why when it became impossible to deny that it occurs in many species, opponents of the theory insisted that it was just a breakdown in social relations—a form of social pathology under stress. This didn't wash for two reasons. First, no one showed that the likelihood of infanticide was related to the amount of ambient stress. Second, and more important, stress is ubiquitous in nature. Stress is what life is about. Evolution thrives on it, and to treat its consequence as a special instance—a pathology—just won't do. Call it pathology if you like, it is nonetheless predictable, and neo-Darwinian theory predicts it.

A more legitimate objection is that many things predicted by sociobiology are predicted by other theories too. For instance, sociobiologists suggest that incest should have been selected against in evolution because it brings hidden genetic defects to the surface. But such other theorists as Westermarck, Freud, and Skinner give us reasons to expect incest avoidance. Even if sociobiology makes more sense in such cases, it doesn't exactly produce surprises.

Consider two instances in which, I believe, it does.

Over the past 15 years systematic research on child abuse and pedicide by Martin Daly and Margo Wilson—research specifically motivated by neo-Darwinian theory—has shown that a child is between 10 and 100 times more likely to be assaulted or killed if he or she lives in a household that includes an unrelated male. Careful studies show that controlling the things we think of first to explain such a finding—socioeconomic status, ethnicity, religion, educational level, and so on—fails to abolish this very large effect. Nor does the finding respect national borders; it appears reliably in four or five countries. Although several of these countries—Canada, the U.S., and Britain—are culturally very similar, comparable effects are seen among the Yanomamo Indians of Venezuela. Because it persists when cultural and sociological variables are controlled, it is difficult to interpret these findings without reference to neo-Darwinian theory. This, we should emphasize, does not explain the mechanism in individual households. But the theory directed researchers' attention to a particular variable and led to a new discovery in a field that, one might have thought, would have known about this phenomenon for decades.

Second, David Buss and others have conducted studies of sex differences in what they call mating strategies. In dozens of different countries—37 and counting, the last time I checked, including Nigeria and Malaysia—men and women consistently respond differently to questionnaires on what they look for in their romantic and sexual partners. All 37 samples are of literate people in their twenties or younger, but these effects are stronger, not weaker, in nonliterate cultures, such as the Ache of Paraguay and the Kipsigis of Kenya, where modernization has had less effect on gender roles. Men value physical appearance more than women do, and women weigh status and income more than men do. Men's ideal mates are a few years younger than they are on average, and women's a few years older. Eleanor Maccoby, a Stanford psychologist, has summarized a lifetime of research on gender in a recent book, *The Two Sexes: Growing Up Apart, Coming Together,* published by Harvard University Press. While she details a complex interaction between initial biologically based differences and the effects of voluntary sex segregation in play (among other social and cultural influences), she concludes that some psychological sex differences are extremely difficult to change. This includes the greater tendency of males to resort to physical measures in conflict, which also shows remarkable cross-cultural consistency.

How should liberals react to such information, assuming that it is scientifically reliable? Surely not by the ostrich method, hoping it will go away. You need to ask yourself: How committed am I to liberal philosophy and policy? Is my viewpoint contingent on certain scientific discoveries, past

> **J**efferson wrote, "In questions of power, let no more be said of confidence in man, but bind him down from mischief, by the chains of the Constitution."

or future, about how biologically based human behavior and human differences are? Or am I committed to policies based on human decency regardless of how large a role biology may play? Do we have to justify equal opportunity with the scientifically untenable claim that it will cause everyone to end up in the same place? Or is it just a matter of fair play, regardless of native ability? In order to share power between men and women, do we first have to prove that the sexes are psychologically equivalent? Or can we resolve, along with "difference feminists" going back to the nineteenth century, that both genders must be represented in any organization not just in spite of, but also because of their differences?

FUNDAMENTAL OR FUNDAMENTALIST?

There is something perversely comforting about the Daly and Wilson finding. Child abuse in the presence of unrelated males is an equal-opportunity scourge, crossing boundaries of class, race, and religion. Sadly, biological mothers as well as stepfathers are guilty of the abuse; it is the presence of the unrelated male in the household that seems to count, whether or not he commits the abuse. Theory notwithstanding, this is a disturbing and puzzling phenomenon, but it is a human one. Or more precisely, it is a human extension of an animal phenomenon, and that perhaps disturbs us most of all.

In recent years, Gould and others have taken to criticizing sociobiology for being overzealous in its application of Darwinian principles. For example, in the *New York Review* of June 12, 1997, Gould pigeonholes his opponents as "Darwinian fundamentalists" or "ultra-Darwinians" who cannot respect any process in evolution other than natural selection. He correctly points out that natural selection is not the be-all and end-all of evolution. Asteroid impacts have drastically changed the earth's climate, flora, and fauna; after one such event the dinosaurs and many of their contemporaries became extinct. Also, many DNA mutations are neutral—they have no adaptive or functional consequence, and so they happen randomly. Finally, there are inertial properties of organisms called developmental constraints, which slow down evolution or shunt it along a finite number of favored paths. These processes are not up for argument. Everyone, including alleged ultra-Darwinians, agrees with Gould that they are important.

The problem is only with Gould's straw man: a Darwinian thinker so ignorant and rigid as to deny the reality of the aforementioned, universally accepted facts. Do "ultra-Darwinians" have difficulty with mass extinction by asteroid impact? Hardly. In fact, such extinctions wipe the slate of life on earth more or less clean, giving natural selection much freer reign for the next few million years as the earth fills with life again. Do "Darwinian fundamentalists" ignore neutral mutations? Of course not, although the "selfish gene" theory itself provides an interesting hypothesis about how DNA can change within a genome without having any effect on the organism, or even having a detrimental effect, by duplicating itself and "hitchhiking" along.

But like asteroid impacts, neutral mutations are random processes that help form the background noise of evolution. It's not that those processes are unimportant, nor even that it's uninteresting to find out how they happen. It's just that in evolutionary biology, as in any other science, the aim is to detect the signal amidst the noise. The signal in this case is natural selection. The noise may be louder and more general, but the signal is more interesting. Focusing on the signal instead of the noise is scarcely proof of fundamentalism.

In a similar vein, in his recent criticism Lewontin has exaggerated sociobiologists' inflexibility on the question of group selection. In a review last October of a book about unselfish behavior by Elliott Sober and David Sloan Wilson in the *New York Review*, Lewontin praises the authors' work as "subversive" and "radical" in the sense of requiring that current orthodoxy be overturned. Lewontin is right to think that a great deal is at stake here, especially for the human sciences. If group selection is powerful and important, then so is group functionalism. And if group functionalism is valid, then the standard social science model—the organic model—is much less vulnerable to Darwinian revision than many of us think. If groups have been selected as functional entities despite individual competition within them, then altruism and cooperation do not need neo-Darwinian explanations.

But, actually, theoretical hostility to group selection has waned considerably among evolutionists, and it has been given a legitimate role even by many like E. O. Wilson, George C. Williams, and John Maynard Smith whom Gould would call "ultras." So when Lewontin characterizes group selection as "anathema" to "nearly all evolutionary biologists," he is substantially behind the curve. Sober and D. S. Wilson are far more open-minded about levels of selection than Gould and Lewontin are; they offer their theory not as a replacement for sociobiology but as an addition. Indeed, the same intellectual developments that Sober and D. S. Wilson call "great insights" and "advances" Gould and Lewontin have viewed as

products of reactionary cultural trends and threats to liberal political philosophy—not to mention being silly and wrong.

Proponents of group theory blur the distinction between kin and group selection, a semantic move that does nothing to advance understanding. The theory has a place, especially in simple asexual organisms. But group selection theorists also aim to change our minds about human altruism and cooperation. They cite ethnographic materials that are unsystematic and biased, taking at face value the claims of functionalist anthropologists of the early twentieth century regarding how cooperative traditional peoples are. Recent studies of the Yanomamo, Ache, Hadza, Kipsigis, and other traditional peoples have tested hypotheses arising from individual and kin selection theory, and these hypotheses hold up as well or better in nonindustrial than in capitalist societies.

In fact, anti-Darwinians, stressing the dangerous social consequences of individual selection, ironically miss the social dangers of group selection theory. Group selection can have been important in human evolution only if groups of our ancestors were quite isolated for long periods. This would suggest that human groups evolved rather separately, a potential comfort to racists. But of course, it is not on this basis that we evaluate the theory, any more than we can evaluate individual selection on the basis of whether or not it comforts capitalists. Either theory stands or falls on the merits.

In the human case, there is no evidence that races, tribes, or other ethnic groups were ever isolated for thousands of generations during our evolution. On the contrary, genetic analysis tells a tale of constant migration and frequent mixing. Yes, there were group conquests and replacements. But these too often resulted in genetic melding, as men and especially women were integrated as servants or slaves. More important, there is endless evidence of conflict within groups, and there is the constant opportunity for defection.

This is key. Defection is the individual's ultimate negative comment on the group, and in human affairs, whether primitive or modern, it is resorted to early and often. Defection more than anything exposes the soft underbelly of the conventional organic model of social organizations. Cells and tissues cannot secede from an organism and otherwise continue their evolutionary process, but individuals can and do secede from groups. They also, through deception, defect internally, enhancing their reproductive success at fellow group members' expense. But it is the act of transfer or group fission that makes group selection implausible.

MARX VS. DARWIN?

With a completed *Das Kapital* in hand, Karl Marx wrote to Charles Darwin, requesting permission to dedicate it to the older, world-famous biologist. Darwin's demurral showed that he was a bourgeois, conservative sort of scientific revolutionary who had troubles enough of his own; but it also showed that there is evolution and then there is evolution. Marx's evolution was that of successive waves of socioeconomic adaptation, each predictably replacing the last through a process of revolutionary transformation.

Marx, of course, was a kind of group selectionist; classes were relentlessly pitted in dialectical conflict. This has proved wrong, partly because of defection (opportunity?) and partly because of the enlightened self-interest of ruling classes, choosing conciliation over chaos. The utopian part of Marx—his version of the Hegelian end of history—was even less compatible with real evolutionary theory, since like all utopian visions it was perfectly cooperative and free of selfishness. In art and poetry the lion may lie down with the lamb, but in evolution the lamb gets eaten. Likewise, within a species, bullies and victims do not rest easily side by side.

For some critics, those last remarks alone make me an apologist for exploitation. This criticism naively confuses "ought" with "is." All major religions and many secular philosophies have declared bad things to be natural and promptly declared a humane war against them. In Judeo-Christian, Platonic, and Confucian thought, among other traditions, we are first endowed with selfish, greedy, and other wicked impulses and then must freely exercise our force of will against them. Far from justifying the impulses by calling them natural, the label does the opposite, emphasizing the human, cultural need to control them.

Even Marxist thought has parallels, in which natural greed, conflict, and oppression lead—through a peculiarly human rise in consciousness—to a willed, chosen, improved course of history and destiny. Indeed, in any body of thought that makes sense, human choices are superimposed on and attempt to control natural tendencies. Why sociobiology's discoveries or claims about what is natural should determine what ought to and will be done is a mystery that the theory's critics have not explained. Sociobiology is trying to be a science, not a philosophy; if it succeeds, any philosophy—including political philosophy—will have to take its findings into account. But what *is* is merely a starting point for determining what *could* or, certainly, what *should* be.

A SOCIAL MACHINE FOR A DARWINIAN CREATURE

As Marx's admiration for Darwin shows, the implications of evolution are not, and never were, inherently conservative. They are, however, inherently materialist and fraught with conflict—something conservatives and revolutionaries are comfortable with but some liberals are not.

The revolutionaries of the nascent American republic certainly were, although not because of evolution. In *The Lost World of Thomas Jefferson*, Daniel Boorstin shows that Jefferson's circle—including psychiatrist-physician Benjamin Rush and other Philadelphia intellectuals—had a strong, detailed concept of human nature. They were scientific materialists. They believed that all human beings were descended from a single pair, giving unifying operational principles to the mind. Under Rush's influence, they maintained a fascination with a fledgling brain science. What Rush called "the anatomy of the mind" was an attempt to put human behavior and psychology on a continuum with the physical sciences and, even more so, with the lives of animals, thus undermining human arrogance. Or as one of the group, Tom Paine, put it, "all the great laws of society are laws of nature," and order in human affairs stems from "the natural constitution of man."

A 1789 monograph from the laboratory of Madison et al. (the one that begins "We the people . . .") described what might be viewed as an epochal social science discovery. It presented the plan for an intricate, elegant device, a sociological invention for keeping human nature in check, while allowing the conflict that seethes in the human breast to leak out through various safety valves. In fact, you could say that they harnessed conflict itself to make the machine run. For unlike most machines, this device was to be built out of people; therefore, its designers had to have some notion of what these human building units were.

Despite agreeing with Paine about the tendency to order, Jefferson—an affiliate of the lab, but absent in Paris when the monograph appeared—had a dark view. "In questions of power," he would write in 1798, "let no more be said of confidence in man, but bind him down from mischief, by the chains of the Constitution." Paine similarly saw the purpose of constitutions as "to restrain and regulate the wild impulse of power." It was these men's great gift to be able to take a Hobbesian view of human life without applying a Hobbesian solution.

Their "natural" view even encompassed individual differences in debate. Jefferson wrote that "the terms of whig and tory belong to natural as well as civil history. They denote the temper and constitution of mind of different individuals." For

Rush, there was "the same variety in the texture of minds, that there is in the bodies of men." But if differences of opinion were really differences in temper, and these in turn inherent brain differences, what could be more hopeless than to seek universal agreement? Instead, the laws would take for granted the permanence of those differences, and create a government that would harness the unremitting energy of conflict.

But we don't really need Boorstin's interpretation; we can read the monograph and infer the theory from it. Human nature is eminently corruptible. People seek power and abuse it, turning it to selfish ends, regardless of how collective and representative its roots. Nepotism, greed, self-aggrandizement, intractable conflict, and suppression of dissent naturally and relentlessly threaten human institutions. A democratic republic is inherently improbable, and will tend to collapse into hereditary dictatorship, oligarchy, or chaos, regardless of how good the intentions of those who began it. As "Publius,"—either Madison or Hamilton—asked in Federalist 51, "But what is government itself, but the greatest of all reflections on human nature? If men were angels, no government would be needed."

What to do? Well—they seem to have thought—let us assume the worst, and under that assumption, invent a device to bully human nature into decency, a "policy of supplying, by opposite and rival interests"—Federalist 51 again—"the defect of better motives." They analyzed human nature, and built a sort of Rube Goldberg machine—almost too complicated, yet so tightly and intricately balanced that it could have been the cotton gin or a mill wheel grinding corn kernels. At one end you could put in a collection of greedy, power-mad people locked in angry conflict, and at the other end something resembling order, peace, and fairness would duly be chucked out.

Creaky, noisy, seemingly ready to crumple or burst at any moment, the machine has more or less worked for a couple of centuries. Brief in evolutionary terms, but a beginning. Inexact working replicas are now cranking away in various places on the planet, threatening to make order out of human nature elsewhere. For those who think our nature is inherently good, unselfish, and cooperative, the result is a poor substitute for a functional, organically coherent, and completely fair society.

But for those of us who see human nature as the unpleasant product of too many eons of individual selection, the machine makes a decent stew out of some pretty iffy meat. Or in Isaiah Berlin's metaphor, it makes from the crooked timber of humanity an acceptable shack—shaky and of course nothing straight, but with occasional repairs, livable. Some people are shut out of it, but that probably means we should add another wing, not that we should tear the thing down and start over. Given the grain of the lumber, we could end up with something much worse.

This perhaps is the enduring implication of Darwin's theory for liberal political philosophy: assume the worst and you can still get something workable, based on Thomas Jefferson and not Thomas Hobbes. Of course, I may merely be spinning pseudoscientific tales to justify the status quo. But at present I fail to see the evidence for a better way to look at evolution.

Personally, I favor political economies like those of northern Europe over the one we have now in the United States, and I have voted that preference to whatever extent possible for more than three decades. Around halfway through that period, I concluded that the neo-Darwinians had a very useful way of looking at evolution, and I accepted it. Why didn't it change my vote?

First of all, because my political views are based as much on "ought" as on "is." I support liberal economic programs because I want to live in a decent community. My definition of "decent" doesn't depend on one or another theory of evolution. But in addition, because I do see human nature as an obstacle to decency, I support programs that buffer us against the loss of it. Newt Gingrich and Milton Friedman must have a far more sanguine view of human nature than I do, or they would surely not be heartless enough to want to give it the free rein of an unalloyed market economy.

In part, it is because I take a dim view of human nature as an evolutionary product that I reject their view. Virtually everyone in the world has decided that economies don't work without more or less free markets at their center. What is up for further discussion is only how much we will care about those who lose out in open competition—including the sick, the old, and the very young. Human nature was not designed by evolution to take care of the needs of these people automatically. Therefore only programs and supports deliberately designed by a collective, humane, political will—a will that also restrains the worst excesses of markets—can, after wide debate, create a decent community and set some limit on selfishness.

TABOO:

Don't Even THINK About It!

In this era of taboo-smashing, writer Michael Ventura—known for his searing essays on everything from our culture of money to the vagaries of romantic love—tells us why America is still, deep down, a country of taboos, where we live our lives by what we cannot say, do, or admit.

TABOOS COME IN ALL SIZES. Big taboos: when I was a kid in the Italian neighborhoods of Brooklyn, to insult someone's mother meant a brutal fight—the kind of fight no one interferes with until one of the combatants goes down and stays down. Little taboos: until the sixties, it was an insult to use someone's first name without asking or being offered permission. Personal taboos: Cyrano de Bergerac would not tolerate the mention of his enormous nose. Taboos peculiar to one city: in Brooklyn (again), when the Dodgers were still at Ebbets Field, if you rooted for the Yankees you kept it to yourself unless you wanted a brawl. Taboos, big or small, are always about

> **In Afghanistan, flying a kite is a sin punishable by beatings, and if two men walk down the street holding hands they may be stoned to death.**

having to respect somebody's (often irrational) boundary—or else.

There are taboos shared within one family: my father did not feel free to speak to us of his grandmother's suicide until his father died. Taboos within intellectual elites: try putting a serious metaphysical or spiritual slant on a "think-piece" (as we call them in the trade) written for the *New York Times*, the *Washington Post*, or most big name magazines—it won't be printed. Taboos in the corporate and legal worlds: if you're male, you had best wear suits of somber colors, or you're not likely to be taken seriously; if you're female, you have to strike a very uneasy balance between the attractive and the prim, and even then you might not be taken seriously. Cultural taboos: in the Jim Crow days in the South, a black man who spoke with familiarity to a white woman might be beaten, driven out of town, or (as was not uncommon) lynched.

Unclassifiable taboos: in Afghanistan, as I write this, it is a sin—punishable by beatings and imprisonment—to fly a kite. Sexual taboos: there are few communities on this planet where two men can walk down a street holding hands without being harassed or even arrested; in Afghanistan (a great place for taboos these days) the Taliban would stone them to death. Gender taboos: how many American corporations (or institutions of any kind) promote women to power? National taboos: until the seventies, a divorced person could not run for major public office in America (it wasn't until 1981 that our first and only divorced president, Ronald Reagan, took office); today, no professed atheist would dare try for the presidency. And most readers of this article probably approve, as I do, of this comparatively recent taboo: even the most rabid bigot must avoid saying "rigger," "spic," or "kike" during, say, a job interview—and the most macho sexist must avoid word like "broad."

Notice that nearly all of our taboos, big and small, public and intimate, involve silence—keeping one's silence, or paying a price for not keeping it. Yet keeping silent has its own price: for then silence begins to fill the heart, until silence becomes the heart—a heart swelling with restraint until it bursts in frustration, anger, even madness.

The taboos hardest on the soul are those which fester in our intimacies—taboos known only to the people involved, taboos that can make us feel alone even with those to whom we're closest. One of the deep pains of marriage—one that also plagues brothers and sisters, parents and children, even close friends—is that as we grow more intimate, certain silences often become more necessary. We discover taboo areas, both in ourselves and in the other, that cannot be transgressed without paying an awful price. If we speak of them, we may endanger the relationship; but if we do not speak, if we do not violate the taboo, the relationship may become static and tense, until the silence takes on a life of its own. Such silences are corrosive. They eat at the innards of intimacy until, often, the silence itself causes the very rupture or break-up that we've tried to avoid by keeping silent.

> If there's a taboo against something, it's usually because a considerable number of people desire to do it.

> It's taboo to be a Christian in China, a Moslem in Israel, a Jew in Syria. And in much of the U.S., it's still taboo to be an atheist.

THE CANNIBAL IN US ALL

You may measure how many taboos constrict you, how many taboos you've surrendered to—at home, at parties, at work, with your lover or your family—by how much of yourself you must suppress. You may measure your life, in these realms, by what you can not say, do, admit—cannot and must not, and for no better reason than that your actions or words would disrupt your established order. By this measure, most of us are living within as complex and structured a system of taboos as the aborigines who gave us the word in the first place. You can see how fitting it is that the word "taboo" comes from a part of the world where cannibalism is said to be practiced to this day: the islands off eastern Australia—Polynesia, New Zealand, Melanesia. Until 1777, when Captain James Cook published an account of his first world voyage, Europe and colonial America had many taboos but no word that precisely meant taboo. Cook introduced this useful word to the West. Its instant popularity, quick assimilation into most European languages, and constant usage since, are testimony to how much of our lives the word describes. Before the word came to us, we'd ostracized, coerced, exiled, tormented, and murdered each other for myriad infractions (as we still do), but we never had a satisfying, precise word for our reasons.

We needed cannibals to give us a word to describe our behavior, so how "civilized" are we, really? We do things differently from those cannibals, on the surface, but is the nature of what we do all that different? We don't cook each other for ceremonial dinners, at least not physically (though therapists can testify that our ceremonial seasons, like Christmas and Thanksgiving, draw lots of business—something's cooking). But we stockpile weapons that can cook the entire world, and we organize our national priorities around their "necessity," and it's a national political taboo to seriously cut spending for those planetcookers. If that's "progress," it's lost on me. In China it's taboo to be a Christian, in Israel it's taboo to be a Moslem, in Syria it's taboo to be a Jew, in much of the United States it's still taboo to be an atheist, while in American academia it's taboo to be deeply religious.

Our headlines are full of this stuff. So it's hardly surprising that a cannibal's word still describes much of our behavior.

I'm not denying the necessity of every society to set limits and invent taboos (some rational, some not) simply in order to get on with the day—and to try to contain the constant, crazy, never-to-be-escaped longings that blossom in our sleep and distract or compel us while awake. Such longings are why even a comparatively tiny desert tribe like the ancient Hebrews needed commandments and laws against coveting each other's wives, stealing, killing, committing incest. That tribe hadn't seen violent, sexy movies, hadn't listened to rock 'n' roll, hadn't been bombarded with ads featuring half-naked models, and hadn't watched too much TV. They didn't need to. Like us, they had their hearts, desires, and dreams to instruct them how to be very, very naughty. The taboo underlying all others is that we must not live by the dictates of our irrational hearts—as though we haven't forgiven each other, or ourselves, for having hearts.

If there's a taboo against something, it's usually because a considerable number of people desire to do it. The very taboos that we employ to protect us from each other and ourselves, are a map of our secret natures. When you know a culture's taboos (or an individual's, or a family's) you know its secrets—you know what it really wants.

FAVORITE TABOOS

It's hard to keep a human being from his or her desire, taboo or not. We've always been very clever, very resourceful, when it comes to sneaking around our taboos. The Aztecs killed virgins and called it religion. The Europeans enslaved blacks and called it economics. Americans tease each other sexually and call it fashion.

If we can't kill and screw and steal and betray to our heart's desire, and, in general, violate every taboo in sight—well, we can at least watch other people do it. Or read about it. Or listen to it. As we have done, since ancient times, through every form of religion and entertainment. The appeal of taboos and our inability to escape our longing for transgression (whether or

> **What desire freezes and fevers you at the same time? What makes you vanish into your secret? That's your taboo, baby.**

not we ourselves transgress) are why so many people who call themselves honest and law-abiding spend so much time with movies, operas, soaps, garish trials, novels, songs, Biblical tales, tribal myths, folk stories, and Shakespeare—virtually all of which, both the great and the trivial, are about those who dare to violate taboos. It's a little unsettling when you think about it: the very stuff we say we most object to is the fundamental material of what we call culture.

That's one reason that fundamentalists of all religions are so hostile to the arts. But fundamentalists partake of taboos in the sneakiest fashion of all. Senator Jesse Helms led the fight against the National Endowment for the Arts because he couldn't get the (vastly overrated) homosexual art of Robert Mapplethorpe or the most extreme performance artists out of his mind—he didn't and doesn't want to. He, like all fundamentalists, will vigorously oppose such art and all it stands for until he dies, because his very opposition gives him permission to concentrate on taboo acts. The Taliban of Afghanistan will ride around in jeeps toting guns, searching out any woman who dares show an inch of facial skin or wear white socks (Taliban boys consider white socks provocative), and when they find such a woman they'll jail and beat her—because their so-called righteousness gives them permission to obsess on their taboos. Pat Robertson and his ilk will fuss and rage about any moral "deviation," any taboo violation they can find, because that's the only way they can give themselves permission to entertain the taboos. They get to not have their taboo cake, yet eat it too.

> **Nearly all of the stuff we call culture— movies, songs, novels, myths, the Bible, Shakespeare— is about people who dare to violate taboos.**

We are all guilty of this to some extent. Why else have outlaws from Antigone to Robin Hood to Jesse James to John Gotti become folk heroes? Oedipus killed his father and slept with his mother, and we've been performing that play for 2500 years because he is the ultimate violator of our deepest taboos. Aristotle said we watch such plays for "catharsis," to purge our desires and fears in a moment of revelation. Baloney. Ideas like "catharsis" are an intellectual game, to glossy-up our sins. What's closer to the truth is that we need Oedipus to stand in for us. We can't have changed much in 2500 years, if we still keep him alive in our hearts to enact our darkest taboos for us. Clearly, the very survival of Oedipus as an instantly recognizable name tells us that we still want to kill our fathers and screw our mothers (or vice versa).

A COUNTRY OF BROKEN TABOOS

Taboos are a special paradox for Americans. However much we may long for tradition and order, our longings are subverted by the inescapable fact that our country was founded upon a break with tradition and a challenge to order—which is to say, the United States was founded upon the violation of taboos. Specifically, this country was founded upon the violation of Europe's most suffocating taboo: its feudal suppression (still enforced in 1776, when America declared its independence) of the voices of the common people. We were the first nation on earth to write into law that any human being has the right to say anything, and that even the government is (theoretically) not allowed to silence you.

At the time, Europe was a continent of state-enforced religions, where royalty's word was law and all other words could be crushed by law. (Again: taboo was a matter of enforced silence.) We were the first nation to postulate verbal freedom for everyone. All our other freedoms depend upon verbal freedom; no matter how badly and how often we've failed that ideal, it still remains our ideal.

Once we broke Europe's verbal taboos, it was only a matter of time before other traditional taboos fell too. As the writer Albert Murray has put it, Americans could not afford

IN SEARCH OF THE LAST TABOO

There is no "last taboo," according to Michael Ventura. But there certainly are a lot of contenders, scattered like clues in a treasure hunt for the heart of our culture. Here, an assortment of last taboos "discovered" by the media in the past few years.

"What a great story: **Incest.** The last taboo!"—*Esquire,* on Kathryn Harrison's memoir *The Kiss.*

" 'The very word is a room emptier,' Tina Brown wrote in her editor's note when, in 1991, Gail Sheehy broke the silence with a story in *Vanity Fair.* . . . **Menopause** may be the last taboo."—*Fort Lauderdale Sun-Sentinel*

"The last taboo for women is not, as Gail Sheehy would have it, menopause, but **facial hair.**"—*New York Times*

"At a time when this is the last taboo, Moreton depicts **erections.**"—*Sunday Telegraph,* describing sculptor Nicholas Moreton's work.

"Virtually no representations of **faith** are seen on television, it's the last taboo."—*Columbus Dispatch*

"Anything with **sex with underage kids** is the last taboo."—*Toronto Star*

"The last taboo: an openly **homosexual** actor playing a **heterosexual** lead."—*Boston Globe*

"With sexual mores gone the way of Madonna, **picking up the tab** has become the last taboo for women."—*Philadelphia Inquirer*

"Most Americans, if they think about **class** at all (it may be our last taboo subject), would surely describe themselves as middle class regardless of a petty detail like income."—*Los Angeles Times Syndicate*

"The Last Taboo Is **Age:** Why Are We Afraid of It?"—headline in the *Philadelphia Inquirer*

"Smash the last taboo! [Timothy] Leary says he's planning the first . . . **interactive suicide.**"—*Washington Post*

"**Money** is the last taboo."—*Calgary Herald*

"**Menstruation** may be the last taboo."—*Manchester Guardian Weekly*

"The real last taboo is that of **privacy and dignity.**"—*Montreal Gazette*

"And then there's **bisexuality,** the last taboo among lesbians."—*Los Angeles Times*

"I think **personal smells** are one of the last taboos."—*The Observer*

"Television's last taboo, long after f-words and pumping bottoms became commonplace, was the **full-frontal vomit.** Now, even that last shred of inhibition has gone, and every drama . . . [has] a character heaving his guts all over the camera."—*The (London) Mail*

"**Tanning.** The last taboo. If you're tan, then your IQ must be lower than the SPF of the sunscreen you'd be using if you had any brains."—*Los Angeles Times*

piety in their new homeland: "You can't be over respectful of established forms; you're trying to get through the wilderness of Kentucky." Thus, from the moment the Pilgrims landed, our famous puritanism faced an inherent contradiction. How could we domesticate the wilderness of this continent; how could peasants and rejects and "commoners" form a strong and viable nation; how could we develop all the new social forms and technologies necessary to blend all the disparate peoples who came here—without violating those same Puritan taboos which are so ingrained, to this day, in our national character?

It can't be over-emphasized that America's fundamental stance against both the taboos of Europe and the taboos of our own Puritans, was our insistence upon freedom of speech. America led the attack against silence. And it is through that freedom, the freedom to break the silence, that we've destroyed so many other taboos. Especially during the last 40 years, we've broken the silence that surrounded ancient taboos of enormous significance. Incest, child abuse, wife-battering, homosexuality, and some (by no means all) forms of racial and gender oppression, are not merely spoken of, and spoken against, they're shouted about from the rooftops. Many breathe easier because of this inevitable result of free speech. In certain sections of our large cities, for the first time in modern history, gay people can live openly and without fear. The feminist movement has made previously forbidden or hidden behaviors both speakable and doable. The National Organization of Women can rail against the Promise Keepers all they want (and they have some good reasons), but when you get a million working-class guys crying and hugging in public, the stoic mask of the American male has definitely cracked. And I'm old enough to remember when it was shocking for women to speak about wanting a career. Now virtually all affluent young women are expected to want a career.

Fifty years ago, not one important world or national leader was black. Now there are more people of color in positions of influence than ever. Bad marriages can be dissolved without social stigma. Children born out of wedlock are not damned as "bastards" for something that wasn't their fault. And those of us who've experienced incest and abuse have finally found a voice, and through our voices we've achieved a certain amount of liberation from shame and pain.

These boons are rooted in our decidedly un-Puritan freedom of speech. But we left those Puritans behind a long time ago—for the breaking of silence is the fundamental political basis of our nation, and no taboo is safe when people have the right to speak.

> We were the first nation on earth to write into law that any human being has the right to say anything without being silenced.

KEEPER OF YOUR SILENCE

In the process, though, we've lost the sanctity of silence. We've lost the sense of dark but sacred power inherent in sex, in nature, even in crime. Perhaps that is the price of our new freedoms.

It's also true that by breaking the silence we've thrown ourselves into a state of confusion. The old taboos formed part of society's structure. Without them, that structure has undeniably weakened. We are faced with shoring up the weakened parts, inventing new ways of being together that have pattern and order—for we cannot live without some pattern and order—but aren't so restrictive. Without sexual taboos, for instance, what are the social boundaries between men and women? When are they breached? What is offensive? Nobody's sure. Everybody's making mistakes. This is so excruciating that many are nostalgic for some of the old taboos. But once a taboo is broken, then for good or ill it's very hard, perhaps impossible, to reinstate it.

But there is another, subtler confusion: yes, enormous taboos have fallen, but many taboos, equally important, remain. And, both as individuals and as a society, we're strained enough, confused enough, by the results of doing away with so many taboos in so short a time, that maybe we're not terribly eager for our remaining taboos to fall. We may sincerely desire that, but maybe we're tired, fed up, scared. Many people would rather our taboos remain intact for a couple of generations while we get our act together again, and perhaps they have a point. But the price of taboo remains what it's always been: silence and constriction.

What do we see, when we pass each other on the street, but many faces molded by the price paid for keeping the silences of the taboos that remain—spirits confined within their own, and their society's, silences? Even this brief essay on our public and intimate strictures is enough to demonstrate that we are still a primitive race, bounded by fear and prejudice, with taboos looming in every direction—no matter how much we like to brag and/or bitch that modern life is liberating us from all the old boundaries. The word taboo still says much more about us than most prefer to admit.

What is the keeper of your silence? The answer to that question is your own guide to your personal taboos. How must you confine yourself in order to get through your day at the job, or to be acceptable in your social circle? The answer to that is your map of your society's taboos. What makes you most afraid to speak? What desire, what word, what possibility, freezes and fevers you at the same time, making any sincere communication out of the question? What makes you vanish into your secret? That's your taboo, baby. You're still in the room, maybe even still smiling, still talking, but not really—what's really happened is that you've vanished down some hole in yourself, and you'll stay there until you're sure the threat to your taboo is gone and it's safe to come out again. If, that is, you've ever come out in the first place. Some never have.

What utterance, what hint, what insinuation, can quiet a room of family or friends? What makes people change the subject? What makes those at a dinner party dismiss a remark as though it wasn't said, or dismiss a person as though he or she wasn't really there? We've all seen conversations suddenly go dead, and just as suddenly divert around a particular person or subject, leaving them behind in the dead space, because something has been said or implied that skirts a silently shared taboo. If that happens to you often, don't kid yourself that you're living in a "free" society. Because you're only as free as your freedom from taboos—not on some grand abstract level, but in your day-to-day life.

It is probably inherent in the human condition that there are no "last" taboos. Or perhaps it just feels that way because we have such a long way to go. But—at least we can know where to look: right in front of our eyes, in the recesses of our speechlessness, in the depths of our silences. And there is nothing for it but to confront the keepers of our silence. Either that, or to submit to being lost, as most of us silently are, without admitting it to each other or to ourselves—lost in a maze of taboos.

Michael Ventura's latest novel is *The Death of Frank Sinatra.*

Mortality Around the World

From Japan to the Netherlands, death is a major part of how we reveal ourselves.

By Lawrence E. Sullivan

I t used to be that nothing was more certain than death and taxes. Not anymore. If you are looking for a fixed point in your universe, bank on taxes. The meaning of death and the practices linked to it is up for grabs. In societies around the world, debate and change stalk death.

Death has long been the center of societal attention, of course. You do not have to visit the Egyptian pyramids to learn this. Any foliage-season tourist to New England can tell you that community graveyards were sited near the central common. Like the communal granary, the burial ground was a center of life, serving as the seedbed for family branches that stemmed outward from hallowed ancestors. *Mortui vivos docent,* "let the dead teach the living," was not only a sober Puritan dictum but the attitude of peoples around the globe for centuries. What are the dead teaching us these days?

In modern times, the face of death has changed. For most of human history, death was the province of the young. Infant mortality and rampant disease struck down people in their prime or before. Though the good may have died young, only the few died old. Nowadays, with average life expectancies rising due to new medicines, technology, and public health programs, death more easily conjures the wrinkled faces of the elderly.

The face of death is also increasingly hidden, kept from sight by modern efficiencies. In car accidents, which are among the most frequent deaths occurring in industrial societies, victims are whisked from the scene to the emergency room and thence to the morgue. Instead of dying at home in our beds before family and friends, we more often expire in hospitals or terminal-care facilities in front of strangers who tend the dying to make a living.

Death and organ transplants in Japan

In Japan, the technological borderland between life and death has been the frontier of a public battle about the nature of death for the past 30 years. For decades, most life-saving transplants of vital organs have been unavailable in Japan. The first heart transplant in Japan, for instance, occurred in 1968; for three decades it remained the only one.

The 800 kidney transplants per year in Japan, compared with the 10,000 performed each year in the United States, involve organs mostly taken from living donors. The problem has not been the lack of know-how. Many Japanese physicians have trained in transplant surgery outside Japan. The problem is death: When does it occur, and, consequently, when can organs be harvested? Without clarity on this issue, transplant surgeons fear prosecution.

Japanese medicine and law have traditionally declared a person dead when his heart finally stops beating. But vital organs deteriorate quickly when the heart stops pumping blood to them, making the prospects of transplant problematic or impossible. In other countries, physicians have kept the heart pumping through artificial means, even after the person's brain ceases to show vital activity. In this state of "brain death," vital organs have been taken for transplant into the living. Japanese practice did not allow organs to be harvested during brain death. In effect, to be "brain dead" was not the same as to be dead.

With the Organ Transplant Law that went into effect in October 1997, the situation has begun to change. But the matter is complicated; the law contains 25 articles.

"Death" now takes on several hues and involves the intentions of the dying person. Under the new law, brain death will be recognized as actual death only when the patient agrees to donate organs in advance and acknowledges in advance and in writing that his eventual state of brain death, should he ever enter it, is tantamount to terminal death. Thus death, for the practical purposes of the organ-harvesting surgeon, indicates not only the state of the organ donor's physical body but also involves somehow his understanding and prior state of mind about it.

The law also stipulates that the patient's family must concur. A Japanese Organ Transplant Network now registers patients seeking heart and liver transplants, and legislators have begun to promote donor registration. By redefining death in a national law, surgeons can proceed to save lives without fearing accusations of murder.

The ambivalence about keeping the body intact at death, on the one hand, and recycling body parts through organ transplantation, on the other, is striking, since in Japan, following Buddhist practice and belief, the corpse is usually cremated

WIDE WORLD

A Buddhist temple west of Tokyo: Japanese women, after having an abortion, bathe and clothe statues that represent their *mizuko* (water child).

and the personality of the individual reenters the cycle of rebirths. This ambivalence about life and rebirth resonates in practices and beliefs associated with abortion as well.

Japanese view of abortion

Increasing attention has been given the religious practices associated with the aborted fetus, or *mizuko* (literally, "water child"). Since 1948, Japan has allowed easy access to abortion. Elective abortion within the first 24 weeks of gestation has been available and legal when performed within medical facilities.

Grounds for legal abortion include economic and social motives as well as to save the pregnant woman's life, physical health, or mental health. Induced abortion on the above grounds requires the consent of a woman or her spouse. In cases of rape or incest, the consent of the woman is not required by law. If a woman is mentally retarded, consent can be given by her guardian.

These broad laws have resulted in large numbers of abortions. According to the Population Policy Data Bank maintained by the Population Division of the UN Secretariat, there were 40.7 abortions per 1,000 women aged 15-44 in 1950; 30 abortions per 1,000 in 1960; 22.5 abortions per 1,000 in 1980; and 14.5 in 1990.

The millions of abortions over the past half century have given birth to one of the largest religious transformations in modern Japan. These devotions center on *mizuko kuyo*, memorial rituals for the fetal child, held at Buddhist temples. From the point of view of many Buddhists, elective abortion is spoken of as a "necessary sorrow."

The memorial rites commemorate the dead child and console the parents. The rites can involve naming the child and inscribing the name on a memorial plaque or roll placed in the temple. One finds, for example, wooden offering sticks, with the child's name written in calligraphy, hung in the middle of a small stream on the temple grounds to betoken the "water child's" suspended state in the stream of rebirth.

Dealing With Death

- A Japanese Organ Transplant Law passed in 1997, making heart and liver transplants easier. Before that, "brain death" was not accepted as physical death.

- The practice of induced abortion is common in Japan, while religious memorializations of aborted children become more intense and public.

- In the Muslim world, the Prophet Muhammad's birthday is celebrated on the day of his death.

- In the Netherlands, many doctors are willing to assist patients who have no terminal physical illness but desire to die.

A young woman who has had an abortion may come to the temple with her mother to wash a small statue just as a mother would bathe a child. They adorn the statue with a child's clothes, bib, and cap and set the statue on a pedestal or between the roots of a tree on the temple grounds. Major pilgrimage temples, like those on the holy mountain of Koyasan, where Japanese come to depose a portion of the cremated remains of family members, contain many huge mounds composed of thousands of embryological statues.

A few Buddhist sects, especially Pure Land groups, object to abortion in principle. But the conflicts linked to abortion in Japan do not generally take the form of public controversies about the legality and availability of abortion as they do in the United States and Europe, though there was bitter debate during the middle nineteenth century in Japan, when Confucian and Shinto thinkers objected strongly to abortion.

Instead, induced abortion continues largely unchallenged in law and practice while, at the same time, the religious memorializations of aborted children grow in intensity and public display, just as do the debates over their meaning and appropriateness. Debate and criticism are pointed toward the practices at temples that host the mizuko kuyo ceremonies and the rising emphasis on guilt, atonement, fear of fetal retribution, and even *tatari*, the vengeance that might befall parents who fail to perform rituals.

From a Buddhist "theological" view, the aborted children are not dead in any final sense. Rather their birth—that is, their entry into this cycle of birth—has been interrupted or postponed, constraining them to wait in *sai no kawara*, a "limbo" or threshold state betwixt and between living existences.

During this time of suspension, the memorializing rites for mizuko maintain relationships between the parents and their fetal children and propel the children along their trajectory through the cycles of rebirth. Over time, the rites are thought to soften the hearts of those who have made the hard decision to induce death through abortion. For reasons that are both psychological and religious, such softening is necessary for the well-being of society and individuals.

LIBRARY OF HISTORIC CHARACTERS

Giving him due praise; Muslims celebrate the birth of the Prophet Muhammad on the same day as his death.

Muslim death

Of course, the custom of memorializing the dead is found throughout the world. In some cases, such memorials have become a mainstay for the religious tradition. The *mawlid an-Nabi*, or celebration of the birthday of the Prophet Muhammad, is celebrated on the very day of the Prophet's death.

The Shiite branch of Islam begins the Muslim year with a very dramatic commemoration of a different kind, called *ta'ziyah*, or "condolence." Ta'ziyah is a passion play that recalls the death of Husayn, son of the fourth caliph, 'Ali. The Shiites acknowledge 'Ali and his descendants as the only legitimate heirs of

COREL

St. Jansgasthuis Hospital, Hoorn, the Netherlands: **How the Dutch treated their terminally ill patients is debated in medical circles.**

because Husayn's death and beheading reconcile his followers with God and help them survive the day of final judgment. His suffering and death benefit them all.

Dutch death

For a last view of the changing face of death in the world today, consider the issue of health care being provided by physicians in the Netherlands. Those monitoring the situation point with concern to the large and growing number of Dutch doctors willing to assist the death of patients who have no terminal physical illness but who, for other reasons, desire to die.

The idea of physicians bringing on the death of their physically healthy patients was recently reviewed by the Dutch Supreme Court. The Supreme Court held that Dr. Boudewijn Chabot did not violate the law when he prescribed lethal pills for his 50-year-old female patient and watched her swallow them and die. She was suffering no physical ailment and no mental derangement.

Dr. Chabot testified that his patient was of sound mind and sound body. She had, however, lost her two sons, one of whom had died of cancer, the other of whom had taken his own life. She wanted to die and asked the doctor's help in doing so. He assented. A three-magistrate panel in the court of the city of Assen acquitted Dr. Chabot of all charges and the district appeals court upheld his acquittal, as did the State Supreme Court of the Netherlands.

Eugene Sutorius, the prominent Dutch attorney who represented Dr. Chabot, announced after the decision that euthanasia, which may have begun as a concept and practice in relation to terminal illness, had now moved to a different plane no longer related to terminal illness. What plane is that? one must now ask.

the Prophet Muhammad. The ta'ziyah are celebrated among Shiite Arab communities in Iraq and elsewhere, as well as by Shiite Turks in Central Asia and by Shiites in India. Nowhere is the commemoration more richly observed than in Iran.

Husayn and his followers were cruelly murdered at Karbala, Iraq, in the year 680. On the first days of Muharram, the first month of the Muslim calendar, devotees recite the details of Husayn's life and perform dramatic public spectacles that involve trancelike dances, self-inflicted wounds, and emotional displays. The crowd divides into two teams of actors, one representing Husayn

and his entourage, the other representing the Umayyads who martyred him. On the tenth day of Muharram the festival of Ashurah is held.

This year Ashurah fell on May 7. Husayn's life and death were reenacted in an intense passion play, and a coffin or tomb, sometimes a very elaborate architectural model, was carried in procession. The occasion reenacts the parade in which Husayn's head was carried by his triumphant enemies, accompanied by those mourning his death. In some versions of the spectacle, the bloody head recites verses from scripture. The community celebrates

In considering euthanasia by physicians, there seems little doubt that the physician is more than a passive element in the process of decision making. From the time of Hippocrates, it has been recognized that the physician's authority, judgment, wise counsel, and lifesaving or death-inducing capabilities make him (or her) a considerable, active ingredient in the life or death process.

Aware of the lethal power of their practices, Hippocrates asked physicians to swear an oath to "do no harm." The influence of physicians' views on the death of their patients is raised anew today, not only by the Dutch case but by a study conducted in Australia and published in the *Journal of Medical Ethics* by Peter Baume, Emma O'Malley, and Adrian Bauman of the University of New South Wales. They assessed the relationship between a physician's religious affiliation and his inclination to consider euthanasia.

In Australia, euthanasia is illegal, yet a quarter of all physicians acknowledge taking steps to bring on a patient's death. Of the 1,200 or more physicians randomly selected for the study, physicians of no religious faith undertook action to end the patient's life 62 percent more often. Physicians who described themselves as agnostics and atheists were more than twice as likely to know other doctors who practiced active euthanasia and were more than three times more likely to claim that hastening a patient's death was right than those doctors who claimed a religious affiliation.

Doctors who thought that administering doses for death was never right based their views on religious principles 81 percent of the time, whereas those who held that actively hastening a patient's death could be right based their view on what they considered to be nonreligious views 74 percent of the time. Since it seems in this study to make a remarkable difference in life or death outcome, you may want to know whether your physician regularly attends religious services.

Can the emptiness of death be redeemed through contemporary reflections on its meaning, its legal standing, or its proper accomplishment through ritual or other means?

Death remains one of the great mysteries integral to human life—mysterious in the sense that, however much we peer into it, its core remains opaque and inscrutable. "Dead men don't talk" is the general rule of human existence. Exceptions to that rule are taken as revelations that form the bases of religious movements and fundamental orientations in life.

Though obscure, death is part of the story we mortals tell about anything important to us. The stories are not necessarily morbid: From *Titanic* and *Terminator* to *Dying Young*, death is entertaining, in the profound sense of the word—holding us in the grip of fascination and giving life to our imagination. Contemplating the many puzzling forms in which death appears in our world may help us piece together a new, life-giving story and allow us to take our proper place in it.

Lawrence E. Sullivan is director of the Harvard University Center for the Study of World Religions.

Marks of Mystery

People respond to scars with fear, revulsion—and fascination. Why do we develop scars, and why are we so captivated by them?

By Elizabeth Austin

Sharon Stone has a scar on her neck. Most moviegoers probably haven't even noticed it, but a group of hardcore fans find the faint pink blemish so fascinating they have created a Web site dedicated to "the mystery and intrigue surrounding the scar on Sharon Stone's neck." Visitors to the site (*http://people.we.mediaone.net/bava/sharon/index.html*) are invited to share their theories about the scar's origin; some call it the aftermath of "routine head transplant surgery," while others blame a "tragic limbo accident." Strikingly, however, the vast majority of their theories revolve around sex.

Why are these people so captivated by a five-inch streak on an actor's neck? And why are they so intent on bandaging an esoteric explanation onto what is, in fact, merely the souvenir of a childhood horseback riding accident? The answer is simple: on a very basic level, we find ourselves riveted by scars and the terrifying or titillating stories they tell. "Scars seem to be fascinating," says Nichola Rumsey, Ph.D., co-editor of *Visibly Different: Coping with Disfigurement* (Butterworth-Heinemann Medical, 1997). "People respond to them with a bit of fear, a bit of revulsion and a bit of excitement."

Why Do We Have Scars?

Our visceral response to scars reaches back through millions of years of human evolution. For reasons no one quite understands, humans develop bigger, thicker scars than any other animals. "Human wound healing appears to have been optimized for quick healing in dirty conditions," says biologist Mark W. J. Ferguson, Ph.D., a scar researcher at the University of Manchester.

The good news is that when we're cut or burned, our immune systems immediately go into overdrive to close and heal the wound, which may be why humans tend to live so much longer than other mammals. But the bad news is that our swift, strong inflammation response sets us up for nasty scars. Surgeon N. Scott Adzick, M.D., who studies scarring at the Center for Fetal Diagnosis and Treatment at the Children's Institute for Surgical Science in Philadelphia, puts it this way: "If you're a caveman or cavewoman running around, and you get bitten by a saber-toothed tiger, it makes sense to patch that wound together as quickly as possible in order to survive, as opposed to devoting the body's energy and resources to healing perfectly."

However, other theorists have offered some different—and intriguing—explanations of human's severe scarring. One theory suggests that human scarring evolved alongside human intelligence. As we started relying on our brains instead of our instincts to get us out of risky situations, scars developed to act as constant reminders of our previous mistakes.

> # The attack on model Marla Hanson made headlines—and, paradoxically, the fine network of scars it left on her face briefly made her a media star.

If, for example, some caveman tried to snag a juicy mastodon chop from the jaws of his cavedog, the scarred bite marks on his forearm would warn him not to try it again.

Another hypothesis suggests that scars serve as sexual attractors; when a cavewoman was courted by a heavily scarred caveman, she got the message that he was brave, bold and had a high-functioning immune system. (Of course, if the scar-as-memory-aid theory holds true, those scars also meant he was a bit slow on the uptake.)

Scars and Sex

To most middle-class Americans, the idea of scars as sexual lures seems bizarre. We think of scars as disfigurements, and try to hide them from view or even remove them completely. Yet our seemingly instinctive recoil is a fairly new and geographically limited phenomenon. Even today, many African tribal cultures still use "body art"—tattooing, branding, piercing and intentional scarring—to proclaim their ancient lineage, display their bravery and attract potential mates.

Women of the southeast Nuba, for example, traditionally received a set of body scars that chronicled their sexual history. When a young girl began to develop breasts, she got her first set of scars; those were followed by a second set marking her first menstruation, then by an elaborate final set incised after she weaned her first child. The Tiv, in Nigeria, have a highly developed esthetic of facial and body scarring, used extensively by both men and women to bring out each individual's most attractive features.

Psychologist Devendra Singh, Ph.D., at the University of Texas, sees a direct connection between the prevalence of scarring among African tribal groups and the continent's high rates of infectious disease. In general, he says, the more disease-ridden a community, the more likely its members—especially its women—will use scarring to show off their healthy immune systems and attract mates. "We found very systematic relationships," he says. "If you live in a society where pathogens are high, female-female competition is also very high." By decorating the breast and belly, particularly the navel, he notes, "you're advertising your femaleness."

In fact, he adds, anthropologists report that among some groups, women with scarred bellies are considered more sexually demanding—and therefore more likely to conceive. A decorated belly also draws attention to a woman's waist-to-hip ratio, which signals youthfulness and potential fertility. Similarly, males scar the face, shoulders and arms to point up their strength and sexual maturity. The sexual content of the scars can be explicit; one Yoruba scarification design for the upper thigh is called "finish at the vagina."

The Western world's apparent immunity to such sexually charged scarring is historically quite recent, insists former anthropology student Raven Rowanchilde, author of the article "Male Genital Modification: A Sexual Selection Interpretation," published in the journal *Human Nature* in 1996. "Westerners are suffering from the smoke damage of Platonic ideals," she says. It was only after Plato embraced the beauty of the idealized, natural human form that the Western world rejected such ancient forms of adornment.

"We went from tribal groups using these marks to symbolize lineage and status to having this pure, untouched body," says Rowanchilde, who now runs a body design studio in Toronto. "The mark of civilization became no marks at all." Judeo-Christian tradition embraced the unmarked body to distinguish itself from surrounding pagans. Leviticus clearly warns: "They shall not . . . make any cuttings in their flesh."

Yet scars can still carry a potent sexual message for Westerners. At the beginning of this century, upper-class Austrian men created a cult of the dueling scar, says historian Kevin McAleer, Ph.D., author of *Dueling: The Cult of Honor in Fin-de-Siecle Germany* (Princeton University Press, 1997). "The *renommier schmiss*, or bragging scar, was a mark of social status," McAleer notes. "It indicated you had been to university," where dueling societies were critical to social life.

These duelists subscribed to an ethos of exaggerated masculinity, in which skilled swordplay and fleetness of foot were less important than stolid fearlessness. Using saber-type weapons, the antagonists—wearing body padding and iron goggles—faced each other for dozens of brief rounds, with each man defending against five whacking strokes and then taking five cuts of his own. "This wasn't footwork, thrust and parry," McAleer says. "It was a mechanical robotic sort of motion," which the opponent would try to fend off until his endurance failed.

"The idea was to stand your man and show courage—not to inflict a wound, but to be wounded," he says. "That's the very strange part of it—the true winner was he who walked away with a nice juicy scar, to show that he'd stood the test. The point was not to get the other guy, but to show that you could take it. You'd get these guys who looked like they'd walked into a propeller. It was pretty gnarly, but the guys were damn proud to look that way."

Women responded ardently to these proudly displayed scars, which the combatants often soaked with beer or stuffed with horsehair, to increase their size and prominence. "The scars showed you had courage and education, and were good husband material," McAleer says. "Anyway, a lot of these kids were rather good-looking, and you didn't have to ruin your whole face in dueling. The scars usually accumulated on the left side of the face, so from the right profile, he still looked good. And even if it was an ugly, knotted scar, women were attracted by everything it implied, and the pride with which the wearer bore it." The cult of the dueling scar has faded, but hasn't entirely disappeared; Professor Ferguson, whose research focuses on scarless healing, claims he was once contacted by an Austrian who actually wanted his modest dueling scar made bigger.

Beautiful But Flawed

Although Americans have never made a cult of scar worship; we tend to find some scars strangely fascinating, particularly if they add character to an otherwise conventionally attractive face. In 1986, Maria Hanson was just one of a thousand pretty models trying to make their fortune in New York City. Then her landlord, angry when she spurned his sexual advances, hired two thugs who used a razor blade to slice her face apart. The attack made headlines—and, paradoxically, the fine network of scars it left on her face briefly made Hanson a media star.

"I imagine it has to do with the background level of facial attractiveness," Rumsey speculates. "If someone is pretty good-looking and they have a scar, I think the unconscious assumption would be that they got scarred in a way that wasn't their fault, because they were terribly brave. I think there's something about those with extreme levels of beauty that can make other people stereotype them as fairly shallow. Maybe a scar makes them a bit more human and desirable."

Many tribal cultures still use "body art"—tattooing, piercing, branding and scarring—to proclaim their lineage, display bravery and attract mates.

A scar on an otherwise flawless face fills us with intense curiosity; we long to hear the sexy or sad story behind it, and we feel slightly disappointed if the story is dull. One perfect example is a scene in the 1988 movie Working Girl, in which actress Melanie Griffith asks Harrison Ford about the (real) scar on his chiseled chin. "Some guy pulled a knife in Detroit," he boasts, then admits the truth: "I was 19 and I thought it'd be cool to have a pierced ear. My girlfriend stuck the needle through and I heard this pop and fainted and hit my chin on the toilet." (According to the many Web pages celebrating Ford's scar, the real story is even more mundane: he hit his chin during a minor traffic accident.)

Scars Intentional and Accidental

The story behind the scar seems to make all the difference in our response to it. "That's our initial response, 'What happened to you?'" Rumsey says. Even in cultures that prize ritual scarification, there's a sharp distinction between nature and culture. Intentional scars are considered beautiful, while random or accidental scars are ugly. To redeem an ugly scar, therefore, the wounded person must create a scenario that tells the story of the scar in an attractive and compelling light.

The ultimate illustration of this desire can be found in the self-portraits of painter Frida Kahlo. As a young woman, Kahlo's back and legs were scarred in a streetcar accident. In her paintings, she often portrayed herself as horribly mutilated, with gore dripping from her many wounds; one painting shows her cut open down the front.

"The scars in her paintings are mostly invented," says Hayden Herrera, a Kahlo biographer. "I think she painted them to force the viewer to respond to her predicament. If her paintings were mawkish, we'd hate them. But because she keeps her face this mask of reserve, and just shows her emotions through the scars and wounds, the scars are sort of noble, in some funny way, rather than self-pitying. She painted herself scarred so she could deal with it. Her paintings don't look like, 'Oh, help, help, I'm hurting.' They're somebody saying, 'This is what's happening to me. This is the way it is. I'm not going to hide it.' These paintings are so beautiful; they're incredibly distant and repressed, yet at the same time jumping

with emotion. Those paintings are like a ribbon around a bomb."

Self-Mutilation

The impulse that drove Kahlo to paint imaginary scars on her body is mirrored in patients who inflict real scars on themselves. "When I look at self-mutilation, I try to understand the meaning behind this supposedly senseless act," says psychiatrist Armando R. Favazza, M.D., author of Bodies Under Siege: Self-Mutilation and Body Modification in Culture and Psychiatry (Johns Hopkins University Press, 1996). For some patients, self-mutilation is a symptom of an underlying psychological problem; patients with borderline personality disorder, for example, often cut or burn themselves in an effort to relieve their overwhelming psychic pain. For other patients, Favazza says, self-mutilation is their primary psychological problem. "It usually starts in early adolescence and goes on for about 15 years, interspersed with periods of eating disorders and substance abuse," he says. "Some people call them multi-impulsive patients"

To outsiders, self-mutilation seems frightening and bizarre. But to the patients themselves, self-inflicted pain makes great internal sense. "It allows for fairly rapid, but short-term, relief from a lot of pathological symptoms," Favazza says. "The major one is intense, intense anxiety; when patients cut, it's like popping a balloon."

Self-mutilation can have great symbolic meaning for patients, as well. "It ties in with cultural ideas of bodily healing, religious salvation and establishment of order," Favazza explains. "When you look at cultural rituals that involve mutilation, the scars are signs of distinction." Similarly, patients can use their wounds and scars to create deeply personal semiotics. "I had one patient who was involved in an old-fashioned Oedipal-type situation, with her Dad coming on to her," Favazza recalls. "She was just cutting and cutting and cutting. She would create the symbol on her body; the gaping wound reminded her of a vagina, the vagina Daddy wanted. Then she'd go to the emergency room and solve the problem by having it sewn shut. Afterward, she'd go home and put baby powder and bandages on the wound. The scar was essentially the baby."

For many patients with self-inflicted wounds, the scars tell the story of their illness and their attempts to heal themselves.

"For patients in the middle of the syndrome, the scars are important," Favazza notes. "Special scars have special meanings. I look at every scar as a sign of the battle the patient has waged. Scar tissue is a sign that the patient has won, and is still alive."

Body Modification

The symbolism of scars reaches so deeply beneath the skin that increasing numbers of American youth are using intentional scarring—called body modification—to chronicle their emotional lives. "They say it's a rite of passage, an initiation into greater mysteries, an opening for beneficial spirits or a healing of the wounded psyche," says Favazza. He cites women who get body piercings after being raped. "By piercing themselves, they're reclaiming their bodies. It gives them a sense of control."

Lisa Romanienko, a sociology doctoral student at Louisiana State University, believes the mostly youthful members of the body modification movement are expressing their alienation from Western civilization, and use their scars, tattoos, brands and piercings as public signs of their disgust and defiance. These "self-symbolizers," as she calls them, actually enhance their self-esteem by offending and repulsing the bourgeois majority. "It's an alternative to political expression, in light of the decline of other organizations to express political views among the Left," Romanienko says. "Anyone can see why kids would be doing this. It's an intentional symbolic message."

Many young body modifiers maintain they're trying to connect themselves to humanity's tribal history, now lost in American civilization. "They see themselves as getting back to some kind of essentialism," says Daniel Wojcik, Ph.D., an associate professor of folklore at the University of Oregon and author of Punk and Neo-Tribal Body Art (University Press of Mississippi, 1995). "They learn about scarring practices in another culture, and then have themselves scarred as a rite of passage." Some, as Romanienko suggests, are primarily motivated by the shock value of their flashy scars. But many neotribalists are very secretive about their body adornments, scarring themselves for personal reasons, not political ones.

"The meanings are very diverse," Wojcik says. "It's dangerous, it's sexy. For some it's an esthetic impulse. Others attribute some transcendent significance to the act, and find

> **Increasing numbers of American youth are using intentional scarring—called body modification—to chronicle their emotional life. "It's a rite of passage, an initiation into greater mysteries, an opening for beneficial spirits or a healing of the wounded psyche."**

some kind of altered state of consciousness that's probably related to the pain involved and the endorphin rush that follows it. It certainly seems to be profoundly meaningful for them." For his book, Wojcik interviewed one unemployed Seattle youth named Perry Farrell, who later went on to fame in the rock bands Jane's Addiction and Porno for Pyros. Farrell's scars and piercings were inspired by photographs he saw in *National Geographic*. For Farrell, the scars were part of a self-made coming-of-age rite. "He told me, 'I need to become a man,' " Wojcik says. "He told me how painful it was, and how he felt transformed afterward."

The trouble is, it's hard to tell where fashionable body modification ends and pathological self-mutilation begins, especially when an individual turns to intentional wounding to mark an emotionally charged life event. "If you've suffered some kind of abuse, this is a way to acknowledge that in some kind of physical way," Wojcik observes. "Then it becomes a ritual, meaningful event. You're responding to a spiritual crisis, and you fortify yourself through these ancient forms of body modification." However, one person's ritual cleansing is another person's Post-Traumatic Stress Disorder.

To Favazza, the distinction is the scar's meaning to its owner—its story. "I define self-mutilation as something that derives from individual psychopathology, the product of loss of control," he says. "You can make a case that when you're symbolically reenacting what was done to you, you're controlling it."

Living with Scars

For the millions of Americans with scars left by accident or surgery, it might seem there's no debate about their meaning or symbolism—only the problem of trying to adjust to a highly visible, permanent and often disfiguring mark. However, Rumsey has found that even with unintended scars, their context plays a critical part in the emotional response of both bearer and viewer. "People who have a story find it much easier to cope," Rumsey says. "We often hear about people who get injured in war, or while saving somebody. They do really well, and come out confident enough to deal with it,

if it's a story they can happily tell that people want to know."

In fact, Rumsey's research indicates that psychological factors are the best predictors of a patient's response to a new scar. "You can't predict the effect of scarring from the size or type of disfigurement," she declares. "Some people get very upset about very minor marks." Instead, patients' future adjustment depends partly on their previous attitudes about physical appearance. "Prior experience and expectation tends to play a part," Rumsey says.

Some patients' attitudes are deeply affected by media depictions of people with scars. "In movies, the ones who have scars tend to be the baddies," Rumsey notes. That's a particularly important issue for children, who tend to be more vulnerable to such messages. Gender also plays a role; a poll by Rejuveness, marketer of alternative scar remedies, found that 65% of women said they were self-conscious about their scars, compared with 35% of men.

But the key factors seem to be the person's self-esteem and social skills, Rumsey believes. In her research, she's found that when people with scars are friendly, relaxed and outgoing, they can overcome strangers' initial recoil. Rumsey began her studies by looking at the impact of scars on basic social interactions. At a first encounter, she says, "I found that people stand about a foot farther away if you've got a disfigurement." That simple fact alone has an enormous impact on any social interaction, she says. "If you take a good step backward, it changes the feeling between the two people, so it's less personal and more distant."

She also found that visible scars had an enormous impact on others' basic helping behaviors. In one study, she and her colleagues posed as market researchers, asking consumers to fill out a questionnaire. Not surprisingly, they found consumers were initially most likely to cooperate with attractive researchers. When the researchers wore artificial scars, they found that significantly fewer people approached them—but those who did offered more help than those who approached unmarked people. "We found that if you could get over that initial approach, people would compensate quite strongly for it."

The researchers then started looking at the behavior of disfigured people them-

selves. Many scarred patients felt self-conscious or defensive, which made them unwilling to hurdle that social barrier. Others overcompensated by behaving rather aggressively, "which further throws things out of balance," Rumsey found. Such shyness and belligerence are socially fatal; in one study, she asked her subjects to rate their responses to a pair of researchers, one displaying great social skills and the other visibly ill at ease. When the researchers wore fake scars, they found that people's responses were polarized. "People rated the skilled person very positively, and the non-skilled person very negatively," Rumsey says. "My conclusion was that if you couldn't change the world's inherent biases, you could do something by attacking social skills and trying to put it a bit more under the person's control."

Rumsey's academic work got a real-world endorsement in 1992 when James Partridge launched Changing Faces, an English support organization for people with facial disfigurements. Partridge, who had been severely burned in a car fire when he was 18 years old, had written a book about living with scars (*Changing Faces: The Challenge of Facial Disfigurement* Phoenix Society, 1992). "There is a point at which my scars became less repellent and more attractive," observes Partridge, now 46. "I don't think it had anything to do with their physical appearance. I think it had a lot to do with the coping skills I developed."

In some ways, Partridge believes, unintended scars can enhance someone's attractiveness by forcing him to develop extraordinary self-assurance. "I doubt very much whether the woman who was attracted to the Austrian duelist was actually attracted by the physical touch of the scars," he says. "It was his stature, his posture, his way of looking her in the eye—his entire physical chemistry, if there is such a term. It's not the scar itself that's attractive, but the person who shines out from behind this scarred face."

The trouble is, many people with facial scars find themselves locked into a social death spiral. When strangers stare or flinch, they respond by withdrawing—which further undermines their social dexterity. So Rumsey began looking for ways to help patients get past those painful first meetings. "You've got to learn how first impressions are formed," Rumsey says. "Let's find techniques of showing them what a witty person you are, what fun you are to be with, and develop a repertoire of things to talk about for a minute or two until that other person settles down. If you can achieve the confidence to depersonalize other people's reactions, it ceases to be a problem."

Rumsey studied the effects of Changing Faces' workshops, which bring together small groups of facially disfigured people to share their experiences and develop some practical strategies for dealing with socially stressful situations. She found that workshop participants did report significant improvement in their ability to handle strangers. However, since all the participants were self-referred, it wasn't clear whether the workshop solutions would work for less-motivated patients. So Rumsey created a pilot project to offer similar interventions to a broader group. "We set up a kind of disfigurement support unit," she says, asking for doctors to refer anyone with a facial scar. That research is still ongoing (slowed, in part, by some medical doctors' resistance

to referring patients for psychological counseling).

Right now, the biggest challenge is convincing doctors and patients that the story behind the injury is just as important to the healing process as the wound itself. "Some injuries are much more difficult to carry, because they're much more difficult to explain," Rumsey says. A scar inflicted during the heroic rescue of a child trapped in a burning building inspires admiration, but no one is likely to be too sympathetic when a scarred person admits being injured while driving drunk. Adds Rumsey: "If you can help them to think up a good reason behind the injury, something they feel more confident and happy with, it's so much easier to handle the inevitable questions."

Those questions, however rude, reflect our hard-wired human curiosity about scars. When we see a scarred face, we instinctively find our eyes drawn to it, and our minds drawn to the story that scar may tell; a few insignificant decades of socialization are no match for millions of years of natural selec-

tion. "If people look different, they almost become public property," Rumsey notes. "You can't sit on a train or walk down a street without people staring. When you walk around with a very visible disfigurement, you know that everyone wants to ask, 'What happened to you?' "

ELIZABETH AUSTIN once saw scars as cosmetic flaws. While writing an article on scar prevention and repair, however, her squeamishness turned into fascination. "It was eye-opening to realize how much sexual meaning scars convey in other cultures—and quite frankly, it forced me to admit that I think Harrison Ford's scar is kind of sexy," she says. In *Marks of Mystery*, Austin makes clear that "it's not the scar itself that intrigues us. It's the story behind it." The 1996 winner of the National Mental Health Association Award for Best Magazine Journalism, Austin has also written for magazines such as *Time, Self* and *U.S. News and World Report.*

Unit Selections

Key Points to Consider

❖ How would you reduce the level of violent crime in this country?

❖ What constitutional rights would you be willing to forgo to reduce crime?

❖ How can we change the criminal justice system to serve the needs of the people better?

❖ What is the cause of increased gang violence in the United States? How should the government and society address the gang problem successfully?

 **Links** **www.dushkin.com/online/**

These sites are annotated on pages 4 and 5.

A few years ago, while on an airplane, I starting talking about crime with the woman seated next to me. She told me that she felt that society had to deal with more than its fair share of crime. Her solution to crime was to shoot all of the criminals. I then asked her whether she really would want to kill all of the criminals. She said yes. I replied that self-report surveys consistently demonstrate that more than 90 percent of Americans commit crimes for which they could be incarcerated, and I asked her whether she wanted to kill 90 percent of the U.S. population. Her response was no, she only wanted to kill real criminals. When I asked her what she meant by real criminals, the response was "murderers and drug dealers." This was her social definition of crime as a form of deviance. The woman's answers were not surprising, because they were consistent with what many Americans believe about crime.

When people think of deviant behavior, they often think of crime. This is not surprising in a society where crime has become an issue so central to our everyday lives. Opening a morning newspaper without reading about the latest murders is impossible. My own town of Jonesboro, Arkansas is still dealing with a school shooting that ended the lives of a schoolteacher and four innocent children. This incident and the media barrage that followed have forever changed the image of our community. Television news brings us many stories on crime. Recently, a producer for a television station in the southern United States was asked why the news shown always started with a crime story and often spent half the show's time dealing with crime. The producer responded that blood and guts sell advertising. That is, the station could build its market share based on having the most graphic news stories in the area. Americans are both fascinated by crime and terrified of its consequences. Stories of crime and violence entertain us wherever we turn the television dial. With shows like *Cops, Law and Order, NYPD Blue*, and countless others, Americans can get their fill of crime. Thus, it is not surprising that when cross-sections of the American public are surveyed about what they perceive as the most serious social problem affecting the United States today, the majority say that it is crime.

The number of crimes committed every year justifiably enrages the American public. Their anger is picked up by the politicians who, interested in maintaining their positions, readily act without considering the causes of crime and the consequences of their actions. As many criminologists recognize, crime is deviant behavior most commonly carried out by teenagers who are 15 to 19 years of age. When our society has many teenagers, it has much crime. Drugs make matters far worse. Historically, cocaine and heroin were the drugs of choice for middle-class white women. These

drugs were incorporated with alcohol into various concoctions and sold as wonder drugs. In the 1940s and 1950s, drug use was confined primarily to young lower-class black males. It was only in the 1960s, when drug use became popular among middle- and upper-class Americans, that crime became an increasingly major problem. Beginning in the middle 1980s and continuing to this day, inexpensive drugs have flooded the market, accessible to anybody with the necessary resources to pay for them. With drugs such as crack cocaine have come increased murder, robbery, and other violent crimes. Increases in such risk factors as teenage parenthood, single-parent households, and children living in poverty have increased the likelihood that many children will grow up in a social setting that create opportunities for criminal activity. The future results are foreboding.

Politicians' "quick fix so you will reelect me" answers have consequences as well. In his speech at the 1992 Democratic National Convention, Jesse Jackson noted that on any given day, one-third of all black males in the United States are under correctional supervision, whether it is prison, jail, probation, or parole. He spoke of the long-term consequences for families, for children, and for this country. When we imprison fathers, they cannot support their families, they cannot serve as role models for their children, and they cost America money. Annually, U.S. taxpayers spend more money to imprison one average inmate than it would cost to send that same inmate to the most expensive college or university in the country. However, out of fear of crime, the American public is willing to build ever more prisons, to house ever more criminals, without regard for the future. Public attention may be less focused on long-term solutions such as drug-use treatment and prevention, education, training, and job creation than on imprisoning criminals.

Violent crime does not choose its victims. Victims could be drug dealers, police officers, spouses, or children. Nevertheless, crime affects everyone—victims' families, friends, and the rest of society as well. Also, we need to consider how violence begets violence. Sometimes victims, or their families, are bent on revenge. In other cases, people are tired of crime, the mistakes of the criminal justice system, and the perceived failure of government to control crime. These citizens may choose to strike out at the government and fellow Americans as a way of dealing with their frustration. They may be justifiably angry, but their actions are no better than those of the people whom they choose to condemn.

The readings for this unit were chosen to provide an overview of crime, particularly violent crime, as the American people perceive it. Different types of violent crime, both in the United States and abroad, are presented.

Maleness and aggression do not have to go together. A "culture of honor" underlies some high murder rates

Men, Honor and Murder

By Richard E. Nisbett and Dov Cohen

Homicide overwhelmingly involves males—as both perpetrators and victims. Evolutionary psychologists Martin Daly and Margo Wilson estimate that across a wide range of cultures a man is more than 20 times more likely to kill another man than a woman is to kill another woman, a finding they explain by arguing that men are more risk prone than women. Moreover, men are more likely to kill women than the other way around. When a woman does commit homicide, she usually kills a man who has repeatedly physically abused her.

These facts, together with the observation that males are the more aggressive sex in nearly all mammals, have led many people to suppose that men are unavoidably aggressive and that homicide is a natural consequence of male biology. Yet the striking variation in homicide rates among different societies makes it clear that, whatever men's predispositions may be, cultures have a great influence on the likelihood that a man will kill. For example, Colombia's rate is 15 times that of Costa Rica, and the U.S. rate is 10 times that of Norway. Marked regional differences exist even within the U.S. We and our colleague

Andrew Reaves have established that in small U.S. cities in the South and the Southwest, the homicide rate for white males is about double that in the rest of the country. We also found that a white man living in a small county in the South is four times more likely to kill than one living in a small county in the Midwest. By making detailed regional comparisons, we have been able to rule out several explanations that have previously been offered to account for similar data, such as the history of slavery in the South, the higher temperatures there and the greater incidence of poverty.

Although there are surely many reasons for regional differences, we believe that one particular set of conditions reliably elicits high rates of homicide. It occurs when men face danger from the actions of other males and the state does not provide protection. Men respond by resorting to self-protection and demonstrating that they are strong enough to deter aggression.

This type of social system is known as a culture of honor. A man establishes his honor by tolerating no challenge or disrespect, responding to insults and threats to his property with threatened or actual violence.

Such a code of behavior deters theft and wanton aggression, but it also requires that violence sometimes be employed: disputants cannot be too willing to back down, or honor will be compromised.

This type of culture dominates almost the entire Mediterranean basin and most of the New World countries influenced by Spanish culture. It is found among the Masai of East Africa, the horsemen of the central Asian steppes and the Native American horsemen of the plains. In the past, it also held sway in Ireland and Scotland, as well as in most of Scandinavia. We have found that it prevails in the U.S. South as well.

What characteristics do these disparate groups have in common? One we think is important is animal husbandry. It plays, or once played, a large role in their economies. Animals are easily stolen, so it is crucial for a man who owns livestock to establish that he is not someone to be challenged lightly. Ethnographer John K. Campbell illustrated the point when he described how critical the first quarrel is in the life of a young Greek shepherd: "Quarrels are necessarily public." To gain respect, a novice shepherd must challenge not only obvious insults but

Rates of Homicide by White Males

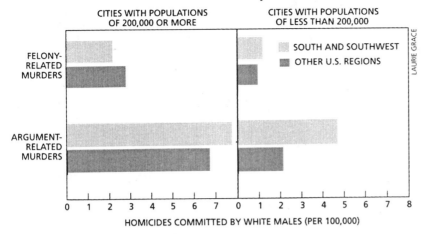

HIGHER RATES OF HOMICIDE in the South and Southwest result from argument-related murders—not felony-related ones. The former are more common in those regions, especially in small cities and rural areas. Large cities in the South and Southwest have more argument-related but fewer felony-related murders than cities elsewhere.

also subtly concocted slights. (The reader may recall people in high school who were gifted at constructing such insults: "You looking at my girlfriend?" "No." "What's a matter, she's not good-looking?")

The U.S. South was settled largely by herdsmen from Scotland and Ireland in the 17th and 18th centuries, when law enforcement was virtually nonexistent. Many of the settlers' descendants relied on keeping hogs and cattle, too. The northern U.S., in contrast, was colonized mainly by tillers of the soil from England, Germany and the Netherlands. Crop growers are at much less risk of having their capital assets stolen, and they must get along with their neighbors. The bluster of the herdsman would not serve them well. We think this is why homicide rates for white males are higher in the South than in the North. (All the statistics we discuss below make reference to white males.)

Many observers have assumed that the South is simply more brutal than the rest of the country. But its lead in the murder department is entirely the result of the number of homicides that, according to data from the Federal Bureau of Investigation, probably stemmed from insults, barroom brawls, lovers' triangles or neighbors' quarrels. Among cities

that have a population of more than 200,000, those in the South and Southwest actually have fewer homicides that occur in the context of a felony such as a robbery or burglary than do those elsewhere. Sociologist John Shelton Reed of the University of North Carolina at Chapel Hill has commented that you are probably safer in the South than in the North if you avoid quarrels and stay out of other people's bedrooms.

Self-Defense in the South

Southerners favor violence in general no more than other Americans. They differ from northerners mainly over the use of force to protect home and property, to respond to insults and to socialize children. Our research shows, for example, that southerners are more likely to think it justifiable to kill to protect one's house. They are more likely to take offense at an insult and to think violence is an appropriate recourse. And they are much more inclined than northerners to say they would counsel their child to fight a bully rather than reason with him.

The differences go beyond attitudes. We conducted an experiment

in which an accomplice insulted a college student by bumping him in a narrow hallway and swearing at him. (The students had agreed to participate in a study but were misled about its nature and were given no clue that the corridor incident was staged.) Northerners tended to shrug off the episode. The angry faces of southerners revealed that they did not take it so lightly. Moreover, their cortisol and testosterone levels—but not those of northerners—surged after the insult, which suggests stress and preparedness for aggression.

For the clincher, we confronted some research subjects with another challenge immediately after the insult. As the subject was walking down the narrow hallway, a six-foot, three-inch, 250-pound accomplice of the experimenter walked toward him down the middle of the corridor. Southerners who had not been insulted stepped to one side when the bruiser was about nine feet away. But those who had been insulted walked to within three feet before they stood aside. Apparently the southerners who had just been offended were in no mood to be trifled with, even by someone else—a dangerous frame of mind when the new antagonist has a 100-pound weight advantage. In contrast, the northern students' decision on how close to approach before stepping aside was unaffected by whether they had been insulted.

We think we have some interesting evidence on what keeps the honor tradition alive. Southerners seem to think they will be regarded as unmanly if they do not respond to an insult, and compared with northerners they perceive more peer support for aggression.

Some of our research subjects knew that another person, whom they were just about to meet, had observed the bump-and-insult incident. After the meeting, we asked the subjects to assess what this observer thought of them. Southern participants, but not northern ones, reported that the observer probably thought they were weak because they had not responded forcefully enough. (They were most likely wrong in this. When shown videotapes of people responding to an insult, students from the South rated aggressive responders whom they watched to be just as unattractive as did northerners.)

In another version of our experiment, done with our colleague Joseph A. Vandello, the insult occurred in front of a group of people. Southerners judged this audience to be more encouraging of aggression than did northerners who watched the same interaction. Such a tendency to perceive support for aggression erroneously could be responsible for maintaining violence as an option.

Institutions in the South also reinforce the culture of honor. We sent retail outlets around the country a job-seeking letter purporting to be from a young man who had killed someone who had been sleeping with his fiancée. Responders from the South were more sympathetic than northerners were. In addition, we sent college newspaper editors around the country a police blotter-style account of a crime of passion that involved an insult. We asked the editors to write up the story for their paper for a fee. Northern accounts strongly condemned the insulted perpetrator; southern accounts were much more sympathetic. A version of the story that contained no insult elicited no comparable differences.

Furthermore, laws and social policies in the South reflect the culture of honor. Southern laws are more likely to exonerate people who

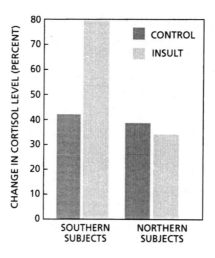
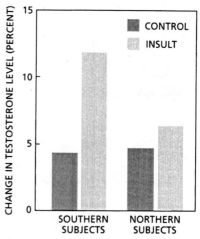

LAURIE GRACE

HORMONE LEVELS surged in southerners who had been insulted in an experiment but changed much less in southerners in a control group who had not been insulted. Northerners in either group were relatively little affected.

shoot someone escaping with their property. And many statutes in the South endorse a "true man" rule, which allows someone to stand his ground and kill rather than forcing him to beat a cowardly retreat from an attacker.

The South's culture of honor will surely change. It has already come a long way since the era when a man would ask a prospective son-in-law if he had ever done any "sparkin' "—putting his life on the line in combat. (If the answer was no, the suit was over.) Economic and social changes, together with immigration from other regions, will eventually erode what remains of the tradition.

In the meantime, the contrast between North and South shows that violence by men is a matter of nurture as much as one of nature. Male aggression is not inevitable. Whether a man reaches for his gun or his civility when insulted is a matter of culture.

The Authors

RICHARD E. NISBETT and DOV COHEN study the relation between culture and thought processes. Nisbett is co-director of the Culture and Cognition Program at the University of Michigan. Most of his research focuses on differences in reasoning resulting from education and culture. He hails from Texas, and while doing the work reported here, he discovered that you can take the boy out of the South but not the South out of the boy. Cohen is assistant professor of psychology at the University of Illinois. He studies how culture affects people, and vice versa.

Further Reading

HONOR. Julian Pitt-Rivers in *International Encyclopedia of the Social Sciences,* Vol. 6. Edited by David Sills. Macmillan, 1968.
HONOR AND VIOLENCE IN THE OLD SOUTH. Bertram Wyatt-Brown. Oxford University Press, 1986.
CULTURE AND HONOR: THE PSYCHOLOGY OF VIOLENCE IN THE SOUTH. Richard E. Nisbett and Dov Cohen. Westview Press, 1996.

WE ARE TRAINING OUR KIDS TO KILL

The desensitizing techniques used for training solders are being replicated in contemporary mass media—movies, television, and video games, giving rise to the alarming rate of homicide and violence in our schools and communities.

by Lt. Col. Dave Grossman

I am from Jonesboro, Arkansas. I travel the world training medical, law enforcement, and U. S. military personnel about the realities of warfare. I try to make those who carry deadly force keenly aware of the magnitude of killing. Too many law enforcement and military personnel act like "cowboys," never stopping to think about who they are and what they are called to do. I hope I am able to give them a reality check.

So here I am, a world traveler and an expert in the field of "killology," when the (then) largest school massacre in American history happens in my hometown of Jonesboro, Arkansas. That was the March 24, 1998, schoolyard shooting deaths of four girls and a teacher. Ten others were injured, and two boys, ages 11 and 13, were jailed, charged with murder.

Virus of Violence

To understand the *why* behind Littleton, Jonesboro, Springfield, Pearl, and Paducah, and all the other outbreaks of this "virus of violence," we need to first understand the magnitude of the problem. The per capita murder rate doubled in this country between 1957—when the FBI started keeping track of the data—and 1992. A fuller picture of the problem, however, is indicated by the rate at which people are attempting to kill one another—the aggravated assault rate. That rate in America has gone from around 60 per 100,000 in 1957 to over 440 per 100,000 in the middle of this decade. As bad as this is, it would be much worse were it not for two major factors.

The first is the increased imprisonment of violent offenders. The prison population in America nearly quadrupled between 1975 and 1992. According to criminologist John A. DiIulio, "dozens of credible empirical analyses . . . leave no doubt that the increased use of prisons averted millions of serious crimes." If it were not for our tremendous imprisonment rate (the highest of any industrialized nation), the aggravated assault rate and the murder rate would undoubtedly be even higher.

The second factor keeping the murder rate from being even worse is medical technology. According to the U.S. Army Medical Service Corps, a wound that would have killed nine out of ten soldiers in World War II, nine out of ten could have survived in Vietnam. Thus, by a very conservative estimate, if we still had a 1940-level medical tech-

Dave Grossman is a voice to be heeded. He believes it is time to take action, by lawsuits if necessary, against manufacturers of video games that train youth to kill. Grossman, a former Army Ranger and paratrooper, is an eminent authority on the subject of motivating killers. His book *On Killing* is an important wake-up call to all who want to stop the wanton carnage in our schools. The fantastic accuracy of the kids who shoot their classmates and teachers happens because they practice killing on their video games. The author notes that some of the kids have shot with greater accuracy than military men who are trained with the very same techniques used in the video games. We are promoting the violence by permitting our kids to be taught to kill skillfully.

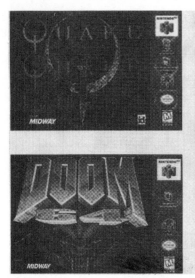

Video games rake in $5.3 billion each year with violent games such as *Quake* and *Doom* at the top of the list; the most violent killing game, *Mortal Kombat,* ranked number one. Eric Harris and Dylan Klebold, the teens responsible for the massacre in Littleton, Colorado, were fond of *Doom,* in which players try to rack up the most kills. Although the entertainment software industry issues warning labels alerting parents that the games are intended for "mature" consumers 17 and older, critics believe that the warning actually makes the games more attractive to the industry's primary audience of preteen boys ages 8 to 13. Senator Orrin Hatch (R-UT) recently noted that a store clerk "recommended" *Quake* and *Doom* to a 12-year-old child. The boy later observed, "I could have bought anything in the store if I had enough money."

nology today, our murder rate would be ten times higher than it is. The murder rate has been held down by the development of sophisticated life-saving skills and techniques, such as helicopter medevacs, 911 operators, paramedics, CPR, trauma centers, and medicines.

Today, both our assault rate and murder rate are at phenomenally high levels. Both are increasing worldwide. In Canada, according to their Center for Justice, per capita assaults increased almost fivefold between 1964 and 1993, attempted murder increased nearly sevenfold, and murders doubled. Similar trends can be seen in other countries in the per capita violent crime rates reported to Interpol between 1977 and 1993. In Australia and New Zealand, the assault rate increased approximately fourfold, and the murder rate nearly doubled in both nations. The assault rate tripled in Sweden and approximately doubled in Belgium, Denmark, England and Wales, France, Hungary, the Netherlands, and Scotland. Meanwhile, all these nations had an associated (but smaller) increase in murder.

This virus of violence is occurring worldwide. The explanation for it has to be some new factor that is occurring in all of these countries. There are many factors involved, and none should be discounted: for example, the prevalence of guns in our society. But violence is rising in many nations with Draconian gun laws. And though we should never downplay child abuse, poverty, or racism, there is only one new variable present in each of these countries that bears the exact same fruit: media violence presented as entertainment for children.

Killing Is Unnatural

Before retiring from the military, I spent almost a quarter of a century as an army infantry officer and a psychologist, learning and studying how to enable people to kill. Believe me, we are very good at it. But it does not come naturally; you have to be taught to kill. And just as the army is conditioning people to kill, we are indiscriminately doing the

same thing to our children, but without the safeguards.

After the Jonesboro killings, the head of the American Academy of Pediatrics Task Force on Juvenile Violence came to town and said that children don't naturally kill. It is a learned skill. And they learn it from abuse and violence in the home and, most pervasively, from violence as entertainment in television, the movies, and interactive video games.

Killing requires training because there is a built-in aversion to killing one's own kind. I can best illustrate this fact by drawing on my own military research into the act of killing.

We all know how hard it is to have a discussion with a frightened or angry human being. Vasoconstriction, the narrowing of the blood vessels, has literally closed down the forebrain—that great gob of gray matter that makes one a human being and distinguishes one from a dog. When those neurons close down, the midbrain takes over and your thought processes and reflexes are indistinguishable from your dog's. If you've worked with ani-

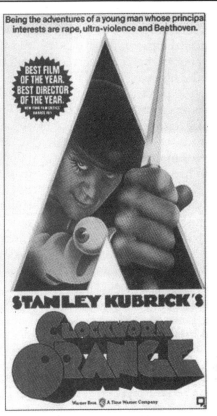

Gruesome violence in movies has long been the target of parents, educators, and experts in social psychology. When Bill Savage, a friend of best-selling author John Grisham, was killed by a young couple who had watched and glamorized *Natural Born Killers*—a move about a disturbed young couple (above) who go on a killing spree—Grisham became involved in a product-liability lawsuit against the film's producer, Oliver Stone, and Time Warner. The lawsuit alleged that the movie had caused injury in the same way a product like cigarettes does, so manufacturers should be held accountable. *A Clockwork Orange* also has been targeted as inspiration for violent copy-cat crimes.

Michael Carneal, the 14-year-old charged with shooting and killing three classmates in Paducah, Kentucky, cited scenes from the movie *Basketball Diaries* as the model for his actions. The victims' parents have filed a $130 million lawsuit against the film's makers of violent video games, including *Doom* and *Quake*, for allegedly training Carneal "how to point and shoot a gun in a fashion making him an extraordinarily effective killer."

mals, you have some understanding of what happens to frightened human beings on the battlefield. The battlefield and violent crime are in the realm of midbrain responses.

Within the midbrain there is a powerful, God-given resistance to killing your own kind. Every species, with a few exceptions, has a hardwired resistance to killing its own kind in territorial and mating battles. When animals with antlers and horns fight one another, they head-butt in a nonfatal fashion. But when they fight any other species, they go to the side to gut and gore. Piranhas will turn their fangs on anything, but they fight one another with flicks of the tail. Rattlesnakes will bite anything, but they wrestle one another. Almost every species has this hard-wired resistance to killing its own kind.

When we human beings are overwhelmed with anger and fear, we slam head-on into that midbrain resistance that generally prevents us from killing. Only sociopaths—who by definition don't have that resistance—lack this innate violence immune system.

Throughout all human history, when humans have fought each other, there has been a lot of posturing. Adversaries make loud noises and puff themselves up, trying to daunt the enemy. There is a lot of fleeing and submission. Ancient battles were nothing more than great shoving matches. It was not until one side turned and ran that most of the killing happened, and most of that was stabbing people in the back. All of the ancient military historians report that the vast majority of killing happened in pursuit when one side was fleeing.

In more modern times, the average firing rate was incredibly low in Civil War battles. British author Paddy Griffith demonstrates in his book *The Battle Tactics of the Civil War* that the killing potential of the average Civil War regiment was anywhere from five hundred to a thousand men per minute. The actual killing rate was only one or two men per minute per regiment. At the Battle of Gettysburg, of the 27,000 muskets picked up from the dead and dying after the battle, 90 percent were loaded. This is an anomaly, because it took 90 percent of their time to load muskets and only 5 percent to fire. But even more amazing, of the thousands of loaded muskets, only half had multiple loads in the barrel—one had 23 loads in the barrel.

In reality, the average man would load his musket and bring it to his shoulder, but he could not bring himself to kill. He would be brave, he would stand shoulder to shoulder, he would do what he was trained to do; but at the moment of

like a 15 percent literacy rate among librarians. And fix it the military did. By the Korean War, around 55 percent of the soldiers were willing to fire to kill. And by Vietnam, the rate rose to over 90 percent.

The method in this madness: desensitization.

How the military increases the killing rate of soldiers in combat is instructive because our culture today is doing the same thing to our children. The training methods militaries use are brutalization, classical conditioning, operant conditioning, and role modeling. I will explain each of these in the military context and show how these same factors are contributing to the phenomenal

watch something happening on television and mimic that action. But it isn't until children are six or seven years old that the part of the brain kicks in that lets them understand where information comes from. Even though young children have some understanding of what it means to pretend, they are developmentally unable to distinguish clearly between fantasy and reality.

When young children see somebody shot, stabbed, raped, brutalized, degraded, or murdered on TV, to them it is as though it were actually happening. To have a child of three, four, or five watch a "splatter" movie, learning to relate to a character for the first 90 minutes and then in the last 30 minutes watch helplessly as that new friend is hunted and brutally murdered, is the moral and psychological equivalent of introducing your child to a friend, letting her play with that friend, and then butchering that friend in front of your child's eyes. And this happens to our children hundreds upon hundreds of times.

Every time a child plays an interactive point-and-shoot game, he is learning the exact same conditioned reflex skills as a soldier or police officer in training.

truth, he could not bring himself to pull the trigger. And so he lowered the weapon and loaded it again. Of those who did fire, only a tiny percentage fired to hit. The vast majority fired over the enemy's head.

During World War II, U.S. Army Brig. Gen. S. L. A. Marshall had a team of researchers study what soldiers did in battle. For the first time in history, they asked individual soldiers what they did in battle. They discovered that only 15 to 20 percent of the individual riflemen could bring themselves to fire at an exposed enemy soldier.

That is the reality of the battlefield. Only a small percentage of soldiers are able and willing to participate. Men are willing to die. They are willing to sacrifice themselves for their nation; but they are not willing to kill. It is a phenomenal insight into human nature; but when the military became aware of that, they systematically went about the process of trying to fix this "problem." From the military perspective, a 15 percent firing rate among riflemen is

increase of violence in our culture.

Brutalization and desensitization are what happens at boot camp. From the moment you step off the bus, you are physically and verbally abused: countless push-ups, endless hours at attention or running with heavy loads, while carefully trained professionals take turns screaming at you. Your head is shaved; you are herded together naked and dressed alike, losing all individuality. This brutalization is designed to break down your existing mores and norms, and force you to accept a new set of values that embraces destruction, violence, and death as a way of life. In the end, you are desensitized to violence and accept it as a normal and essential survival skill in your brutal new world.

Something very similar to this desensitization toward violence is happening to our children through violence in the media—but instead of 18-year-olds, it begins at the age of 18 months when a child is first able to discern what is happening on television. At that age, a child can

Sure, they are told: "Hey, it's all for fun. Look, this isn't real; it's just TV." And they nod their little heads and say OK. But they can't tell the difference. Can you remember a point in your life or in your children's lives when dreams, reality, and television were all jumbled together? That's what it is like to be at that level of psychological development. That's what the media are doing to them.

The Journal of the American Medical Association published the definitive epidemiological study on the impact of TV violence. The research demonstrated what happened in numerous nations after television made its appearance as compared to nations and regions without TV. The two nations or regions being compared are demographically and ethnically identical; only one variable is different: the presence of television. In every nation, region, or city with television, there is an immediate explosion of violence on the playground, and within 15 years there is a doubling of the murder rate. Why 15 years? That is how long it takes for the brutalization of a three- to five-year-old to reach the "prime crime age." That is how long it takes for you to reap what you have sown when you brutalize and desensitize a three-year-old.

Today the data linking violence in the media to violence in society are superior to those linking cancer and tobacco. Hundreds of sound scientific studies demonstrate the social impact of brutalization by the media. *The Journal of the American Medical Association* concluded that "the introduction of television in the 1950s

them. And one by one, a select few Japanese soldiers would go into the ditch and bayonet "their" prisoner to death. This is a horrific way to kill another human being. Up on the bank, countless other young soldiers would cheer them on in their violence. Comparatively few soldiers actually killed in these situations, but by making the others watch and cheer, the Japanese were able to use these kinds of atrocities to classically condition a very large audience to associate pleasure with human death and suffering. Immediately afterwards, the soldiers who had been spectators were treated to sake, the

titions of this, he associates violence with nausea. And it limits his ability to be violent.

We are doing the exact opposite: Our children watch vivid pictures of human suffering and death, and they learn to associate it with their favorite soft drink and candy bar, or their girlfriend's perfume.

After the Jonesboro shootings, one of the high-school teachers told me how her students reacted when she told them about the shootings at the middle school. "They laughed," she told me with dismay. A similar reaction happens all the time in movie theaters when there is bloody violence. The young people laugh and cheer and keep right on eating popcorn and drinking pop. We have raised a generation of barbarians who have learned to associate violence with pleasure, like the Romans cheering and snacking as the Christians were slaughtered in the Colosseum.

"We have raised a generation of barbarians who have learned to associate violence with pleasure ... a phenomenon I call AVIDS—Acquired Violence Immune Deficiency Syndrome."

caused a subsequent doubling of the homicide rate, i.e., long-term childhood exposure to television is a causal factor behind approximately one half of the homicides committed in the United States, or approximately 10,000 homicides annually." The article went on to say that "... if, hypothetically, television technology had never been developed, there would today be 10,000 fewer homicides each year in the United States, 70,000 fewer rapes, and 700,000 fewer injurious assaults" (June 10, 1992).

Classical Conditioning

Classical conditioning is like the famous case of Pavlov's dogs they teach in Psychology 101. The dogs learned to associate the ringing of the bell with food, and once conditioned, the dogs could not hear the bell without salivating. The Japanese were masters at using classical conditioning with their soldiers. Early in World War II, Chinese prisoners were placed in a ditch on their knees with their hands bound behind

best meal they had in months, and to so-called comfort girls. The result? They learned to associate committing violent acts with pleasure.

The Japanese found these kinds of techniques to be extraordinarily effective at quickly enabling very large numbers of soldiers to commit atrocities in the years to come. Operant conditioning (which we will look at shortly) teaches you to kill, but classical conditioning is a subtle but powerful mechanism that teaches you to like it.

This technique is so morally reprehensible that there are very few examples of it in modern U.S. military training, but there are some clear-cut examples of it being done by the media to our children. What is happening to our children is the reverse of the aversion therapy portrayed in the movie *A Clockwork Orange*. In *A Clockwork Orange*, a brutal sociopath, a mass murderer, is strapped to a chair and forced to watch violent movies while he is injected with a drug that nauseates him. So he sits and gags and retches as he watches the movies. After hundreds of repe-

The result is a phenomenon that functions much like AIDS, a phenomenon I call AVIDS—Acquired Violence Immune Deficiency Syndrome. AIDS has never killed anybody. It destroys your immune system, and then other diseases that shouldn't kill you become fatal. Television violence by itself does not kill you. It destroys your violence immune system and conditions you to derive pleasure from violence. And once you are at close range with another human being, and it's time for you to pull that trigger, Acquired Violence Immune Deficiency Syndrome can destroy your midbrain resistance.

Operant Conditioning

The third method the military uses is operant conditioning, a very powerful repetitive procedure of stimulus-response, stimulus-response. A benign example is the use of flight simulators to train pilots. An airline pilot in training sits in front of a flight simulator for endless hours; when a particular warning light goes on, he is taught to react in a certain way. When another warning light goes on, a different reaction is required. Stimulus-response, stimulus-response, stimulus-response. One day the pilot is actually flying a jumbo jet; the plane is going down, and 300 people are screaming behind him. He is wetting his seat cushion, and he is scared out of his wits; but he does the right thing. Why? Because he has been conditioned to respond reflexively to this particular crisis.

When people are frightened or angry, they will do what they have been conditioned to do. In fire drills, children learn to file out of the school in orderly fashion. One day there is a real fire, and they are frightened out of their wits; but they do exactly what they have been conditioned to do, and it saves their lives.

The military and law enforcement community have made killing a conditioned response. This has substantially raised the firing rate on the modern battlefield. Whereas infantry training in World War II used bull's-eye targets, now soldiers learn to fire at realistic, man-shaped silhouettes that pop into their field of view. That is the stimulus. The trainees have only a split second to engage the target. The conditioned response is to shoot the target, and then it drops. Stimulus-response, stimulus-response, stimulus-response—soldiers or police officers experience hundreds of repetitions. Later, when soldiers are on the battlefield or a police officer is walking a beat and somebody pops up with a gun, they will shoot reflexively and shoot to kill. We know that 75 to 80 percent

of the shooting on the modern battlefield is the result of this kind of stimulus-response training.

Now, if you're a little troubled by that, how much more should we be troubled by the fact that every time a child plays an interactive point-and-shoot video game, he is learning the exact same conditioned reflex and motor skills?

I was an expert witness in a murder case in South Carolina offering mitigation for a kid who was facing the death penalty. I tried to explain to the jury that interactive video games had conditioned him to shoot a gun to kill. He had spent hundreds of dollars on video games learning to point and shoot, point and shoot. One day he and his buddy decided it would be fun to rob the local convenience store. They walked in, and he pointed a snub-nosed .38 pistol at the clerk's head. The clerk turned to look at him, and the defendant shot reflexively from about six feet. The bullet hit the clerk right between the eyes—which is a pretty remarkable shot with that weapon at that range—and killed this father of two. Afterward, we asked the boy what happened and why he did it. It clearly was not part of the plan to kill the guy—it was being videotaped from six different directions. He said, "I don't know. It was a mistake. It wasn't supposed to happen."

In the military and law-enforcement worlds, the right option is often not to shoot. But you never, ever put your money in that video machine with the intention of not shooting. There is always some stimulus that sets you off. And when

he was excited, and his heart rate went up, and vasoconstriction closed his forebrain down, this young man did exactly what he was conditioned to do: he reflexively pulled the trigger, shooting accurately just like all those times he played video games.

This process is extraordinarily powerful and frightening. The result is ever more "homemade" sociopaths who kill reflexively. Our children are learning how to kill and learning to like the idea of killing; and then we have the audacity to say, "Oh my goodness, what's wrong?"

One of the boys involved in the Jonesboro shootings (and they are just boys) had a fair amount of experience shooting real guns. The other one, to the best of our knowledge, had almost no experience shooting. Between them, those two boys fired 27 shots from a range of over 100 yards, and they hit 15 people. That's pretty remarkable shooting. We run into these situations often—kids who have never picked up a gun in their lives pick up a real gun and are incredibly accurate. Why? Video games.

Lt. Col. Dave Grossman, an expert on the psychology of killing, retired from the U.S. Army in February 1998. He now teaches psychology at Arkansas State University, directs the Killology Research Group in Jonesboro, Arkansas, and has written On Killing: The Psychological Cost of Learning to Kill in War and Society *(Little, Brown and Co., 1996). This article was adapted from a lecture he gave at Bethel College, North Newton, Kansas in April 1998.*

STOPPING
Abuse in Prison

Lawyers for women behind bars and human rights groups are making a difference

BY NINA SIEGAL

Widespread abuses of women behind bars barely received notice until seven or eight years ago. Across the country, there were incidents of prison or jail staff sexually molesting inmates with impunity. Slowly but surely, the nation's correctional facilities are responding to this abuse.

"Ten years ago, I think we knew it was going on, but we hadn't named it," says Brenda Smith, a Practitioner-in-Residence at Washington College of Law at American University. "Until you raise it as a problem, and until people start coming forward and talking about it, it is not perceived as a problem."

The changes are the result of several landmark legal cases, a shift in government policy, and the attention of human-rights groups. Still, problems remain. Guards continue to rape women inmates. But now there's a process to bring them to justice.

The stories were too consistent to be ignored. Numerous female inmates in three Washington, D.C.,

Nina Siegal is a reporter for "The City" section of The New York Times and a frequent contributor to The Progressive.

prison and jail facilities said they had been awakened at two or three in the morning for a "medical visit" or a "legal visit" only to be led into the kitchen, the clinic, the visiting hall, or a closet to have sex. Many inmates were becoming pregnant in a system that allowed no conjugal visits.

"There were a lot of places where people could have sex," says Smith. "A lot of it was in exchange for cigarettes." Prison employees offered other deals: " 'I will give you phone calls, I will make sure you get a better job assignment, I'll give you drugs if you have sex with me.' The sex involved not just correctional officers. It involved chaplains, administration, deputy wardens, contractors, and food-service workers. It involved not just male staff but female staff as well," Smith says.

In 1993, the National Women's Law Center and a District of Columbia law firm filed a class-action suit, *Women Prisoners vs. District of Columbia Department of Corrections,* in U.S. District Court. The suit alleged a pattern of discrimination against women in the jail, the Correctional Treatment Facility, and the Lorton Minimum Security Annex, a D.C. facility in Lorton, Virginia. A large portion of the case focused on issues of sexual misconduct, based on evidence that the law firm had collected during an investigation.

The following year, a judge found that there was a pattern and practice of misconduct so severe that it violated the Eighth Amendment protection against cruel and unusual punishment. The decision was appealed and is still in court.

As extreme as the D.C. situation was, it was not unique.

Lawyers in Georgia had been preparing a class-action suit on behalf of men and women in the state's prisons for almost ten years when they began to come across striking charges of sexual misconduct in the Georgia Women's Correctional Facility in Milledgeville and the nearby camp, Colony Farm. The alleged activities included rape, criminal sexual contact, leering, and abusive catcalling of inmates. One lieutenant had sex with at least seven prisoners from 1987 to 1991, directing women to meet him in various locations in the prisons for sex.

In 1992, the lawyers for the suit, *Cason v. Seckinger,* amended their complaint to add allegations of sexual abuse that had taken place over a period of fourteen years. Seventeen staff members were indicted. None were convicted, though several were dismissed from their jobs as a result of the lawsuit. The suit resulted in a number of federal court orders requiring the department to rectify many of its practices. It also influenced the department to close Milledgeville and move all the female inmates to a different facility.

These two suits—and the criminal prosecutions that ensued—were the first major legal attempts to address a problem that had been plaguing the criminal justice system for decades.

One of the biggest cases for the rights of women prisoners was settled last year. The case (*Lucas vs. White*) involved three inmates of a federal facility in Pleasanton, California, called FCI Dublin, who were sold as sex slaves to male inmates in an adjoining facility. Inmates paid guards to allow them into the cells of female inmates who were being held in the men's detention center, which is across the street from Dublin.

The plaintiffs settled their civil suit against the Federal Bureau of Prisons for $500,000 and forced the agency to make dramatic changes in the way it handles allegations of misconduct. According to the settlement, the Bureau of Prisons was to set up a confidential hotline, or some other reporting mechanism, so that inmates and staff can inform the authorities of problems inside. It was also supposed to provide medical and psychological treatment for inmates who have been victimized and establish new training programs for staff and inmates.

Geri Lynn Green, one of the two attorneys for the *Lucas* case, has been monitoring the changes at the prison since the case settled. After the lawsuit and the subsequent training, she says, "it appears there was a tremendous impact."

Brett Dignam, clinical professor of law at Yale University, agrees that the *Lucas* case made a big difference: "More prison staff members are resigning over issues of sexual misconduct."

Human rights advocates, too, have taken up the cause. In 1996, the Women's Rights Project at Human Rights Watch issued "All Too Familiar: Sexual Abuse of Women in U.S. Prisons."

The 347-page report detailed problems in California, Washington, D.C., Michigan, Georgia, and New York. "We have found that male correctional employees have vaginally, anally, and orally raped female prisoners and sexually assaulted and abused them," says the report. "We found that in the course of committing such gross misconduct, male officers have not only used actual or threatened physical force, but have also used their near total authority to provide or deny goods and privileges to female prisoners to compel them to have sex or, in other cases, to reward them for having done so."

Last June, the United Nations sent a special rapporteur, Radhika Coomaraswamy, to the United States to investigate sexual misconduct in the nation's women's facilities. She argued that stronger monitoring was needed to control widespread abuses.

"We concluded that there has been widespread sexual misconduct in U.S. prisons, but there is a diversity—some are dealing with it better than others," Reuters reported her saying in December. "Georgia has sexual misconduct but has set up a very strong scheme to deal with it. In California and Michigan, nothing has been done and the issue is very prevalent." In April, Coomaraswamy will give a final report to the U.N. Commission on Human Rights.

This March, Amnesty International released its own report, " 'Not Part of My Sentence': Violations of the Human Rights of Women in Custody," which includes a section on sexual abuse. "Many women inmates are subjected to sexual abuse by prison officials, including: sexually offensive language, observation by male officers while showering and dressing, groping during daily pat-down searches, and rape." In addition to the problems detailed in the Human Rights Watch report, Amnesty investigators found problems in Illinois, Massachusetts, New Hampshire, Texas, West Virginia, and Wyoming.

Lawyers and human rights groups have won some important reforms. In 1990, only seventeen states had a law on the books defining sexual misconduct in prisons as either a misdemeanor or a felony offense. Today, there are only twelve states left that do not criminalize sexual relations between staff and inmates—Alabama, Kentucky, Massachusetts, Minnesota, Missouri, Montana, Nebraska, Oregon, Utah, Vermont, West Virginia, and Wisconsin—according to Amnesty International, which is campaigning to get all these states to pass their own laws.

The U.S. Justice Department is also taking a more active role. It has filed two suits charging that the correctional systems in Michigan and Arizona were responsible for violations of prisoners' constitutional rights. The suits cite numerous allegations of abuse, including rape, lack of privacy, prurient viewing, and invasive pat searches. Both cases are still pending.

Meanwhile, state prison systems are training personnel. Andie Moss was a project director with the Georgia Department of Corrections in 1992 when the department was asked to help interview inmates for the class-action lawsuit. She ended up culling information from women who said they had been subjected to misconduct over a fourteen-year period. Today, Moss works with the National Institute of Corrections, part of the Bureau of Prisons. Her primary responsibility is to develop training programs to educate both staff and inmates about sexual misconduct, the new laws, and their rights.

Since her program, "Addressing Staff Sexual Misconduct," was initiated in early 1997, Moss and her team have provided training for more than thirty state correctional systems, and she expects to complete training for all fifty states by the end of 1999.

The training involves four basic elements: clarifying the departments' sexual misconduct policy, informing inmates and staff of the law in their state, telling inmates and staff how to report abuse that they witness, and giving examples of how people have intervened in the past.

"We know it's still an issue. We know corrections departments still need to work diligently on this," says Moss. "It's a constant effort because it is a cultural change. But if you could follow the change in the law, the change in policy and practice, there's been an amazing effort in the last three years."

Despite all the positive steps, however, women are still being abused in America's prisons and jails. Investigators from a number of California-based law firms who recently visited the Valley State Prison for Women in Chowchilla, California, heard stories of at least a dozen assaults by specific guards. They also found "a climate of sexual terror that women are subjected to on a daily basis," says Ellen Barry, founding director of Legal Services for Prisoners with Children, based in San Francisco.

"The instances of both physical and sexual abuse are much higher than any other institution where I've interviewed women," she says. "The guards are really brutalizing women in a way that we really haven't seen before."

Valley State Prison inmate Denise Dalton told investigators that a doctor at the facility groped her and conducts inappropriate pelvic exams. "If I need Tylenol, all I need to do is ask him for a pelvic and he will give me whatever I want," she said.

But most of the abusive conduct was of the type that, Barry says, made for "a climate of sexual terror" in the prison. Coreen Sanchez, another inmate, said that in December, she entered the dayroom at the facility and asked a correctional officer if the sergeant had come in, and he responded by saying, "Yeah, he came in your mouth." She also reported seeing correctional officers flaunt their erections in front of inmates.

Advocates for prisoners say there still needs to be a dramatic cultural shift within the system before women are safe from the people who guard them behind bars.

"I think we have to keep in perspective the limitations of litigation and advocacy work for truly making a change in this arena," says Barry.

One problem that advocates cite is the recalcitrance of the unions that represent prison guards. "The people we really have to win over are not legislators, but the unions," says Christine Doyle, research coordinator for Amnesty International U.S.A. "Guards look at this as a workplace violation, as something fun to do on the job. They don't look at these women as human beings. The message

that these are human beings they are exploiting isn't getting through."

For them to get that message, says Doyle, corrections officers will have to hear it from within the unions, and not from any set of codes, procedures, or laws. "We have states that have legislation, and some of them are just as bad, if not worse, than states without legislation," Doyle says. "So, obviously, that doesn't work. If it comes from within, and the unions themselves say, 'We can do this internally,' workers will respond better."

Human rights groups, for now, are focusing on legislative solutions. In 1996, Human Rights Watch recommended that Congress require all states, as a precondition of receiving federal funding for prisons, criminalize all sexual conduct between staff and inmates. It also urged the Department of Justice to establish secure toll-free telephone hotlines for reporting complaints.

Amnesty International's new report takes an additional step, arguing that the role of male staff be restricted in accordance with the United Nations' Standard Minimum Rules for the Treatment of Prisoners, which state that "women prisoners shall be attended and supervised only by women officers."

Debra LaBelle, a civil rights attorney who filed a class-action suit on behalf of abused women inmates in Michigan, says she would like to see men taken out of women's institutions altogether.

"I resisted going there for a long time, but I don't know another solution," she says. "When we started out, they didn't do any training, much supervision, investigation. In the last three years, they've changed countless policies and yet it is still happening. Get them out of there. It's not like they're losing employment opportunities. There are, unfortunately, many more facilities that men can work in."

Sheila Dauer, director of the Women's Human Rights Program for Amnesty International, says the group's report aims to persuade the final thirteen states without laws against sexual misconduct to initiate legislation, starting with eight state campaigns this year. She says the campaign will also lend support to a federal bill that would do the same thing,

Amnesty's report, she says, is designed to "wake up the American public to the horrible abuses that women inmates are suffering in prison and stop the suffering."

Can hackers be stopped?

In an epic cyberspace battle, white hats are pitted against black hats

By Brendan I. Koerner

Christopher Klaus's north Atlanta office can charitably be described as bland. Cramped and colorless, with furniture inherited from an insurance company and a view of the highway, it seems an unlikely place for a cherubic *wunderkind* to do battle with the anonymous thousands who break into computer networks. Here, his X-Force of software wizards has tangled with hacker groups like Cult of the Dead Cow, devoted to making life miserable for Microsoft, and Hacking for Girlies, masterminds behind the takedown of the *New York Times* Web site last September.

Klaus, the 25-year-old founder of Internet Security Systems, has earned a tidy fortune—well over $200 million at last count—protecting the computer systems of major corporations from crackers, the preferred term for criminal hackers. Inspired by tales of cyberspace cowboys in the classic sci-fi novel *Neuromancer,* Klaus, a Georgia Tech dropout, realized early on that Internet security would grow into one of the computer world's most lucrative sectors, and that the tug of war between "white hats" and "black hats"—defenders versus attackers, the establishment versus the outlaws—would become its most thrilling subplot.

Six years after Klaus began running ISS out of his grandma's house, the company has blossomed into a leader in "adaptive network security," making software designed to stave off the kinds of intrusions that have become front-page staples lately. In the past 12 months alone, black hats have hacked the Web sites of eBay, Ameritech, Bell South, Packard Bell, even the White House. The break-ins have exposed the laughable inadequacy of most conventional security measures, which often fail to stop intruders armed with only the most rudimentary skills. In a recent survey of top corporations and government agencies by the FBI's Computer Intrusion Squad and the Computer Security Institute, 30 percent of respondents admitted that their systems had been penetrated by outsiders last year, while 55 percent reported unauthorized access by insiders.

For businesses that live and die by Web traffic, having a site disabled by mischief makers can be costly. In the FBI-Computer Security Institute survey, 163 organizations reported combined losses of nearly $124 million last year from computer security breaches. Experts say huge losses often go unreported, as most corporate victims want to avoid bad publicity. If they choose to, crackers can do serious damage: In March 1997, a teenager who went by the alias Jester started poking around the system of NYNEX, now Bell Atlantic, in Worcester, Mass. He eventually disabled the network, knocking out the town's phone service and disrupting radio transmissions at a nearby airport.

The stakes for consumers are also getting higher, as banking records, monetary transactions, and personal data rapidly become little more than 1s and 0s zipping through the Internet. Credit card numbers, the lifeblood of E-commerce, are particularly ripe for pilfering. Last August, two members of Hacking for Girlies made off with 1,749 credit card numbers.

Last summer also witnessed the debut of "Back Orifice," which grants unauthorized users remote access to machines running either Windows 95 or Windows 98, the operating system of choice for most home computers. Once installed on a targeted machine, perhaps disguised as an innocuous E-mail attachment, Back Orifice gives hackers more control of the computer than the person at the keyboard has, according to Cult of the Dead Cow, its creators. The program is available free of charge on the group's Web site and requires little in the way of technical know-how to operate.

National-security officials fear much darker forces lurking in cyberspace—hostile nations boasting computer-proficient shock troops. "The major threat is from foreign countries," says Richard A. Clarke, the National Security Council's most senior adviser on infrastructure protection. "The only thing I can say on an unclassified basis is we know there are foreign governments interested in our critical infrastructure, and they are developing plans to go after it."

There are no official estimates as to how many black hats are bouncing around cyberspace, but there are clearly enough to draw the rapt attention of law enforcement. This past Memorial Day weekend, the FBI conducted an 11-city sweep of 20 suspected crackers. (The more common label—hacker—is reserved for those who refrain from using their skills for malice, although some system administrators dispute the distinction.)

Muscle flexing. The FBI raid was retaliation for the hacking of the White House Web site on May 9 by a gang calling itself gH, or Global Hell, which defaced the page with a picture of flowered panties. "For those who think that this is some sort of sport, it will be less fun when the authorities do catch up with them," warned White House Press Secretary Joe Lockhart. But the FBI's muscle flexing has failed to impress most experts. "I would say the FBI is pretty much grasping at straws," says Mike Hudack, editor of *Aviary-mag.com,* an online information security magazine. He believes that little evidence will be gleaned from the suspects' seized computers. Crackers are using near-unbreakable encryption, "so what's the point?" Hudack asks.

One target of the raid, who goes by the nickname "mosthated," was similarly unimpressed by the operation—despite being subjected to a three-hour interrogation. "I agree with what they did. I can't get mad at them for busting me for what I did," the 18-year-old Houston-area resident told *U.S. News.* After he signed a statement "admitting that I had had access to servers in 14 countries around the world," mosthated was released without being charged—minus his computer, which was retained by the FBI. He has since replaced it. "At least they were nice enough to leave me with my monitors and my scanners," he says.

Though a midlevel gang may occasionally get busted, the concern is that top-tier black hats are so skilled, so far ahead of their government pursuers, that capture seems a remote possibility. "The script kiddies will get stopped," says Greg Shipley, a freelance security consultant with close ties to the hacker community. He is referring to amateurs

> **FINDING HOLES.**
> The X-Force races to discover vulnerabilities before its foes. At the quality assurance labs, engineers test new countermeasures on every known operating system.

who use prefabricated attacks—copies of hacking tools that they simply download, rather than program themselves. "The ones a notch above get caught when they are careless. But the ones that are good—I mean, really good—continue to go undetected. You never read about them, and they are the biggest threat."

Playing catch-up. Scott Charney, chief of the Department of Justice's Computer Crime and Intellectual Property Section, disputes the notion that the elite are untouchable. "Some very good hackers are serving time." But he admits that authorities are playing catch-up. "The law enforcement community is relatively new to this and has a steep learning curve," he says. "The number of technically literate prosecutors and agents is growing. But the technology keeps changing."

The script kiddies are considered especially dangerous. Many expert hackers trespass on systems strictly for the challenge and will patch holes on the way out or notify system administrators about how they broke in. Script kiddies, by contrast, revel in breaking things, whether on purpose or by accident; a typical example is the case of two California teens, "Makaveli" and "TooShort," who rummaged through a group of high-level military servers last year. "If they get into a network, they don't know what they're doing. They don't patch up the holes," says mosthated. "They really do some things that are destructive."

Hackers point out that it is vendors, not they, who are responsible for the gaping holes that permeate so many products. With companies releasing software as fast as possible, proper se-

curity often gets lost in the rush toward store shelves. "As complexity increases, the opportunity for vulnerability increases," says Steven Foote, a senior vice president at the Hurwitz Group, which analyzes strategic business applications.

Security professionals deride Microsoft operating systems, in particular, as porous and unreliable, often crashing and leaving themselves open to attack. "Windows NT is slow, it's buggy, and we don't trust it," says Marcus Ranum, founder of the security software company Network Flight Recorder, who faults NT-centric networking strategies for contributing to decreased security. Sites geared toward E-commerce, which are constructed to be open and accessible to visitors, also provide particularly appealing targets. "With E-business, you're allowing customers into your data center," says Foote. "Then there's ample opportunity for customers to hack deep into your environment."

Inside jobs. In the past, system administrators kept out intruders by installing a fire wall, a device that vets requests for service and turns away those lacking proper authorization. But fire walls have become practically useless as stand-alone defenses. They don't guard against attacks by insiders—disgruntled employees, password thieves—which account for up to 65 percent of all incidents. Different networks often use the same popular brand, so figuring out how to crack one fire wall can give a perpetrator instant access to thousands of sites.

The white-hat response has been to develop new tools. Some assess security risks; others alert administrators to attacks in progress. At ISS, the two flagship products are Internet Scanner, a "virtual hacker" that probes systems for hidden weaknesses, and RealSecure, a veritable "burglar alarm," or intrusion-detection system. Big organizations, such as AOL, Microsoft, NASA, and 21 of the nation's top 25 banks, depend on ISS products for protection, a client list that has pushed the publicly traded company into the elite ranks of profitable Internet ventures, with earnings of $1.3 million last quarter.

Thwarting black hats requires staying abreast of their tricks. At ISS, that task falls to the X-Force, a team of around 50 researchers charged with keeping an ear to the computer underground. Headed by Chris Rouland, 27, the group monitors security-oriented Web sites, chat rooms, and mailing lists in search of the latest exploits. Internet Scanner and RealSecure can only defend against known attacks, and therefore they rely on frequent updates from the X-Force, which has so far uncovered over 2,100 potential vulnerabilities. At the same time, team members pick apart new software releases, trying to sniff out holes and miswritten code before their enemies do.

"We have to hire people who have all the capabilities of the bad guys," says Tom Noonan, ISS's CEO, who turned down a cushy post at Oracle to join the company in 1994. The back and forth between the X-Force and its adversaries has occasionally been ferocious, most notably at last year's DefCon, an annual computer security convention in Las Vegas. That is where Cult of the Dead Cow released Back Orifice, ostensibly to expose Microsoft's security shortcomings. Hours after its public debut, Rouland got a copy to Jon Larimer, the X-Force's "back door" guru. "I knew they'd used some encryption, and we needed to have a way for RealSecure to track that," says Larimer, a Penn State dropout whose slight build and shy demeanor make him seem even younger than his 20 years. Fueled by free sodas and his own adrenalin, he churned out

a decode in a single night. ISS released a countermeasure within days.

ISS is hardly the only adaptive network security outfit, with a slew of rivals jockeying for a piece of a market expected to generate at least $700 million in sales by 2002, up from $45 million two years ago. Axent Technologies, router giant Cisco Systems, and Network Associates are all fierce competitors, with a crop of startups, like Ranum's Network Flight Recorder, nipping at their heels.

Though Noonan asserts his company "wouldn't hire anyone on the dark side," rivals charge ISS with keeping black hats on its staff. Ranum claims an underground figure known as "ReDragon" was an ISS employee while co-editing the popular hacker zine *Phrack.* (Michele Norwood, an ISS spokeswoman, says the employee in question was asked to resign his position at *Phrack* as soon as it was discovered and that he later left the company.)

Behind the curve. The real competition, of course, is not Axent and Cisco, but the black hats. "I really believe we are ahead of 99 percent of the hackers out there that are criminals," boasts Klaus. Those close to the computer underground, however, claim that ISS and its white-hat peers are woefully behind the curve. "ISS makes products that are

in the upper crust of products available," says "NeonSurge," a member of Rhino9, a group of security experts. "Personally, to me this doesn't mean much because all products out there are always two to three months behind the latest techniques being used."

The crew at ISS acknowledges that security-assessment and intrusion-detection products are not silver bullets. "We'll never reach a point where every known attack is defended against," says Mark Wood, head of ISS's intrusion detection team. The goal, instead, is "to reduce the number of people who can attack to two or three in the world. But can those two or three defeat RealSecure if they really want to? Yes."

Rouland and the X-Force do not have the time to fret over such matters. Their summer promises to be a busy one. Rouland has advance information that Cult of the Dead Cow will be releasing "Back Orifice 2000," and the X-Force is already gearing up to respond. The summer months are also the traditional high season for cyberattacks. School's out, notes Rouland, so kids have plenty of time to poke around the world's hole-filled networks.

With Doug Pasternak and David E. Kaplan

Stolen identity

It can ruin your credit. And that's just the beginning

By Margaret Mannix

When Jessica Grant and her husband went to the bank in December to refinance their home, they thought it would be routine. After all, the couple, who live in Sun Prairie, Wis., were refinancing with their existing mortgage lender, and they prided themselves on their credit history. So it was quite a shock when the bank officer turned them down, pointing to their credit report, which listed numerous accounts in arrears.

It turns out that a woman in Texas had applied for credit *19* times using Grant's name and Social Security number. In all, she had made purchases totaling $60,000, leaving a trail of unpaid debt that Grant is desperately trying to prove is not hers: a $25,000 loan for a mobile home, two car loans, credit card bills, and charges for a cellular phone and other services. "She torched my credit to the point where even *she* was denied," says Grant.

Grant is a victim of a crime of the '90s: identity theft. It happens when one individual uses another's personal identification—name, address, Social Security number, date of birth, mother's maiden name—to take over or open new credit card and bank accounts, apply for car and house loans, lease cars and apartments, even take out insurance. The perpetrators don't make the payments, and the victim is left to deal with the damage—calls from collection agencies and creditors, the endless paperwork that results from trying to expunge fraudulent accounts from a credit record, the agony of waiting to see if more phony accounts pop up. Meanwhile, the proliferation of black marks on a credit report can be devastating. Victims of identity theft are often unable to get loans; some run into trouble applying for a job. A few have even been arrested after the thief committed a crime in the victim's name.

Many identity thieves use stolen personal information to obtain driver's licenses, birth certificates, and professional licenses, making it easier to get credit. Most victims don't even know how the criminals pulled it off; data have been stolen from desk drawers in the workplace, mailboxes, job application forms, and the Internet. False identification cloaks a thief in anonymity, and the impostor can often use the alias for a prolonged period of time; thieves typically have the bills sent to an address that is not the victim's, concealing the scheme for months, even years. Most victims aren't aware that their credit has taken a nose-dive until, like Grant, they apply for credit themselves or receive a call from a bill collector.

Proof positive. In the '80s, criminals who wanted free plastic simply made up counterfeit credit cards with the correct number of digits. To thwart them, the industry instituted sophisticated security

There's no law on the books to stop credit bureaus from selling personal information

measures involving holograms and algorithms. Now criminals are taking advantage of what some see as the weakest link in the credit system: personal identity. "There is nothing in the system that

Since lawyer Mari Frank's identity was stolen, she carries a police report with her at all times just to prove she's not the criminal.

demands proof that I am the person I say I am," says James Bauer, deputy assistant director of the U.S. Secret Service's Office of Investigations, which has jurisdiction over credit fraud and false documents. "Our personal identifiers are now, more than ever, a valuable commodity to criminals."

That's evident in a soon-to-be-released U.S. General Accounting Office report obtained by *U.S. News*. While no single agency tracks identity fraud, statistics collected by the GAO point to a growing problem. Trans Union, for example, one of the three major credit bureaus, says two thirds of all consumer inquiries relate to identity fraud. Those inquiries numbered 35,235 in 1992; last year there were 522,922. "The costs of identity fraud can be very high," states the report: The Secret Service says losses to victims and institutions in its identity-fraud investigations were $745 million in 1997, up from $442 million in 1995. "It's a problem that Congress has to address," says Rep. Jerry Kleczka, the Wisconsin Democrat who requested the GAO study. He has introduced legislation prohibiting credit

Despite its impact, only a handful of states have made identity theft a crime

bureaus from giving out facts like Social Security numbers and dates of birth—details thieves crave. But that's only part of the problem.

Identity fraud is a relatively new phenomenon, and it's not a crime, except in a handful of states like Arizona and California that have recently made it so. (Legislation is pending to make it a federal crime.) Most victims call the police. But in states with no statute, some police departments refuse to take a report because the law sees the victim in a case of identity fraud as the party that granted the credit (the bank or the merchant, for example), not the person impersonated. "That's frustrating to the victims because they often need a report to prove they are not the bad guys," says Beth Givens, director of the Privacy Rights Clearinghouse in San Diego.

Victims need proof because the attitude they often encounter when dealing with creditors is guilty, guilty, guilty. "Every person I talk to has been skeptical, condescending, and hostile," says Chris Scurlock of Laurel, Md., who is still trying to clean his credit report of 20 bounced checks, written to stores in Arizona in 1994 on a bank account opened fraudulently in his name. "That really aggravates me," says Scurlock,

who has already been turned down for a mortgage. Victims often have to play detective, coming up with clues, leads, and even the basic evidence that a fraud has been committed. "You have to do all the footwork yourself," says Kathy Brown of Albany, Ore.

The kitchen sink. Typically, creditors ask an identity-theft victim to fill out an affidavit certifying he or she did not incur the debt. Some require much more: One collection agency told Grant it needed a copy of her driver's license, her Social Security card, her birth certificate, and any lease or mortgage contract for the past five years—all for a $43 cable bill. In the end, Grant neither paid the bill nor sent the copies to prove her innocence, opting to explain the $43 item on her credit report to future creditors. As with many victims of identity theft, sensitive documents were the last thing she wanted to send to a stranger.

The belligerence that victims encounter from some creditors is particularly irksome to those who suspect a creditor's negligence in the first place. "Many creditors do not take the proper steps to verify the identity of the credit applicant," says Givens. Mari Frank, of Laguna Niguel, Calif., points to a credit card application that started an impostor on a crime spree in her name: The application was preprinted with the impostor's name and address, but the impostor had crossed off her own name—leaving her address—and written in Frank's name, Social Security number, and occupation. The bank gave the impostor a credit card with a $10,000 credit line, leading Frank to ask: "Wouldn't a reasonable person say something is fishy

here?" Bankers, meanwhile, insist they are on the ball. "All the banks have systems that detect fraud," says Nessa Feddis, senior federal counsel at the American Bankers Association. "They have to modify them for every new scheme that comes up."

Dialing for dollars. To make matters worse, two weeks after Frank notified the bank that the account was fraudu-

Says Kathy Brown of Albany, Ore.: "I am not the criminal but I am the one who is looking over my shoulder waiting for her to do it again."

lent, the bank sold it to a collection agency, and she and her children started receiving threatening phone calls and letters. It didn't stop there. The card triggered an avalanche of preapproved credit offers to the phony Frank's mailbox: One different address on a credit account was all it had taken for one of the credit bureaus to switch Frank's credit-file address to the impostor's. "They came to her like candy," says Frank. Some credit bureaus won't change a file address until three creditors report a new address, but a criminal

When the worst happens . . .

Victims of identity theft have a growing number of resources to guide them:

■ **Credit bureaus.** Victims of identity theft are entitled to free copies of their credit reports from the three major credit bureaus. To report fraud, call Equifax at (800) 525-6285, Experian at (888) 397-3742, and Trans Union at (800) 680-7289. If you want to obtain your report to check it, you can call Equifax at (800) 685-1111, Experian at (888) 397-3742, and Trans Union at (800) 888-4213.

■ **Interest groups.** The Privacy Rights Clearinghouse and the California Public Interest Research Group (CALPIRG) distribute a free fact sheet, "Identity Theft: What to Do If It Happens to You." Send a stamped, self-addressed envelope to Privacy Rights Clearinghouse, 1717 Kettner Avenue, Suite 105, San Diego, CA 92101 or visit its Web site at *www.privacyrights.org*. For details about the Victims of Identity Theft support group in California, write CALPIRG at 926 J Street, Suite 523, Sacramento, CA 95814, or E-mail *pirg@pirg.org* (subject: "VOIT"). Victims trade tips on how to deal with identity theft—emotion-

ally as well as strategically. Other state chapters are forming.

■ **Help from one who knows.** Attorney Mari Frank of Laguna Niguel, Calif., whose own identity was stolen, has written *From Victim to Victor: A Step-By-Step Guide for Ending the Nightmare of Identity Theft*. It's pricey at $39.95 plus $6.95 for shipping and handling, but it's comprehensive—it includes sample letters to insurers and creditors. For more information, visit *www.privacyrights.org/idtheftkit* or call (800) 725-0807.

on a spree can quickly cross that threshold.

It's not easy getting a credit report back on track. "The credit bureau says contact the creditor, the creditor says contact the credit bureau, and the consumer just gets ping-ponged back and forth," says Ed Mierzwinski, consumer program director for the U.S. Public Interest Research Group in Washington, D.C. The bureaucracy can be maddening: Grant recently received a letter from the credit bureau Experian saying it was reinserting a disputed item. The letter did not say which of the 19 accounts it referred to.

One of the few weapons victims have to protect them is a "fraud alert," which credit bureaus will put in consumer credit files. This notifies anyone who pulls the report that the subject is a victim of fraud and that he or she should be called to verify any credit application. The alert isn't foolproof. Edwin Walters, of San Francisco, says two credit issuers opened accounts for someone using his name in February despite the fraud alerts posted in his credit files—and even though he already had cards from both. "It just doesn't make sense," says Walters.

Credit bureaus might want to step up their efforts at finding a solution before more aggrieved consumers turn to the courts. Last month a Clarksdale, Miss., man won a lawsuit against Trans Union for failing to clean up his credit report. The award: $4.5 million.

Meanwhile, the credit reporting industry has formed a task force to tackle identity theft. Among solutions being considered are taking files of theft victims off line and sharing fraud alerts among credit bureaus more quickly. Individual creditors are also taking steps to stem their losses and prevent future ones. In San Francisco, Cellular One routinely flags suspect applications and compares details with credit reports. That's how Tiffany Dela Rosa in San Francisco found out her identity had been compromised: Last year a woman applied for service using Dela Rosa's identity, but Cellular One's fraud department thought the application looked suspicious and phoned her to check. Moreover, it alerted competitors in the area that they might be the next targets.

Identity theft is a crime that comes back to haunt its victims, and many are taking determined measures to prevent its recurrence. Grant and her husband have taken an unusual vow: When they have children, they will not get them Social Security numbers—even though that means no tax deduction. To her way of thinking, safeguarding her children's identity is far more valuable.

Unit Selections

Key Points to Consider

❖ How has the concept of marriage changed over time?

❖ Who should get the kids when a couple splits up, and why do you feel this way?

❖ How is polygamy similar to, and different from, marital infidelity?

❖ What are the consequences of abuse for a battered woman?

❖ Why may women choose to have an abortion? Under what circumstances would you support a friend having an abortion, and why do you feel that way?

❖ How does deviance in the family fit the four perspectives of the social definition of deviance?

 **Links** **www.dushkin.com/online/**

11. **Child Abuse: Statistics, Research, and Resources**
    http://www.jimhopper.com/abstats
12. **Divorce Source: Family Law, Custody, Alimony, Support, and Visitation**
    http://www.divorcesource.com
13. **National Data Archive on Child Abuse and Neglect**
    http://www.ndacan.cornell.edu
14. **Polygamy Page**
    http://www.familyman.u-net.com/polygamy.html
15. **Single Parent Resource: Articles**
    http://www.parentsplace.com/family/singleparent/

These sites are annotated on pages 4 and 5.

The stereotypical family has a husband/father, wife/mother, and 2.7 children. In that family the parents work as a team to make sure that the entire family unit thrives, everyone is considerate of each other's feelings, and nobody goes out of the way to hurt anyone else. A family, like other social concepts, is socially defined. Social workers may define family as two or more persons living together that are perceived as a family. This definition may or may not include the traditional married couple with children. The family may or may not be composed of unmarried persons living together with children. The family may or may not include several spouses living together in a polygamous relationship with children. The stereotypical couple has typically been of one race or another, and interracial relationships have often been viewed as deviant. Today, interracial marriage is far more common and acceptable than it was in the past. Randall Kennedy introduces us to how that change has occurred over time. In other words, while there may be a stereotypical family unit, the social definition of family, like the social definition of deviance, is relative.

Deviance in the family can take on many forms. One form is abuse. Domestic violence is an often-secret form of family deviance. While it occurs throughout society, we rarely see it or even hear about it. Often, it only becomes public because of some especially heinous act involving severe injury or death. Abuse can be physical, sexual, or emotional, and it can involve neglect. Domestic violence does not discriminate by age, sex, or race. It occurs in the best and worst of families. Social class is not a barrier to being a victim or an offender. Often the victims are too embarrassed and scared to tell anyone, and their abusers are too scared or too bold to admit that they have a problem. Family members who know of the abuse are often incapable of preventing it, either out of fear, disbelief, or embarrassment. It is only when knowledge of the abusive acts becomes public information that people begin to ask questions. However, just because the abuse becomes public does not guarantee that it will end.

Many reasons for abusive behavior exist. One hypothesis states that male children who observe their fathers abuse their mothers may grow up to be men who believe that it is normal for a husband to beat his wife. A related hypothesis is that persons who are abused as children grow up to be adults who abuse children. That is, domestic violence is intergenerational.

Domestic violence can lead to murder. Lenore Walker described what she called the cycle of violence. The first stage of the three-stage cycle is tension building. Tension building may be characterized by nonviolent marital discord including emotional abuse. The second stage involves physical violence. The third stage is a cooling-off or loving stage, when the abusive person may beg forgiveness and promise never to abuse the spouse again. Without intervention, however, the cycle will continue. At some point, the cooling-off stage disappears, and the cycle moves back and forth between the tension-building and violent stages. At this point an intervention is necessary. If no intervention occurs, it is likely that the tension stage will disappear, and only violence will exist. At this point, the experts believe that the abusive spouse will kill the victim, or the victim will kill the abuser in self-defense.

An example of behavior that was at one point in time thought to be deviant is having an abortion. For better or worse, abortion is as common a life experience for women as is divorce. Twenty-five years after *Roe v. Wade*, abortions are safe, legal, and *not* rare.

The Problem with Marriage

Steven L. Nock

A *Call to Civil Society* warns that the institutions most critical to democratic society are in decline. "What ails our democracy is not simply the loss of certain organizational forms, but also the loss of certain organizing ideals— moral ideals that authorize our civic creed, but do not derive from it. At the end of this century, our most important challenge is to strengthen the moral habits and ways of living that make democracy possible." I suggest that American institutions have traditionally been organized around gender and that the loss of this organizing principle explains many of the trends discussed in the report. Specifically, the continued centrality of gender in marriage— and its growing irrelevance everywhere else—helps explain many contemporary family problems. The solution is to restore marriage to a privileged status from which both spouses gain regardless of gender.

The family trends we are now seeing reflect a conflict between the ideals central to marriage and those that define almost all other institutions. Growing numbers of Americans reject the idea that adults should be treated differently based on their gender. But it is difficult to create a new model of marriage based on such a premise. For many people, assumptions about gender equality conflict with the reality of their marriages. It may hardly matter if one is male or female in college, on the job, at church, in the voting booth, or almost anywhere else in public. But it surely matters in marriage. The family, in short, is still organized around gender while virtually nothing else is. Alternatively, marriage has not been redefined to accommodate the changes in male-female relations that have occurred elsewhere. This, I believe, is the driving force behind many of the problematic trends identified in *A Call to Civil Society.*

Stable marriages are forged of extensive dependencies. Yet trends toward gender equality and independence have made the traditional basis of economic dependency in marriage increasingly problematic. The challenge is to reinvent marriage as an institution based on dependency that is not automatically related to gender. Both partners, that is, must gain significantly from their union, and both must face high exit costs for ending it.

Despite dramatic changes in law and public policy that have erased (or minimized) distinctions between men and women, married life has changed more slowly and subtly. In the last four decades, the percentage of married women in the paid labor force increased from 32 percent to 59 percent, and the number of hours that wives commit to paid labor increased apace. While men do not appear to be doing much more housework today than they did two decades ago, women are doing less in response to their commitments to paid labor. Women did 2.5 times as much household labor as their husbands in 1975. By 1987, the ratio was 1.9. Wives' share of total (reported) household income increased marginally, from 35 percent in 1975–1980 to 38 percent in 1986–1991. In such small ways, husbands and wives are increasingly similar. Still, marriages are hardly genderless arrangements. My research for *Marriage in Men's Lives* showed that most marriages in America resemble a traditional model, with husbands as heads of households, and wives who do most housework and child care. Given the pace at which gender distinctions have been, or are being, eliminated from laws, work, school, religion, politics, and other institutions, the family appears to be curiously out of step.

One reason gender is still a central motif in marriage is because masculinity (and possibly, femininity) are defined by, and displayed in marriage. As the title of Sara Berk's book proclaimed, the family is *The Gender Factory.* Consider the consequences of unemployment for husbands. If spouses were economically rational, then the unemployed (or lower-paid) partner would assume responsibility for housework. Sociologist Julie Brines found just the opposite. After a few months of unemployment, husbands actually *reduced* their housework efforts. The reason is that housework is much more than an economic matter. It is also symbolic. "Men's" work means providing for the family and being a "breadwinner," whereas "women's" work means caring for the home and children. Such assumptions are part of our cultural beliefs. Doing housework, earning a living, providing for the family, and caring for children are ways of demonstrating masculinity or femininity. When wives are economically dependent on their husbands, doing housework is consistent with traditional assumptions about marriage. Such women conform to cultural understandings about what it means to be a wife, or a woman. However, a dependent husband departs from customary assumptions about marriage and men. Were he to respond by doing more housework, his deviance would be even greater. Marriage is still the venue in which masculinity and femininity are displayed.

The husband and wife who construct a new model of marriage that doesn't include gender as a primary organizing principle will face challenges. The husband who decides to be the primary child-care provider or the wife who elects to be the sole wage earner will find these unusual marital roles difficult but not impossible to sustain. Relationships with parents may be awkward. Friends may struggle to understand the arrangement if it differs from their own. Employers may also find such an arrangement difficult to understand and accept. Yet as difficult as it may be to forge a new model of marriage, it seems certain that some change is necessary if marriage is to endure.

The title of Goldscheider and Waite's recent book asks a stark question: *New Families,* or *No Families*? In "new" families, husbands and wives will share family economic responsibilities and domestic tasks equitably. The alternative, according to these authors, is "no" families. Quite simply, marriage must be redefined to reflect the greater gender equality found everywhere else, or women will not marry. Or those who do will face increasing difficulties reconciling their public and private lives. Indeed, young women today value marriage less than young men do. Three in four (75 percent) never-married men under age 30 described getting married as important for their lives in 1993. A smaller percentage (66 percent) of comparable women replied that way (1993 General Social Survey).

Research confirms that most women who marry today desire marriages that differ importantly from those of their grandmothers because women's lives have changed in so many other ways in recent decades. However, though the options available to women have expanded in other respects, the basic pattern of marriage is pretty much the same as it has been for decades. The revolution in gender has not yet touched women's marriages. Part of the reason is that men have been excluded from the gender revolution. While almost any young woman today will notice enormous differences between her life options and those of her great-grandmother, the differences between men and their great-grandfathers are minimal, at most. The script for men in America has not changed. In short, despite enormous changes in what it means to be a woman, marriage does not yet incorporate those changes. Neither men nor women have yet figured out how to fashion "new" families.

Many of our problems are better seen as the result of institutional change than of individual moral decline. The *personal problems* that lead to family decline are also legitimate *public issues.* Institutions like the family are bigger than any individual. So when large numbers of people create new patterns of family life, we should consider the collective forces behind such novel arrangements. And if some of those innovations are harmful to adults or children, fixing them will require more than a call for stronger moral habits (though there is certainly

nothing wrong with such advice). Fixing them will require restructuring some basic social arrangements.

Since *A Call to Civil Society* focuses on *institutional* decline, I want to consider the meaning of an institution. A society is a cluster of social institutions, and institutions are clusters of *shared* ideals. Only when people agree about how some core dimension of life should be organized is there a social institution. The family is a good example.

Although individual families differ in detail, collectively they share common features as a result of common problems and tested solutions. In resolving and coping with the routine challenges of family life such as child care, the division of household labor, or relations with relatives, individuals draw on conventional (i.e., shared) ideals. As disparate individuals rely on shared answers to questions about family life, typical patterns emerge that are understood and recognized—mother, father, son, daughter, husband, and wife. To the extent that such ideals are widely shared, the family is a social institution. Were individuals left completely on their own to resolve the recurring problems of domestic life, there would be much less similarity among families. Alternatively, were there no conventional values and beliefs to rely on, the family would not be an institution. The family, as an institution, differs in *form* from one culture to another. Yet everywhere, it consists of patterned (i.e., shared and accepted) solutions to the problems of dependency (of partners, children, and the elderly).

The problem today is that an assumption that was once central to all social institutions is no longer so compelling. Beliefs about gender have long been an organizing template that guided behaviors in both public and private. Yet while gender has become increasingly unimportant in public, neither women nor men have fully adjusted to these changes in their private married lives. If men and women are supposed to be indistinguishable at work or school, does the same standard apply in marriage? Americans have not yet agreed about the answer. As a result, the institution of the family (the assumptions about how married life should be organized) no longer complements other social arrangements. Increasingly, the family is viewed as a problem for people because the assumptions about domestic life no longer agree with those in other settings. When husbands and wives return home from work, school, church, or synagogue, they often struggle with traditional ideals about marriage that do not apply in these other areas. No matter what her responsibilities at work, the married mother will probably be responsible for almost all child care at home, for instance. Responsibilities at work are unlikely to be dictated by whether the person is male or female. But responsibilities at home are. This contradiction helps explain the trends identified in *A Call to Civil Society.*

High rates of divorce, cohabitation, and unmarried childbearing are documented facts, and all have clearly increased this century. Do such trends suggest that the family is losing its institutional anchor? In fact, the traditional arrangements that constitute the family are less compelling today than in the past. In this respect, the institution of the family is weaker. To understand why, I now consider the traditional basis of the family, legal marriage.

Legal Marriage and the Institution of the Family

The extent to which the family *based on legal marriage* is an institution becomes obvious when one considers an alternative way that adult couples arrange their intimate lives. Certainly there is no reason to believe that two people cannot enjoy a harmonious and happy life without the benefit of legal marriage. In fact, growing numbers of Americans appear to believe that unmarried *cohabitation* offers something that marriage does not. One thing that cohabitation offers is freedom from the rules of marriage because there are no widely accepted and approved boundaries around cohabitation. Unmarried partners have tremendous freedom to decide how they will arrange their legal and other relationships. Each partner must decide how to deal with the other's parents, for example. Parents, in turn, may define a cohabiting child's relationship as different from a married child's. Couples must decide whether vacations will be taken together or separately. Money may be pooled or held in separate accounts. If children are born, cohabiting parents must decide about the appropriate (non-legal) obligations each incurred as a result. In such small ways, cohabiting couples and their associates must *create* a relationship. Married couples may also face decisions about some of these matters. However, married spouses have a pattern to follow. For most matters of domestic life, marriage supplies a template. This is what cohabiting couples lack. They are exempt from the vast range of marriage norms and laws in our society.

A man can say to his wife: "I am your husband. You are my wife. I am expected to do certain things for you, and you likewise. We have pledged our faithfulness. We have promised to care for one another in times of sickness. We have sworn to forego others. We have made a commitment to our children. We have a responsibility and obligation to our close relatives, as they have to us." These statements are not simply personal pledges. They are also enforceable. Others will expect these things of the couple. Laws, religion, and customs bolster this contract. When this man says to someone, "I would like you to meet my wife," this simple declaration says a great deal.

Compare this to an unmarried couple living happily together. What, if any, are the conventional assumptions that can be made? What are the limits to behavior? To whom is each obligated? Who can this couple count on for help in times of need? And how do you complete this introduction of one's cohabiting partner: "I would like you to meet my . . . "? The lack of a word for such a partner is a clear indication of how little such relationships are governed by convention. Alternatively, we may say that such a relationship is *not* an institution, marriage is. I believe this helps explain why cohabiting couples are less happy, and less satisfied with their relationships than married couples.

Almost all worrisome social trends in regard to the family are actually problems related to *marriage*: declining rates of marriage, non-marital fertility, unmarried cohabitation, and divorce. Any understanding of the family must begin with a consideration of marriage. I now offer a *normative definition of marriage*; a statement of what Americans agree it *should be,* the assumptions and taken-for-granted notions involved. In so doing, I will lay the foundation for an explanation of family decline.

In *Marriage in Men's Lives,* I developed the details of normative marriage by consulting three diverse sources. First, I examined large national surveys conducted repeatedly over the past two decades. Second, I read domestic relations law, including state and federal appellate decisions. Finally, I consulted sources of religious doctrine, especially the Bible. Throughout, my goal was to identify all aspects of marriage that are widely shared, accepted as legitimate, and broadly viewed as compelling.

A normative definition of marriage draws attention to the central idea that marriage is more than the sum of two spouses. As an institution, marriage includes rules that originate outside the particular union that establish boundaries around the relationship. Those boundaries are the understood limits of behavior that distinguish marriage from all other relationships. Married couples have something that all other couples lack; they are heirs to a system of shared principles that help organize their lives. If we want to assess changes in the family, the starting point is an examination of the institutional foundation of marriage. Six ideals define legal marriage in America.

1) *Individual Free Choice.* Mate selection is based on romantic love. In the course of a century, parents have come to play a smaller and smaller role in the choice of married partners. Dating supplanted courtship as compatibility, attractiveness, and love replaced other bases for matrimony. National surveys show that "falling in love" is the most frequently cited reason for marrying one's spouse, and that the most important traits in successful marriages are thought to be "satisfying one another's needs" and "being deeply in love." Western religious ceremonies admonish partners to love one another until death, and every state permits a legal divorce when love fails ('incompatibility', 'irreconcilable differences' or similar justifications). Love is associated with feelings of security, comfort, companionship, erotic attraction, overlooking faults, and persistence. Since love and marriage are so closely related, people expect all such feelings from their marriages.

2) *Maturity.* Domestic relations law defines an age at which persons may marry. Throughout the U.S., the minimum is 18, though marriage may be permitted with

approval by parents or the court at earlier ages. Parental responsibilities for children end with legal *emancipation* at age 18. Thus, marriage may occur once parents are released from their legal obligations to children, when children are legally assumed to be mature enough to enter binding contracts, and once children are assumed able to become self-sufficient and able to provide for offspring. Traditional religious wedding ceremonies celebrate a new form of maturity as Genesis states: "A man leaves his father and mother and cleaves to his wife and they become one flesh."

3) *Heterosexuality*. Traditionally, and legally, the only acceptable form of sex has been with one's spouse. Sex outside of marriage (fornication or adultery) is still illegal in half of U.S. states. And sexual expression within marriage has traditionally been legally restricted to vaginal intercourse (sodomy laws). Though such laws are rarely enforced even where they exist, they remind us of the very close association of marriage and conventional forms of heterosexual sexuality. Recent efforts to legalize homosexual marriage have been strenuously resisted. Since the full-faith-and-credit clause of the Constitution requires that marriages conducted legally in one state be recognized as legal in others, the possibility of legal homosexual marriage in Hawaii prompted an unprecedented federal "Defense of Marriage Act" in September 1996. This law will allow states to declare homosexual Hawaiian marriages void in their jurisdiction. Despite growing acceptance of homosexuality, there is very little support for homosexual marriages. The 1990 General Social Survey showed that only 12 percent of Americans believe homosexuals should be allowed to marry.

4) *Husband as Head*. Though Americans generally endorse equality between the sexes, men and women still occupy different roles in their marriages. Even if more and more couples are interested in egalitarian marriages, large numbers of people aren't. The 1994 General Social Survey shows that adults are almost evenly divided about whether both spouses should contribute to family income (57 percent approve of wives working, and in fact, 61 percent of wives are employed). Four in ten adults endorse a very traditional division of roles, where the wife takes care of the home and family, and the husband earns all the income. Traditional religious wedding ceremonies ask women to "honor and obey" their husbands. In reality, most husbands have more authority than their wives do. The spouse who is primarily responsible for income enjoys more authority, and in the overwhelming majority of American marriages, that is the husband. Demands made of husbands at work are translated into legitimate demands made on the family. So most husbands have more authority than their wives do, regardless of professed beliefs.

5) *Fidelity and Monogamy*. In law, sexual exclusivity is the symbolic core of marriage, defining it in more obvious ways than any other; Husbands and wives have a legal right to engage in (consensual) sex with one another.

Other people may not have a legal right to engage in sex with either married partner. Adultery is viewed as sufficiently threatening to marriages that homicides provoked by the discovery of it may be treated as manslaughter. Extramarital sex is viewed as more reprehensible than any other form, including sex between young teenagers, premarital sex, and homosexual sex. Eight in ten adults in the 1994 General Social Survey described extramarital sex as "always wrong." Adultery, in fact, is rare. Recent research reported by Laumann and his colleagues in *The Social Organization of Sexuality* revealed that only 15 percent of married men and 5 percent of married women have ever had extramarital sex. Among divorced people these percentages are only slightly higher, 25 percent for men and 10 percent for women. Monogamy is closely related to fidelity because it restricts all sexual expression to one married partner. With the exception of Utah where some Mormons practice polygamy (against the canons of the Mormon Church), monogamy has gone largely unchallenged in the United States since 1878 when the U.S. Supreme Court upheld the conviction of a Mormon who practiced polygamy.

6) *Parenthood*. With rare exceptions, married people become parents. Despite high rates of unmarried fertility, there is little to suggest that married couples are less likely to have, or desire to have children today than they were several decades ago. Only 13 percent of ever-married women aged 34 to 45 are childless today. Two decades ago, the comparable figure was 7 percent. The six-point difference, however, is due to delayed fertility, rather than higher childlessness. Overall completed cohort fertility (i.e., the total number of children born to women in their lifetime) has remained stable since the end of the Baby Boom. And while the legal disabilities once suffered by illegitimate children have been declared unconstitutional, marital and nonmarital fertility differ in important respects. Unmarried fathers may, through legal means, obtain the custody of their children, although few do. Indeed, a vast legal apparatus exists to enforce the parental obligations of men who do not voluntarily assume them. On the other hand, married men are automatically presumed to be the legal father of their wife's children, and nothing (except the absence of "unfitness") is required of them to establish custody.

Challenges to Normative Marriage

This ensemble of behaviors and beliefs describes how most Americans understand marriage. Even if particular marriages depart in some ways from this model, this should be the starting point when attempting to assess family change. If "the family" has declined, then such change will be obvious in one or more of the foregoing dimensions. Widespread attempts to change normative marriage, or wholesale departures from it, are evidence that Americans do not agree about the institution. I now briefly review three obvious challenges to the normative model of marriage just outlined. High divorce rates, late ages at marriage, and declining rates of remarriage are a reflection of an underlying theme in such challenges. That theme is the importance of gender in marriage

The increasingly common practice of unmarried *cohabitation* is an example of a challenge to normative marriage. In 1997, 4.1 million opposite-sex cohabiting couples were counted by the U.S. Bureau of the Census, the majority of whom (58 percent) have never married, and one in five of whom (22 percent) is under 25 years old. Research on cohabiting partners has identified a central theme in such relationships. Cohabiting individuals are more focused on gender equality in economic and other matters than married spouses. They are also less likely to have a gender-based division of tasks in most forms of household labor except the care of infants.

Yet another challenge to normative marriage is unmarried childbearing. One in three children in America is born to an unmarried woman; six in ten of those children were conceived outside of marriage (the balance were conceived prior to a divorce or separation). The historical connection between sexual intercourse and marriage weakened once effective contraception and abortion became available. Without contraception, married women became pregnant if fecund. There was no reason to ask a married woman why, or when she would have a child. Parenthood in an era of universal contraception, however, is a choice. It is now possible to ask *why* someone had a child. Since childbearing is thought to be a choice, it is viewed as a decision made chiefly by women. And the type of woman who chooses to have children differs from the childless woman because motherhood now competes with many other legitimate roles in a woman's life. Research has shown that women who choose motherhood give occupational and income considerations lower priority than childless women.

By the late 1960s, feminists who argued that wives should not be completely dependent on husbands joined this critique of the exclusive breadwinner role of husbands. Just as the exclusive breadwinner role for men was criticized, the exclusive homemakermother role for married women was identified as oppressive. And, of course, such women are the statistical exception today. Maternity must be balanced with many other adult roles in women's lives, and traditional marriage is faulted as creating a "second shift" for women who return home from work only to assume responsibility for their households with little help from their husbands.

All significant challenges to marriage focus on various aspects of gender. The traditional assignment of marital roles based on sex (i.e., husband as head of household) is the core problem in marriage. Other dimensions of normative marriage are less troublesome. There is little evidence of widespread disagreement about the ideas of free choice of spouses, fidelity, monogamy, heterosexual marriage, maturity, or parenthood.

Whether Americans are now less committed to common moral beliefs than in the past is an empirical question. Values (i.e., moral beliefs) are researchable issues, and it would be possible to investigate their role in matters of family life. Increases in divorce, cohabitation, illegitimacy, or premarital sex are certainly evidence that some beliefs are changing. However, social scientists have yet to identify all the various causes of these family trends. Undoubtedly there are many, including demographic (e.g., longer life, lower fertility), technological (e.g., contraception, public health) and cultural (e.g., shifting patterns of immigration). Changing values about gender are but one cause of family change. Still, I suspect they are the most important. When something as basic and fundamental as what it means to be a man or woman changes, virtually everything else must change accordingly. Now we must incorporate such new ideas into the institution of marriage.

New Families

It is easy to imagine how a new model of marriage would look. None of the basic elements of normative marriage are likely to change except the gender assumptions about who heads the family. Husbands and wives are already familiar with this new model of marriage, even if we have yet to acknowledge it. In 1995, virtually all (95 percent) of married men with children in the household were employed. Two-thirds (65 percent) of wives in such families were employed. Husbands are still breadwinners, but so are wives. While employment does not typically eliminate a wife's dependency on her husband, it does mean that husbands are also dependent on wives. Most American marriages now involve a pooling of incomes. The resulting lifestyle, therefore, is produced jointly by wives and husbands. Income pooling has increasingly replaced the breadwinner/homemaker pattern.

These new economic realities of married life have not been fully incorporated into the institution of normative marriage—the way we think about marriage. Husbands and wives have yet to reconcile their joint economic dependency with the routine of married life. Even if most married couples today depend on one another's earnings, traditional patterns of domestic responsibilities persist. Such gendered marriages are a problem because they do not fit with the assumptions about men and women in all other spheres of their lives.

The trends in the family that worry us might better be viewed as a consequence of redefining the institution. We are now struggling to resolve ideas about what is proper in our marriages with ideas about what is proper outside of them. Repeated studies have shown that conflicts over gender (Should the wife work? Who should do what?) are leading causes of divorce. Growing numbers of women find it difficult to live in marriages that appear to devalue their roles as breadwinners. On the other hand, full-time housewives feel that housework is devalued. Growing numbers of couples opt for "informal" marriage, or cohabitation, as a way to live without strict gender assumptions. Large numbers of women decide to pursue parenthood without the limitations and restrictions that would be imposed by marriage. It is easy to see why people make these choices. But though understandable, they are costly. Adults and children thrive in stable, nuclear families, even if they are not always happy. No feasible alternative comes close in its economic or emotional benefits for children or adults.

But the solution is not complete independence in marriage. Cohabitation has taught us that two soloists do not make a very good duet. Such equal partnerships do not last very long, and cohabiting couples report low levels of happiness and satisfaction. That is probably because nothing binds cohabiting couples together except love and affection. As desirable as those emotions are, they are a flimsy basis for an enduring relationship without alternative bonds. Stable, enduring marriages must be forged of extensive dependencies. Each person must depend on the other for many things. But such dependencies need not be inequitable or unfair.

What is the problem with marriage? The problem is the role of gender in the institution. More accurately, the problem is how to deal with widespread social change in matters of gender. But there is good reason to believe that we will come to terms with such challenges. Few boys today will grow up with mothers who are not employed. Young men are unlikely to inherit their fathers' or grandfathers' traditional views about marriage or women. Fewer men work with colleagues who openly view women and wives in traditional restricted roles. More and more of the youthful life course is spent in nontraditional families or outside of families altogether. Children, especially boys, who experience such childhoods (employed mothers, divorce, non-family living) are more accepting of women's new roles and options and are willing to perform more housework. It is not, therefore, a dramatic change in the basic institution of normative marriage that we need. Rather, it is a recognition and accommodation to the changes in women's lives and patience for intergenerational (cohort) change to catch up with current expectations. And men must become a part of the gender revolution. Even if this is not a fundamental redefinition of marriage, it will have profound consequences for how marriage is experienced because the tension between public and private lives will be reduced.

Marriage and Public Policy

Social institutions can be changed intentionally, but not easily, not quickly, and not without widespread discussion and debate. I have been studying covenant marriage in Louisiana for the past year. In that state (and in Arizona) couples may elect one of two marriage regimes; the traditional one based on no-fault divorce rules, and covenant marriage which requires premarital counseling, and is governed by traditional fault-grounds for divorce. Covenant marriage laws are the first in over 200 years in America designed explicitly to make *marriage more permanent and divorce more restrictive*. Not surprisingly therefore, they are extremely controversial. It is much too early to know if this legal innovation will affect divorce rates. But one thing is clear. The passage of more restrictive divorce laws, even if optional, has provoked intense debate and discussion about the meaning of marriage and the role of the state in family affairs. Covenant marriage is discussed and debated almost weekly in the Louisiana media. A public discussion about marriage has begun in that state. Only through such *megalogues*, as Etzioni calls them, will institutions change. Social change is not being legislated. It is simply being encouraged, debated, and discussed.

Proposals that marriage be recognized, promoted, and protected by revisions in federal tax codes, increased use of pre-marital counseling, and revisions in divorce laws are a good start. I believe we must go further, however, to create and reinforce dependencies in marriage. Dependency based automatically on gender will eventually be purged from marriage, as it is now being purged from work, school, and other public realms. The transition is clearly difficult and painful as we now can see. But what will bind couples to such new families? The answer is that bases of dependency other than gender must be created. Significant benefits must flow from the marriage, and significant exit costs must exist for both partners.

The most sensible, though controversial way to achieve these goals is for states to establish a preference for married couples in the distribution of discretionary benefits. My research on covenant marriage has convinced me that any attempt to privilege marriage over other statuses will be controversial and resisted, especially by those who see traditional marriage as unfair to women. Since the inequities in marriage are being resolved, I would focus on ways to privileged marriage by granting significant economic benefits to couples willing to commit to a restrictive regime. The purpose would be to create a new distinction between married and unmarried persons, though not one automatically based on gender. If marriage is to thrive, significant benefits *other than emotional ones* must flow from the status. And men and women alike must benefit from the status of marriage.

Marriage has traditionally been founded on dependencies of many types. But unequal (i.e. women's) economic dependencies are the most obvious (and often the source of inequity). In a world where men and women may each be economically independent, the benefits of pooled incomes may not suffice to sustain couples during those inevitable times when love fades. What the authors of *A Call to Civil Society* refer to as "the philosophy of expressive individualism—a belief in the "sovereignty of the self" is fostered by gender equality and individual economic independence. In the absence of unequal economic dependencies, marriage must become a privileged status again, or else divorce rates will remain high, and marriage rates will continue to fall. To make it a privileged status, we should establish significant economic incentives. To the extent that people benefit economically in obvious and large ways by virtue of their marriages, (and to the extent that such benefits are not available to unmarried people) each spouse is dependent on *the union, per se* (dependency is typically measured by the costs of exiting a relationship).

The state has an enormous economic interest in promoting stable marriages. Strangely, the *macroeconomic* costs of divorce are rarely discussed in deliberations about public policy. Yet the *microeconomic* consequences are well known. Divorce and single-parenthood take a toll on earnings, educational attainment, labor-force attachment, subsequent marital stability, and the likelihood of poverty for the adults and the children involved. The aggregate consequences of all such individual losses are vast, even if unknown. Promoting marriage makes very good economic sense, beyond any other benefits to children or adults.

There are many ways we might promote marriage. Here I offer one example. We should consider significant tax credits for some married couples to create an economic interest in the marital union and significant exit costs for both partners. Americans will not tolerate mandatory family policy, so states should follow the lead of Louisiana in offering couples the option of two marriage regimes. Any couple could elect to be married under the customary no-fault divorce system without requirements for pre-marital and marital counseling. The more restrictive marriage regime would require premarital and marital counseling (as a prerequisite for a divorce), and would apply prevailing "best interests of the child" custody standards in granting a divorce. Divorce would be denied if the court determined that it was not in the best interest of the child (or children) involved. ("Best interests of the child" divorce proposals have been considered in several states, though never enacted.)

Couples who marry under the more restrictive marriage regime would qualify for very significant tax credits. Such credits must be quite large—$2,500 or $3,500 a year—sufficient to offset the costs of a college education for the children of married parents, or to underwrite the costs of a home, for example. Such tax credits would create a financial interest in the marriage *per se,* a benefit that flows to married couples by virtue of their marital status and nothing else. It also creates a significant exit cost at divorce. Both partners benefit so long as they remain married, both lose at divorce. How will we pay for such generous benefits? In fact, it is not certain that there would be net costs. A more appropriate question is how we will continue to pay for single parenthood and divorce.

Such a proposal seeks to restore marriage to a privileged status. It also addresses the need for a new basis of dependency in modern marriages where both spouses are likely to be breadwinners. It is intended to foster higher rates of marriage, lower rates of unmarried childbearing, and delays in divorce. Were any policy to be partially successful in having these consequences, the long-term economic ledgers (i.e., costs and benefits) may balance. Even if they didn't, such proposals would surely provoke discussion and debate about the importance of marriage in America. *A Call to Civil Society* asks us to begin such a debate about the loss of organizing ideals. Let's start with a consideration of the centrality of gender to the problem with marriage.

Steven L. Nock is professor of sociology at the University of Virginia. His most recent book, Marriage in Men's Lives *explains how and why marriage changes men. He is currently conducting a five-year study of covenant marriage in Louisiana.*

I'm O.K.

You're O.K.

So Who Gets the Kids?

By **Susan Douglas**

IT'S 3:47 A.M. HOUR OF THE WOLF. THAT DEEP POCKET IN THE NIGHT when anxieties and self-doubts gnaw at already ragged psyches. I get up and go to my daughter's room. I got home from work too late the night before to put her to bed. I brush the hair off her face and kiss her warm, sweet-smelling forehead. And I wonder if Robert Young is doing the same, only with a much more desperate sense of urgency and impending loss. And his ex-wife, Alice Hector, also up in the night, staring into her daughters' empty rooms, her stomach in a knot?

I am up because I hate this story. It's too upsetting. But that pales beside Young's and Hector's battle: for both of them, their daily relationship to their daughters, ages 10 and 13, is on the line. In a highly publicized case, Alice Hector, once a partner in a prominent Miami law firm and now head of her own, lost custody of her two daughters in June 1998 because an all-male three-judge panel ruled that her work schedule was too demanding for her to remain their primary caretaker. They overturned a trial judge's decision to keep the girls with their mother, and awarded custody to Robert Young, the girls' father, who until two years ago was a stay-at-home dad, and who now has a job with flexible work hours. Hector appealed the ruling in December and, as of this writing, awaits a decision. Her ex-husband, by all accounts a deeply involved and devoted father, insists that their daughters get a much higher quality of love and attention with him than they would at Hector's home, because she must relegate much of their care to a housekeeper.

Young had done things like start a Brownie troop for their younger daughter when none existed, organize a soccer team

for the elder daughter when that didn't exist either, and then coach the team, as well. He also volunteered at school. Hector couldn't do these kinds of things. But she did get up at the crack of dawn so she'd have time with the girls in the morning, she devoted her weekends to them, and she claimed in court that in the middle of the night, when either one of them was sick, they came to her. Young and his attorneys have been very careful not to label Hector a bad mother; on the contrary, they have praised her efforts to juggle her work as a litigator with the demands of motherhood. Young's point is simple: we're both devoted parents, we both love our kids, but I'm home much more than she is and have much more time to take care of the kids, so they should live with me.

Florida does not favor joint custody, as many other states do. Florida law assumes that moving back and forth between parents' homes is bad for kids. Instead, the law promotes "shared parental responsibility," meaning that both parents are supposed to remain active in the children's lives, but the kids maintain a primary residence with only one of the parents. This is, in part, where the battle started. Both sides say they agreed to share the house while they worked out the divorce settlement—an arrangement that kept the parents in daily touch with the kids but may have exacerbated their intense competition over who deserves custody.

Deep resentments and intransigent stereotypes snarl through the case. Hector and Young got married in New Mexico in 1982, when she was a public interest lawyer making a moderate salary and he was a successful architectural designer and

ALICE HECTOR HAS BEEN STEREOTYPED AS A SELFISH, UNCARING MOTHER, WHILE ROBERT YOUNG HAS SAID, "I WAS ONLY PERCEIVED AS ALICE'S HUSBAND."

home builder. His business collapsed in the aftermath of the 1987 stock market crash, and Hector and the couple's two

---

Mom is still suspect if she isn't standing in the doorway at 3:30 P.M. in a cookie-dough-smeared apron offering baked goods to her kids as they come home from school.

---

daughters moved to Florida in 1989 after she got a better-paying job at a major law firm. Young followed six months later, but couldn't find work in a new location where he had few professional contacts. Hector claims she never wanted Young to be a stay-at-home dad, but instead encouraged him to try to find work. She increasingly resented having the burden of supporting the family entirely on her shoulders, and clearly felt it was unfair for her to have to put in 60-hour weeks while her husband did no work outside the home.

IT IS VERY DIFFICULT FOR MOST WOMEN, HOWEVER LIBERATED, TO OVER-come our culture's easy equation of bringing home the bacon and true manhood. Difficult for the courts, too: during the initial hearing, when Hector won custody, the judge said to Young, "Maybe I'm missing something. Why don't you get a job?" Young found himself dismissed elsewhere, as well, for staying home with the kids. He recalled a partner in his wife's law firm greeting him with "It's nice to meet you, Mr. Alice." In a comment feminists should find poignant, he told a reporter, "I was only perceived as Alice's husband." Hector, of course, has been stereotyped, too, as a selfish, uncaring mother who brought legal briefs with her to a child's recital. "There is the idea that I wanted this life and this was the life I chose," Hector said in an interview. "The opposite is true. I'm not saying I don't enjoy my work—I do—but it is not my first choice."

Which one of them should I be rooting for? Why is this a contest, a war? Does being a feminist mean that I automatically root for her, no matter what? If my husband and I ever found ourselves in divorce court, would I, too, face losing custody of my daughter because there have been nights, like last night, when I wasn't home for dinner and didn't tuck her in? Or could he be suddenly ripped out of the daily routine of her life—even though he takes her back and forth to school almost every day, helps her with her homework, and wouldn't be able to stand not seeing her for days on end—simply because I'm the mother? According to David Chambers, a professor of law at the University of Michigan, in most custody cases the courts prefer to place a child with the parent who is the primary caretaker, and in the overwhelming majority of cases, this is the mother. The primary caretaker presumption was designed, in part, to thwart the potential threat by fathers to sue for custody so their ex-wives would give in on other aspects of a divorce settlement, like money. But what if you're both the primary caretakers?

It's easy, as a feminist, to have a knee-jerk reaction to the Hector-Young case: how dare three men take away a woman's daughters just because she works? But I guess that one of the reasons I hate this story is that this case, more than many other custody battles that have received media attention, does, in fact, require us to confront our contradictory stances about what we want and expect from fathers now that we're 30 years into the women's movement. Three decades ago, we argued that our treatment before the law should be gender-blind because when it wasn't, we lost. We've also been insisting, with some limited success, that fathers become more involved in child rearing. Those of us who work outside the home are tired of the utter unfairness of the second shift, when both parents come home from work, but Dad gets to read the paper while Mom makes dinner, helps with geometry homework, fends off telemarketers, and does ten loads of laundry.

And many of our husbands have responded.

SO IF SOME MEN HAVE BECOME EQUAL, OR EVEN MORE THAN EQUAL, partners in child rearing, as we'd hoped, then shouldn't those men have the same rights that women would in court? I do know men who are, indeed, more conscientious and better parents than their wives and would very much merit primary custody if their marriages were to end. But if we grant this, are we opening the floodgates to thousands of frivolous and even unjust custody challenges by fathers who work but won't face the same prejudices in court about their commitment to their children as a working mother automatically does? In a custody battle, if Dad knows the name of the kids' dentist and went to one PTA meeting, he's the Albert Schweitzer of parenting; if Mom gets up at 5:00 A.M. to do the laundry and read files from work so she can have more time with her kids, she's still suspect if she isn't standing in the doorway at 3:30 P.M. in a cookie-dough-smeared apron offering baked goods to her kids as they come home from school. A 1989 report commissioned by Michigan's Supreme Court found that stereotypes bias judges against working mothers: they granted custody to fathers showing the most minimal interest in parenting, and they viewed mothers who placed emphasis on their careers to be less fit as parents than fathers who did exactly the same thing.

Many feminists, women lawyers, and women's organizations have expressed outrage over the ruling against Hector. After all, this case has not occurred in a vacuum: it comes on the heels of quite a few well-publicized and outrageous cases in which mothers lost custody of their children simply because they work outside the home, or work "too many hours." Some studies claim that when custody disputes end up in court, fathers win more than 60 percent of the time, and women lose custody for behavior that is utterly acceptable for men, such

PAMELA MCGEE'S EX-HUSBAND, THE REV. KEVIN E. STAFFORD, ASSERTED THAT A CAREER AND MOTHERHOOD ARE MUTUALLY EXCLUSIVE: MCGEE'S "LEVEL OF ACHIEVEMENT," HE ARGUED, "IMPAIRS HER ABILITY TO PARENT HER DAUGHTER."

as having ambitious career goals. The list is long and infuriating. In 1994, Sharon Prost, deputy chief counsel of the Senate Judiciary Committee, lost custody of her two sons because a female judge determined that she devoted too much time to her job. It didn't matter that Prost got up at 5:30 A.M. to fix breakfast and drive her older son to school or that she brought

This case comes on the heels of quite a few outrageous cases in which mothers lost custody of their children simply because they work.

her younger son with her to the Senate day care center every day, usually had lunch with him, and often left for home before 6:00 P.M. It didn't matter that a court-appointed psychologist affirmed that Prost's children were attached primarily to their mother. Nor did it matter that her ex-husband, Kenneth Greene, insisted that the couple retain an au pair, even when he was unemployed and at home for over a year, or that when he was employed, he put in extremely long workdays himself. After the new arrangement, according to *Time* magazine's Margaret Carlson, Greene reportedly sent along the kids' dirty laundry when he dropped them off with Prost. Recently the couple agreed to share joint custody. It came about only after Prost began to put in fewer hours at work, while her ex-husband continued to work full time.

Also in 1994, Jennifer Ireland, who had a child when she was 16 and subsequently won several scholarships to attend the University of Michigan, lost custody of her daughter because she placed the child in day care for 35 hours a week while she was in school. The child's father wasn't asserting that he would be the primary caregiver, but rather that his mother would. Judge Raymond Cashen found this arrangement superior because, as he put it, day care meant that the child would be "supervised by strangers." This case, too, ultimately ended in a joint custody solution after Cashen's ruling was successfully appealed in the spring of 1996.

Meanwhile, shortly after Hector lost custody of her daughters, *Sports Illustrated* reported that Pamela McGee, who plays for the WNBA's Los Angeles Sparks, lost custody of her four-year-old daughter while the court investigated whether McGee's work prevented her from being a good mother. In his motion for temporary sole custody, McGee's ex-husband, the Rev. Kevin E. Stafford, asserted that a career and motherhood are mutually exclusive: McGee's "level of achievement," he argued, "impairs her ability to parent her daughter." At issue, according to *Sports Illustrated*, was whether McGee's travel schedule—she's on the road about four weeks a year—took her away from her daughter too much. The court was not

investigating whether Stafford's travel schedule—he's on the road seven to eight weeks a year—made him an unfit father.

Many male judges are so prejudiced against working mothers and day care that they will award custody to the father and his new wife if she stays at home, insisting that a stepmom is superior to a working mother. In 1982, a father who had refused to acknowledge paternity, wouldn't pay child support, and didn't visit his son until he was 15 months old sued for custody after the mother tried to get child support. He won, because the mother had worked two jobs to support her son, while his new wife didn't have a job and could be home with the child. This mother has had to watch her child be raised by another woman. When sexist judges with outdated and inaccurate biases against day care apply the "best interests of the child" standard, working mothers can easily lose. And child care providers, whether housekeepers, baby-sitters, or day care centers, are routinely dismissed as inferior, second-rate caretakers.

So it's no surprise that we feminists have our hackles up. We see a vengeful backlash against mothers who work outside the home in which we detect a barely disguised glee in meting out the most painful punishment there can be: separating us from our children. There seems to be a real blood lust—not just in the courts, but in much of the culture—to take working women down a peg, especially if they are more successful than their ex-husbands. At its core, this trend of taking children away from their working mothers is about punishing women for having what is perceived to be too much power. This has occurred within the broader backlash against feminism that continues unabated, where we see an assault on women's reproductive rights, punitive policies toward poor mothers, ridicule of women's studies programs, trivialization of date rape, and calls by a bevy of antifeminist women for us to get back into the kitchen.

Because so much of what we fought for in the 1970s was either undermined or never realized, the prerogatives of motherhood have seemed, until recently, one of our last few privileged outposts. Of course we're going to protect our rights and interests here: we feel under siege in so many areas, and now they want to take our kids away, too? And one thing that court documents can never establish is the endless mental work of mothering: anticipating the children's immediate and long-term needs, and tending to them in advance. The kids' needs are most often in a mother's head, integrated in her psychic "to do" list, because that's what's expected of mothers, and that's what they're supposed to do.

Yet too many feminists, in our understandable outrage over this punitive trend, have been dismissive of Young. He has had to pay for every sexist judge's decision, every mother wronged

JENNIFER IRELAND, WHO HAD A CHILD WHEN SHE WAS 16, LOST CUSTODY OF HER DAUGHTER BECAUSE SHE PLACED HER IN DAY CARE FOR 35 HOURS A WEEK WHILE SHE ATTENDED COLLEGE. THE CHILD'S FATHER WASN'T ASSERTING THAT HE WOULD BE THE PRIMARY CAREGIVER.

in court. His feminist attorney, Barbara Green, who saw this as a case about gender equality, has been stung by reactions from other women attorneys who now treat her like a traitor. We should admit to the other truth that we also know: many fathers are deeply connected to their children and then, after a divorce, are relegated to every-other-weekend cameo appearances. I think we've let this case be too easy for us, and we've used Hector and Young as caricatures onto whom we can project a host of fears, rages, and anxieties about work and the family.

> **We know many fathers are deeply connected to their children and then, after a divorce, are relegated to every-other-weekend cameo appearances in their kids' lives.**

BUT I ALSO WONDER HOW MANY OF US REALLY WANT FATHERS TO BE absolutely equal partners in parenting. As gender roles shift and blur, isn't it our dirty little secret that we want to preside over at least a few of the old preserves, that we need to be seen as the better parents, that we bitch about how much more we have to do than fathers but also cherish our essentialist claims to superiority? Motherhood in America is an ongoing contest, a competition, but mostly between ourselves and celebrity moms, or our friends, or the bad mothers in the media that women are urged to feel superior to, like Susan Smith or welfare mothers. Against some of these women we lose, and against others we win. But to lose to a man?

There are other cases—L.A. Sparks player Pamela McGee's, for example—that feminists should see as emblematic of men trying to demonize working mothers. But I don't see the Hector-Young case as the exemplar of the attack on working mothers, because he truly has been a pretty unusual father. The number of stay-at-home fathers in the U.S. appears to be very small. And not many mothers make over $300,000 a year, as Hector did, or put in her hours, although increasing numbers of mothers—and fathers, for that matter—are facing expanding work schedules and speed-ups. Rather, this case embodies another crucial feminist lesson: negotiation is always preferable to battle.

As Ellen Lyons, the feminist attorney who handled "Young's successful appeal, put it, "I always tell my clients to settle." The emotional costs of going through a trial and an appeal are enormous, she emphasizes, and can produce intense pain. "People should think twice before going to battle," she warns, "because the scars are so deep, so bloody." This couple should have settled, but the legal system in which divorcing parents find themselves should make it harder, not easier, to end up in court. Florida's paternalistic attitudes toward joint custody, however well intentioned, and its insistence on someone being the victor—the parent with whom the children make their primary residence—make contests over custody even more heavily charged than they already are.

The case also dramatizes how very far we still have to go as a culture to devise family-friendly work environments. For most professional people, being overworked means you're important and productive. It also means you have less time for your family. While women rightly want the same opportunities as men, feminists once had a dream that we could humanize the workplace; many of us didn't want to have to become just like workaholic, absentee men. Cases like Hector-Young allow us to focus on particular individuals—the classic way the news media covers major trends—instead of on the deep systemic problems of overwork as laid out by Juliet B. Schor in *The Overworked American*. I'm betting that despite feminists' strong reactions to this case, most of us see ourselves in neither Young nor Hector, but in the imagined parent between the two of them.

It is impossible for me not to feel torn by this case. If one is committed to gender equity, and to granting custody to the primary caretaker, Robert Young should retain custody. In my head, I am with him. But in my heart, I am with Hector. Because I know that if I ever found myself in a courtroom, it wouldn't matter that I know the names of all my daughter's dolls, or that I lie in bed with her at night to talk about friendship, or decimals, or god, or that I know which kind of socks she loves and which ones she absolutely refuses to wear. It would only matter that I work longer hours than my husband, and so, as a working mother, I am a bad mother. Until the courts banish this stereotype, it is going to be impossible for many feminists, however deeply committed they are to gender equity, to support the sort of role reversals we once celebrated in our dreams.

Susan Douglas teaches communication studies at the University of Michigan. Her most recent book is "Listening In: Radio and the American Imagination" (Times Books).

How Are We Doing with *Loving?*

RACE, LAW & INTERMARRIAGE

"Almighty God created the races white, black, yellow, malay and red, and he placed them on separate continents. And but for the interference with his arrangement there would be no cause for such marriages. The fact that he separated the races shows that he did not intend for the races to mix."

BY RANDALL KENNEDY

THE HISTORICAL U.S. SUPREME COURT case titled *Loving v. Virginia* arose from the fact that in 1958, two Virginians, Richard Loving and Mildred Jeter, married one another in Washington, D.C. and then returned to their native state to live together as man and wife. The problem was that Richard was white and Mildred was black and that the state of Virginia outlawed such marriages.

Virginia had barred interracial marriages continuously since 1691 when it restricted English persons from intermarrying with Negroes, mulattos, or Indians to prevent the "abominable mixture and spurious issue" that were fearfully expected from such unions. The statute under which the Lovings were prosecuted was enacted in 1924. Entitled "An Act to Preserve Racial Purity," the law narrowed existing racial definitions of whiteness and decreed that in Virginia no white person could marry anyone other than another white person. Not only did this law criminalize interracial marriage within the state; it also criminalized entering into an interracial marriage outside the state with the intent of evading Virginia's prohibition.

The Act to Preserve Racial Purity also declared that an interracial marriage was void which meant, among other things, that children born to such a union were deemed in the eyes of the state to be illegitimate and without the protections and privileges accorded to the children of lawfully wedded parents.

The Lovings pleaded guilty to violating the Act to Preserve Racial Purity and were sentenced to one year in jail, though the trial judge gave them the option of avoiding incarceration on the condition that they leave the state and not return together for 25 years. In the course of the proceedings the trial judge asserted that "Almighty God created the races white, black, yellow, malay and red, and he placed them on separate continents. And but for the interference with his arrangement there would be no cause for such marriages. The fact that he separated the races shows that he did not intend for the races to mix."

After Virginia's Supreme Court of Appeals affirmed the conviction, the Supreme Court of the United States reversed it on the grounds that the federal constitution prohibits states from barring interracial marriage. In the process of doing so, the Court also implicitly invalidated similar laws then in existence in 15 other states.

The Supreme Court issued its ruling on June 12, 1967. Given that 32 years has elapsed since that landmark decision, it seems appropriate to ask how we are doing with *Loving*.

Loving occupies a totally secure niche in American constitutional law. Its significance is sufficiently vibrant to have caused a principal to lose his job in Wedowee, Alabama for voicing opposition to interracial dating and marriage, and that such relationships have become sufficiently acceptable that by 1991 Senator Strom Thurmond, once a fire-eating segregationist, debated unreservedly on behalf of the imperiled Supreme Court nomination of Clarence Thomas, a black man who resided in Virginia and lived in married bliss with a white woman.

In the post-*Loving* regime, at least in terms of race, no one has to worry about governments counteracting or prohibiting desires to marry.

So how are we doing with *Loving?* Although the marriage market remains racially segmented, white-black marriages have increased. According to the calculations of Douglas Besharov and Timothy Sullivan, in 1960, about 1.7% of married blacks had a white spouse. In

From *InterRace* Magazine, Vol. 9, No. 3, 1999, pp. 14-16. © 1999 by Randall Kennedy. Reprinted by permission.

1990, the percentage had risen to about 5.9%. Moreover, the pace of increase in marriage across the black-white racial frontier is quickening, especially in terms of white men and black women. (In 1980, black women married white men in only 0.7% of all marriages involving a black bride; by 1993, black women were marrying white men in 3.9% of the marriages involving black brides.)

Besharov and Sullivan contend approvingly that the realities reflected by these numbers show "a strong, unambiguous trend toward integration within American families." They note that "African Americans are substantially less likely to marry whites than are Hispanics, Asians, or Native Americans. But that rather bland formulation obscures the fact that, in Nathan Glazer's words, "Black and White After Thirty Years": "Blacks stand out uniquely among the array of American ethnic and racial groups in the degree to which marriages remain within the group."

The pattern of intermarriage of other peoples of color with whites have increased over time. Of marriages involving a person of Japanese ancestry in the 1940s, for example, about 10 to 15 percent involved intermarriages with whites. By the 1960s, nearly half of the marriages involving a person of Japanese ancestry involved intermarriages with whites. There has been a lesser degree of intermarriage with other groups, such as people of Chinese and Korean ancestry. But the rates at which individuals in these groups intermarry with whites has always been greater than white-black rates of intermarriage. There is considerable reluctance to view the relatively low rates of black-white intermarriage as a problem.

One source of reluctance is a desire to avoid nourishing an already swollen racial self-importance that afflicts many whites; some people understandably fear that suggesting intimate association with whites as a valuable commodity will only heighten the vice of white racial pride.

Another source of reluctance is that portraying low rates of white-black intermarriage as a problem will reinforce longstanding beliefs that blacks lack a decent sense of racial self-respect and want nothing more than to become intimate, especially sexually intimate, with whites.

A third source of reluctance stems from the sense that marriage should be based upon tender feelings of love therefore it occupies a wholly different plane than jobs, or housing, or schooling or any of the other institutions, goods, or services that are the typical subjects of debate in discussions over race relations policy.

Each of these concerns point towards political and analytical difficulties that make the subject of white-black intermarriage treacherous terrain. In my view, however, the relative fewness of white-black intermarriages is an important problem that warrants attention and discussion. That blacks intermarry with whites at strikingly lower rates than others is yet another sign of the uniquely encumbered and peculiarly isolated status of African Americans.

It is also an obstacle to the development of attitudes and connections that will be necessary to improve the position of black Americans and, beyond that, to address the racial divisions that continue to hobble our nation. Marriage matters. That is why white supremacists invested so much time, thought, and energy into prohibiting marriage across racial lines. Marriage plays a large role in governing the intergenerational transfer of wealth. It also is central to maintaining a stable race line. After all, when people intermarry and produce children of mixed race, racial identifications, racial loyalties, and racial kinships blur.

Granted the social significance of intermarriage, what should one's stance toward it be? In my view, white-black intermarriage is not simply something that should be tolerated. It is a type of partnership that should be applauded and encouraged.

Intermarriage is good because it signals that newcomers or outsiders are gaining acceptance in the eyes of those in the dominant population and perceived by them as persons of value. Intermarriage is also good because it breaks down the psychological boundaries that distance people on racial grounds, opening up new expectations and experiences that would otherwise remain hidden.

Intermarriage encourages the learning of transracial empathy that is crucial for enabling people to place themselves in the shoes of others racially different than themselves. Few situations are more likely to mobilize the racially-privileged individual to move against racial wrongs than witnessing such wrongs inflicted upon his mother-in-law, father-in-law, spouse, or child. Fortified by such lessons and animated by a newly drawn map of racial self-interest, participants in interracial marriage are likely to fight against racial wrongs that menace loved ones.

There are, of course, powerful forces against increased rates of white-black intermarriage. One impediment is the residual influence of white opposition. Some polls suggest that as much as 20% of the white population continues to believe that interracial marriage should be illegal. Some of these people express their disapproval in ways that go beyond answering the questions of pollsters. Through stares, catcalls, and even violence, they put a shadow over interracial intimacy, driving up its costs and frightening off some who might otherwise explore its possibilities.

It is a terrible fact that in many locales, mixed couples face a substantial risk that they will be subjected to abuse by those who feel affronted by a form of loving that they perceive as "unnatural."

A second impediment is the centrifugal force of black solidarity. In *Mixed Blood*, an illuminating study of intermarriage that focuses on Jews, blacks, and Japanese Americans, Paul R. Spickard writes:

[W]here there were clusters of Black people, Japanese Americans, or Jews along with ethnic institutions such

as synagogues and fraternal organizations, the communities actively discouraged intermarriage.... Where such social networks were lacking, individuals were more likely to override any personal internal constraints and marry outside the group.

Blacks who intermarry with whites can expect to be viewed with skepticism, if not hostility, by many other blacks who will consider them to be racial defectors. It does not matter that there are many examples of blacks who, though intermarried with whites, have consistently and militantly fought to improve the fortunes of African Americans; Frederick Douglass, Walter White, Richard Wright, James Farmer, and Marian Wright Edelman, for example.

A third impediment has to do with the brutal consequences of deprivation: the fact that, because of historical and ongoing oppression, many blacks will simply have less to offer in the marriage market. Black people live shorter lives, typically have less education, are objects of discrimination, face all manners of racial obstacles in the struggle for upward mobility. The extent to which this is true, blacks will seem less of a "good catch" to many people, particularly whites, in the marriage market. Marriage often involves an entire array of delicate and mysterious feelings and motivations—lust, love, and the deepest springs of self-identity—however, marriage also triggers concerns about dollars and cents, social advancement, finding a good catch.

As long as black people are kept in a state of relative social, political, and economic deprivation, others will be less inclined to want to marry them. What is to be done?

First, the legal system ought to carry through completely with the anti-discrimination agenda. The most pertinent context in which it has failed to do so is the realm of transracial adoption.

As a matter of law or practice, many jurisdictions exercise a preference for placing orphaned or abandoned children of a given race in the care of adults of the same race. This practice is known as race matching. Race matching is premised on the belief that it is more natural and thus better for a child to be raised by adults of the same race as the child.

Abolishing race matching would respond to the immediate benefit of children in need of foster care or adoptive homes by removing an impediment which currently slows or prevents child placements when parents of the "correct" race are not on hand. Getting rid of race matching would also have a broader, long-term beneficent consequence by signaling in a vivid way that, in the eyes of the law, same-race families are no better than, and cer-

> **I look back on *Loving v. Virginia* with gratitude, and hope that more people will take advantage of this enlarged area of freedom.**

tainly entitled to no preference over, racially mixed families.

Recently, Congress prohibited any public or private agency that receives funding from the federal government from delaying or denying the placement of a child for adoption or into foster care because of the race of the child or of the prospective parents. There is, however, a big difference between prohibiting a deeply-ingrained practice and its actual disappearance.

Second, people who embrace my view should openly and unapologetically express their opinion on the subject to their mothers and fathers, sisters and brothers, colleagues and friends. Consider the following scenario: A white man friend lets it be known that he would like to be introduced to a nice woman. It just so happens that around the same time a black woman friend indicates that she would like to be introduced to a nice man.

My impression is that many people would steer the white man to a white woman and the black woman to a black man. What one should do is introduce these two people to one another as potential romantic partners. Furthermore, if, after the blind date, either party complains about the racial politics of the matchmaking, people of my ideological persuasion should openly, calmly, but resolutely question the basis of the complaint and through discussion attempt to persuade friends to reconsider whether they want to remain committed to inherited conventions and formulas that limit their choice of potential partners.

Finally, people should militantly support policies that elevate the status of black Americans. The more secure, accepted, and prosperous they are, the more attractive they will be in the marriage market, further spurring the modest increase in intermarriage that we have witnessed over the past decade. This will help to bring about the type of society I want: a cosmopolitan society in which race no longer impedes the ability of people to appreciate the human qualities of one another, a society in which interracial loving is not only tolerated but so normal that it ceases to be an object of sensational wonderment.

The coming of this society will be both heralded and made possible by more interracial marriages. That is why I support the practice—not simply tolerate it but encourage it. That is also why I look back on *Loving v. Virginia* with gratitude, and hope that more people will take advantage of this enlarged area of freedom.

Randall Kennedy is a professor of law at Harvard University and an advocate of transracial adoption and interracial marriage.

The perils of polygamy

An incest case in Utah highlights the controversy over 'plural marriage'

By Vince Beiser in Salt Lake City

It's a sunny afternoon in Manti, a bucolic little central Utah town dominated by an incongruously imposing Mormon temple. Inside a tidy yellow-brick house on a quiet street, Jim Harmston, looking like a cowboy patriarch with his combed-back grey hair and denim shirt and jeans, is leafing through back issues of *National Geographic* and chatting with three women ranged around him on two living-room sofas. The peaceful tableau could be set in any middle-class house in any small American town, except for one detail: all three women—and five more besides—are Harmston's wives. "Nothing on earth sanctifies the soul like the institution of plural marriage," says wife Jeannine Harmston, a kindly looking woman in her 50s.

Remarkably, that seemingly archaic institution—better known as polygamy—has never been stronger. Despite being banned both by law and mainstream Mormon doctrine, the practice is not only thriving in heavily Mormon Utah and other parts of the U.S. West, but appears to be growing. The issue has burst into the open with the high-profile trials of two brothers, David and John Daniel Kingston. Last year, one of John Daniel's daughters, then 16, told police he had forced her to

marry her uncle David—who already had 14 wives. When the girl fled home after four sexual encounters with her uncle, she testified, her father beat her with a belt. Amid a blaze of media attention, John Daniel pleaded no contest to child abuse charges in April, and is now serving a 28-week sentence. On July 9, David was sentenced to up to 10 years in prison for incest and unlawful sexual conduct with a minor.

Such stories of intra-family mating and violence are nothing new to Carmen Thompson. Now 41, Thompson spent 13 years as one of a Salt Lake City Mormon man's eight wives, a harem that she says included the man's sister and 14-year-old niece. She finally left him, taking their five children, after what she describes as years of beatings, poverty and emotional neglect. Last year, Thompson helped found Tapestry of Polygamy, the first-ever support group for women and children leaving polygamous marriages. Since the beginning of the year, the group has fielded over 300 calls from people seeking help. "In polygamous families, the patriarch has all the power," says Thompson. "When there's that kind of imbalance, abuse comes naturally."

But polygamy's adherents say that as consenting adults they should have the right to live however they want. "We abhor abuse of any kind, and people like the Kingstons should be prose-

cuted," says Mary Potter, formerly one of a policeman's three wives and recent founder of a pro-polygamy women's group, the Women's Religious Liberties Union. "But abuse is also rampant in monogamous marriages. Why blame our religion?"

Polygamy was widely practised in the 1800s among the Mormon pioneers who settled the arid, remote territory that would become Utah. As a condition for receiving statehood, Utah banned the practice in the 1890s. Conveniently, the Mormon religious leadership received a divine revelation around that time that plural marriages should cease. A few diehards continued the practice underground, however, and in the 1930s a resurgent Mormon fundamentalist movement spawned openly polygamous breakaway factions. Today, there are an estimated 20,000 to 100,000 people living in polygamous families—more than when plural marriage was official Mormon doctrine.

And the population appears to be growing, due to conversions and the high birth rates in the secretive, closed-off fundamentalist clans. The largest single polygamous community comprises some 5,000 people in the small town of Hildale on the Utah-Arizona border. That group also has branches scattered across the western United States, Mexico and British Columbia. Canadian authorities brought the B. C. group to trial in 1992, but

Vince Beiser is a senior editor at *Mother Jones'* online sister publication, *The Mojo Wire* (www.motherjones.com).

the courts concluded that laws banning plural marriages violated the constitutional guarantee of religious freedom. Those established groups have been joined in recent years by newer factions. Among them is Harmston's 300-member True and Living Church of Jesus Christ of Saints of the Last Days. One of the more extreme fundamentalist groups, it teaches children that Saturday morning cartoons are the tool of Satan. There are also the so-called independents, people like Mary Potter who are not affiliated with any formal group but practise polygamy because that is what the original 19th-century Mormon prophets prescribed. Utah is also home to a small non-Mormon Christian polygamist movement.

For all, the bottom line is the same: God, they believe, wants his true followers to live polygamously. As a bonus, they say, the lifestyle also offers practical benefits. With multiple mothers in a family, there is no need for day care, hired help or hurried microwaved meals. "As a monogamous mother of six, I about went nuts trying to be everything to everybody," says Harmston's wife Laura, a former main-stream Mormon who left her husband to join the Manti group. "In a plural marriage, you have help."

Lillian Bowles, however, was miserable growing up as one of 40 children in a cloistered polygamous community near Salt Lake City. Her father had eight wives and she saw him only once a week, on Saturday nights when it was her mother's "turn." "He had very little interaction with our lives, but an incredible amount of control," says Bowles, 26. "We couldn't even play at a friend's house without getting his permission. You can talk about consenting adults, but the kids have no choice."

Even supporters concede polygamy has its downsides. "The jealously was very hard to take," admits Harmston's first wife, Elaine, with whom he had been married over 30 years before taking his subsequent wives. Thompson, the anti-polygamy activist, says the result is a kind of brainwashing. "It's incredibly emotionally degrading to lie in bed and hear your husband having sex with another woman on the other side of the wall," she says. "But you're taught that jealousy is a sin against God that you should fight. You learn to deny your emotions."

Finances are often a problem, too. It is hard to find, let alone afford, housing for a family that includes three or four wives and a dozen or more children. "We'd go dig food out of the dumpster behind the grocery store every week," says Bowles. "There were lots of other families who did the same."

Polygamy's suddenly high profile is proving embarrassing to tolerant Utah state authorities. Only a handful of offenders have been prosecuted for the crime since the 1950s, when the state quit making occasional raids on polygamous enclaves. "There's a large amount of tacit support for polygamy, because it's part of our state's history," says Utah state Senator Ron Allen. University of Utah psychology professor Irwin Altman argues that polygamous families are taking a place alongside other non-traditional households, from same-sex couples to single-parent homes, that have become fixtures of American life. "This movement," says Altman, who spent nearly a decade studying polygamous communities, "is here to stay."

The Consequences of Violence against Women

Violence is a vicious cycle that harms women and their families

by Lisa A. Mellman, M.D.
Columbia University

Society is riddled with violence. In 1995 some eight million people were assaulted in the U.S. Homicide was the second leading cause of death among 15- to 24-year-olds and the principal cause of death for 15- to 24-year-old black men. Of the several thousand women murdered each year (4,654 in 1995, according to the Department of Justice), one quarter to one half are killed by their male partners—and many were battered by these men in previous incidents. The homicide rates for children and adolescents have doubled since the early 1960s, and teenage girls are at least 13 times more likely to have been raped or sexually assaulted than teenage boys. The impact of this violence is pervasive, with profound physical, psychological, economic and social consequences for everyone.

Because violence against women largely takes place at home, it has a particularly insidious character and effect. Women are seven times more likely than men are to experience violence committed by someone close to them, by a lover, spouse or ex-lover. This corruption of trust and intimacy means that primary relationships are disrupted throughout the household and that a vicious cycle is set in motion—one that is at risk of being perpetuated by the next generation.

Violence and neglect beget violence and neglect. All children can become scarred and depressed by abuse that they observe or receive. Although most mistreated children do not become violent adults, one third may become abusive or neglectful parents; one third are at risk of becoming violent. Only by realistically assessing and facing the full scope and consequence of violence against women can health care professionals and political advocates make some headway in combating it. Fortunately, better-designed epidemiological studies are clarifying prevalence and are

Police and doctors are called in for only a small number of cases of domestic violence.

increasingly documenting the long-term medical and psychological effects of violence on women and their children.

Numbers at Odds

Arguments revolving around statistics have long plagued discussions about how to gauge the prevalence of violence. In part, the problem has arisen from semantics. Survey results differ depending on how exactly terms are defined. For instance, various studies have imprecisely defined terms such as "rape" or "domestic violence." Domestic violence has sometimes been interpreted as being hit repeatedly and other times as being grabbed once in the course of a relationship. The same problem applies to the ambiguous phrases "intimate relationship" and "physical injury." In addition, methodology shapes outcome. Face-to-face interviews, for example, yield higher numbers than do those conducted over the telephone. (The figures given in this article are the best ones available to date, but it is certain that some of them also suffer from these confounding factors.)

Only recently have epidemiologists precisely clarified their terms. Today we know from solid studies that 36 percent of American women—that is, more than 34 million women—report experiencing violent events (including rape and sexual or physical assault) or the homicide of someone they knew well. And between 9 and 12 percent of women report being raped at least once.

The data on violence by intimate partners remain less clear, however. Research using more exact methodology and larger samples is under way, including a large study funded by the Centers for Disease Control and Prevention (CDC) and the National Institute of Justice (NIJ). Results from this study will be available later this year. But for now we have to rely on older estimates: every year between 1.8 and four million women are battered by their partners.

Assessing the medical and psychological aftermath of this violence has been difficult to quantify as well, but for reasons other than terminology. Instead the challenge has been establishing causality between a violent event and a later physical or psychiatric symptom. Women often experience more than just violence: familial dysfunction and neglect usually coexist with physical or sexual abuse, or both. This confluence makes it difficult for physicians to tease apart which factors are contributing to an illness. In addition, abused women may develop more than one psychiatric disorder and may show symptoms long after a traumatic event took place.

These complexities are further compounded by the stigma and shame that abused women feel. According to a report by the Commonwealth Fund, 90 percent of women who described themselves as physically abused by their partner or spouse had never told a doctor. Even when directly asked, women often deny being beaten or assaulted. Some feel embarrassed about their situation and frightened of their batterer; others are understandably terrified about addressing the serious problems of their relationship. To confront the batterer means risking his denial or revenge. To leave means facing the daunting task of securing housing and work—efforts often complicated by the need for child care and the lack of economic or emotional self-sufficiency.

A Nightmare of Body . . .

Although precise numbers remain elusive for the time being, the medical and psychological effects of domestic violence are nonetheless becoming terribly clear. In 1991 the American Medical Association began a campaign to educate physicians—and the country at large—about domestic violence. Studies have documented that victims of violence and their children make more visits to physicians and have more medical complaints than most people do. Indeed, researchers found that the average number of physician visits increased 31 percent for assaulted women and 56 percent for rape victims in the year after the crime against them. Only in the past few years, however, have physicians begun to be trained to recognize and treat abuse.

Even a cursory look at the injuries women incur explains why the resulting medical costs for domestic violence in the U.S. have been

Domestic violence leaves lasting scars, emotionally and sometimes physically.

estimated at between $5 billion and $67 billion annually. Women suffer not only transitory injuries such as bruises, cuts, broken bones, concussions and urinary tract infections but also permanent ones: joint damage, hearing or vision loss, chronic pain, irritable bowel syndrome and sexually transmitted disease, including HIV infection.

Pregnant women are especially at risk of complications related to abuse. Studies indicate battered women have almost twice the number of miscarriages as nonbattered women do. Battered women often start prenatal care late in pregnancy and may have a greater number of low-birthweight babies. Because substance abuse is more prevalent among abused women, their fetuses are more likely to suffer drug- and alcohol-related complications.

. . . and of Mind

The psychiatric consequences of violence are also proving to be wide-ranging and severe. Survivors often describe a pervasive sense of terror and loss of control during and after the assault. Acute stress disorder (ASD) or posttraumatic stress disorder (PTSD) often follows violent events. Both are characterized by flashbacks and nightmares, numbness and avoidance, and heightened alertness—including irritability, vigilance, overresponsiveness to touch or sound, and an increased capacity for being startled.

Stress disorders are much more prevalent in victims of physical and especially sexual assault than they are in people who have not experienced such violence. In one survey, more than 94 percent of women who had been raped developed ASD within the first month, and 47 percent of these women had PTSD after three months. Extrapolation from several studies suggests that of the estimated 12 million or so American women who have been raped, almost four to five million have suffered PTSD.

Physiological studies demonstrate that the stress response evoked in PTSD is distinct from the normal stress response—and from the response reported in other psychiatric disorders. Individuals with PTSD have low cortisol levels and greater cortisol fluctuation, which indicates that their stress response has been biologically altered. These chemical changes may translate into a more reactive heart rate and a tendency to startle easily.

Violence and abuse are frequently associated with other disorders as well: depression, anxiety, substance abuse and feelings of being disconnected from reality. Women who were repeatedly raped in childhood are three times more likely to develop depression and almost five times more likely to develop anxiety disorders than women who have not suffered in this way. Abused women also suffer from low self-esteem and poor interpersonal skills and feel inherently bad or dirty. They blame themselves for what has happened. These feelings make them unwilling to take care of themselves—and thus unwilling to seek help or to comply with medical care.

Many women who have been victimized are at higher risk of having chronic sexual problems, mutilating themselves, running away from home as teenagers and entering into prostitution. They are more likely to abuse substances; according to one report, 75 percent of women in substance-abuse treatment programs have a history of sexual abuse. The risk of attempted suicide increases dramatically in women who were sexually assaulted before age 16.

The implications for children are immeasurable. Not only is it damaging to grow up with a primary caretaker who is consistently depressed or suffering from PTSD, but as targets of and witnesses to violence, children are deeply harmed. Basic trust, the first developmental stage in psychoanalyst Erik H. Erikson's life-cycle theory, is completely disrupted. Normal expectations—that parents and caretakers are protectors, that daily life is predictable, that your body is your own—may be permanently crushed. When violence is enacted toward a child, it may disrupt normal development, setting the stage for lifelong difficulty.

At least three million children in the U.S. witness parental abuse annually; between 40 and 70 percent of children entering battered women's shelters are abused, mostly by the mother's abuser but sometimes by the mother herself. Children suffer behaviorally and intellectually from seeing violence in abusive environments and from the nomadic life that may ensue. Many develop the same problems that plague abused adults: PTSD, anxiety, depression, suicidal thoughts. Male children are at greater risk of committing a violent offense if they have a history of abuse or neglect; female children who have been sexually abused are twice as likely as nonabused children to be abused in adulthood by their partners.

As more research emerges, the social implications of violence against women are becoming increasingly apparent. The circle of violence set in motion in the home moves out onto the streets and then back into homes, ruining the childhood of another generation and setting the stage for the perpetuation of all forms of violence and abuse. Violence against women is not a discrete phenomenon but one that underlies many aspects of our culture. It is time it was addressed as such.

LISA A. MELLMAN is an associate clinical professor at Columbia University, where she is also the associate director of residency training. Mellman directs the psychotherapy clinic for training and research at the New York State Psychiatric Institute.

The Department of Health and Human Services has a nationwide, 24-hour domestic violence hotline: 800-799-SAFE.

Unit 4

Key Points to Consider

❖ How do the four perspectives of deviance apply to organizational deviance?

❖ How can organizational acts such as mountain-leveling impact the society that surrounds the mountain?

❖ How might organizational deviance be prevented?

❖ If the financial results of corporate crime are beneficial to the corporation and/or to the economy, should the behavior be allowed to flourish? Why or why not?

 **Links**   **www.dushkin.com/online/**

These sites are annotated on pages 4 and 5.

Organizational Deviance

Organizational deviance deals with the deviant acts of organizations. When deviance is committed by corporations, it may be called corporate crime. For example, tax-exempt, not-for-profit organizations that fail to pay taxes on their for-profit revenues risk being labeled deviant. Organizational deviance also occurs within governmental agencies and is usually called governmental deviance. One example is the failure of the United States Department of Agriculture to adequately ensure the safety of the nation's food supply. Another example is the failure of medical boards to properly regulate the medical profession to prevent incompetent surgeons from performing dangerous and unnecessary surgeries.

It has been suggested that there are at least three types of costs associated with corporate crime. The *financial* costs of corporate crimes are believed to far exceed the financial costs of street crimes. Whereas a robber may get a few hundred to a few thousand dollars from a crime, a corporation may net millions, if not billions, of dollars in profits from a single offense.

The *human* costs of corporate crime can be staggering. Some researchers believe that each year approximately 100,000 Americans fall sick and/or die as a direct result of corporate crime. For example, more than 64,000 children annually are injured in accidents while engaged in agricultural

labor. Injuries may range from minor cuts and bruises to the loss of body parts and even death. One example of the human costs of organizational deviance concerned a tire manufactured by Firestone. The tire, called the 500, was so poorly designed that at freeway speeds it had a propensity to explode. Many drivers and passengers were killed or severely injured in the resulting crashes. Initially, the company denied that there was a problem with the tire. It took a government investigation and recall before Firestone would admit that there was a problem.

The *social* costs of corporate crime can be severe as well. If a company engages in criminal actions that become public knowledge, consumers can lose respect for the company and may choose not to purchase its products. The resulting loss of profits may lead the company to lay off workers, whose loss of income can lead to other problems. In addition, corporations often profit from their crimes because their revenues exceed any possible penalties. When the public learns of this, the consequence may be a loss of respect for the government and the corporation. Corporations and unions that pay no more than lip service to female employees' claims of sexual harassment risk social and financial costs that outweigh any benefit derived from ignoring the behavior.

an american sweatshop

The women at the Lion Apparel factory in Beattyville, Kentucky, are part of a largely female workforce of 15,000 nationwide that sews U.S. military uniforms. The Defense Department keeps costs as low as possible, and these workers ultimately pay the price.

by Mark Boal

THE TWO-LANE ROAD INTO BEATTYVILLE, KENTUCKY, WINDS through breathtaking Appalachian foothills, past rusty machinery and heaps of broken coal left over from the last strip-mining boom. Little handmade signs offer acreage for sale. But there is no demand for land like this—too rocky for commercial farming and too remote for development. Beattyville (population 1,800) is less a town than a three-light strip bordered by aluminum shacks and a pine forest.

These days, the chief economic activity in town can be found in the parking lot of the local garage, where teenagers offer a visitor deals on moonshine by the gallon and homegrown marijuana at $2,500 a pound, about half what it would cost in an urban area. Legitimate work opportunities, after all, remain limited. There's a private prison and a data processing center, but both require a high school education, and since half the population never graduates, most seek jobs elsewhere. Inevitably, many of the women turn to Lion Apparel, which operates a sewing factory on the edge of town.

Lion, meanwhile, takes full advantage of its labor pool. Carol Shelton, 48, friendly but blunt, says that every day for the nine years she worked at Lion she would come home exhausted, her hands swollen from pushing stiff fabric past a moving needle. She had to work fast to meet quotas kept by a timekeeper, and if she slowed down or had to redo a seam, her hourly income dropped to the base rate, which usually hovered around minimum wage. Besides the low pay, the job gave her back pain from hunching over old sewing machines held together with spare parts and electrical tape. Fumes from formaldehyde, a suspected carcinogen used to keep fabric stiff, would cling to her clothes, make her short of breath, give her headaches, and cause rashes on her arms. During the

sweltering summers, the plant had no air conditioning. One winter, Shelton says, the water in the toilets froze.

In May 1998, Shelton was fired after refusing to perform a job she feared would hurt her back, and she says she has spoken to a lawyer about filing a workers' compensation claim. Meanwhile, five former and two current employees corroborate her description of work conditions at Lion. According to their accounts, the factory fits the definition of a sweatshop as specified by the laws of more than a dozen U.S. cities and counties that ban using public funds to buy from such places. Those criteria include wages so low that workers can't meet basic needs, dangerous working conditions, and intimidation when workers try to unionize. Lion, in a written response to questions from *Mother Jones*, categorically denies these conditions exist.

The responsibility for the environment these women endure doesn't rest solely with Lion, but also with its main client: the U.S. government. The 650 employees at Lion's facilities are among an estimated 15,000 apparel workers nationwide who produce uniforms for the military, which spends more than $800 million annually on clothing for its 1.4 million personnel. (Lion, based in Dayton, Ohio, is among the top three private suppliers, with a $51 million contract.)

These factories are located in some of the most rural and impoverished communities in America: isolated hamlets in the Appalachian mountains of Kentucky and Tennessee, and small towns in Louisiana. In many of these communities, the stories are similar to Shelton's. Joyce Bennett, a 58-year-old mother of five, says that in the four years she stitched collars on Navy uniforms at Doyle Shirt Manufacturing in Spencer, Tennessee, she never made

From *Mother Jones* Magazine, May/June 1999, pp. 46-51, 78-79. © 1999 by the Foundation for National Progress. Reprinted by permission.

After the public shaming of Kathie Lee Gifford whose Wal-Mart clothing line was made in sweatshops, the Department of Labor and the White House urged retailers to pledge not to exploit workers. But the Department of Defense has never offered such promises to contract workers.

more than minimum wage and had to supplement her income with food stamps.

In Beattyville, the drive to Shelton's faded-blue clapboard house (the last home on a gravel road with no sign) follows the route Lyndon Johnson took 35 years ago when he toured the area to announce the War on Poverty, his plan for helping the nation's poor join the Great Society. While the resulting social programs managed to reduce the most extreme poverty in Appalachia, the government's role has since changed dramatically. Even though the women of Beattyville work for a large Department of Defense contractor, their dismal workplace conditions remain virtually unregulated by the government. And instead of trying to assist them, the U.S. government trades on their labor for the highest possible return.

WHEN KATHIE LEE GIFFORD'S FACE WAS SPLASHED ACROSS THE tabloids in 1996 after her line of Wal-Mart clothing was exposed as the work of underpaid laborers in New York City's Chinatown, the Department of Labor and the White House teamed up to denounce such practices. With much fanfare, the Clinton administration launched the "No Sweat" campaign, which pressured retailers and manufacturers to submit to periodic independent audits of their workplace conditions.

This campaign urged manufacturers to sign the Workplace Code of Conduct, a promise to self-regulate that has since been adopted by a handful of retailers and many of the nation's largest manufacturers, including Liz Claiborne, Nicole Miller, Nike, Patagonia, and L.L. Bean. Absent, however, is the Department of Defense, which has a $1 billion garment business that would make it the country's 14th-largest retail apparel outlet, right behind Talbots and just ahead of Charming Shoppes, whose stores include the Fashion Bug chain.

Without the Defense Department's voluntary adherence to the code, the job of stopping public-sector sweatshops falls to the Department of Labor. Federal contractors that violate wage laws or safety and health codes can lose their lucrative taxpayer-financed contracts. But Suzanne Seiden, a deputy administrator at the department, says that to her knowledge the agency has never applied that rule to government apparel manufacturers. "I just assume that

they are adhering to safety and health [requirements]," she says. According to records obtained by *Mother Jones* through a Freedom of Information Act request, the Occupational Safety and Health Administration has cited Lion 32 times for safety and health violations in the past 12 years. Furthermore, a 1996 General Accounting Office report estimated that 22 percent of all federal contractors had been cited by OSHA for violating safety standards.

In 1997, Arleenna Lawson, a worker at Lion's plant in West Liberty, about a half-hour drive from Beattyville, began waking up with small bumps on her face. At first she thought it was nothing, but in two weeks the bumps grew into large lumps. When she showed a manager at work, she was told not to worry about it. An allergist later determined she was suffering a reaction to the formaldehyde in the permanent-press fabrics she sewed at work, and recommended that Lawson be given an assignment away from the offending chemical. "But they just moved me to another line for a few days, and then I was back doing collars," she remembers. "It got so bad I had to quit."

Before she did, Lawson wrote a letter to OSHA. The agency performed an inspection, concluding that "several women had rashes and were complaining about formaldehyde exposure." OSHA also ruled that Lion should have sent Lawson to the doctor when she complained of illness, and that by not doing so had failed to behave appropriately when "a substantial probability that death or serious physical harm could result." Lion's punishment? A $975 fine. (Lawson eventually won an unemployment benefits claim against Lion.)

Lawson's case was the most recent in a history of violations. In 1987, Lion was cited for failing to give employees proper face protection. In 1990, it was fined for not training employees how to handle hazardous chemicals. It was cited seven times in 1993 for a variety of violations, and nine times in 1996 for, among other reasons, failing to train employees how to use portable fire extinguishers in a plant loaded with flammable materials.

In the absence of effective enforcement, union leaders have pushed for legislative protection for all workers employed through federal contracts. In February 1997, Vice President Al Gore championed the cause, proposing an executive order that would require companies that do business with the government to maintain clean OSHA records and permit union activity. "If you want to do business with the federal government, you had better maintain a safe workplace and respect civil, human, and union rights," Gore told an appreciative AFL-CIO audience. But the proposal caused an outcry among Republicans and has remained on the back burner ever since. Chris Lehane, a Gore spokesman, says, "You have to realize these things don't happen overnight."

WHEN *MOTHER JONES* ASKED LION IF IT HAD EVER THREATened to close the Beattyville plant if workers unionized, the company's president, Richard Lapedes, wrote back: "No, and we have been happy to state clearly and openly that we would never do such a thing." The Union of Needletrades, Industrial, and Textile Employees (UNITE) tried to organize Lion in 1997 but failed, union leaders claim, because of the management's swift and unyielding opposition. Several memos circulated by Lion to its workers, and obtained by *Mother Jones*, would appear to support UNITE's interpretation; in one case, the company seems to narrowly evade federal labor laws that prohibit employers from threatening plant closings. The memo reads: "Why [is UNITE] trying to get information which they may want to use to hurt Lion's business? If that happens, that could hurt all of our jobs."

The memos did manage to instill fear in some of the workers. "We had to hide this one girl down in the floorboards of the car whenever we went out to talk about the union," says Tamara Sparks, 23, who is Carol Shelton's daughter. Sparks and her mother are very close, celebrating their weddings (Tamara's first, Carol's third) together in 1991, and working side by side at the Lion factory for three years. Sparks was a union supporter at Lion, and signed a letter, along with seven other employees, that requested outside oversight to prevent the company from retaliating against pro-union workers.

Written with UNITE's help, the letter was sent to Gore, as well as to eight Kentucky congressmen and the state's U.S. senators, telling them: "Some of us have been told point-blank that if we get a union, the plant will close. . . . They've spied on people to see who took union leaflets, and they've told individuals who work here that if we talk to the union we will be fired. Up 'til now, people here have been too afraid to file any official charges, but we'd like to talk to you or someone from your staff about what can be done."

It's not clear how, but shortly thereafter, the letter was forwarded to Lion's management, which then posted it on the company's bulletin board. Soon after that, the union drive sputtered out.

The drive does appear to have had some benefits. Lion's payroll administrator, Tina Ward, says that last year, when Lion raised the hourly pay 30 cents to $5.80—65 cents more than the minimum wage—it was in response to the unionizing efforts.

In Lion's written response, Lapedes told *Mother Jones*: "We believe we are one of the most progressive companies, certainly in our industry, if not any industry in the United States." Lapedes conceded that the plant had no air conditioning, but stated that "investment capital has become available, so that air-conditioning all of our facilities has become a viable option." The same day *Mother Jones* received Lapedes' statement, according to current Lion employees, the company began installing air-conditioning systems at the Beattyville plant.

MEANWHILE, THE GOVERNMENT IS IMPRESSED BY LION'S EFFIciency. "We are obviously pleased with them as a vendor," says Lynford Morton, a spokesman for the Defense Logistics Agency (DLA), the Defense Department office responsible for most outside contracts. A recent DLA annual report even goes so far as to highlight Lion as a success story, attributing annual savings of $4.5 million to the company's finesse.

The DLA has, in turn, received the admiration of Gore, who has honored the agency's efficiency with 51 Hammer Awards, one of the highest honors his office can bestow. The DLA's job is to secure the lowest bid it can for a contract. The agency's officials, proud of their private-sector partners, say they have no desire to revisit the days before Ronald Reagan and, more recently, Bill Clinton, both of whom eased regulations covering government contracts. "We're getting out of the big daddy thing," explains Morton. "We have no right to tell our suppliers how to do their business."

In 1997, the DLA spent $811.8 million on uniforms and textiles for the Defense Department, and ultimately sold them for $996.9 million, a 22.8 percent markup. Of these uniforms, 97 percent were sold to the U.S. armed services, though the DLA also sells uniforms to foreign governments, including El Salvador ($1 million from 1995 to 1999 in coveralls, flight boots, flight jackets, signal flags, and camouflage cloth), and Saudi Arabia ($17.9 million from 1995 to 1999 in jackets, tents, boots, tarpaulins, helmets, and assorted clothing).

> "We're getting out of the big daddy thing," explains one Defense Department spokesman. "We have no right to tell our suppliers how to do their business."

The DLA says that it does not profit from uniform sales, and that the markup is used to cover bureaucratic overhead. But the numbers don't add up. In 1997, the DLA's overhead amounted to 9.3 percent of the cost of purchasing the uniforms, which left an additional $109.6 million unaccounted for. When an internal Defense Department task force reviewed the DLA's 1997 budget, it reported that profits were slated to fund other Defense Department programs, specifically referring to $20 million that was budgeted for the military's operations in Bosnia. The Defense Department has since claimed that the transfer was incorrectly labeled. Members of the task force, meanwhile, are tight-lipped, but stand by their report. "We reported accurately based on the facts we had at the time," says Navy Capt. Barbara Brehm. The Coast Guard's Robert Gitschier says task force members maintain "a level of doubt" about the military's denials.

There are other, more direct ways the military profits from uniform sales. Military clothing stores, for example, which are run by the Army and Air Force Exchange Service (AAFES), sell what they describe as "optional uniform" clothing to its troops. Usually of better quality than the standard uniforms issued to recruits—thicker fabric, better tailoring—optional uniforms are purchased from other outside vendors. A survey of these 40 manufacturers shows that 12 of them have received a total of 207 OSHA violations in the past 10 years.

In 1998, $3.4 million in profits from these stores was allocated to the Army's Morale Welfare and Recreation fund, described by a Defense Department official as a network of programs to improve "productivity, mental and physical fitness, individual growth, positive values, esprit de corps, and family well-being." Among the projects underwritten by the fund are Shades of Green, an Army hotel in Florida that features heated swimming pools and free transportation to Disney World; a beachside resort in Hawaii; and an 18-hole golf course at Fort Knox, Kentucky, not more than 120 miles west of Beattyville.

GOLF ISN'T THE RECREATION OF CHOICE IN BEATTYVILLE. I DROVE Tamara Sparks and her husband, Cecil (with whom she no longer lives), around one night in my rented car, and we talked about what they do for fun. "We party hard, son," Cecil says. That, according to the couple and their friends, means Xanax trips that last for days and moonshine that'll make you want to walk naked down Main Street. There's also racing old Buicks along the back roads, with pit stops in the woods for a little of what Sparks elusively refers to as "scroggin' and scotchin'."

Sparks is vivacious and talkative, but her insecurity comes out in offhand comments, such as when she refers to herself as "just a hillbilly redneck." She doesn't delude herself about life in Beattyville, and becomes anxious when talk turns to the future of her family. She tells Cecil that a cousin told her that "there's lots of work in Texas and I could find a job, no problem." But Cecil, the father of her children, is hesitant to go. While work remains scarce in Appalachia (unemployment estimates reach 24 percent), outside opportunities are hard to imagine in an area where only 5 percent of the population has college degrees.

Besides, Beattyville is home, and those who live here have grown to rely heavily on one another. One of Sparks' brothers-in-law grows and distributes tomatoes and beans; Carol Shelton's husband, Herbert, hunts rabbit and deer, which she then makes into sausage; people trade labor for building supplies and staples; and every month, the church hands out 50-pound sacks of potatoes.

At her current job working at a gas station, Sparks doesn't have health insurance, so her mother lends her money for a doctor when one of the children gets sick. Sparks says she prefers the gas station to Lion, except that the pay's not very good. Unemployment, she says, proved more lucrative. During the time she stayed home after leaving Lion, she explains, she could save the $50 a week she now spends for a babysitter. Her lower earnings also forced her to give up an apartment with lots of space in a big cement dwelling—low-income housing built with government aid. For now, she has moved back to her mother's little blue house.

Razing Appalachia

by Maryanne Vollers

First they dug out the land. Then they strip mined it. Now Big Coal is leveling the mountains themselves—and tearing communities apart.

"Hear that quiet?" Larry Gibson asks as he climbs through the highland cemetery where nearly 300 of his kin lie buried. "You know they're about to set off a shot when they shut down the machines." Gibson, a 53-year-old retired maintenance worker and evangelist of the environmental cause, hunkers down with some visitors to wait for the blast.

Gibson knows the routine by heart. After all, the Princess Beverly Coal Company has been blowing up the hills around his family's 50-acre "homeplace" in West Virginia for more than a decade. When the demolition team is ready down below, the "Ukes"—heavy shovel trucks—back away from a line of high explosives drilled into solid rock. Then the warning horn sounds: two minutes.

The graveyard sits atop Kayford Mountain, a modest, leafy peak that sticks out of the shattered landscape like a fat, green thumb. The view from the edge of the cemetery looks more like the Tunisian outback than a West Virginia mountain range: The ground drops 300 or 400 feet into a dust bowl of raw coal and rubble, crosscut by dirt tracks. In the distance, what used to be forested ridges now resemble flat-topped buttes crusted over with rough grass and a few stunted trees.

West Virginia has been mined since the mid-18th century, but nobody has seen annihilation like this before. In the past 20 years, environmentalists claim, 500 square miles of the state have been stripped and gutted for their coal. In the most apocalyptic form of strip mining, called mountaintop removal, whole peaks are razed to extract layers of relatively clean-burning low-sulfur coal, while the excess rock and earth "overburden" is dumped into the valleys. Hundreds of miles of streams have been buried under these "valley fills," and dozens of mountains have been flattened into synthetic prairies.

Now, an environmental group called the West Virginia Highlands Conservancy and seven coalfield residents are taking state and federal regulators to court for the first time, claiming not only that mountaintop removal devastates the environment, but that existing laws designed to mitigate the damage are not being enforced. Coal companies and their proxies defend the practice as necessary for the economy, and assert that there is no proof it permanently damages the environment. Since last year, both sides have been presenting their cases in a federal court. What's at stake is the future of surface coal mining in West Virginia, the economies of several countries, the way of life of thousands of people, and, environmentalists contend, the ecological health of the northern Appalachian watershed.

Whatever the outcome of the lawsuit, most of Kayford Mountain is destined to be strip-mined one way or another. But Larry Gibson won't let the coal companies take it all. He represents the large extended clan that owns that 50-acre parcel atop Kayford, the remnant of a mountaintop farm dating back to the 18th century. It's one of the rare private holdings in West Virginia's southern highlands, where most land is owned by corporations and leased to coal companies. Millions of dollars in coal lie beneath the picnic ground and vacation cabins, but the family trust won't sell.

"The man from the coal company told me, 'We haven't seen anything we can't buy,' " Gibson recalls. "I said, 'You're not buying this land.' If we sell, we sell our heritage. We have no past after that. Where can we show our family where their roots are?"

As we watch, a huge explosion wallops a coal-streaked bench below the cemetery, flinging up plumes of yellow dust and sending cascades of dirt and shale overburden into the valley. The hillside shudders with the shock wave.

"That warn't nothing," observes Gibson's cousin, Carl "Red" Fraker, a 70-year-old retired miner who lives in a

From *Mother Jones* Magazine, July/August 1999, pp. 36-43, 86-87. © 1999 by the Foundation for National Progress. Reprinted by permission.

half-deserted village along Cabin Creek, below Kayford. "The big ones roll the ground like an earthquake."

Fraker was born on Kayford Mountain, and he intends to be buried here some day. But most of his friends and neighbors have moved on. Aside from the environmental damage caused by mountaintop removal, the practice is killing a way of life in West Virginia's hollows. Explosions shower dust and rocks down on people who live below the mountaintop mines. The foundations of their houses crack and their wells dry up. Whole towns are disappearing as people sell their homes and move away.

Machines do almost all the work in these modern mines; the coal miners and their communities are now an inconvenience. Thousands of people once lived in simple woodframe houses along Cabin Creek. Now the road that follows the streambed is lined with ghost towns with names like Red Warrior and Acme and White Row, casualties of the conversion from underground mining to strip mining and now mountaintop removal. After the shops and movie theaters were shuttered and shacks were emptied, the bulldozers came. All that remains now are worn patches in the mountainside, and a few stubborn clusters of daffodils planted long ago in now-vanished gardens.

Up above, when the dust clouds settle after the latest blast, the Ukes start chugging up the hill to scrape out the exposed coal. Red Fraker takes another look out at the black wasteland below. "I want to ask, what's gonna happen to West Virginia when all the coal's gone?" he says. "Ain't no timber on it. No dirt left. Nothin'. What's it gonna be?"

T HAT WAS PRECISELY THE QUESTION MEMBERS OF CONGRESS WERE asking when they passed the Surface Mining Control and Reclamation Act, SMCRA (familiarly known as smack-ra), back in 1977. The gist of the law is this: If you mine it, you have to restore the land to the same or better condition than it was in before you got there. The law also provides detailed regulations designed to reduce the environmental impact of such destructive mining. According to SMCRA, strip mines, including mountaintop mines, cannot be allowed within 100 feet of active streams unless it can be shown that the streams won't be damaged. The law further requires "contemporaneous reclamation"— meaning that soil replacement and reseeding must occur soon after the coal is removed. The land must be returned to its "approximate original contour," or AOC. The permit holder can be granted a variance from the AOC rule only after submitting a detailed plan for post-mining flatland development, such as a school, airport, or shopping center that would benefit nearby communities.

West Virginia's Department of Environmental Protection (DEP) is charged with enforcing SMCRA, with the oversight of the federal Office of Surface Mining. Unfortu-

"I was born in this hollow and I'm gonna die here. They'll have to bulldoze me out before I go."

—James Weekley, longtime resident of Blair, West Virginia

nately, there has been very little regulation by the DEP, whose ranks are filled with former coal-industry employees, and even less supervision from the weak and understaffed federal agency.

When SMCRA was written, mountaintop removal was still an unusual practice. It became more prevalent in the 1980s, when 20-story-tall, rock-eating machines called draglines were brought in to make the technique profitable. Ironically, it was stricter environmental laws that increased the demand for West Virginia's low-sulfur coal. More than 80 percent of America's coal is consumed by coal-burning electric power plants, which in turn provide the nation with 56 percent of its electricity. Following passage of 1990's Clean Air Act, power plants were forced to reduce the sulfur content of smokestack emissions, which react with the atmosphere to cause acid rain. Some of the purest and hottest-burning coal in the nation is found in thin, multiple seams high in West Virginia's southern mountains. Rather than mine this coal out of the mountains, industry accountants found, it's cheaper and faster to take the mountains off the coal.

In recent years, the DEP has kept up with the demand for low-sulfur coal by granting permits for more and bigger surface mines. Since 1995, the agency has approved permits subjecting 27,000 new acres to mountaintop removal. (In contrast, journalist Ken Ward, Jr. discovered while researching a prizewinning series of articles for the *Charleston Gazette*, the state's largest and most influential newspaper, fewer than 10,000 acres were permitted during the 1980s.) Anywhere from a tenth to two-thirds of the mining permits issued in West Virginia in 1997 (the number depends on whether you consult state regulators or the *Gazette*'s Ward) are for mountaintop-removal mines, which account for 16 percent of the state's coal output. Environmentalists assert that some mountaintop mining areas are now 10 miles wide, and that the largest will eventually gobble up 20,000 acres.

But it is not just the size of a given mining area that's worrisome; nobody has studied what the cumulative impact of so much disruption will be on the environment of northern Appalachia. "It might be a different story if it was a 200-acre plot here, and 500 acres in another county," says Cindy Rank of the West Virginia Highlands Conservancy. "But mountaintop removal is spreading and connecting all through the areas where there are coal reserves." If permits continue to be approved at the pace set over the past decade, environmentalist say, half the peaks in some southern counties would be lopped off.

Despite assurances from coal companies that the technique is perfectly safe, environmentalists are focused on an array of problems associated with mountaintop removal. They worry about increased acid runoff from these giant gashes, particularly since they estimate that 75 percent of West Virginia's streams and rivers are already polluted by mining and other industries. They fear the loss of groundwater in the land below flattened mountains that were once laced with springs and aquifers. And even though coal-industry technicians insist that the gargantuan valley fills behave "like sponges" and are actually a form of flood control, other experts remain skeptical. "What you see in a lot of these valley fills has no engineering method to it at all," says Rick Eades, a hydrogeologist who used to work in the mining industry and is now an environmental activist. "It's just dirt and rock being pushed over the side of a hill and filling in vertically several hundred feet." Although none of the valley fills has failed since they became a part of West Virginia's landscape 25 years ago, Eades fears a disastrous flood within the next 25. "Nature will cut those valley fills right out of there, given time. And there's no way that the mountains can heal in a way that will resemble the original ability of the land to hold back the water during heavy rains, hold back sediments, and retain groundwater." Such concerns led two West Virginia conservation groups to put the DEP on notice in January of this year of their intent to sue the agency for not assessing the "cumulative hydrological impacts" of mountaintop removal during the permitting process.

Still more problems exist. "Mountaintop removal destroys the beauty of the state, which is somewhat intangible," says William Maxey, West Virginia's former chief forester. "More tangible is the fact that it deforests the state." Maxey says that, as of 1997, 300,000 acres of hardwood forest had been destroyed by mountaintop removal. He characterizes the mining industry's preferred reforestation methods as "bogus," saying they are "totally superficial and will not work." After Maxey failed to convince the DEP to require adequate reforestation of mountaintop mines, he resigned from his job in disgust.

KING COAL RULES WEST VIRGINIA LIKE A PETULANT MONARCH, one used to getting its way. Coal production accounts for 13 percent of West Virginia's gross state product, commands an annual payroll of $900 million, and provides more than a third of the state's business-tax revenues. King Coal also finds campaign contributions a good investment, and is famously generous with them. For instance, Gov. Cecil Underwood, a former coal executive, is the recent beneficiary of $250,000 in campaign donations from coal companies.

The last two years have set new records for West Virginia coal production, with 182 million tons extracted in 1997 alone.

Arch Coal vice president David Todd and other industry spokesmen tout the positive effects of mining reclamation, but conservationists warn of longterm environmental damage from the intensive mining techniques.

(An additional quarter-million was contributed to cover the cost of his inauguration party.) It was Underwood who pushed a bill through the state legislature last year to make mountaintop-removal mining even easier and more profitable. It allowed companies to obliterate up to 480 acres of the drainage above any stream (up from 250 acres) before paying mitigation costs to the state—of $200,000 per buried acre.

But the blatant coal-industry giveaway backfired—leading to the bill's repeal—when it roused public interest, even outrage. City people started paying more attention to what was going on out of sight, up in the remote coalfields. A 1998 opinion poll showed that 53 percent of West Virginians opposed mountaintop removal, versus 29 percent in favor.

At the same time that Underwood was lobbying for the pro-industry bill in March 1998, the *Charleston Gazette* was employing the Freedom of Information Act to obtain 81 mining permits issued by the DEP, which it then reviewed against federal laws such as SMCRA and the Clean Water Act. The investigation revealed some startling facts: The DEP didn't keep complete records of how many permits it issued, so there was no way to track the cumulative effects of mining. The U.S. Army Corps of Engineers routinely gave general "nationwide" permits for valley fills that should have required more rigorous individual permits. And in almost all cases, mountaintop-removal AOC variances were issued without post-mining development plans. In those cases when plans were submitted, most of them were for "timberland" or "wildlife habitat"—uses not recognized by SMCRA.

The Office of Surface Mining conducted its own investigation, which essentially confirmed the newspaper's findings. In other words, for 20 years the DEP had been stretching the law to please the coal companies, and the U.S. government had been letting them get away with it.

In response to an increasing public outcry over mountaintop removal, Gov. Underwood appointed a task force to investigate the issue. It came up with recommendations for more studies and increased vigilance by the regulators.

But old hands at this game don't believe coal companies can be regulated. Ken Hechler, West Virginia's 84-year-old secretary of state, is a longtime nemesis of the coal industry. As a West Virginia congressman from 1959 to 1977, Hechler tried to abolish strip mining altogether.

"I still feel that it is impossible to have either strip mining or mountaintop removal and have adequate reclamation, which I characterize as putting lipstick on a corpse," he says. He recently appeared at an environmental rally at the capital and sang a song, to the tune of John Denver's "Take Me Home, Country Roads." It began: "Almost level, West Virginia/Scalped-off mountains, dumped into our rivers."

Meanwhile, Arch Coal, the country's second-largest coal company, was trying to push through a 3,100-acre mountaintop-removal permit to expand its giant Dal-Tex mine in Logan County. It would be the largest permit ever granted—amounting to about five square miles of what the DEP calls "total extraction." The Dal-Tex mine had already filled in dozens of hollows on the west side of the Spruce Fork River along state Highway 17. All but 40 of the 200 families that once lived in the hamlet of Blair had already moved away. That was when James Weekley, a 58-year-old grandfather and former miner, began to fear that Arch Coal wanted the rest—including the headwaters of Pigeonroost Branch, in the leafy hollow where he and his family have lived for generations.

In July 1998, Weekley and nine other coalfield residents joined with the West Virginia Highlands Conservancy to sue the Army Corps and the DEP for ignoring SMCRA, the Clean Water Act, and other laws. (Three of the original plaintiffs have since dropped out.) Although no coal companies were specifically sued, the purpose of the lawsuit was to make sure the mines comply with the law.

Pro-coal letter writers to West Virginia newspapers labeled Weekley and the other plaintiffs environmental radicals. "I'm not an environmentalist—I'm a citizen!" says Weekley. "I was born in this hollow and I'm gonna die here. They'll have to bulldoze me out before I go."

Last December, the plaintiffs decided to settle part of the case against the federal government. They agreed that the Army Corps, in conjunction with other federal and state agencies, would conduct a two-year environmental impact study to assess and deal with the cumulative damage caused by mountaintop removal in West Virginia. Meanwhile, new permits, and ones already in the pipeline, would be subjected to closer scrutiny to ensure their compliance with existing regulations and standards. But after Arch Coal, responding to pressure from the U.S. Environmental Protection Agency that was unrelated to the lawsuit, made significant changes in its permit application—including reducing the lifetime of the Dal-Tex expansion mine from 12 to five years and scaling back its proposed valley fills—the federal defendants argued that the Dal-Tex permit should be exempted from new, stricter scrutiny, and that mining should be allowed to begin.

> **"It's impossible to have strip mining or mountaintop removal and have adequate reclamation. [It's like] putting lipstick on a corpse."**
>
> —Ken Hechler,
> **West Virginia secretary of state**

But Weekley and the other plaintiffs balked at exempting the Dal-Tex mine. They asked U.S. District Chief Judge Charles Haden for a preliminary injunction to delay the permit until the rest of the lawsuit could be resolved in a trial scheduled for this July.

To the astonishment of almost everyone, the conservative republican judge—who had visited Pigeonroost Hollow and flown over the coalfields—granted the preliminary injunction. In doing so, he cited the "imminent and irreversible" harm that would be done to the Weekleys, and to the stream flowing through Pigeonroost Hollow, if the mining were to proceed, and distinguished it from the "purely temporary economic harms" that Arch would endure from the delay in its operations. The judge then noted that the other legal questions the plaintiffs had raised regarding the conduct of mountaintop removal would be addressed in the future trial. Meanwhile, Arch Coal would have to wait for its permits.

The coal company responded to the ruling by laying off 30 miners at its Dal-Tex mine, and promising to shut down its operation and put 300 more employees out of work by summer. The loss of jobs and tax revenues would poleax the economy of Logan County, one of the poorest counties in a poor state. Less money would be available for schools, police—everything would be affected. The president of the Logan County Commission declared, "It's a war!" and the commission vowed to fight to keep the mine open. Days after the Haden decision, 1,500 miners, along with union and business leaders from Logan County, marched on Charleston to protest.

The United Mine Workers of America (UMWA) found itself in a terrible position. The stark reality of labor in West Virginia is this: At the end of World War II there were more than 100,000 union coal miners in the state. Now, of the fewer than 19,000 who remain, only 40 percent belong to the UMWA. The union's president, Cecil Roberts, perceived as a moderate on the issue of mountaintop removal, had already come out in favor of protecting communities from the technique's excesses. But the imminent loss of one of the biggest union mines in the state was more than he could take. Roberts called for observation of April 2, 1999, as a "memorial day" without pay for the nation's 35,000 union miners to protest the situation in West Virginia. He was hoping that up to 10,000 would attend a rally in Charleston. Perhaps because it was the Easter weekend, only about 500 miners and family members showed up at the Capitol steps.

Roberts, a wiry, bearded, native West Virginian, shouted like a preacher at the modest crowd that day, telling them they'd all been "kicked in the teeth again by the environmental community. We're fed up and we're fired up!"

Roberts has been busy leading the union in its fight with the Clinton-Gore administration over U.S. support for the Kyoto treaty on global warming, which he fears will put the nation's coal industry out of business and cost his workers their jobs. He told the crowd, "You can't say 'Don't burn it' in Washington and 'Don't mine it' in West Virginia and say you're not trying to take the jobs of every coal miner in the United States. And I'm here to say no, no, and hell no!"

Some in West Virginia have accused Roberts of stirring up an already volatile situation in the coalfields. Roberts responds that he's been reasonable for the past year, trying to negotiate a solution to the mountaintop-removal problem. "We were working to find a compromise for workers to keep their jobs and at the same time protect the environment. I believe you can do both," he told *Mother Jones.* "We argued that we shouldn't eliminate mountaintop mining at that moment. It wasn't fair to the workers, wasn't fair quite frankly to the companies that had invested literally millions and millions of dollars in West Virginia."

Secretary of State Hechler, who has a long history of supporting the UMWA, is disappointed in Roberts' stance. "Like all wars," he says, "a war against the mountains creates employment. But you don't keep fighting just to supply jobs. In any event, we ought to start diversifying our economy early on instead of making such a heavy dependence on coal, which pollutes the streams, pollutes the politics, and is a finite resource."

The coal hasn't quite run out yet. In fact, the last two years have set new records for West Virginia coal production, with 182 million tons extracted in 1997 alone. Furthermore, most of the mining jobs eliminated over the past half-century were lost to mechanization of the mines and a conversion to surface mining—not a decline in coal production.

But Hechler is right: The coal will run out some day. And the big lie of Big Coal is that West Virginia depends on mining for its prosperity. Skeptics ask: What prosperity? West Virginia is 49th among the 50 states in household income. And in this very poor state, the poorest counties are the ones with the most coal mines.

"No state has given more to the American Dream and gotten less back from it than West Virginia," says Norm Steenstra, director of the West Virginia Citizen Action Group and a former coal operator himself. "The corrupt political system, the dead streams, the severed mountains, the fraud, the dust, the noise, the air pollution—what for? All to supply the voracious American appetite for cheap electricity."

I T'S A RISKY BUSINESS CALLING UP A COAL COMPANY AND SAYING you're with *Mother Jones.* But David Todd, vice president and spokesman for Arch Coal, is a good sport, and he agrees to a tour of the Hobet 21 mine near Madison, West Virginia. The mine is a cousin of the Dal-Tex operation, 40 miles south of here, and a showcase for mountaintop removal.

We climb into a 4 × 4 truck to have a look at a section that was mined 20 years ago. In fact, the reclaimed parts of Hobet 21 are quite handsome. There are rolling, grassy hills, stands of small trees here and there, a number of ponds where ducks like to nest. To my eyes, it looks more like western Nebraska than West Virginia. But to Todd, and to the regulators who approved this reclamation, this is a fine example of restoring the approximate original contour of the land. "The hills are smaller but with similar rolls as the original mountains," says Todd, sweeping his hand across the pastures to the forested bumps on the horizon. "This is just more manicured-looking."

Secretary of the Interior Bruce Babbitt (who oversees the Office of Surface Mining) took a similar tour of the Hobet 21 mine in the summer of 1996. Impressed, he announced that the Hobet mine was "a rebuke to those who say, Jobs or the environment. This landscape shouts out: You can have both!" Babbitt also said something that continues to haunt the foes of mountaintop removal: "The landscape has changed. It is a better landscape in many ways, a different landscape—a savanna of forests coming back, of fields." The local headline read "Landscape improved, Babbitt says." And Arch Coal helpfully provides copies of the story in its press kit.

Before we wrap up the afternoon tour, Todd wants to get something off his chest about the mountaintop-removal controversy and the Dal-Tex permit problem.

"If you detect a level of frustration, sometimes even anger, I don't deny it," says Todd, a fair-haired man in a white hard hat. "Because, dammit, we've done everything and more that people have asked us to do throughout the years." He says Arch Coal has bent over backward to get the right permits and keep the mine running, taking a loss of $1 million a month since September 1998 in the process. "All we ask is, tell us what the standard is, how we should comply with the law, the permits we need, and we will do that!" he says, throwing up his hands. "Meantime, shutting us down and costing 300 jobs at Dal-Tex is unconscionable!"

It's touching to hear a coal executive so concerned about the loss of jobs. In the past year, 900 union miners have been laid off in West Virginia due to reduced domestic demand (after a pair of mild winters) and a general consolidation in the coal industry. Nobody marched on Charleston when those cuts were announced, and no corporate vice presidents expressed their anger and frustration. Most of the coal-mining jobs are moving to the Powder River Basin of Wyoming, where there are no unions, and where seams 75 feet thick lie right below the gentle, rolling surface of the land. Arch Coal recently purchased Atlantic Richfield Company's giant strip mine there and, a few days after Judge Haden's decision, began to dismantle one of its 340-ton coal shovel trucks to ship to Wyoming.

Ricky Light of Sharples, West Virginia, used to drive that truck. Light, 32, who has a wife, three young daughters, and payments to make on a new modular home, was one of the first to be laid off at Dal-Tex. He used to make $55,000 a year; now he receives unemployment income of $1,200 a month, though his bills amount to $1,800, not including groceries. He and his wife, Samantha, may be shutting off the phone soon, and are considering moving in with her mother. "We planned our life around 15 more years of mining," says Light, a slender, dark-haired man in a Nike swoosh cap. "I didn't believe it'd go this far. I thought they'd get the permits."

Light says he has a "few good possibilities" for another job. He's been told he could relocate to Arch's new mine, near Gillette, Wyoming, but Light doesn't want to leave his hometown. Like the business leaders in Logan, Ricky Light doesn't fault Arch Coal or the grim realities of mining for his predicament. He blames the people who brought the lawsuit, some of them his neighbors.

"There's a lot of hard feelings here," he says. "It's just getting started. 'Cause you don't take things off people's tables. You don't mess with people's livelihoods."

PIGEONROOST HOLLOW IS JUST A MILE OR SO EAST OF BLAIR Mountain, which was the site of the biggest union battle in the history of West Virginia. That was in 1921, when a young firebrand named Bill Blizzard—whose great-nephew happens to be UMWA president Cecil Roberts—led 15,000 men on a march to unionize the southern coalfields. Famed organizer Mary Harris "Mother" Jones herself tried to stop the confrontation, but she couldn't turn them back. The union men met the sheriff's private army on the slopes of Blair Mountain. As many as 20 people were killed; nobody knows the exact number. Blizzard ended up in jail. It took another decade and still more blood to organize the West Virginia mines.

Another war is now being fought in the shadow of Blair Mountain. The barriers seem harder to define, and the sons and daughters of those union foot soldiers are dug in on both sides of the line. It's a battle over jobs and the environment, tradition and change—a fight that is going on here in the coalfields, and out in the redwood forests of California, and in the copper mines of Montana, and overseas where the natural resources are running dry.

There used to be a historical marker at the foot of Blair Mountain describing the great union war. But somebody stole it, and the sign was never replaced. Soon the mountain itself will be gone, consumed by the dragline and converted into an artificial pasture big enough for a hundred future Wal-Marts, although there will be hardly anyone left to shop there. There may not even be a marker to commemorate the battle, or the times when Mother Jones walked up the creeks to organize the coal camps because the coal company owned the roads. The creeks themselves will be buried under tons of dirt and rock, buried like the mountain and the memory of a time when the people of the coalfields and their union knew which side they were on.

It's What's for Dinner

BY PAUL CUADROS

Most everyone heard about Hudson Foods's twenty-five million-pound recall of bacteria-contaminated ground beef last summer. It was the largest recall in U.S. history. But not many heard what Hudson planned to do with the contaminated beef after the company got it back.

Two weeks following the recall, Hudson Foods sought to cook and resell the ground beef that was contaminated with Escherichia coli O157:H7, a deadly pathogen that killed four children in the infamous Jack-in-the-Box outbreak in 1993. The bacteria was first discovered in ground meat in 1992. Cooking the meat at high temperatures would kill the bacteria and make it usable for such prepackaged foods as pizza toppings, chili, and taco meat. But when word about Hudson's plan leaked out in the press, the company did a quick about-face and gave up on cooking and selling the product. Why? The bacteria is found only in feces. Selling the product "cooked" would result in bacteria-free food, but not food that is free of fecal material.

Hudson Foods was doing nothing wrong or illegal in seeking to cook bacteria-contaminated meat. The U.S. Department of Agriculture says it's OK for meat processors to serve you fecal-contaminated food, just so long as the pathogens are not present. Think of that the next time you get a craving for a hamburger.

"If it goes through a processing plant where the bacterium can be destroyed, it's perfectly wholesome food,

Paul Cuadros is an investigative reporter who works for the Center for Public Integrity in Washington, D.C.

nutritious food," says Jacque Knight, a spokesperson for the USDA's Food Safety and Inspection Service, which oversees meat inspection and recalls in the United States.

There's not much the USDA can do anyway. If Hudson's managers wanted to cook the contaminated meat and resell it, the USDA could not have stopped them. "We don't have the authority to command them to destroy it," Knight adds. The agency doesn't even have the authority to mandate a recall from a company.

Ever since Hudson's voluntary recall, Secretary of Agriculture Dan Glickman has been seeking mandatory recall authority for his agency. But so far he has not won it.

The USDA cannot do an adequate job of protecting the American public from contaminated meat. It lacks serious enforcement authority, it is unable to recover the majority of recalled contaminated meat, and it permits the product that is recovered to be recycled, cleaned up, and served as wholesome food to an unsuspecting public. No labels identify recalled and recycled meat products.

While it might not kill you to eat food with cooked feces in it, most consumers would prefer not to. But the inspection and recall system is geared around an industry that doesn't want

to lose money on recalled product, not around consumers' best interests.

Twelve times since 1990 companies have recalled their meat product without destroying it, according to information received through a Freedom of Information Act request by the Center for Public Integrity, an investigative government watchdog group in Washington, D.C. The total amount of meat product reworked, reprocessed, cooked, and sold again comes to 1.7 million pounds out of 5.2 million pounds recalled. The recalls were for a variety of problems including bacteria such as listeria, E. coli O157:H7, stones, bones, black spots, swollen cans, undercooked food, and spoilage.

H ere are a few examples of recalled meat products that were cleaned up and resold or distributed to consumers as normal, high-quality goods:

- In November 1994, Monfort, Inc., which is owned by ConAgra, recalled more than 595,000 pounds of ground beef that had been contaminated with the deadly E. coli 0157-H7 bacteria. The company was able to recover a total of 124,000 pounds in the recall. It destroyed 5,600 pounds. It cooked and resold 18,400 pounds to unsuspecting consumers, who ate the fecally contaminated product in their prepackaged foods.

- In February 1995, Hudson Foods recalled 3.1 million pounds of finely ground turkey that was found to have bones in the product. According to the USDA, more than 269,000 pounds was recovered and reworked. The ten-pound packages of "Delightful Farms Finely Ground Turkey" were originally distributed to retail food stores in fourteen states. Of the 269,000 pounds of turkey recovered, more than 188,000 pounds went to make pet food, about 8,000 was condemned, and more than 77,000 was approved by the USDA and exported, according to Archie Schaffer, a spokesperson for Tyson Foods, Inc., which bought Hudson Foods in January for a reported $600 million.

- In February 1993, Seitz Foods, Inc., of St. Joseph, Missouri, recalled 800,000 pounds of hot dogs contaminated with the sanitizer Control-It. The company added 0.5 gallons of the sanitizer to a 550 gallon of brine solution in an effort to extend shelf life, according to the USDA. More than 723,000 pounds of hot dogs were recovered and reworked.

- Beech Nut Nutrition Corporation recalled 528,760 pounds of contaminated baby food that had black spots on the product. Beech Nut officials say the spots were only cosmetic defects and that the food was safe to eat. They donated the product to starving children in Armenia and the country of Georgia.

- In 1995, the Jack-in-the-Box fast-food chain had more than 200,000 pounds of ground beef recalled from two different suppliers on two separate occasions. The recooked meat then went into their tacos with the USDA's blessing, according to a September 1997 Cox News Service article.

"It's disgusting," says Felicia Nestor, food safety director of the Government Accountability Project, which has monitored sanitary conditions at U.S. meat-processing and packing plants. She doesn't think the government should let companies reprocess contaminated meat. "One of the things that I really don't like about it is it decreases the incentive to produce a wholesome product to begin with."

There is also a real and increasing danger of food-borne illness. The General Accounting Office, the investigative arm of Congress, estimated in a 1996 report that as many as eighty-one million people become sick due to food-borne diseases each year, and that approximately 9,000 die as a result. The report also said that the number of pathogens is growing.

E. coli 0157:H7 is one of the new deadly pathogens to have emerged in the past twenty years. The USDA's Economic Research Service estimates that up to 20,000 people are poisoned each year with this pathogen. If meat is found to contain E. coli 0157:H7, it's because the product has been fecally contaminated.

"My mama told me not to eat it when I was little. She said, 'It's not good for you,'" says Jesse Privett, laughing. Privett is a USDA inspector at a processing plant in Texas. He cracks jokes about fecal matter in the meat. But he also worries about the serious health effects of less-than-stellar industry standards. With more than twenty years' experience on the line, he's seen it all. When asked if the meat processors would do well by their customers to listen to his mama's advice, he replies, "Yeah, but they're not. They listen to the cash register. That's the problem."

"We have always maintained that we don't want to eat cattle feces, fully cooked or not," says Nancy Donley, president of Safe Tables Our Priority, a food safety advocacy group. Donley's six-year-old son, Alex, died in 1993 after eating a hamburger contaminated with E. coli O157:H7.

The USDA argues that E. coli O157:H7 is present only in minute amounts. "We're not talking visible fecal contamination in that product," says Knight. "Visible fecal contamination would have to be trimmed and then reworked. If the fecal contamination had been, say, on a carcass, the carcass would be trimmed but there still could be some microbes there."

Jesse Majkowski, the director of the Food Safety and Inspection Service's Emergency Response Division, said that before the product can be cooked it is reexamined by government officials for visible signs of fecal contamination.

But even if E. coli O157:H7 is found only in minute amounts, it still means that the product has been fecally contaminated. In light of the fact that the USDA has a "zero tolerance" standard for fecal contamination, as a consumer you'd think that even minute traces

mean that the standard has not been met.

Knight says otherwise: "The zero tolerance for fecal contamination is for visible fecal—if you saw visible fecal contamination."

Reworking or reprocessing a product in a process plant happens all the time. "Here's what's happening in a packing plant," says John Gould, the American Meat Institute's director of inspections and a former USDA meat inspector. "You're making frankfurters and you get broken frankfurters or they're off weight, they'll rework them. It means they'll put them back into a new production." Gould says that the Institute has no policy on cooking recovered recalled product.

But handling bacteria-contaminated meat is different. "If they had a chili-manufacturing operation, or someone that wanted to do it for them, that would be acceptable," says Gould. "Obviously, for public interest, there's not too many people who are looking for that product. Most of it is dumped. A named chili company doesn't want it to be known that they go around and buy salvaged product, even though there's nothing wrong with it."

The last thing a meat-processing plant wants is unsold product. "We had condensation coming off a roof onto cattle and we weren't sure if there was bacteria or whatever in it, but it was not an edible surface, so we sent that to a chili plant because it cooks it to an internal temperature of 160 degrees," recalls Privett. Condensation, filth, fecal contamination, and bacteria are not the only things that lead to meat being reworked or reprocessed. "There's measle beasts, that's what we call them," Privett says. "It's a little parasite, a tape worm that gets into the muscle and if it's all over the carcass, it's condemned, but if you only find one or two in the head and carcass, then they're shipped out to a plant that cooks them."

Sometimes reworking a product means using a metal detector to scan for metal shavings. "We had some product a couple of years ago, chicken that was contaminated with flakes of metal and the company came in with a presentation on how they were going to run this through a metal detector," Majkowski says. The agency required the company to run the product through the detector twice in different positions. "We do have a directive on foreign material contamination. The machine has to be capable of getting down to $\frac{1}{32}$ of an inch. That's about the size of a pepper grain, or smaller than that, and it's something that you can't feel in your mouth."

But that doesn't satisfy Privett. "There is no way to rework ground product, for aesthetics, or physical contaminants like fecal. You can cook it and kill the E. coli, but the physical contaminant is still in there. Which, for us old-timers, is not acceptable," he says.

Caroline Smith DeWaal, food safety director of the Center for Science in the Public Interest, has a different concern. "I would rather have that product cooked than sent to the landfill," she says. "If you take that product and just dump it, the bacteria will have the opportunity to grow and possibly spread into the water supply." But she adds, "It's definitely a lower quality product than one that isn't contaminated. It should be fully cooked and it should be worthless."

In January, the country's largest meatpacking plants implemented a new system to control contamination. It's called Hazard Analysis of Critical Control Points, an industry-designed monitoring system that relies on companies to spot and then fix problems in the production line, where contamination could occur. USDA inspectors monitor each plant's control efforts. The system also calls, for the first time, for microbial testing. The USDA tests for salmonella, and the industry tests for generic E. coli contamination of samples.

The system was created in response to the growing number of incidents of new pathogens in the meat industry that made people sick, and in some cases killed them.

Three months into the new program, government inspectors have detained more than one million pounds of product, issued 265 warning letters to plants for violations of the law, coordinated fifty-three administrative actions, and managed USDA participation in eleven criminal cases in federal courts. Despite all those violations, the government also reports that the 300 plants that began using the new inspection system have a 92 percent compliance rate with the regulations.

Too bad the USDA and industry don't have a similar success rate when it comes to recovering recalled meat product. According to the USDA, there were 272 recalls from 1990 to 1997, with more than thirty-five million pounds of product recalled. But the USDA and the companies managed to recover only fifteen million pounds, or 43 percent of the tainted product. This means that approximately twenty million pounds of bad food was most likely consumed. Of the more than 9.7 million pounds of bacteria-contaminated meat recalled, the USDA and industry recovered only 4.5 million or 47 percent, according to USDA records.

The figures are even worse when it comes to E. coli O157:H7, the deadly pathogen. Since 1990, 1.5 million pounds of meat, mostly ground beef, was recalled for this pathogen, but only 403,379 pounds were recovered—26 percent.

With all the emphasis on catching microbial contamination, inspectors like Privett fear that the traditional inspections for healthy animals will be left behind. Privett says the meat industry is now paying less attention to catching traditional problems like carcasses with tumors, growths, abscesses, fecal matter, pus, and other problems that may not kill the consumer but are nonetheless unappetizing.

The biggest change is allowing industry to police itself more under the new inspection system.

"We're paper-pushers now," says Gerald Lorge, a federal meat inspector. "We have to spend so much of our time trying to check [the plant's] documentation that we really don't have time to check the product anymore." Lorge is president of a local meat inspector's union.

"The bottom line is a company has to make a profit or it's going to replace the management people," adds Privett. "If they are super quality-conscious, they're going to catch most of it, but if they start going in the red, they're going to let it go."

Prevention is the key, according to Donley. "We need to have slower processing speeds to prevent contamination in the first place, and we also need to be doing on-farm research and dealing with the problem in the animals and keeping it out of the food chain."

Meanwhile, the millions of pounds of ground beef recovered from the Hudson Foods August recall sits frozen, in storage, in northwest Arkansas, waiting for the USDA's investigation to be completed and for someone to decide what to do with it.

Will they cook it up and serve it to consumers? "We have not ruled out anything," says Tysons' Schaffer. "All I can tell you is no decision has been made."

What Doctors Don't Know

HMOs aren't the only thing wrong with American Medicine

By Michael L. Millenson

IN EDGAR ALLAN POE'S "THE PURLOINED LETTER," the protagonists overlook the crucial clue that is sitting right in plain sight: a letter left casually on a desk. Today, a similar near-willful blindness prevails among those who present the managed care industry as the leading threat to the quality of American medicine. Implicitly, this view defines high-quality care as consisting of immediate access to treatment. While that is obviously important, the critics ignore a separate issue whose equal significance should be glaringly obvious: What happens to the patient once he or she actually reaches the doctor or hospital?

It would be nice if good medical care simply consisted of preferring the physician's judgment over that of "insurance company accountants," as President Clinton put it in his 1998 State of the Union address. Indeed, the argument that the public is faced with a choice between medical decisions made by "good" doctors or "bad" bureaucrats (albeit private-sector bureaucrats) has been sounded by everyone from anti-managed care politicians to (surprise) indignant representatives of various physician organizations. Preserving physician freedom is presented as the way to "preserve" high-quality care; any other path leads inexorably to ruin.

Unfortunately for the health of patients, this story line is a gross oversimplification. There's no question that the business ethic of some health plans can dangerously distort medical decision-making and has sometimes done so. Yet the larger truth about our health-care system is at once more complicated and much more unsettling.

From ulcers to urinary tract infections, tonsils to organ transplants, back pain to breast cancer, asthma to arteriosclerosis, scores of thousands of patients are dying or being injured every year because the best scientific information on how to care for them is not being put into practice by physicians. If one counts the lives lost to preventable medical mistakes, the toll jumps even higher.

In the scientific literature, the struggle to put medical theory into practice goes by the genteel term "evidence-based medicine." Kenneth I. Shine, president of the Institute of Medicine, phrases the problem this way: "If we asked the question of whether physicians have based their practice on scientific principles," he says, "it is clear that the profession has been sorely lacking."

Put in Clintonian campaign terms, however, the problem is easy for a layperson to understand: "It's the doctors' decisions, stupid."

What Doctors Don't Do

Most patients would be surprised to know what their doctors don't know—or don't put into practice. Even the best-trained doctors go about their work with an astonishingly shallow base of knowledge concerning the link between what they do and how it affects a patient's health. For instance, more than half of all medical treatments, and perhaps as many as 85 percent, have never been validated by clinical trials. But even when there is scientific evidence about what works best, large numbers of doctors don't apply those findings to actual patient care.

A prime example of the latter problem is the treatment of ulcers, a common and painful condition that will afflict an estimated 25 million Americans at some point in their life. Back in 1988, the prestigious British journal *The Lancet* published the results of a clinical trial that showed that most ulcers were actually caused by a bacteria called *H. pylori*. Patients didn't have to spend their lives taking anti-ulcer medications to control acidic secretions; the bacteria could be eradicated and the ulcer cured.

A study replicating this research appeared in a major American journal in 1991. A consensus panel from the National Institutes of Health endorsed the anti-bacteria ulcer treatment in 1994. Yet today, half of all U.S. doctors still aren't testing their ulcer patients for *H. pylori* and prescribing the right therapy, according to the federal Centers for Disease Control and Prevention. Managed-care financial incentives have nothing to do with this

---

Michael L. Millenson, *a Chicago based consultant, is the author of* Demanding Medical Excellence: Doctors and Accountability in the Information Age (*University of Chicago Press*)

problem. Indeed, if anything they should work in the opposite direction—it's cheaper to cure a patient than to keep paying for maintenance drugs.

But to truly understand the consequences of failing to apply evidence to practice, one need only look at treatment of heart disease, the number one killer of both men and women in the United States. Heart disease is common, and it is expensive (total health care costs for cardiovascular disease are more than $150 billion annually). To listen to the managed-care debate, one might think the most pressing problem in cardiac care is getting people directly to the hospital emergency room without waiting for pre-approval from their health plan. (And forget for a moment that only 1 of every 9 visits to the emergency room for chest pain results in a confirmed heart attack.) The medical literature, however, paints a very different story than the one heard on the nightly news. It's a tale of wasted money and of unnecessary patient deaths and complications that has nothing to do with health plans. To give just a few examples:

• Inappropriate invasive procedures are distressingly prevalent. Harvard University researchers found that one quarter of the heart bypasses, angioplasties and catheterizations (measuring blood flow and blood pressure in the heart) performed on elderly heart attack victims have no effect on patient survival. In other words, thousands of these expensive treatments—which pose a significant risk of complications or death—could probably be eliminated.

• Proven drug therapies, meanwhile, go unused. A New Jersey study found that just one-fifth of eligible heart attack victims received beta blocker therapy that could have increased their chances of survival by as much as 43 percent. Other studies have found much the same problem. By one estimate 18,000 people die each year from heart attacks because they did not receive effective interventions. Meanwhile, one-third of heart-attack survivors in one study left the hospital without their doctor telling them to take an aspirin a day to help prevent another attack.

• Some hospitals are performing heart surgery even when their doctors haven't performed the operation often enough to keep their skills up. There is a long and well-documented connection between a hospital's performing a high volume of bypass surgeries and increased patient survival. Yet nearly one-third of the 1,023 U.S. hospitals performing open-heart surgery in 1994–95 performed fewer than the 200 cases per year that groups such as the American Heart Association recommend as a minimum, according to Medicare data. In California, 56 percent of the hospitals were below the 200-case minimum, a recent study found. It makes a difference. In New York State in 1995, one hospital that performed only about half the recommended number of bypasses had a morbidity rate *over twice* the state average. Traditionally, bypass surgery has traditionally been a prestigious and highly profitable service. That may or may not explain why the profession has not enforced its own standards.

Reports like these led to a damning indictment of the quality of care by the prestigious National Academy of Sciences' Institute of Medicine. The IOM report, in the September 16, 1998 issue of the *Journal of the American Medical Association* (JAMA), cited some of the above examples and concluded that "serious and widespread quality problems exist throughout American medicine... very large numbers of Americans are harmed as a direct result." The IOM consensus report added pointedly, "Quality of care is the problem, not managed care."

The Making of a Non-Scandal

One would think that the glaring disconnect between research-based medicine and everyday practice would be a national scandal. The evidence, after all, is in plain sight. Moreover, some big names in the policy world are even starting to talk about the problem.

Earlier this year, the presidential Advisory Commission on Consumer Protection and Quality issued an extraordinary indictment. The commission wrote: "Exhaustive research documents the fact that today, in America, there is no guarantee that any individual will receive high-quality care for any particular health problem." American medicine, it added, was plagued by "overuse, underuse and misuse." In other words, the heart disease examples cited earlier are the rule, not the exception.

The press, however, glued to the politically hot "patient bill of rights," has virtually ignored other causes for the wildly varying quality of patient care. The reaction to reports on deaths due to preventable medical mistakes has been ho-hum. Earlier this year, when the Centers for Disease Control and Prevention released a report stating that 50,000 people die each year from infections caused by their hospitalization, *The New York Times* put the story on page A12. A close reading of the story revealed that the last time the CDC looked closely at infections in hospitals was nearly 25 years ago! What went unstated in the report is that no governmental or private agency requires hospitals to have either a standardized definition of an infection or report on its infection rate to anyone.

So where is the outrage? In large part, the absence of scandal may be due to the equal absence of identifiable victims. The classic medical expose is about "bad" doctors. A man who has had the wrong foot amputated by a surgeon or a woman who has been sexually molested by her internist knows something went wrong. And, indeed, incompetent or impaired doctors remain a problem. Public Citizen Health Research Group estimates that one percent of doctors nationwide "deserve" some disciplinary action each year, yet Federation of State Medical Boards data show an average of just 3.84 actions per 1,000 physicians in 1997. Moreover, patients in a state like Florida may wait as long as two years for their complaint even to be heard.

Similarly, health-plan members with access problems often know when they've been mistreated, as was the case with the Washington representative of a health-care organization who was told that being taken unconscious to the ER was no excuse for not getting pre-authorization approval.

By contrast, the heart-attack patient who doesn't receive beta blocker therapy or isn't told to take an aspirin on discharge most likely won't have a clue that his life was put at risk. That's particularly true if some sort of therapy is prescribed and the doctors and nurses appear to be working hard and doing their best. (Of course, a few patients don't take any chances. An older physician I know who lives in a rural area carries beta blockers and aspirin in his wallet, along with instructions to the hospital on their use, just in case.) Similarly, the patient who receives an unnecessary angioplasty has no way of knowing that it was unneeded—except, perhaps, when some health plan reviewer objects, and the patient becomes outraged that the HMO is rationing care. And in the case of hospitals doing a low-volume of bypass surgery, it's hard to prove that any individual patient was harmed.

Perhaps the best example of a quality lapse where the victim is unlikely to complain involves autopsies. A recent JAMA study of autopsy results found that doctors failed to diagnose cancer properly in a shocking 44 percent of cases. Yet the frequency of autopsies is at a record low, in part because an unperformed autopsy is likely to generate a grateful family, not a dissatisfied one ready to complain to its local TV news team.

But it's not only the lack of easily-identifiable victims that's kept evidence-based medicine off the public radar screen. There are also political and economic reasons. Take the American Medical Association, which for a time actively sought out HMO horror stories for the media and Congress. While the AMA's scientific arm is a leader in the fight for evidence-based medicine, its political arm is devoted to protecting doctors' autonomy. Sometimes, that's propatient, as when the AMA battles unreasonable managed-care rules. Other times, it's pro-pocketbook of doctors, as when the AMA defines quality of care as forcing plans to contract with "any willing provider." That kind of arrangement takes away a plan's ability to compete on quality, because it's no longer free to decide which doctors will be part of the plan.

Public discussion of evidence-based medicine might lead some to wonder whether unchecked physician autonomy is really such a good thing. Those whose memories stretch back more than two news cycles might even remember that the Health Maintenance Organization Act of 1973 emerged out of widespread public disgust with a fee-for-service system then run by doctors.

Indeed, in 1976, a time when less than 10 percent of the population belonged to an HMO, the *Times* ran a five-part, page-one series about medical errors, overprescribed drugs and other failings of American medicine. The date of those articles should be noted by the nostalgia-mongers who loudly contrast today's system with the days of "Marcus Welby-style medicine? Nineteen seventy-six was the year that Marcus Welby, M.D. finally left the prime-time airwaves. Even in Marcus Welby's time, Marcus Welby-style medicine was not a reality for patients; it was just a TV show.

While the physician groups have an economic agenda that can cause them to slight evidence-based medicine, some consumer groups have a political one. Liberal organizations like Public Citizen seem to want to discredit managed care in order to pave the way for Canadian-style national health insurance. While that's a worthy goal (and one this magazine has long supported) it's unlikely to succeed in the current climate. More to the point, addressing the legitimate problem of access to care by the millions of Americans without health insurance says nothing about the quality of care received once access is assured. Conservative groups such as the National Center for Policy Analysis are as obsessed as the liberals with access and financing issues. But unlike the liberals, they want to replace managed care with a national system of medical savings accounts, another policy fantasy.

Given these ideological and economic interests, today's medical scandals follow a predictable script. For example, the refusal of some health plans to allow some breast cancer patients to stay in the hospital overnight after a mastectomy created a national uproar. Yet there is persuasive medical evidence that suggests a one-night stay can be perfectly safe—if health plans and hospitals choose the patients carefully and put the proper support services in place. More to the point, if breast-cancer victims are the real concern, then we should consider the lack of attention given a study appearing about the same time as the "drive-through mastectomy" debate erupted.

This study, by Dartmouth Medical School researchers, found that "geography is destiny" when it comes to care for breast cancer (as well as a number of other conditions). For example, fewer than three out of every 200 breast-cancer patients in Rapid City, S.D. received breast-conserving surgery versus a mastectomy, while in Elyria, Ohio, 96 out of 200 did. The two procedures have roughly equal therapeutic efficacy.

Which is worse: being given a too-short hospital stay after a mastectomy or unnecessarily losing a breast to surgery in the first place? To even pose that question exposes the shallowness of viewing high-quality care as synonymous with deference to individual physician judgment.

Since women's health issues are so politically attractive, here's another example of practice variation every woman will understand. When family practitioners in Washington State were asked about treating a simple urinary tract infection, one of the most common of female complaints, eighty-two physicians came up with an extraordinary 137 different strategies! It defies common sense to believe that every patient of each of those doctors is receiving equally high-quality care.

(Speaking of non-scandals: why is hospital "dumping" of poor patients without insurance—which once made front-page news—now relegated to the trade publications? Are the only certifiable "victims" the victims of health plans?)

The good news is that there are, in fact, some successes by health plans, hospitals and doctor groups in implementing science-based medical practice. The efforts of United Healthcare, a national for-profit plan, were even profiled recently in *The Wall Street Journal*. There are others. In Boston, for instance, Harvard Pilgrim Health Care has pioneered a program to involve asthmatic children, their parents, and the plan's doctors in applying "best care" The program cut inpatient admissions and emergency room visits by kids by more than three-quarters. Not only that, the children reported a significant increase in their ability to function at school or home.

The heart-attack patient who doesn't receive beta-blocker therapy won't have a clue that his life was put at risk.

Yet many organizations hesitate to share their successes at making use of medical procedures that are already on the books. A moment's thought makes it obvious why: A hospital or doctor who excels at using scientific advances that have already been in the medical literature risks being greeted by the question: What were you doing before this? The questioner might even be a lawyer.

Despite these barriers, I've seen a number of hospitals that are dedicated to operationalizing better care. In Pittsburgh, for instance, Forbes Regional Hospital used evidence-based clinical guidelines to improve the recovery time of seriously-ill pneumonia patients and dramatically cut the death rate of those who were less ill. In South Carolina, changes in heart-attack care at the Anderson Area Medical Center saved the lives of an estimated two patients a month who previously would have died. In Los Angeles, Cedars-Sinai Medical Center's systematic review of the medical literature on a heart condition in infants called Tetralogy of Fallot found that one treatment meant to prevent respiratory infections in these newborns actually increased the infection rate!

The common thread in all these improvement stories is this: There are no "bad guys" The doctors involved were neither evil nor incompetent. They are your doctor and mine—which may be the most powerful explanation of all for why the problem of evidence-based medicine has attracted so little attention. Whatever the failings of doctors in general, "to distrust one's [own] doctor is to be vulnerable in the most fundamental and undesirable

of ways," as one medical sociologist wrote. "The image of the doctor in America continues in large part to be an idealization that reflects people's hopes rather than their actual experiences"

Yet "good" doctors don't follow best practice for a variety of reasons. There is a failure to keep up with an overwhelming flood of medical literature, a reluctance to get caught up in new therapies that may be fads and uncertainty over which patients are best-suited for which therapy. Certainly, financial incentives can play a part in overuse, underuse and misuse. But ideologues who believe there is a perfect payment system that guarantees high-quality care will be disappointed. The problem of medical mistakes and a failure to practice evidence-based medicine is international. And, of course, there remains the problem of treatments where the evidence is ambiguous or simply unavailable.

A Better Way

When it comes to protecting patients, the same kind of pressures being brought on health plans should also be applied to the actual providers of care. While President Clinton has declared that passing a patient bill of rights will be a top 1999 priority, legislation that focuses only on speedy access to care will ultimately fail to truly protect patients. Providing every patient with the most appropriate and effective care—"doing the right thing and doing the right thing right"—must be just as much a priority as guaranteeing access to that care.

Those physicians who are working hard to bring change to our present system need financial and political encouragement, just as those who are reluctant to change need a mixture of financial and political incentives to rethink their position. Take, for instance, the connection between low volumes of surgery and higher mortality rates. If the patient bill of rights guarantees the right to go to the emergency room without delay, then how about the right to know, before the anesthesia takes effect, how many times the hospital or an individual surgeon has performed heart surgery? Medicare rule-making could go a long way to encourage this type of disclosure.

Similarly, what about a system of disclosing hospital infection rates that parallels the ratings used by health departments for restaurants? Right now, hospital lobbies across America display a certificate of accreditation from the Joint Commission on Accreditation of Healthcare Organizations, a group whose workings few patients understand. On the other hand, the difference between an "A" and a "C" grade on a certificate rating infection control would be an instant conversation-starter for patients and their doctors.

At the same time, legislators must be careful not to undermine internal hospital improvement efforts. Organizing information in a more systematic way, particularly through the use of computers, will both give doctors useful data at their fingertips and allow outside overseers to control better. Software now available can provide doctors with treatment protocols based on the latest science or a database of drug interactions designed to protect patients against possibly deadly adverse reactions. Other software, involved in electronic medical records, can help doctors and hospitals track the outcome of care in different groups of patients and continuously improve it. Unfortunately, the news stories highlighting legitimate worries about privacy of electronic medical records have not given equal play to the improvements in patient care that electronic medical records can bring.

Meanwhile, those researching how to apply evidence more effectively to practice could use far more funding than their present few crumbs. While Congress and the president heap billions more onto NIH's plate, the little-known Agency for Health Care Policy and Research makes do with a budget in the $100 million range. Funding applications work in medicine is like buying bullets and boots for the military; it's not glamorous, but it can mean the difference between success and failure.

Evidence-based medicine may be moving toward a higher profile. The Washington-based National Coalition on Health Care and the Boston-based Institute for Healthcare Improvement has just launched a quality initiative called Accelerating Change Today (ACT) for American Health. The explicit aim is to put best practices into common practice. Similarly, several corporate coalitions including some of the most prominent names in American business have quietly been holding talks about coordinating their efforts in a national effort to upgrade standards of care.

As the cost of medical care starts to accelerate again, it is becoming more urgent than ever to provide only that care which is the most appropriate and most effective. The alternative is grim: buying whatever care is cheapest. It's about time we started measuring the performance of health professionals and of health plans alike—and insisting that both groups be held accountable for results.

SEX @ WORK

What are the rules?

HARASSMENT OR HANKY-PANKY? These days, a lot of people, faced with a confusing and sometimes contradictory array of state and federal laws and individual company policies, are unable to tell the difference. Is offensive behavior automatically harassment? What about harassment that isn't sexual? Confusion about questions like these, along with a deliberate distortion of the meaning of the law, has plunged the nation into a rancorous, passionate debate about what is—and is not—sexual harassment. In the meantime, the President of the United States stands accused of sexual harassment (as well as other questionable sexual behavior).

   We decided it was time to sort out the issues. What follows are factual articles, deeply felt opinions, and the voices of the best experts: women who have been harassed and who, in the process, learned something about themselves and their rights in the workplace.

—The Editors

Confused by the Rules

By Gloria Jacobs with Angela Bonavoglia

Ruby S. was working late one night when the supervisor of her department at a large banking firm came up behind her and started massaging her back. She hadn't been working for the company long; didn't know the guy very well; and didn't particularly like him: "He was a little too slick for my taste." She turned to him and said, "Thanks for the back rub, but I have to go; I'm meeting someone in a few minutes." He laughed, let go of her shoulder, and asked, "Who's the lucky guy?" As he helped her on with her coat, he brushed his hand over her hair, tucking a strand behind her ear. She grabbed her things and got out of there, even though she still had a lot of work to do on an important project that was due the following week. "He gave me the creeps," she says, "but I never felt like I could be more firm about telling him to leave me alone, because it had taken a long time to find that job, and I really liked it except for him. I didn't

want to risk losing it." After about six months, she switched to another department with another supervisor. Her ex-boss stayed right where he was.

   What exactly was going on in Ruby's office? Was it sexual harassment? Was it illegal? Was it someone trying to be friendly who just wasn't Ruby's type? And who gets to decide? Ruby? Her boss? Her company? A judge?

   If you asked ten different people those questions, you'd probably get ten different answers. The truth is that just as the United States has become mired in media overkill on the topic of sexual harassment—was it or wasn't it? did he or didn't he?—many people of perfectly good intentions have absolutely no idea what such harassment really is. Short of the most egregious cases, we still don't "get it."

   The lack of clarity at all levels has left corporate counsels shaking in their boots, haunted by visions of financial ruin (sales of employment practices insurance, which covers sexual harassment settlements, more than doubled in the last 18 months, from $100 million to over $200 million, according to *U.S. News & World Report*). Government employees and workers in companies and universities all across the country, private and public, large and small, are completely confused—many are convinced that the new rules forbid everything from flirting to joking to falling in love with your cubicle-mate.

Confusion may be inevitable when it comes to personal relations: so much of it is based on nuance, anyway. But it's also true that sexual harassment law, perhaps more than most, is constantly evolving as each new case comes before the courts and establishes new precedents. Thus, what today would be a perfectly obvious (and winnable) case of harassment—a woman loses her job because she won't sleep with her boss—was far from obvious to judges in the early 1970s.

Discrimination based on race, color, religion, national origin, or sex was outlawed in 1964 by Title VII of the Civil Rights Act. But over the next decade more than one sexual harassment case was lost when judges ruled that being punished for refusing to have sex with your boss had nothing to do with discrimination per se—these were "personal" relationships—and therefore did not fall under Title VII. Eventually several cases were successfully argued—by lawyers who claimed that because of the sexual stereotyping of women, an unwanted sexual advance by a person with supervisory power did amount to discrimination. In 1980, the Equal Employment Opportunity Commission (EEOC), which enforces federal antidiscrimination laws (some states have their own laws, in addition), issued specific guidelines on sexual harassment. Title VII covered nonsexual harassment as well, the kind used to keep women from competing with men for jobs—such as tampering with their work or equipment, threatening them, or deliberately jeopardizing their safety. But the EEOC emphasized sexual relations—the guidelines focused only on harassment between members of the opposite sex, and so have the courts over the years. It was not until March 4, 1998, that the Supreme Court declared same-sex harassment (whether against gays or straights) illegal.

The EEOC's guidelines identified two types of harassment: quid pro quo and hostile environment. As more and more cases were won using these categories, legal precedents were established, and expectations of what was acceptable behavior began ponderously but steadily shifting, like tectonic plates lumbering under the earth. As with many of the changes feminism has brought about, the idea that men—and some women—would have to question male prerogatives has elicited hostility and hosannas, as well as bewilderment and confusion. This discomfort, along with fear of litigation, has frequently led employers to overreact: if they don't know for sure where the line is, they'll draw it far enough back so hardly anyone can claim they didn't know they were stepping over it. Often companies end up with policies that don't make distinctions between office romances (given all the hours we spend at work, where else are we going to find a date or a mate?) and harassment.

Quid pro quo is Latin for "this for that"—it involves a boss demanding sexual favors in exchange for things like a job, a promotion, a raise, or benefits. Sexual favoritism is an offshoot of quid pro quo: it postulates that if a boss has sex with an employee and gives her promotions, better hours, and other benefits in return, the other women on the job can argue that they're being penalized for not sleeping with the boss.

It took 12 years for quid pro quo to be recognized by the courts. In 1976 in *Williams v. Saxbe*, a district court in Washington, D.C., finally ruled that sexual harassment is a form of unlawful sex discrimination. A year later, a higher court, the D.C. court of appeals, one of the most influential courts in the country, concurred. In *Barnes v. Costle*, the court ruled that having a job be "conditioned upon submission to sexual relations" was illegal. In response to *Barnes* and several big settlements that followed it, many employers took drastic steps, banning all romantic involvement between supervisors and their subordinates. The same thing happened in universities that created policies forbidding teachers from having a sexual relationship with students.

Employers develop exhaustive lists of all the behaviors that won't be tolerated, which they generally post and distribute.

Not surprisingly, there's a lot of disagreement about the effect of such sweeping policies. Some people believe they are essential, others say they rob us of the ability to make personal decisions. Last year, the president and chief operating officer of Staples, the office supply giant, resigned after it was revealed that he had had a consensual affair with his secretary. Staples' policy was that anyone in a close reporting relationship with another employee is prohibited from sexual relations with that person. That resignation received a great deal of media attention and set off a lot of second-guessing—the man was considered a top-notch leader, and if the woman consented, and he didn't show her any favoritism at work, who was harmed?

What is surprising in all the debate about no-dating's pros and cons is that, despite backlash rantings in the media against puritanical feminists, few feminists involved in workplace issues actually support policies like Staples'. "A no-dating policy is a quick-fix solution," insists Ellen Bravo, codirector of 9to5, a working women's advocacy group, "and a foolish policy." Carol Sanger, who teaches sexual harassment law at Columbia University in New York City, says these policies simply set women up as victims. "What women don't need is for the law to say, 'Guess what, you thought you were consenting to have sex, but we say you couldn't possibly have, because you're in an inferior power position, you're only a secretary.' Women's sexuality has been repressed too long. Let them consent." On the other hand, warns Sanger, if the initiator of an unwanted sexual advance is the person with more power, they must be willing to pay the price, if necessary: "If you fuck around with your young employees or your students, and they decide they're injured, then the risk should be on your head."

The Supreme Court first addressed the issue of sexual harassment in a 1986 ruling that set precedent by recognizing "hostile environment" harassment. In *Meritor Savings Bank v. Vinson*, the Court ruled that harassment could occur even if the victim hadn't lost any job benefits. In this case, the plaintiff had slept with her boss, but the justices said that he had sexualized the workplace to such an extent that it amounted to a hostile environment—which, according to the EEOC guidelines, consists of "unwelcome sexual advances, requests for sexual favors, and other verbal or physical conduct of a sexual nature" when it affects employment, interferes with work performance, or creates "an intimidating, hostile, or offensive working environment."

Since *Meritor,* the largest number of legal cases brought to the courts involve hostile environment. It is also the murkiest area of the law. What type of sexual conduct are we talking about exactly? When does harmless workplace behavior morph into a potentially hostile environment? When a guy e-mailing "The 50 Worst Things About Women" to several of his buddies hits the "all" key by mistake? When a man asks a female coworker for a date by e-mail, then voice mail, then sends a fax, then goes back to e-mail again, even though she has said no each time? When a male manager insists on checking a problem with a female coworker's computer and leans over her shoulder and whispers compliments in her ear? When the guys in the mail room begin the day with the latest raunchy joke, within obvious earshot of an older woman worker? When a male professor uses *Hustler* to teach female anatomy despite students' concerns? When a female administrator whose office brims with posters and cartoons that rag on men is assigned a male office mate?

With the exception of the e-mail of the "50 Worst Things" (assuming it was a one-time mistake, and recognizing the risk of using company e-mail for personal communiqués), all of the other examples may amount to sexual harassment. "Sexual harassment is deliberate, repeated, unwelcome, not asked for, and not returned," says Susan Webb the author of *Shades of Gray*, a guide on sexual harassment in the workplace. Her Seattle-based consulting firm that advises corporations on preventing harassment was one of the first to enter the field.

Firms like Webb's are multiplying because most companies feel they're on shaky ground when it comes to figuring out what a hostile environment is. "Sexual harassment is not black and white," says Webb. "You've got to take the whole thing in the context in which it occurred." It's not surprising that some of the examples given above could leave people scratching their heads. And many companies have established guidelines that go beyond the EEOC or their state laws. So you could lose your job for having violated company rules, but not have committed an illegal act. Companies are creating these policies because they are legally liable if they knew or should have known that harassment existed and failed to act. So far,

the courts have said that the company is somewhat less liable for a hostile environment than for quid pro quo harassment, but most employers are trying to avoid as much risk as possible. With the sheer potential for liability—there are 137.6 million people working in the U.S.—and the damage that can be done to a carefully honed corporate image by one sensational suit, many employers have gone off the deep end in their efforts to control personal behavior.

VO!CES *"I was more angry than frightened."*

DEBORAH WITHERSPOON, 43 • CURRENT JOB AND JOB WHEN HARASSED: SECURITY GUARD IN BANKING INDUSTRY I work midnight to 8 A.M. I'm one of only two females on that shift. I started being sexually harassed last year when one of my bosses started making little innuendoes, flirting with me, and from there it just escalated. He became more aggressive because I was ignoring him. He started coming out to where I lived and would watch me come and go. I became very hostile and I kept telling him to leave me alone. But he took it like a joke—he paid it no mind.

Then he began to use his power as my boss to threaten me. He would say: "You're going to be transferred!" If I came in five or ten minutes late, he would record it. He told me the company wasn't satisfied with my performance.

One night, I was the only guard posted when he came in and closed the door and started talking some trash—telling me, "Now we can get it on." I became very frightened. I thought maybe he was going to attack me. I told him to get away from me and that the cleaning man was nearby. When I said that he left.

I'm not the type of person who likes to start problems or cause anyone to lose their job, but after that incident, I grew concerned. A girlfriend told me, "Look, it's not going to stop," so I took the situation to his boss, the vice president.

He seemed concerned and immediately rushed me over to human resources, where I gave them a statement. But the human resources person told me it was my word against his, and that he had said he didn't want to transfer. She asked me if I wanted to transfer. I told her I thought it was very unfair that she suggest I transfer when I wasn't the one who did anything wrong. What did she mean it was my word against his? Did she think I just picked him out of a crowd?

I stayed at my job. I'm not going to give up a good job for something someone else did to me. For a while the man who was harassing me stayed away from me. But recently he's started to come over to where I work. He hasn't said anything out of order yet, but I think he's getting more comfortable. Whenever he's around, I'm on my guard.

I surprised people by speaking out the way I did. And I think, at first, I got more respect from the other men because of it. People saw that I wasn't somebody you could push over. I will stand my ground for what I believe is right.

Overall, this situation made me more angry than frightened—until I was cornered that night. But even then I was angry. I don't like people to treat me like they can do what they want to me, as if I have no say. And what makes me angrier is how human resources dealt with the situation. Harassment is very serious.

I think that this type of behavior is wrong, and women should stand up against it even though there are consequences when you do. I should be respected just like the next person, regardless of the fact that I'm a female. I do my work, and I respect people. I demand that that same respect be given to me.

—ALL "VOICES" INTERVIEWED BY KATIE MONAGLE

Often, they've turned to what are known as "zero tolerance" policies. These say, in effect, one wrong move and you're out the door. But how to interpret that wrong move? Employers develop exhaustive lists of all the behaviors that won't be tolerated, which they generally post and distribute. Some behaviors on the lists are understandable: no unwelcome physical contact; and some are unrealistic: absolutely no touching. "One of my favorite examples of the stupidity of these lists," says Freada Klein, a longtime consultant on corporate policy, "is when some corporation did the typical thing after a lawsuit. They overreacted and put in a policy that said no touching ever. One of the first complaints came from someone who had observed a manager embracing his secretary—well, she had just found out her mother had died and he came out and consoled her."

When it comes to the people who truly use these behaviors to harass, the lists don't do much good, insists Klein. "Do you really think that someone who would engage in that kind of behavior, if they had a laminated card in their pocket with dos and don'ts, would decide not to act that way?" This rigid approach is "bizarre, insulting, infantalizing, and ineffective." She adds: "For every other workplace issue, we're talking about driving decision-making down. On this one, we say, 'You can't think for yourself, you're not a grown-up, you will only do as you're told.' "

Schools are another place where a "dos and don'ts" approach to harassment can melt down into the ludicrous. In 1996, two little boys, ages 6 and 7, were accused of sexual harassment for stealing kisses (and, in one case, the button of

At the core of sexual harassment law lies a concept that the "victim" gets to decide if she has been victimized.

a dress) from female classmates. Each was briefly suspended from his school. The impetus was fear of liability by the schools involved: families have been successfully suing school districts for sexual harassment involving kids. And plenty of awful cases abound. A study by the American Association of University Women has shown that harassment of teenage girls in middle and high schools is pervasive and has devastating effects.

Based on its own studies, as well as reports like the AAUW's, and complaints received by the agency, in 1997 the U.S. Department of Education issued guidelines for stopping student-to-student harassment, as well as harassment between students and teachers, that hold schools responsible for their implementation. Unfortunately, despite the fact that the guidelines made distinctions according to age, cases like the ones involving the two little boys indicate, as in corporate America, a tendency to overreact, to see discipline problems involving children of different genders as harassment, and to disregard what any good educator should know: moral standards develop with age. "A 12-year-old's understanding of what is right and

---

VO!CES   *"He got away with it, that's the long and the short of it."*

ANONYMOUS, 34 • CURRENT JOB AND JOB WHEN HARASSED: UNION TECHNICIAN IN ENTERTAINMENT INDUSTRY I'm an apprentice technician. Before I was sexually harassed, I was a rising star. I was using cutting-edge technology and had achieved a lot of prestige and recognition in my field.

One day, I was working alone in a room with my boss on a particular job, and he pushed me over, sat in the chair with me and kissed me on the head. The next day I was in a warehouse, alone again, and he came up from behind me and wrapped his arms around me and kissed me. I squirmed. I didn't say anything. I was scared to the point of paralysis. That night I couldn't sleep at all. So the next day I call him up at home and say, "Your behavior yesterday and the day before was inappropriate, and I want to have a strictly professional relationship." He says, "You're absolutely right, I was out of line and I should stop—but I want to talk to you about it." So on a coffee break the next day he tells me, "I have been totally infatuated with you ever since I met you. The main reason why I hired you is because I'm attracted to you."

I documented the entire incident in a memo—including all the specific details, like dates, places, the number of times. I went to the union business agent, who's the head of the union. I wanted him to tell this guy to leave me alone. I didn't want him brought up on charges because I didn't want anyone else to know about this. In my field it can be very hard to get people to take me seriously because I'm a woman, and women doing what I do is very unusual. I already have to work twice as hard for respect. This would make things worse. Also, I was ashamed that this had happened to me at all.

The agent talked to him and he apologized for his actions. Shortly after, there was a three-month break on that job, so I took another assignment. I wasn't in touch with him at all until it was time to return. I called him to check in, and he said, "Oh, by the way, I've changed your rate of pay." Basically, he cut my pay.

Again, I went straight to the union business agent, who controls what jobs I get and who is ultimately responsible for my pay. But I could not convince the agent that the reason my boss had cut my pay was because I had busted him on sexual harassment. The business agent saw a legal loophole to explain my pay cut, and that's the story he stuck with. So there was nothing I could do. The business agent was totally against bringing this guy up on charges, and without the agent's support, I could never win in a grievance procedure in the union, because he had been there 30 years and was rarely challenged. I agreed to take another job with the union at the same location but doing something different, for less money, and in a different department from my harasser.

Recently, a new, younger business agent and president took over the union. They found work for me at different locations because the guy continued to harass me. I'm happy with this work, but not with how things turned out. If justice was ultimately what I wanted, I should have brought him up on charges right away. But the price for justice would have been so high, that in hindsight I don't have regrets. I just wish the world were different. He got away with it, that's the long and the short of it. I would have had to sacrifice my whole career to make him pay.

wrong on this subject can be very different from what a 7-year-old thinks," Gwendolyn Gregory, who was the deputy general counsel for the National School Boards Association at the time of the incidents, told the Washington *Post*.

The cases involving these young boys were exceptional, but they received an enormous amount of derogatory press, some of it implying that sexual harassment as a concept was so off the wall, it made these kinds of cases inevitable. "By playing up the ridiculous, the exaggerations, or the aberrations, what the right wing tries to do is make it seem that that's the main thing that's going on, and it isn't," argues Ellen Bravo. "The main thing going on in the schools is not a 6-year-old being kicked out for kissing a girl on the cheek, but grabbing, groping, and sexual assault that borders on criminal behavior. By trivializing sexual harassment that way, they can dismiss it."

VO!CES — "Was it all in my head?"

ANONYMOUS, 22 • HIGH SCHOOL STUDENT WHEN HARASSED; CURRENTLY A COLLEGE STUDENT I was an easy target—I had "victim" written all over me. I was a junior in high school and I wasn't doing great academically. I had just moved to a new school and wasn't close with a lot of people there. Plus, I was going through a lot of emotional stuff at home. He was my U.S. history teacher and he always chose one girl to pick on every year. That year it was me.

In class he would try to make me look stupid, try to provoke me into arguing with him. I was really quiet and I tried to be almost invisible. The last thing I wanted was someone pointing me out, always being after me. Outside of class he would make comments about my appearance and proposition me. One time he cornered me and said, "I just need to know—do you want to have a teacher-student relationship, or do you want something more?"

There would be these really intense periods in which he'd make comments, touch my hair, grab my hand, things like that. Then it would be followed by a week when he wouldn't talk to me or acknowledge me in the classroom, even if I were to try to ask a question, or hand in a test. I got to a point where I had no idea what was real. It made me think I was going crazy because I would think maybe it wasn't really going on, maybe it was all in my head. At the same time, I was afraid that he would attack me. I thought it probably wouldn't happen at school, but I just didn't know. I also feared that my grade could be affected.

For a long time, I thought it wasn't such a big deal. But now I see that it had a huge impact on how I perceived myself. I became less confident. I started to wear baggy sweaters so that I would appear less sexual. By the end of that year I wouldn't even wear a skirt or anything that could have been seen by him as suggestive.

To me, there weren't any options in dealing with this. I didn't feel that there was anyone I could go to. I wasn't close enough to my mom to say anything to her, and my best friend was actually having an affair with one of her high school teachers. I didn't think that people would believe me or take me seriously. I figured they would think I was leading him on or encouraging him in some way. How else could this happen? It just seemed implausible that a high school teacher was saying these things to his student.

Later I realized that having "victim" written all over me didn't mean that it was my fault or that I necessarily deserved how he victimized me. I'm glad I never have to be 16 again. My only regret is that I didn't do anything about the harassment because he's probably still doing it to other students.

At the core of sexual harassment law lies a concept that the "victim" gets to decide if she has been victimized. (This strikes fear in the hearts of many—and may have contributed to employer overreaction.) If a coworker tells dirty jokes in your presence, and they don't bother you—you laugh along with everyone else—that's not harassment. If a coworker tells those same jokes as part of a pattern of hostility that makes you so uncomfortable it's hard to do your job, it's harassment. To those who have to implement the law, this can seem like a fairly subjective standard. Especially when it comes to trying to win a case in court. Recognizing that, the courts have ruled that the standard must be that of the so-called reasonable person. Because most plaintiffs in sexual harassment cases have been women, the standard is often referred to as that of a "reasonable woman."

This woman is a kind of Jane Doe/Everywoman: not too sensitive, not too idiosyncratic, sort of "just right," like Goldilocks' porridge. It would seem like an impossible task to figure out what's "reasonable" under such an amorphous standard. But the point, many lawyers insist, is that women do have a certain experience of the world that the courts should take into account. "We realize there's a broad range of viewpoints among women as a group," says Carol Sanger, "but we believe many women share common concerns which men do not necessarily share. For example, because women are disproportionately victims of rape and sexual assault, women have a stronger incentive to be concerned with sexual behavior. If a man gets a note from a female coworker who's been making sexual overtures, he's not afraid she's going to come up behind him in the parking lot one night."

But this attempt to give some flexibility to the law and prevent frivolous lawsuits has led to endless legal debates about just what is "reasonable" in a multicultural society, anyway. One of the biggest areas of contention involves the issue of speaking up. Because the law gives the victim the power to define the offense, many lawyers feel strongly that, when possible and safe, women ought to let the potential harasser know that his behavior is offensive. One law professor describes an incident when she served as ombudsman for her students. "A girl comes in and tells me that a guy says to her, 'I'd love to see you naked.' I say to her, what did you do? And she says, 'Well, I giggled and ran into my room.' That wasn't good enough. All you have to do is say, 'Don't do that to me again.'" A few days later, the woman came back, furious that she was expected to confront her fellow student. The professor eventually convinced her to write a letter, if for no other reason than to document his behavior should he repeat it. In this case, says the professor: "He really didn't know it was wrong. This is a guy who lives in a completely sexualized culture and he's a complete nerd and he's trying to be cool."

Others argue that men should know by now when their behavior is unacceptable, it shouldn't be up to women to teach them, and it isn't always possible to speak to a harasser. "In principle, it makes sense," says Katherine Franke, a professor of law at New York City's Fordham University, who specializes in sexual harassment. "But as a practical matter, a lot of women don't feel in a position to say to their boss, cut that out. What the law requires is often very different from what people feel empowered to do."

Topping off the debate on what's reasonable is the question of bigotry. Is someone's homophobia, for example, reasonable because a lot of people might share it? Vicki Schultz, a professor at Yale Law School in New Haven, Connecticut, describes a case in which a gay man was sued by a female coworker for sex harassment because he talked about his sex life at work. Although the woman lost, Schultz cautions, "I can see this being a very punitive measure in the hands of socially conservative people who don't want to hear people they perceive to be sexually deviant talk about their lives at all."

So here we are, women at the turn of the century who have transformed the workplace and the rules that govern it, by our presence. The good that has come from that transformation is now inevitably bogged down in the messy, complicated task of trying to make sure all the pieces of this particular puzzle fit together. It's a task that makes many people uncomfortable, and feminists have taken the brunt of the backlash. "The accusation lies there: you're just a frigid feminist, all you want to do is regulate sexuality," says Sanger. "But what kind of lives have people led that they don't know what awaits women?"

Ellen Bravo makes the point that "people have described in a trivializing, minimizing, and parodying way those of us who fight sex harassment, as if what we want is a repressive workplace where no one can tell a joke, no one can flirt, no one can date. This is not what we want. We want an end to unwelcome, offensive behavior of a sexual nature."

That is what we want, but nevertheless, the question remains—and it's a huge one—how can the average well-intentioned person figure out what behavior is acceptable in the workplace, especially when the damage is always in the eye of the beholder? The answer, say those who help devise the corporate rules, is deceptively simple: respect. Nearly everyone agrees that you can't just teach people a set of rules, expect them to memorize them, and that's it. It takes communication and discussion over a period of time. Not a one-day training session. Not handing people a manual and saying, "Read this." It takes a willingness to listen, respect for the concerns and fears of others, and an ability to honor differences, in order to reach some common ground. "Boilerplate policies are preposterous," says Freada Klein. "You have to respect the culture of the organization. Many of us are not in the same businesses, and even when we are, one company may be much looser than another." So the company has to set the tone and the standard.

Several companies are starting to do just that. DuPont, for example, has created a sexual harassment training program called A Matter of Respect. It consists of several workshops, some lasting several hours, some several days. The workshops use role playing, videos, and group discussions to help all levels of employees understand harassment. According to the company, about 75 percent of its 60,000 workers have attended some part of the program. Dupont diversity consultant Bob Hamilton says the goal is to "get people to build relationships so that they can talk freely, and so that if someone does something that bothers them, they can feel comfortable knowing they have the support of management and the organization to say something."

DuPont is one of the leaders in the attempt to create policies that rely on judgment and communication rather than specific rules. Even those who are most in favor of such policies say the effort is not easy. It demands that people do some second-guessing of themselves. One female executive says she now controls her impulse to touch her staff. "All of a sudden I realized I can't go out there and stand behind one of my employees and put my hand on his shoulder. That may be offensive to him and may be misinterpreted by him. So I've had to change my behavior."

Other executives say it's possible to get to a point where the decision-making about what's acceptable is more couched in the moment and the context. Burke Stinson, a spokesman for AT&T, which has an antiharassment program based on individual judgment, says women and men are definitely more comfortable about where to draw the line now. "If colleagues from different offices run into each other, there will be a hug, a 'God-it's-good-to-see-you' exchange that is nonsexual, nonthreatening, nongroping, based on one human being to another. Five or six years ago, I would say each party would have thought three times about it, and then just shaken hands."

People are more relaxed, Stinson believes, because they know the company will support them if there is a problem. "Employees who grew up in the work environment of the seventies and eighties feel that corporate America's hallways are not as threatening, are more secure, that there is recourse if there is some nasty business with words, deeds, or actions, a policy to fall back on. We're beginning to see a new sense of confidence."

Let's hope he's right. And that, along with that sense of confidence, there is a willingness to continue to struggle to figure out what's right, rather than resorting to inflexibility and archaic notions of women's "protected" status.

Gloria Jacobs is the editor of "Ms." Angela Bonavoglia, the author of "The Choices We Made: 25 Women and Men Speak Out About Abortion" (Random House), conducted research for, and helped to develop, this article.

Unit 5

Unit Selections

21. **Addicted,** J. Madeleine Nash
22. **Passion Pills,** Judith Newman
23. **Crank,** Walter Kirn
24. **More Reefer Madness,** Eric Schlosser
25. **Beyond Legalization: New Ideas for Ending the War on Drugs,** Michael Massing

Key Points to Consider

❖ How did certain drugs become illegal? Discuss whether or not the sale and use of marijuana should be legalized.

❖ Should legal drugs be sold if they are beneficial for their stated purpose, even if they may cause other health problems? Why or why not?

❖ Discuss whether or not, given their harmful effects, alcohol and tobacco should remain legal.

 **Links** | **www.dushkin.com/online/**

19. **The Center for Alcohol & Addiction Studies**
    http://center.butler.brown.edu
20. **DEA—Home Page**
    http://www.usdoj.gov/dea/index.htm
21. **Indiana PRC—Drug Statistics Master Page**
    http://www.drugs.indiana.edu/drug_stats/home.html
22. **The Institute of Alcohol Studies**
    http://www.ias.org.uk
23. **Yahoo!—Substance Abuse Search Index**
    http://www.yahoo.com/Health/Mental_Health/Diseases_and_Conditions/Substance_Abuse/

These sites are annotated on pages 4 and 5.

In the past, a large proportion of the white middle-class population legally used drugs such as cocaine, heroin, and marijuana. Pharmacies across the United States sold heroin mixed with alcohol as a cure-all. They sold potions such as Ayer's Cherry Pectoral for such ailments as arthritis, colds, and "women's problems." Cocaine, a stimulant drug derived from the juice of the coca leaf, popular until the early 1900s, was the active ingredient that gave Coca Cola drinkers a boost. The Pure Food and Drug Act of 1906 required truth in labeling and banned the adulteration of foods and drugs, generally ending over-the-counter sales of strong stimulants and narcotics. Marijuana, a member of the *cannabis* family, used to be grown as hemp for making rope. Smoking marijuana to elicit a "high" became popular during the 1930s when Mexican farm workers introduced the behavior into the United States. Marijuana became popular with poor young black males after World War II and through the 1950s. It was only during the 1960s that marijuana became one of several drugs popular with young, white, middle- and upper-class Americans. Following the lead of the pop psychologist Timothy Leary, many young people made it a practice to "turn on, tune in, and drop out" with LSD, a powerful hallucinogenic drug with long-term psychologically and physically damaging effects. Heroin, a narcotic, was a popular drug of the urban subculture during the 1960s and 1970s. Cocaine, in powdered form, reemerged as a "rich man's high" during the 1980s. Its use was generally limited to the upper and middle classes due to its high market price. The average price during the 1980s was approximately $125 per gram, which made it unaffordable to most people. In the late 1980s and into the 1990s, crack cocaine, a powerful and particularly addictive hardened form of the drug, became popular because it is far more affordable than powdered cocaine. In the 1990s, methamphetamine, a powerful stimulant drug also known by its aliases of "crank" or "crystal meth," has become popular with rural users. Recent reports in the media suggest that over one-third of Americans have tried marijuana. Also, the media recently reported that during the first half of the 1990s, the use of drugs such as marijuana, heroin, LSD, and cocaine increased drastically, after a marked decline during the 1980s. This trend was particularly true among teenagers, especially those whose parents had a history of drug use or whose friends used drugs. The media reports also suggested that marijuana was the major entry-level drug for users of the more potent illegal drugs.

Most illegal drugs became illegal as the result of changes in the social definition of the drugs and the social acceptability of their use. For example, marijuana became illegal largely because using it was a behavior practiced by a minority ethnic group that was unpopular with most of the population. When heroin and cocaine became the drugs of choice for poor and minority Americans, they then became illegal. We still see remnants of this in the federal sentencing guidelines for possession of different types of cocaine. Under the current guidelines, the sentence for possession of 5 grams of crack cocaine is the same as for possession of 500 grams of powdered cocaine. Crack cocaine is the drug of choice for minority, poor users, while powdered cocaine is the drug of choice for white, rich users. In 1995, when legislation to reduce the perceived inequity in sentencing failed in the Congress, the result was mass rioting in prisons across the United States.

Drugs have not only been socially defined as deviant due to who uses them, but also because their use and abuse have led to an increase in many other social problems. For example, in 1993 there were more than 24,000 murders in the United States. Many of those murders may be directly attributable to drug distribution and sales. Rival dealers may kill each other to gain market share, and they may kill informants for giving information on dealers to the police. The financial cost of illegal drugs has produced a massive drain on the nation's economy. An ongoing study sponsored by the Office of National Drug Control Policy found that in 1993 alone, an estimated $49 billion was spent on the purchase of illegal drugs. Many substance abusers may have no legitimate means for paying for their drugs and as a result may commit crimes to pay for them. For instance, in large cities, it is common to hear of women working as prostitutes in exchange for drugs. The media sometimes report on instances of mothers' selling their children to pay for drugs. Many cases of spousal abuse, child abuse, and neglect may be related to drug use by one or more members of a family. Many formerly successful people have ruined their lives and families as a result of becoming dependent on illegal and legal drugs.

This unit deals with both legal and illegal drugs. Drugs need not be illegally obtained to be addictive and/or dangerous. Until approximately 20 years ago, Valium, an antianxiety drug, was commonly prescribed by physicians as a way to take the edge off life, legally. Amphetamines such as Dexedrine, sold for weight loss, can also be addictive. Drugs sold both by prescription and over-the-counter can have unintended side effects. Drugs such as Naprosyn, which is sold over-the-counter as Aleve, can result in stomach problems. Ritalin, a legal stimulant given to children for the treatment of the symptoms of hyperactivity, is increasingly being given to nonhyperactive children by their parents, in hopes that their grades will improve. In addition, an illegal market for Ritalin has developed, with pills selling for between $3 and $15 each.

Alcohol is another drug that can be legally obtained and consumed, even though it may have dangerous side effects: It can increase the risk of developing cancers, strokes, and heart attacks. Also, drunk driving has become the number one cause of death for young people in this country. As a result, a number of states have taken action to prevent drunk driving among teenagers. For example, in the state of Arkansas, the maximum blood alcohol concentration for a teenage driver is only 20 percent of that allowed for an adult driver. The average teenage driver need only consume more than 2 ounces of beer to exceed the legal limit. Nationwide, the blood alcohol concentration (BAC) for finding adults legally drunk is .10 percent, and there is a national move afoot to lower the adult BAC to .08 percent.

Cigarettes and other tobacco products are legal drugs that also have deleterious effects on their users. It is estimated that over 300,000 persons annually succumb to tobacco-related illnesses.

One might reasonably ask why it is legal to purchase and consume alcohol and tobacco if they are so dangerous, while other drugs are illegal to purchase and consume. The answer seems to lie in the social definition of alcohol and tobacco as socially acceptable drugs. What makes alcohol and tobacco use deviant is not the substances themselves as much as the manner in which they are used and the damaging effects they incur.

A D D I C T E D

Why do people get hooked? Mounting evidence points to a powerful brain chemical called dopamine

By J. MADELEINE NASH

IMAGINE YOU ARE TAKING A SLUG OF WHIS-key. A puff of a cigarette. A toke of mari-juana. A snort of cocaine. A shot of heroin. Put aside whether these drugs are le-gal or illegal. Concentrate, for now, on the chemistry. The moment you take that slug, that puff, that toke, that snort, that shot, tril-lions of potent molecules surge through your bloodstream and into your brain. Once there, they set off a cascade of chemical and elec-trical events, a kind of neurological chain re-action that ricochets around the skull and rearranges the interior reality of the mind.

Given the complexity of these events—and the inner workings of the mind in gen-eral—it's not surprising that scientists have struggled mightily to make sense of the mechanisms of addiction. Why do certain substances have the power to make us feel so good (at least at first)? Why do some peo-ple fall so easily into the thrall of alcohol, cocaine, nicotine and other addictive sub-stances, while others can, literally, take them or leave them?

The answer, many scientists are con-vinced, may be simpler than anyone has dared imagine. What ties all these mood-al-tering drugs together, they say, is a remark-able ability to elevate levels of a common substance in the brain called dopamine. In fact, so overwhelming has evidence of the link between dopamine and drugs of abuse

become that the distinction (pushed primar-ily by the tobacco industry and its support-ers) between substances that are addictive and those that are merely habit-forming has very nearly been swept away.

The Liggett Group, smallest of the U.S.'s Big Five cigarette makers, broke ranks in March and conceded not only that tobacco is addictive but also that the company has known it all along. While RJR Nabisco and the others continue to battle in the courts—insisting that smokers are not hooked, just ex-ercising free choice—their denials ring increasingly hollow in the face of the grow-ing weight of evidence. Over the past year, several scientific groups have made the case that in dopamine-rich areas of the brain, nicotine behaves remarkably like cocaine. And late last week a federal judge ruled for the first time that the Food and Drug Ad-ministration has the right to regulate to-bacco as a drug and cigarettes as drug-delivery devices.

Now, a team of researchers led by psychiatrist Dr. Nora Volkow of the Brook-haven National Labo-ratory in New York has published the

strongest evidence to date that the surge of dopamine in addicts' brains is what triggers a cocaine high. In last week's edition of the journal *Nature* they described how powerful brain-imaging technology can be used to track the rise of dopamine and link it to feelings of euphoria.

Like serotonin (the brain chemical affected by such antidepressants as Prozac), dopamine is a neurotransmitter—a molecule that ferries messages from one neuron within the brain to another. Serotonin is associated with feelings of sadness and well-being, dopamine with pleasure and elation. Dopamine can be elevated by a hug, a kiss, a word of praise or a winning poker hand—as well as by the potent pleasures that come from drugs.

The idea that a single chemical could be associated with everything from snorting co-caine and smoking tobacco to getting good

PRIME SUSPECT

They don't yet know the precise mechanism by which it works, but scientists are increasingly convinced that dopamine plays a key role in a wide range of addictions, including those to heroin, nicotine, alcohol and marijuana

DOPAMINE MAY BE LINKED TO GAMBLING, CHOCOLATE AND EVEN SEX

grades and enjoying sex has electrified scientists and changed the way they look at a wide range of dependencies, chemical and otherwise. Dopamine, they now believe, is not just a chemical that transmits pleasure signals but may, in fact, be the master molecule of addiction.

This is not to say dopamine is the only chemical involved or that the deranged thought processes that mark chronic drug abuse are due to dopamine alone. The brain is subtler than that. Drugs modulate the activity of a variety of brain chemicals, each of which intersects with many others. "Drugs are like sledgehammers," observes Dr. Eric Nestler of the Yale University School of Medicine. "They profoundly alter many pathways."

Nevertheless, the realization that dopamine may be a common end point of all those pathways represents a signal advance. Provocative, controversial, unquestionably incomplete, the dopamine hypothesis provides a basic framework for understanding how a genetically encoded trait—such as a tendency to produce too little dopamine—might intersect with environmental influences to create a serious behavioral disorder. Therapists have long known of patients who, in addition to having psychological problems, abuse drugs as well. Could their drug problems be linked to some inborn quirk? Might an inability to absorb enough dopamine, with its pleasure-giving properties, cause them to seek gratification in drugs?

Such speculation is controversial, for it suggests that broad swaths of the population may be genetically predisposed to drug abuse. What is not controversial is that the social cost of drug abuse, whatever its cause, is enormous. Cigarettes contribute to the death toll from cancer and heart disease. Alcohol is the leading cause of domestic violence and highway deaths. The needles used to inject heroin and cocaine are spreading AIDS. Directly or indirectly, addiction to drugs, cigarettes and alcohol is thought to account for a third of all hospital admissions, a quarter of all deaths and a majority of serious crimes. In the U.S. alone the combined medical and social costs of drug abuse are believed to exceed $240 billion.

For nearly a quarter-century the U.S. has been waging a war on drugs, with little apparent success. As scientists learn more about how dopamine works (and how drugs work on it), the evidence suggests that we may be fighting the wrong battle. Americans tend to think of drug addiction as a failure of character. But this stereotype is beginning to give way to the recognition that drug dependence has a clear biological basis. "Addiction," declares Brookhaven's Volkow, "is a disorder of the brain

no different from other forms of mental illness."

That new insight may be the dopamine hypothesis' most important contribution in the fight against drugs. It completes the loop between the mechanism of addiction and programs for treatment. And it raises hope for more effective therapies. Abstinence, if maintained, not only halts the physical and

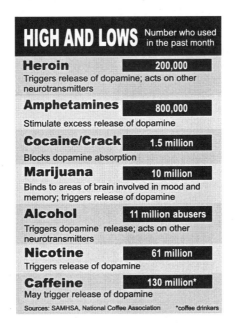

HIGH AND LOWS	Number who used in the past month
Heroin	200,000
Triggers release of dopamine; acts on other neurotransmitters	
Amphetamines	800,000
Stimulate excess release of dopamine	
Cocaine/Crack	1.5 million
Blocks dopamine absorption	
Marijuana	10 million
Binds to areas of brain involved in mood and memory; triggers release of dopamine	
Alcohol	11 million abusers
Triggers dopamine release; acts on other neurotransmitters	
Nicotine	61 million
Triggers release of dopamine	
Caffeine	130 million*
May trigger release of dopamine	

Sources: SAMHSA, National Coffee Association   *coffee drinkers

psychological damage wrought by drugs but in large measure also reverses it.

Genes and social forces may conspire to turn people into addicts but do not doom them to remain so. Consider the case of Rafael Rios, who grew up in a housing project in New York City's drug-infested South Bronx. For 18 years, until he turned 31, Rios, whose father died of alcoholism, led a double life. He graduated from Harvard Law School and joined a prestigious Chicago law firm. Yet all the while he was secretly visiting a shooting "gallery" once a day. His favored concoction: heroin spiked with a jolt

WHAT ELSE?

Preliminary evidence suggests that dopamine may be involved even when we form dependencies on things—like coffee or candy—that we don't think of as drugs at all

of cocaine. Ten years ago, Rios succeeded in kicking his habit—for good, he hopes. He is now executive director of A Safe Haven, a Chicago-based chain of residential facilities for recovering addicts.

How central is dopamine's role in this familiar morality play? Scientists are still trying to sort that out. It is no accident, they say, that people are attracted to drugs. The major drugs of abuse, whether depressants like heroin or stimulants like cocaine, mimic the structure of neurotransmitters, the most mind-bending chemicals nature has ever concocted. Neurotransmitters underlie every thought and emotion, memory and learning; they carry the signals between all the nerve cells, or neurons, in the brain. Among some 50 neurotransmitters discovered to date, a good half a dozen, including dopamine, are known to play a role in addiction.

The neurons that produce this molecular messenger are surprisingly rare. Clustered in loose knots buried deep in the brain, they number a few tens of thousands of nerve cells out of an estimated total of 100 billion. But through long, wire-like projections known as axons, these cells influence neurological activity in many regions, including the nucleus accumbens, the primitive structure that is one of the brain's key pleasure centers. At a purely chemical level, every experience humans find enjoyable—whether listening to music, embracing a lover or savoring chocolate—amounts to little more than an explosion of dopamine in the nucleus accumbens, as exhilarating and ephemeral as a firecracker.

Dopamine, like most biologically important molecules, must be kept within strict bounds. Too little dopamine in certain areas of the brain triggers the tremors and paralysis of Parkinson's disease. Too much causes the hallucinations and bizarre thoughts of schizophrenia. A breakthrough in addiction research came in 1975, when psychologists Roy Wise and Robert Yokel at Concordia University in Montreal reported on the remarkable behavior of some drug-addicted rats. One day the animals were placidly dispensing cocaine and amphetamines to themselves by pressing a lever attached to their cages. The next they were angrily banging at the lever like someone trying to summon a stalled elevator. The reason? The scientists had injected the rats with a drug that blocked the action of dopamine.

In the years since, evidence linking dopamine to drugs has mounted. Amphetamines stimulate dopamine-producing cells to pump out more of the chemical. Cocaine keeps dopamine levels high by inhibiting the activity of a transporter molecule that would ordinarily ferry dopamine back into the cells that produce it. Nicotine, heroin and alcohol trigger a complex chemical cascade that raises dopamine levels. And a still unknown chemical in cigarette smoke, a group led by Brookhaven chemist Joanna Fowler reported last year, may extend the activity of dopamine by blocking a mopping-up enzyme, called MAO B, that would otherwise destroy it.

The evidence that Volkow and her colleagues present in the current issue of *Nature* suggests that dopamine is directly responsible for the exhilarating rush that reinforces the desire to take drugs, at least in cocaine addicts. In all, 17 users participated in the study, says Volkow, and they experienced a high whose intensity was directly related to how extensively cocaine tied up available binding sites on the molecules that transport dopamine around the brain. To produce any high at all, she and her colleagues found, cocaine had to occupy at least 47% of these sites; the "best" results occurred when it took over 60% to 80% of the sites, effectively preventing the transporters from latching onto dopamine and spiriting it out of circulation.

SCIENTISTS BELIEVE THE DOPAMINE system arose very early in the course of animal evolution because it reinforces behaviors so essential to survival. "If it were not for the fact that sex is pleasurable," observes Charles Schuster of Wayne State University in Detroit, "we would not engage in it." Unfortunately, some of the activities humans are neurochemically tuned to find agreeable—eating foods rich in fat and sugar, for instance—have backfired in modern society. Just as a surfeit of food and a dearth of exercise have conspired to turn heart disease and diabetes into major health problems, so the easy availability of addictive chemicals has played a devious trick. Addicts do not crave heroin or cocaine or alcohol or nicotine per se but want the rush of dopamine that these drugs produce.

Dopamine, however, is more than just a feel-good molecule. It also exercises extraordinary power over learning and memory. Think of dopamine, suggests P. Read Montague of the Center for Theoretical Neuroscience at Houston's Baylor College of Medicine, as the proverbial carrot, a reward the brain doles out to networks of neurons for making survival-enhancing choices. And while the details of how this system works are not yet understood, Montague and his colleagues at the Salk Institute in San Diego, California, and M.I.T. have proposed a model that seems quite plausible. Each time the outcome of an action is better than expected, they predicted, dopamine-releasing neurons should increase the rate at which they fire. When an outcome is worse, they should

decrease it. And if the outcome is as expected, the firing rate need not change at all.

As a test of his model, Montague created a computer program that simulated the nectar-gathering activity of bees. Programmed with a dopamine-like reward system and set loose on a field of virtual "flowers," some of which were dependably sweet and some of which were either very sweet or not sweet at all, the virtual bees chose the reliably sweet flowers 85% of the time. In laboratory experiments real bees behave just like their virtual counterparts. What does this have to do with drug abuse? Possibly quite a lot, says Montague. The theory is that dopamine-enhancing chemicals fool the brain into thinking drugs are as beneficial as nectar to the bee, thus hijacking a natural reward system that dates back millions of years.

The degree to which learning and memory sustain the addictive process is only now being appreciated. Each time a neurotransmitter like dopamine floods a synapse, scientists believe, circuits that trigger thoughts and motivate actions are etched onto the brain. Indeed, the neurochemistry supporting addiction is so powerful that the people, objects and places associated with drug taking are also imprinted on the brain. Stimulated by food, sex or the smell of tobacco, former smokers can no more control the urge to light up than Pavlov's dogs could stop their urge to salivate. For months Rafael Rios lived in fear of catching a glimpse of bare arms—his own or someone else's. Whenever he did, he remembers, he would be seized by a nearly unbearable urge to find a drug-filled syringe.

Indeed, the brain has many devious tricks for ensuring that the irrational act of taking drugs, deemed "good" because it enhances dopamine, will be repeated. PET-scan images taken by Volkow and her colleagues reveal that the absorption of a cocaine-like chemical by neurons is profoundly reduced in cocaine addicts in contrast to normal subjects. One explanation: the addicts' neurons, assaulted by abnormally high levels of dopamine, have responded defensively and reduced the number of sites (or receptors) to which dopamine can bind. In the absence of drugs, these nerve cells probably experience a dopamine deficit, Volkow speculates, so while addicts begin by taking drugs to feel high, they end up taking them in order not to feel low.

PET-scan images of the brains of recovering cocaine addicts reveal other striking changes, including a dramatically impaired ability to process glucose, the primary energy source for working neurons. Moreover, this impairment—which persists for up to 100 days after withdrawal—is greatest in the

prefrontal cortex, a dopamine-rich area of the brain that controls impulsive and irrational behavior. Addicts, in fact, display many of the symptoms shown by patients who have suffered strokes or injuries to the prefrontal cortex. Damage to this region, University of Iowa neurologist Antonio Damasio and his colleagues have demonstrated, destroys the emotional compass that controls behaviors the patient knows are unacceptable.

Anyone who doubts that genes influence behavior should see the mice in Marc Caron's lab. These tireless rodents race around their cages for hours on end. They lose weight because they rarely stop to eat, and then they drop from exhaustion because they are unable to sleep. Why? The mice, says Caron, a biochemist at Duke University's Howard Hughes Medical Institute

CRACK

Prolonged cocaine use deadens nerve endings in the brain's pleasure-regulation system. A brain scan of a cocaine abuser shows a marked drop in the number of functioning dopamine receptors

laboratory, are high on dopamine. They lack the genetic mechanism that sponges up this powerful stuff and spirits it away. Result: there is so much dopamine banging around in the poor creatures' synapses that the mice, though drug-free, act as if they were strung out on cocaine.

For years scientists have suspected that genes play a critical role in determining who will become addicted to drugs and who will not. But not until now have they had molecular tools powerful enough to go after the prime suspects. Caron's mice are just the most recent example. By knocking out a single gene—the so-called dopamine-transporter gene—Caron and his colleagues may have created a strain of mice so sated with dopamine that they are oblivious to the allure of cocaine, and possibly alcohol and heroin as well. "What's exciting about our mice," says Caron, "is that they should allow us to test the hypothesis that all these drugs funnel through the dopamine system."

Several dopamine genes have already been tentatively, and controversially, linked to alcoholism and drug abuse. Inherited variations in these genes modify the efficiency

COKE'S HIGH IS DIRECTLY TIED TO DOPAMINE LEVELS

A.A.'S PATH TO RECOVERY STILL SEEMS THE BEST

with which nerve cells process dopamine, or so the speculation goes. Thus, some scientists conjecture, a dopamine-transporter gene that is superefficient, clearing dopamine from the synapses too rapidly, could predispose some people to a form of alcoholism characterized by violent and impulsive behavior. In essence, they would be mirror images of Caron's mice. Instead of being drenched in dopamine, their synapses would be dopamine-poor.

The dopamine genes known as D2 and D4 might also play a role in drug abuse, for similar reasons. Both these genes, it turns out, contain the blueprints for assembling what scientists call a receptor, a minuscule bump on the surface of cells to which biologically active molecules are attracted. And just as a finger lights up a room by merely flicking a switch, so dopamine triggers a sequence of chemical reactions each time it binds to one of its five known receptors. Genetic differences that reduce the sensitivity of these receptors or decrease their number could diminish the sensation of pleasure.

The problem is, studies that have purported to find a basis for addiction in variations of the D2 and D4 genes have not held up under scrutiny. Indeed, most scientists think addiction probably involves an intricate dance between environmental influences and multiple genes, some of which may influence dopamine activity only indirectly. This has not stopped some researchers from promoting the provocative theory that many people who become alcoholics and drug addicts suffer from an inherited condition dubbed the reward-deficiency syndrome. Low dopamine levels caused by a particular version of the D2 gene, they say, may link a breathtaking array of aberrant behaviors. Among them: severe alcoholism, pathological gambling, binge eating and attention-deficit hyperactivity disorder.

The more science unmasks the powerful biology that underlies addiction, the brighter the prospects for treatment become. For instance, the discovery by Fowler and her team that a chemical that inhibits the mopping-up

enzyme MAO B may play a role in cigarette addiction has already opened new possibilities for therapy. A number of well-tolerated MAO B inhibitor drugs developed to treat Parkinson's disease could find a place in the antismoking arsenal. Equally promising, a Yale University team led by Eric Nestler and David Self has found that another type of compound—one that targets the dopamine receptor known as D1—seems to alleviate, at least in rats, the intense craving that accompanies withdrawal from cocaine. One day, suggests Self, a D1 skin patch might help cocaine abusers kick their habit, just as the nicotine patch attenuates the desire to smoke.

Like methadone, the compound that activates D1 appears to be what is known as a partial agonist. Because such medications stimulate some of the same brain pathways as drugs of abuse, they are often addictive in their own right, though less so. And while treating heroin addicts with methadone may seem like a cop-out to people who have never struggled with a drug habit, clinicians say they desperately need more such agents to tide addicts—particularly cocaine addicts—over the first few months of treatment, when the danger of relapse is highest.

REALISTICALLY, NO ONE BELIEVES better medications alone will solve the drug problem. In fact, one of the most hopeful messages coming out of current research is that the biochemical abnormalities associated with addiction can be reversed through learning. For that reason, all sorts of psychosocial interventions, ranging from psychotherapy to 12-step programs, can and do help. Cognitive therapy, which seeks to supply people with coping skills (exercising after work instead of going to a bar, for instance), appears to hold particular promise. After just 10 weeks of therapy, before-and-after PET scans suggest, some patients suffering from obsessive-compulsive disorder (which has some similarities with addiction) manage to resculpt not only their behavior but also activity patterns in their brain.

In late 20th century America, where drugs of abuse are being used on an unprecedented scale, the mounting evidence that treatment works could not be more welcome. Until now, policymakers have responded to the drug problem as though it were mostly a criminal matter. Only a third of the $15 billion the U.S. earmarks for the war on drugs goes to prevention and treatment. "In my view, we've got things upside down," says Dr. David Lewis, director of the Center for Alcohol and Addiction Studies at Brown University School of Medicine. "By relying so heavily on a criminalized approach, we've only added to the stigma of drug abuse and prevented high-quality medical care."

Ironically, the biggest barrier to making such care available is the perception that efforts to treat addiction are wasted. Yet treatment for drug abuse has a failure rate no different from that for other chronic diseases. Close to half of recovering addicts fail to maintain complete abstinence after a year—about the same proportion of patients with diabetes and hypertension who fail to comply with their diet, exercise and medication regimens. What doctors who treat drug abuse should strive for, says Alan Leshner, director of the National Institute on Drug Abuse, is not necessarily a cure but long-term care that controls the progress of the disease and alleviates its worst symptoms. "The occasional relapse is normal," he says, "and just an indication that more treatment is needed."

Rafael Rios has been luckier than many. He kicked his habit in one lengthy struggle that included four months of in-patient treatment at a residential facility and a year of daily outpatient sessions. During that time, Rios checked into 12-step meetings continually, sometimes attending three a day. As those who deal with alcoholics and drug addicts know, such exertions of will power and courage are more common than most people suspect. They are the best reason yet to start treating addiction as the medical and public health crisis it really is.

—With reporting by Alice Park/New York

PASSION PILLS

A NEW CROP OF DESIGNER DRUGS IN THE WORKS WILL ALLOW YOU TO PICK A POTION THAT GUARANTEES GOOD SEX EVEN IF YOU —OR YOUR PARTNER—DON'T MUCH FEEL LIKE IT

BY JUDITH NEWMAN

OK, *so it doesn't look much like a love nest. No candles, no Persian rugs, not one Barry White CD: just a drab hospital room equipped with a Barcalounger.*

But romance—or at least its off-spring, arousal—is what it's all about here at the Women's Sexual Health Clinic at the Boston University School of Medicine. This room is a testing ground for new generations of drugs to treat women who have lost their zest for sex—and therefore, suggest researchers at the center, for life.

Right now, the drug being tested is the one already proven wildly successful for men: Viagra. Here's what happens. A woman takes the blue diamond-shaped pill, then waits the requisite hour for the drug to work. She settles into the reclin-

ing chair and straps on a pair of 3-D glasses. For the next 15 minutes or so, she tunes in to an erotic video created for women (it has a plot), a movie with a title like *Dinner Party II* or *The Bridal Shower*. She is told to use a vibrator to excite herself—doctors are trying to make the conditions of sexual arousal similar from patient to patient. Before long, clinic director Jennifer Berman enters the room.

Berman, whose youth and blond good looks seem better suited to the cat-walk than the science lab, gauges the woman's physiological responses using a variety of special instruments: an ultrasound device that measures blood flow, a pH probe that measures alkalinity, another probe to measure the lengthening and widening of muscle tissues,

and a biothesiometer to determine sensitivity to applied pressure. The preliminary results of this ongoing study reveal that Viagra significantly improves sexual response in some women.

Berman and a handful of other researchers across the country are trying to answer a question that has puzzled humanity since Ovid first suggested onions were aphrodisiacs: What causes passion? And—more important to the pharmaceutical companies investing billions in search of the answer—can it be bottled?

The introduction of Pfizer's Viagra last year ushered in a season of sexual reawakening for millions of men. If clinical trials are successful, Viagra will eventually be made available for women, although Pfizer has yet to announce marketing plans.

A QUESTION HAS PUZZLED HUMANITY SINCE OVID: WHAT CAUSES PASSION?

DRUG TESTING: A LONG AND WINDING ROAD

Wonder why Viagra costs a whopping 10 bucks a pill? Well, consider that a drug can take from three to 10 years to get to market, a gestation period during which expenses inevitably mount up. The new sex drugs must go through several testing stages. Phase I involves preliminary safety tests with healthy humans: Will the drug harm you? In Phase II, manufacturers move on to studies with larger populations to test effectiveness: Does this drug work? Phase III is the stage for double-blind, placebo-controlled studies in which some subjects receive the drug and some don't. This phase is crucial for Food and Drug Administration approval. Even after granting initial approval, the FDA often requires Phase IV as feedback comes in from the general population. "When millions are taking a drug, that's when you're really going to find the problems," says FDA spokesperson Laura Bradbard. –J.N.

DRUG NAME:	SILDENAFIL	PHENTOLAMINE MESYLATE	APOMORPHINE	ESTROGEN/ TESTOSTERONE DERIVATIVE	TESTOSTERONE PATCH	PT-14
BRAND NAME:	MEN: Viagra WOMEN: None yet	MEN: Vasomax Women: Vasofem	MEN: Uprima WOMEN: None yet	WOMEN: Estratest	WOMEN: None yet	MEN: None yet Women: None yet
DELIVERY:	MEN AND WOMEN: Oral tablet	MEN: Oral tablet Women: Likely vaginal suppository	MEN AND WOMEN: Sublingual tablet	WOMEN: Oral tablet	WOMEN: Dermal patch	MEN AND WOMEN: To be determined
WHAT IT DOES:	Enhances blood flow	Enhances blood flow	Enhances blood flow	Boosts libido	Boosts libido	Triggers response through central nervous system
POTENTIAL SIDE EFFECTS:	MEN: Headache, facial flushing, indigestion, hazy light blue vision Women: Unknown	MEN: Nasal congestion, dizziness Women: Unknown	MEN: Nausea WOMEN: Unknown	Nausea	Unknown	MEN AND WOMEN: Yawning and stretching
STATUS:	MEN: Available. Women: In Phase II trials. Earliest availability– several years from now.	MEN: Finished Phase III trials. Earliest availability– late 2000. WOMEN: Phase II trials begin late 1999.	MEN: In Phase III trials. Anticipated availability, mid- year 2000. WOMEN: Phase II trials began July 1999.	Available now for relieving various symptoms of menopause. Additional tests under way for effectiveness as a libido booster.	WOMEN: In Phase II trials. Earliest availability– several years from now.	MEN AND WOMEN: Phase I trials expected to begin in 2000. Earliest availability– several years from now.

In the meantime, numerous new drugs for enhancing sexual function—for both men and women—are in the pipeline. Pharmaceutical companies clearly heard the siren call of Pfizer's sales—$1 billion in one year—and they are answering with a vengeance.

To compete with the 800-pound blue gorilla, the competition must come up with drugs that do what Viagra does— increase blood flow to sex organs—but do it better. Or they must come up with a blockbuster pharmaceutical that does what Viagra definitely doesn't do—create a desire for sex, not just the ability to have it if you already want it.

The likelihood that drug manufacturers will achieve the latter goal is good, so imagine, if you will, pillow talk in the year 2003: *"You're not in the mood? What does that mean?"*

The story of scientific progress is often the story of serendipity, and that is certainly true with the new breed of designer sex drugs in the works. Just as sildenafil, the active ingredient in Viagra, began its life as a treatment for angina, so several of the new sex drugs originally had another use entirely—until some smart person figured out that those frequent erections being reported by test subjects weren't just the result of youth and good health.

Several of the new treatments being tested are, like Viagra, vasodilators. All strive for essentially the same end result of increasing blood flow in the genitals. And it is thought that these vessel dilators work in clitoral tissue just as they do in penile tissue. Each drug company working on a new vasodilator is trying hard to outdo Viagra.

Zonagen's Vasomax apparently works in 15 to 30 minutes, as compared with Viagra's one hour. But only 30 to 40 percent of the men who try Vasomax find it helpful compared with about 70 percent of the men who try Viagra. A female version of Vasomax is also in the works. Testing of Vasofem, which may be formulated as a vaginal suppository rather than a pill, began last December. "We think vaginal delivery will increase blood flow and lubrication," says Jean Anne Mire, a spokesperson for Zonagen.

Apomorphine, another blood vessel dilator, has been used for years to treat tremor-causing Parkinson's disease. It turned out that many male Parkinson's patients experienced an unexpected side effect: improved erections. Apomorphine acts on the central nervous system, helping to send electrical impulses

SEXUAL DYSFUNCTION: THE GENDER GAP

When Pfizer entered the world of impotence treatment with Viagra, there was a consensus on what male sexual dysfunction was," says Irwin Goldstein, a professor of urology at Boston University School of Medicine. "There were outcome parameters. International conferences existed in the field." But for women, says Goldstein, "we couldn't agree on what sexual dysfunction was. What if you can get aroused but can't have an orgasm? What if you can have an orgasm but generally don't get there because you feel no desire in the first place? What if you have three orgasms a week but want three per session?"

In an article submitted to the *Journal of Urology,* Goldstein and 18 leading researchers studying women's sexual response came to a consensus. They define four classes of female sexual dysfunction: lack of desire; inability to be sufficiently aroused, including problems with lubrication and sensation; problems having an orgasm; and sexual pain, including the involuntary contraction of the vaginal muscles and severe genital discomfort.

Given the myriad issues that may confront a woman, the treatment will most likely be more multifaceted than "Take pill. Swallow. Wait."—*J.N.*

from the hypothalamus in the brain down through the spinal cord to increase blood flow to the genitals. Uprima, an apomorphine tablet from TAP Pharmaceuticals Inc., helped 40 to 60 percent of men who tried it in three tests. The tablet is placed under the tongue and works in 15 to 20 minutes. One drawback: It makes some users nauseous.

Tests on women began in July. "Eventually, apomorphine may be taken with Viagra," says Ragab El Rashidy of Pentech Pharmaceuticals, which is producing a sublingual apomorphine tablet for women. "Together, the two drugs should have about an 80 percent effectiveness rate."

With various Viagra copycats about to flood the market, the question for researchers studying female sexual dysfunction is: Will they really work for women? Because vaginal dryness and inability to reach orgasm are often found in women who have vascular disease, there's some reason to believe that insufficient blood supply to a woman's genitals impedes her sex life. So for women whose problem is lack of lubrication or narrowing of the blood vessels, vasodilators may provide some relief. In the United States 43 percent of women experience some form of sexual dysfunction, according to a 1999 survey from the University of Chicago, but they don't all have problems with their blood vessels. Some have problems with their libidos. They'd

rather be doing something altogether different.

Vasodilators like Viagra may restore physical function, but they cannot give a woman a sex drive. That seems to be the job of hormones. Specifically, the hormone we associate with the male sex drive: testosterone.

Certainly Carol Gruwell, a 43-year-old mother from Springfield, Illinois, is convinced. Three years ago she had two children, four dogs, two cats, and a very happy marriage. But her life changed abruptly when severe endometriosis necessitated the removal of her uterus and ovaries. She was catapulted into premature menopause—and complete sexual paralysis. "My husband and I had sex, but I was just going through the motions," she says. "I tried to hide my feelings, but I didn't even feel like being affectionate."

Standard estrogen replacement therapy to prevent hot flashes, mood imbalances, and the atrophying of vaginal tissue was not enough for Gruwell. Eventually, Gruwell's doctor recommended Estratest, a pill from Solvay Pharmaceuticals that combines estrogen and a testosterone derivative. In women, both the ovaries and the adrenal gland secrete minute amounts of testosterone—about 20 times less than the amount secreted by men. But researchers increasingly believe that this smidgen of hormone may be just as responsible for female libido as it is for its male counterpart.

Estratest has been on the market for more than 30 years as an alternative to standard estrogen therapy. But along with a decrease in hot flashes, many patients were reporting an increase in energy and sexual enjoyment. The people at Solvay knew a good thing when they saw it. "About 70 percent of women on estrogen therapy alone discontinue use after one year because their symptoms haven't been relieved or they don't like the side effects," says Roland Gerritsen van der Hoop, head of clinical research and development at Solvay. "Based on prescription renewal figures, loyalty to Estratest is much greater."

And now, no one is more loyal than Carol Gruwell. "At first, it was almost too much." she says. "My nipples became so easily aroused that for the first two weeks just clothing rubbing against me would be a turn-on." After about a year she lowered her dosage from two capsules to one a day, "which is still great but normal."

There is enough promise in hormone therapy so that even consumer goods giant Procter & Gamble is getting in on the act. Testosterone patches have long been available to treat hypogonadism, a condition suffered by millions of American men who do not secrete enough testosterone and generally have little or no sexual desire. In a recent study for Proc-

APOMORPHINE HAS BEEN USED FOR YEARS TO TREAT PARKINSON'S DISEASE. IT TURNED OUT THAT MANY MALE PATIENTS EXPERIENCED AN UNEXPECTED SIDE EFFECT: IMPROVED ERECTIONS.

ter & Gamble and TheraTech Inc., Glenn Braunstein of Cedars-Sinai Medical Center in Los Angeles found that the patches, in smaller doses, restored energy and libido to some women whose testosterone levels were below normal because their ovaries had been removed.

Nobody knows the long-term effects of testosterone replacement. There is concern that increasing testosterone levels in women may heighten the chances of heart disease. One thing is likely: Companies will have to offer different patches with sizably different doses, because women seem to have quite a range of sensitivity to the hormone. Most women, like Gruwell, suffer no ill effects, but testosterone can sometimes cause acne, voice deepening, and hirsutism. So a dose that is one woman's lust producer may be another woman's electrolysis bill.

Perhaps the most startling area of hormone research involves work on PT-14, a peptide molecule derivative of a melanocyte-stimulating hormone that's being investigated by Palatin Technologies. The hormone is naturally present in the body. It has several functions, among them the production of melanin to protect the nuclei of skin cells from the ravages of the sun. Norman Levine, a dermatologist at the University of Arizona Health Sciences Center, was investigating the possibilities of giving the hormone to very fair-skinned people. He noticed that some of his patients were not only getting great suntans but also great erections. Earlier studies had revealed that the hormone, when injected by a catheter into brains of rats, "made the male rat get an erection and elicited a mating position in the female," says Carl Spana, chief technology officer and a researcher for Palatin. In a study completed in May, Levine and a urologist gave PT-14 to ten men with erectile dysfunction and found it helped nine of them. If additional trials go well for men, testing on women should begin in about two years.

Vasodilators require sexual desire to create an erection or vaginal lubrication; testosterone seems to create sexual desire. But a guy on PT-14 can be thinking

NEW DRUGS: THE SCIENTIFIC JACKPOT

The failure rate for scientists struggling to bring new drugs to market is about 95 percent, says Nicholas Terrett, the man dubbed "the father of Viagra" by the British press. Terrett, a bespectacled chemist who works out of Pfizer's Sandwich site in southern England, was part of the team that discovered sildenafil, the active compound in Viagra. "I've had two compounds I discovered go into clinical development but only one to market," says Terrett, who claims he does not regret that his compound has earned hundreds of millions for Pfizer but has not made him personally rich. "Most researchers can be supported by the company for their entire lives and not find anything that comes to market," he says. "Pfizer is one of the most successful companies in the world. And Sandwich is a major part of our discovery efforts. There have been three or four drugs discovered in Sandwich in the last 20 years. You have about 200 chemists and 200 biologists at least. The people who have the good fortune to bring something to market are few and far between." Terrett insists that the process of discovery itself is what gives him the most satisfaction. "There is such aesthetic pleasure in developing a nice new crystalline compound," he says. "Or in taking a compound that's somewhat efficacious, and making it better."

By the way, Terrett knows you must be curious. "Never tried Viagra," the 41-year-old chemist says with a grin. "I hope I never will."—*J.N.*

about his income tax returns and still achieve a level of tumescence a character in a gothic romance novel would be proud of. "Normally, with an erection, as you start to think about sex there's a feedback loop: There's a subset of nerves that get stimulated, and the vessels in the penis undergo vasodilation," says Spana. "With PT-14, if your circulatory system is functioning, you get an erection whether or not you're sexually aroused. There are advantages and disadvantages to this. The drug may be for men who have impotence for purely psychogenic reasons." In other words, there's nothing wrong with their plumbing but the men may have some psychological hang-ups about sex. "But with PT-14," Spana adds, "an erection is pretty much guaranteed."

The fact that we might soon have an arsenal of pharmaceuticals available to treat sexual dysfunction begs a question: Do we need to medicalize yet another fact of nature, that some people don't have as strong a sex drive as others? Weight loss drugs suggest that you are ill—and perhaps irresponsible—if you don't slim down.

Baldness cures suggest there's something abnormal about a shiny pate. Drugs for depression are targeted toward compulsive shoppers and the severely shy. Are we using medicine to shrink diversity in the range of human behavior? And what will we lose if everyone's alike? If Henry James had had a vigorous sex drive, would he have only written greeting cards?

Certainly there is ambivalence among researchers about using medicine for social engineering. "If there's something that can be done to enhance a woman's possibility for reaching her full sexual potential, I'm all for it," says sex therapist Laura Berman, who runs the Women's Sexual Health Clinic at Boston University with her sister Jennifer. "That said, there are a couple of potential backlashes. It's just like antidepressants. A person may suffer from depression for all sorts of good reasons—family problems, death of a loved one—and taking an anti-depressant may relieve the symptoms but not the problems. Well, with drugs for sexual dysfunction, women can use them as Band-Aids and not resolve real issues in their lives—like abusive relationships or

DO WE NEED TO MEDICALIZE THE FACT THAT SOME PEOPLE DON'T HAVE A STRONG SEX DRIVE?

body image problems." In her practice, Berman already has women patients who ask for Viagra—for themselves—as a way of dealing with their husbands' premature ejaculations. Rather than slow the men down, which is easily accomplished without drugs, the women want Viagra to speed themselves up.

Berman also sees a risk that men and women—but especially women—may begin to have unrealistic expectations of their own sexuality. "It's like the prevalence of breast implants has changed our expectation of what a perfect breast should be," she says. "These drugs could do the same thing. Women may begin to think that every orgasm must be super-powerful and super-easy in order to be correct."

Other health specialists fervently disagree. "This isn't about medicalizing—it's about improving our understanding of sexuality, particularly how men's and women's sexuality differ," says Marianne Legato, director of the Partnership for Women's Health at Columbia University in New York who ran a symposium this year on Gender and Human Sexuality in Washington, D.C., which was sponsored by Pfizer and Proctor & Gamble. "We're on a quest for real information about female sexuality. For the most part, sexuality has only been studied in men."

An outgrowth of the symposium was a survey of 500 Americans' attitudes toward human sexuality; 92 percent of the women queried said that sexual enjoyment adds to quality of life at any age, and 60 percent didn't think waning sexual desire should have to be accepted as part of aging.

Carol Gruwell, for one, finds it frustrating that so many women she knows who've had their uteruses or ovaries removed still have not heard about vasodilators to make sex more comfortable or testosterone to make sex more desirable. The doctors who are used to thinking that a man without an erection is not a man are often the same doctors who think that a woman with sex problems is just . . . well, either getting on in years or one of "those" women. "A man gets Viagra and the news is all over the world," says Gruwell. "But women have to fight tooth and nail for this stuff. It aggravates me."

The drug once called speed has come roaring back as a powdery plague on America's heartland. Here, a close look at one place in the grip of . . .

CRANK

By WALTER KIRN
BILLINGS

IT'S A FULL-MOON FRIDAY NIGHT, AND JENnifer, 25, a hardcore loker (smoker of methamphetamine known as crank) has been wide awake around the clock for almost four days. She isn't yet seeing plastic people, shadow men or transparent spiders—just three of the fabled hallucinations of the Billings, Mont., crank scene, a hyperstimulated subculture sickeningly rich in slang and folklore. But she is feeling pangs of remorse about her three-year-old. On Monday, when she left her parents' house, where she has been living since dropping out of college, she promised the daughter she calls "my angel" that Mommy would be right back. Sadly, though, crank squeezes time like an accordion, and since Jennifer swore her solemn maternal oath, approximately 100 hours have passed in a sleepless, virtually food-free blur of hurried parking-lot drug deals, marathon bouts at the video poker machine and frantic cigarette runs to the mini-mart.

Now, perched at the bar of a downtown dance club where her dealer boyfriend ditched her ages ago with just $4 for drinks, Jennifer scratches at her wrists and elbows; her eyes dart from pool table to door; and her butt compulsively scoots around inside her baggy jeans. Crank kills the appetite, just wipes it out, and while many women she knows view this as a selling point, Jennifer doesn't want to lose more weight. Hoping to supplement the child-support check that turns to drugs the day it hits her mailbox, she'd applied for a job as a cocktail waitress, but her meth-shrunken breasts didn't fill the skimpy costume.

"This drug makes you lose everything," she says, gulping a shot of bourbon and root-beer schnapps to calm her freaking neurotransmitters. "I'm not afraid, though. I've

cranked for seven years," Jennifer says. (Her name has been changed by TIME, as have the names and various identifying details of other crank users cited.) "I'm getting pretty used to losing everything."

All over Billings (pop. 91,000), the scappy hub city of the northwestern Great Plains,

> **"How are you going to cut off the supply of something you can produce at home?"**

home to oil refineries, regional medical centers and countless smoke-filled fistfight barrooms where cowboys from Wyoming to South Dakota come for some urban R. and R., people are losing everything to crank—their families, their jobs, their homes, their bank accounts and, perhaps irretrievably, their minds. The potent, man-made stimulant—invented 80 years ago in Japan, issued to soldiers in World War II, prescribed to chunky housewives in the '50s, known to '60s hippies as speed and now sometimes passed out to antsy third-graders with attention-deficit disorder—is, at least in its crum-

bly, powdered street form, an upper that leads straight down.

This isn't the carefully calibrated dose of methamphetamine dispensed by pharmacists in pill form. This is crank—smoked, snorted or injected—and it makes people live like coyotes, says a cop standing outside a southside Billings bungalow while agents from the Drug Enforcement Administration toss the place for drugs. "This town is coming unhinged," another cop says. As if to prove their point, the suspected crank house whose street-side picture windows are sheathed with tinfoil (sunlight is the cranker's natural enemy) starts belching evidence of criminal lunacy—hypodermic needles clogged with meth, automatic pistols of several calibers and an AK-47 with a loaded 100-round clip.

Next come the makings for amateur bombs: jars of gunpowder, lengths of pipe and a homemade blasting cap fashioned from fuse cord and a rifle shell. Given crank's capacity for rendering even casual users clinically psychotic (the transparent spiders weave webs inside the brain after the meth has left one's system), the arsenal is probably unnecessary, real weapons amassed for a figmentary showdown.

Marijuana and cocaine were this city's illegal substances of choice until about four years ago, when a blizzard of crank swept in. "It's pretty much all we deal with now," says Sergeant Tim O'Connell, who heads the city's multiagency drug task force. For law enforcers, methamphetamine is a tough drug to pin down. It's sold hand to hand behind closed doors, in homes and motel rooms, in the style of a Tupperware party. Worse, its production requires little overhead. Ephedrine, an over-the-counter cold medication, can be combined with a shopping list of chemicals easily obtained from stores and industrial-supply companies (common drain cleaners figure in some formulas) and cooked in a kitchen sink from recipes downloaded from the Internet. Billings cops call these homely setups "Beavis and Butt-head labs."

Why crank? And why now? The crank epidemic is new enough, and its mostly white, often rural victims quiet enough, that those questions are just starting to be asked. "The current culture is 'Keep going, keep moving and do it all.' That would be the initial draw, I think," says Nancy Waite-O'Brien, Ph.D., director of psychological services at the Betty Ford Center in Rancho Mirage, Calif. Add to this the wannabe-supermodel factor. "Women," observes Waite-O'Brien, "get into meth because they think it will manage weight. Which I suppose it sometimes does—at first."

AMERICAN DRUG WARRIORS, WELcome to your nightmare—a do-it-yourself guerrilla narcotic spread by paranoid insomniacs who think they see federal agents through every keyhole, even when it's just the Domino's Pizza man. In cities large and small across the West and Midwest crank belt, from Oregon to Iowa, where the drug is known as the poor man's cocaine in towns that barely had cocaine in the first place, the drug arrives nonstop from every direction and by every imaginable route. Wrapped by the ounce and the pound in duct-tape eggs that can be stashed in the air vent of a car, crank comes up the interstate from California and Mexico, where it's produced in massive quantities by organized criminal gangs.

Sometimes it even comes by UPS. In one of Billings' biggest recent crank seizures, O'Connell, wearing the company's brown uniform, intercepted a 5-lb. package at the UPS warehouse one morning (street value: a quarter of a million dollars) and delivered it to the address on the label. The men who answered the doorbell were arrested. Dennis Paxinos, the Yellowstone County attorney, requested that the men's bail be set at $250,000, but the judge involved reduced the sum to a mere $1,000. Paxinos publicly called the decision "asinine." Within a few hours of his release, one of the suspects was back in jail on another charge.

A lot of Billings crank has to travel no farther than across the street, from the apartment building where it's made to the tavern or motel room where it's sold. So pervasive is this bathtub crank that a Billings teenager trying to kick drugs had to quit her job as a hotel maid because she was constantly finding traces of meth in the bathrooms she cleaned. While on assignment for this story, TIME's writer and photographer watched from the lobby of their motel as a notorious Billings crank dealer, facing state charges at the time, received a steady stream of pre-

"This town is coming unhinged."— a Billings cop at the scene of a drug raid

dawn customers in a room directly across the courtyard. ("You know he's in," the night clerk said, "when the phone lines all light up at once.") Approached for an interview about his trade, the wanted man, a tattooed giant on a bed surrounded by a clutch of weary party girls, merely said, "I'm busy. I don't have time now." Last week the alleged dealer was arrested in another Billings motel in a raid that netted several ounces of what police identified as meth. Said a motel employee about her fugitive lodger: "The only problem is that when he leaves, the mirrors in his room are always broken and all the light bulbs are missing." (Lokers without a pipe at hand typically smoke crank from a broken light bulb.)

"How are you going to cut off the supply of something you can produce at home?" asks Mona Sumner, chief operations officer of the Rimrock Foundation, Billings' (and Montana's) largest drug-rehab facility. Sumner, in her 30 years at Rimrock, has seen many a drug craze come and go, but she has never felt this frightened or frustrated. Crank admissions to her facility have tripled in the past four years.

Crank is too cheap, too available, and too addictive, Sumner says. "Honestly, I don't know where it's going." The crankers who show up at the clinic require, on average, four weeks of detox, often with the use of antipsychotic drugs, before the counselors can even get through to them. On a wall in the Rimrock recreation room hangs a homemade poster showing a medevac helicopter like those that land at nearby St. Vincent Hospital. The poster is intended to reassure paranoid recovering crankers, but many are so unstrung that they fear the helicopter is after them.

DELUSIONS ABOUT SINISTER AIRcraft are among the milder symptoms of the Billings area's mounting crank plague. East on Interstate 90, in the town of Livingston, the body of a young woman, Angela Brown, was found rotting in a river, and local law-enforcement officials are investigating a Billings meth connection. A few months earlier, south of Billings, in Hardin, an admittedly cranked-out 17-year-old, Jonathan Wayne Vandersloot, whose head hadn't touched a pillow in

days, allegedly shot dead his sleeping grandparents, scooped up some jewelry, guns and cash, and took off in their pickup. Vandersloot's first trial ended in a hung jury. Prosecutors plan to retry him this fall.

Farther south, crank has decimated the Northern Cheyenne Reservation, populated by descendants of the warriors who routed Custer at the Battle of the Little Big Horn. "Crank will do to the reservations what Custer couldn't," says Bonnie Pipe, clinical director of a tribal recovery center in the town of Lame Deer. When James Walksalong, chairman of the local school board, brought in a team of drug-sniffing dogs last year, kids climbed out of classroom windows, and by the end of the day the dogs had detected 30 instances of drug residue. On reservations throughout Montana and Wyoming, the drug has led to increased domestic abuse, a flurry of audacious daylight burglaries and overloaded medical facilities.

David Morales, a truant officer for Billings School District 2 and a recovering addict, deals with the meth problem too often in the form of 10- and 11-year-olds either on the drug or suffering abuse at the hands of spun-out relatives. "I call them the ghost children," he says. "I see them all the time."

Recently Morales called into his office a beautiful little six-year-old girl who had been missing a lot of school. "I asked her if she needed an alarm clock to help her wake up on time," he recalls, "and all of a sudden she breaks down crying." It seems that under the nose of her allegedly crank-addicted mother, the girl had been raped repeatedly by a teenage relative, a sadistic sort given to dousing his hands in fingernail-polish remover, setting them aflame and then blowing out the fire before he was burned. He warned the girl that he would ignite her if she spoke out. Morales tells of another girl, 11, whose meth-crazed mother prostituted her for a onetime windfall of $360. The girl thought this was normal life, Morales says. Mom needed the money.

The E.R. doctors at Deaconess Billings clinic have their own ugly tales to tell. The crank casualties who appear in the E.R. break down into three basic types, according to Dr. Larry McEvoy, who heads the emergency-medicine department: "First there's the 'I've hit bottom' presentation. They've used for 10 days, haven't eaten or slept and have run out of drugs. They're wiped out, feel heavy and can hardly move. Type 2 is the acute public-disturbance person. They start fighting with people or screaming in the street. Often they're impossible to interview because they're so paranoid. Third are people who use crank a lot and notice that their arms are numb or they're having trouble breathing."

MCEVOY HAS SEEN A RADICAL increase in all three types: "The amounts we see are overwhelming. As a physician, I regard it as the worst possible drug. It really burns people out." And it can do so almost instantly, in McEvoy's experience.

"One night a boy came in so out of control he thought I was the police and the police were trying to kill or kidnap him. He was incredibly violent—biting, slapping, grabbing doctors' private parts. We got hold of his folks and found out he's usually a good student. Even if he does this only once every two years, given his psychotic reaction to the drug, he could end up killing someone.

"I've seen 14-year-old girls with infected arms who have been stuck a bunch of times by people who aren't very good at hitting veins. And I'm frequently surprised by the number of people who don't use it every day but don't feel bad about dabbling in it. They seem to be unaware of the precipice they're hanging over."

Janet Cousrouf, Rimrock's director of nursing, says crank carries with it almost a two-week residue of paranoia. "Since the detox time is longer than most companies are willing to pay for, our biggest problem is insurance."

Cousrouf frankly despairs about the crank plague and in particular its spread from generation to generation. "A lot of the crankers are products of crank mothers, or they have fetal alcohol syndrome. And we're seeing a whole new era of fetal drug syndrome—underdeveloped brain stems, SIDS deaths." Cousrouf believes crank is one of the main culprits in these cases.

But from their sober point of view, doctors and nurses can tell you only so much. The best way to see what crank has done to Billings—and perhaps understand the appeal of a drug made from drain-cleaning crystals—is to spend time with crankers, both active and reformed. A group of them loiter outside the Montana Rescue Mission, a private Christian charity that offers a bed to crash in and, if they choose, a religion-based recovery program, Reality and Christ.

Tom, 24, a husky blond kid who says he has been drug free for 17 days, is fresh out of jail for stealing a handgun he planned to sell for drug cash. The gun belonged to his girlfriend's father, who happened to be a deputy sheriff. "How dumb can you get?" Tom asks. After flashing a driver's license photo to show how much thinner he was in his meth days, Tom effuses about his newfound love of Christ. A few minutes later he reaches into his jeans jacket and pulls out a scorched, homemade glass crank pipe.

"To be honest," he says, "if I had some now, I'd smoke it."

Huddled on the ground against a wall, Justin and Kim, 24 and 18, scoff at Tom's pipe. They're bangers—they shoot their crank—and anyone who does different is crazy, they say. "We've been off it 11 days," says Justin. "I'm trying to get my tolerance back down so it won't take me so much to get spun out," he explains. As narcotics go,

CRANK BREAKDOWN

■ **METHAMPHETAMINE HY-DROCHLORIDE** (a.k.a. crank) can be smoked, injected, snorted or swallowed. It stimulates massive release of the pleasure-causing neurotransmitters adrenaline and dopamine in the brain and inhibits their breakdown

■ **IMMEDIATE EFFECTS** (lasting from 2 to 14 hrs. per dose) include euphoria, sexual arousal, elevated heart rate, tremor, dry mouth, loss of appetite, insomnia and paranoia, followed by agitation and irritability

■ **LONG-TERM EFFECTS** include malnutrition, psychosis, depression, memory loss and possible damage to the heart, brain, lungs and liver

■ **PHARMACEUTICAL VERSIONS** of the drug (Desoxyn Gradumet) are approved for treatment of obesity and attention-deficit disorder

crank is famously cheap—a $20 bundle keeps you buzzing for up to 12 jaw-grinding, heart-pounding hours—but frequent users still have trouble affording it. For one thing, they tend to get grandiose while high. A recovering addict (in his one year of crank use, he went from reigning as high school homecoming king to serving a robbery sentence in a state penitentiary) remembers buying drinks for the house every time he set foot in a strange bar.

When asked how he's staying away from the needle, Justin produces a plastic medicine dropper and pokes his arm with it. "Calms me down," he says. "I quit smoking the same way, by sucking on a crayon." Like so many other Billings geeters—yet one more slang term—Justin is a teller of wild tales. He shows off the sunken veins in his arms and describes how he once had to gaff his shot of crank—inject it straight into his jugular vein—while watching himself in a rearview mirror. "The jugular," he says, nodding earnestly, "the only vein in the body that won't roll over on you."

Hovering in the mission's doorway, a sweatshirt hood drawn over his pale, thin face, is Dracula. That's what the others call him, and he answers to it. Trembling, high and radically withdrawn, Dracula refuses to speak a word, but he does show off an arm full of tattoos. The intricate, dense, almost abstract blue-green filigree seems to say, "This is your brain on crank." The next show-and-tell item is the eyeglass case in which Dracula keeps his syringe and razor

blade. The case's interior is obsessively decoupaged with tiny, interlocking pictures snipped from magazines.

Dracula is a great artist, Justin says, and if art is defined as manic pattern-making for no apparent purpose, he's right.

Across town, at a table in the modest apartment where she supposes she'll have to go on living until she finds a job, Alicia is quitting crank. Once an upwardly mobile employee of a FORTUNE 500 company based in a large Southwestern city, Alicia is in her mid-30s but looks 50. Her face is pocked and pitted from her attempts to pick out the crystals of methamphetamine that, she swears, used to form under her skin. Alicia moved to Montana several years ago in hopes of escaping the bigger city's crank scene. She says the subcutaneous crystals aren't a problem now; the Billings meth is not so pure. Not that it matters, because she's quitting.

Tomorrow.

Right now, however, she's lighting one last pipeful in a ritual as intricate as a Japanese tea ceremony. She ignites a propane torch and holds the blue flame beneath the smudge of powder in her clear glass pipe. Crank is smoked differently than crack cocaine; it takes less heat and melts instantly (burning away the impurities, Alicia says). Once the drug vaporizes in a white cloud, Alicia inhales. She then repeats the process. The residues in the pipe, called frosties, are infinitely valuable to crankers, and Alicia keeps torching them until they're gone.

But such solitary crank use isn't the norm in Billings. Crank is a party drug here, a social thing, smoked, injected and snorted by tight-knit groups holed up in houses behind blacked-out windows, talking nonstop about their hopes and dreams and smoking a joint now and then or drinking a beer to mellow out the high.

"You think you're with your best friends in the whole world," remembers the toppled homecoming king. "You stay up all night saying things like 'Man, I'd die for you,' and then in the morning everybody crashes and you realize you hate these people. They disgust you."

Paula, 19, who has been clean for six months following a stay at Rimrock, remembers crank parties as surreal blendings of light and darkness, reality and dreams. "The sun goes up and down and you lose track, and pretty soon you're hearing laughs and whispers and seeing things dart around on the floor. Then the other people turn into monsters."

Boyish, sardonic and stunningly intelligent, Paula, who has never been anywhere else, calls Billings the crank capital of the universe: "The people in my neighborhood all learned crank from their parents. I mostly hung out with 13- and 14- year-olds. It's getting younger and younger every year."

"I call them ghost children. I see them all the time."—David Morales

Part of crank's appeal to Paula, and apparently to most users, is that it helped her get things done. It made her feel capable, on top of things. She could party into the wee hours (often having sex with virtual strangers because, as she puts it, once you've stayed up all night with someone, you feel pretty close to them), go to work the next day, then come home and clean her room. "I even started depending on it to go to school," she says.

THEN CAME WHAT PAULA CLAIMS WAS A three-month-long, nearly sleepless crank run that left her homeless, expelled from school and seeing ghouls behind every tree. Crankers tend to exaggerate, but her memories of the streak have that patented methamphetamine exactitude. "I knew I had to get nutrition, so every day I had a pudding snack, an applesauce and a little carton of milk," she says.

Her diet wasn't all so wholesome, though. "Also, I was smoking tons of pot just to calm my nerves."

For Jennifer, the conscience-stricken mother, the party's still not over. Another crank-warped week has passed; another Friday night has rolled around; and though she's thinner, paler and less coherent, she's feeling considerably richer owing to the arrival this morning of her monthly child-support check. Swaying nautically on her favorite barstool, she reports that she has made some changes in her life in the past few days. She's moved out of her parents' place, leaving her daughter behind, and has taken up residence in a rented house with two male roommates who share her taste for meth and, unlike her family, don't "make me feel guilty every time they look at me."

That's where the party continues when the bars close. The tiny house, across the tracks and across the freeway, is supernaturally tidy. In the spotless kitchen, at a spotless table next to a box filled with hundreds of empty beer cans all conscientiously rinsed and crushed (when crankers decide to clean house, they clean house), Jennifer and her roommates smoke and jabber while clock hands turn from 3 to 4 to 5. The oldest roommate—his fortyish, gaunt face so stiff and lifeless it looks taxidermied—veers from a fond recollection of a camping trip to a paranoid rant about "hidden cameras" and warnings to TIME's photographer and reporter that "we know how to protect ourselves in this house."

With daybreak nearing, disaster strikes. Jennifer discovers she has lost her purse, child-support check and all. A panic ensues. The house is searched, and the driveway. Someone hatches a plan to drive downtown and retrace Jennifer's steps, which won't be easy. "Where did you leave it?" her friends keep asking, but she just sighs and insists she can't remember.

Probably the same place she left her looks, her education, her jobs, her little angel. Somewhere out there in crank city, in the dark—a dark that, no matter how hard Jennifer tries to stop it, always turns to dawn.

—With reporting by Patrick Dawson on the Northern Cheyenne Reservation

More Reefer Madness

by ERIC SCHLOSSER

Marijuana gives rise to insanity—not in its users but in the policies directed against it. A nation that sentences the possessor of a single joint to life imprisonment without parole but sets a murderer free after perhaps six years is, the author writes, "in the grip of a deep psychosis"

EIGHT years ago Douglas Lamar Gray bought a pound of marijuana in a room at the Econo Lodge in Decatur, Alabama. He planned to keep a few ounces for himself and sell the rest to some friends. Gray was a Vietnam veteran with an artificial leg. As a young man, he'd been convicted of a number of petty crimes, none serious enough to warrant a prison sentence. He had stayed out of trouble for a good thirteen years. He now owned a business called Gray's Roofing and Remodeling Service. He had a home, a wife, and a two-year-old son. The man who sold him the drug, Jimmy Wilcox, was a felon just released from prison, with more than thirty convictions on his record. Wilcox was also an informer employed by the Morgan County Drug Task Force. The pound of marijuana had been supplied by the local sheriff's department, as part of a sting. After paying Wilcox $900 for the pot, which seemed like a real bargain, Douglas Lamar Gray was arrested and charged with "trafficking in cannabis." He was tried, convicted, fined $25,000, sentenced to life in prison without parole, and sent to the maximum-security penitentiary in Springville, Alabama—an aging, overcrowded prison filled with murderers and other violent inmates. He remains there to this day. Under the stress of his imprisonment Gray's wife attempted suicide with a pistol, survived the gunshot, and then filed for divorce. Jimmy Wilcox, the informer, was paid $100 by the county for his services in the case.

Gray's punishment, although severe, is by no means unusual in the United States. The laws of at least fifteen states now require life sentences for certain nonviolent marijuana offenses. In Montana a life sentence can be imposed for growing a single marijuana plant or selling a single joint. Under federal law the death penalty can be imposed for growing or selling a large amount of marijuana, even if it is a first offense.

The rise in marijuana use among American teenagers became a prominent issue during last year's presidential campaign, fueled by Republican accusations that President Bill Clinton was "soft on drugs." Teenage marijuana use has indeed grown considerably since 1992; by one measure it has doubled. But that increase cannot be attributed to any slackening in the enforcement of the nation's marijuana laws. In fact, the number of Americans arrested each year for marijuana offenses has increased by 43 percent since Clinton took office. There were roughly 600,000 marijuana-related arrests nationwide in 1995—an all-time record. More Americans were arrested for marijuana offenses during the first three years of Clinton's presidency than during any other three-year period in the nation's history. More Americans are in prison today for marijuana offenses than at any other time in our history. And yet teenage marijuana use continues to grow.

The war on drugs, launched by President Ronald Reagan in 1982, began as an assault on marijuana. Its effects are now felt throughout America's criminal-justice system. In 1980 there were almost twice as many violent offenders in federal prison as drug offenders. Today there are far more people in federal prison for marijuana crimes than for violent crimes. More people are now incarcerated in the nation's prisons for marijuana than for manslaughter or rape.

In an era when the fear of violence pervades the United States, small-time pot dealers are being given life sentences while violent offenders are being released early, only to commit more crimes. The federal prison system and thirty-eight state prison systems are now operating above their rated capacity. Attempts to reduce dangerous prison overcrowding have been hampered by the nation's drug laws. Prison cells across the country are filled with nonviolent drug offenders whose mandatory-minimum sentences do not allow for parole. At the same time, violent offenders are routinely being granted early release. A recent study by the Justice Department found that in 1992 violent offenders on average were released after serving less than half of their sentences. A person convicted of murder in the United States could expect a punishment of less than six years in prison. A person convicted of kidnapping could expect about four years. Another Justice Department study revealed that almost a third of all violent offenders who are released from prison will be arrested for another violent crime within three years. No one knows how many violent crimes these released inmates commit without ever being caught. In 1992 the average punishment for a violent offender in the United States was forty-three months in prison. The average punishment, under federal law, for a marijuana offender that same year was about fifty months in prison.

Even legislation aimed at reducing violent crime has been subverted by the legal underpinnings of the drug war. According to a report by the Center on Juvenile and Criminal Justice, California's much-heralded "three strikes, you're out" law has imprisoned twice as many people for marijuana offenses as for murder, rape, and kidnapping combined.

The vehemence of marijuana's opponents and the harsh punishments routinely administered to marijuana offenders cannot be explained by a simple concern for public health. Paraplegics, cancer patients, epileptics, people with AIDS, and people suffering from multiple sclerosis have in recent years been imprisoned for using marijuana as medicine. The attack on marijuana, since its origins early in this century, has in reality been a cultural war—a moral crusade in defense of traditional American values. The laws used to fight marijuana are now causing far more harm to those values than the drug itself. In order to eliminate marijuana use, state and federal legislators have sanctioned an enormous increase in prosecutorial power, the emergence of a class of professional informers, and the widespread confiscation of private property by the government without trial—legal weapons reminiscent of those used in the former Soviet-bloc nations. The long prison sentences given to growers and dealers have pushed marijuana prices skyward, creating a domestic industry whose annual revenues now rival those of cotton, soybeans, or corn. U.S. public officials, like their counterparts in Mexico, Colombia, and Bolivia, are being corrupted with drug money. Millions of ordinary Americans have been arrested for marijuana offenses in the past decade, and hundreds of thousands have been imprisoned, yet marijuana use is increasing and has regained its status as a symbol of youthful rebellion. Instead of debating the wisdom of our current policies, members of Congress and of the Administration are competing to see who can appear toughest on drugs. For years the war on drugs has been driven by political concerns, without regard to its consequences. But at the state and local levels, where the costs of that war are most keenly felt and unlikely alliances have begun to form, there are signs that madness may give way to common sense.

The Legacy of Len Bias

THE 1986 Anti-Drug Abuse Act marked a profound shift not only in America's drug-control policy but also in the workings of its criminal-justice system. The bill greatly increased the penalties for federal drug offenses. More important, it established mandatory-minimum sentences, transferring power from federal judges to prosecutors. The mandatory minimums were based not on an individual's role in a crime but on the quantity of drugs involved. Judges in such cases could no longer reduce a prison term out of mercy or compassion. Prosecutors were given the authority to decide whether a mandatory-minimum sentence applied.

This new law did not represent the culmination of a careful deliberative process. Nor did it reflect the thinking of the nation's best legal minds. The mandatory-minimum provisions were written and enacted in a matter of weeks without a single public hearing. The most important drug legislation in a generation—the enforcement of which would more than triple the size of the federal-prison population and whose sentencing philosophy would influence state drug laws across the country—was prompted by the death of a popular basketball player shortly before a congressional election.

Len Bias was a local hero in Washington, D.C., clean-cut and all-American, a University of Maryland basketball star who had been drafted by the Boston Celtics at the age of twenty-two. On June 17, 1986, Bias attended a ceremony in Boston to sign a contract with the Celtics. Two days later he died of heart failure, allegedly caused by crack cocaine. When Speaker of the House Tip O'Neill returned to Boston for the Fourth of July congressional recess, everyone seemed to be talking about the death of the Celtics' first-round draft pick. As fears of crack cocaine swept the nation, O'Neill grew worried that the Democratic Party might be labeled soft on drugs. He returned to Washington in mid-July determined to pass an omnibus drug-control bill before the upcoming election. The legislation had to be drafted within a month. Eric E. Sterling, who was then the assistant counsel for the House Subcommittee on Crime, recently told me that staff members scrambled to assemble a bill. The process of selecting drug quantities to trigger the mandatory-minimum sentences was far from scientific, according to Sterling: "Numbers were being picked out of thin air."

The drug-control bill left the subcommittee in mid-August, while many academics and government officials were away on vacation. There had been little time to study the potential costs of the legislation or its ramifications for the criminal-justice system. In the absence of public hearings there had been no input from federal judges, prison authorities, or drug-abuse experts. President and Mrs. Reagan were calling for tough new drug-control measures, and House Democrats rushed to provide them. Only sixteen congressmen voted against the bill, which passed in the Senate by a voice vote. Reagan signed the final version of the bill on October 27, just a week before Election Day.

In *Smoke and Mirrors*, which was published last year, Dan Baum, a former *Wall Street Journal* reporter, gives a definitive account of the politics surrounding Reagan's war on drugs. Conservative parents' groups opposed to marijuana had helped to ignite the Reagan Revolution. Marijuana symbolized the weakness and permissiveness of a liberal society; it was held responsible for the slovenly appearance of teenagers and their lack of motivation. Carlton Turner, Reagan's first drug czar, believed that marijuana use was inextricably linked to "the present young-adult generation's involvement in anti-military, anti-nuclear power, anti-big business, anti-authority demonstrations." A public-health approach to drug control was replaced by an emphasis on law enforcement. Drug abuse was no longer considered a form of illness; all drug use was deemed immoral, and punishing drug offenders was thought to be more important than getting them off drugs. The drug war soon became a bipartisan effort, supported by liberals and conservatives alike. Nothing was to be gained politically by defending drug abusers from excessive punishment.

Drug-control legislation was proposed, almost like clockwork, during every congressional-election year in

POLITICIANS ARE REFUSING TO ADMIT

THE TRUE COST OF THE NATION'S DRUG LAWS. "WE'RE NOT BEING HONEST TO THE PUBLIC OR TO OURSELVES," SAYS STEWART J. GREENLEAF, A PENNSYLVANIA STATE SENATOR WHO WROTE A TOUGH DRUG-SENTENCES LAW THAT HAS FLOODED HIS STATE'S PRISONS WITH LOW-LEVEL OFFENDERS WHO CANNOT BE PAROLED. "THESE LAWS JUST HAVEN'T WORKED AS WE PLANNED."

the 1980s. Election years have continued to inspire bold new drug-control schemes. On September 25 of last year Speaker of the House Newt Gingrich introduced legislation demanding either a life sentence or the death penalty for anyone caught bringing more than two ounces of marijuana into the United States. Gingrich's bill attracted twenty-six co-sponsors, though it failed to reach the House floor. A few months earlier Senator Phil Gramm had proposed denying federal welfare benefits, including food stamps, to anyone convicted of a drug

crime, even a misdemeanor. Gramm's proposal was endorsed by a wide variety of senators—including liberals such as Barbara Boxer, Tom Harkin, Patrick Leahy, and Paul Wellstone. A revised version of the amendment, limiting the punishment to people convicted of a drug felony, was incorporated into the welfare bill signed by President Clinton during the presidential campaign. Possessing a few ounces of marijuana is a felony in most states, as is growing a single marijuana plant. As a result, Americans convicted of a marijuana felony, even if they are disabled, may no longer receive federal welfare or food stamps. Convicted murderers, rapists, and child molesters, however, will continue to receive these benefits.

Forfeitures and Informers

FEDERAL prosecutors now have an extraordinary amount of power in drug cases. A U.S. attorney can determine the eventual punishment for a drug offense by deciding what quantity of drugs to list in the indictment, whether a mandatory-minimum sentence should apply, and whether to press charges at all. Drug offenses differ from most crimes in being subject to federal, state, and local laws. The federal government could prosecute any and every marijuana offender in the United States if it so desired, but in a typical year it charges fewer than one percent of those arrested. By choosing to enter a particular case, a federal prosecutor can greatly affect the penalty for a marijuana crime. In 1985 Donald Clark, a Florida watermelon farmer, was arrested for growing marijuana, convicted under state law, and sentenced to probation. Five years later the local U.S. attorney decided to prosecute Donald Clark under federal law for exactly the same crime. Clark was found guilty and sentenced to life in prison without parole. A Justice Department spokesman quoted in *Smoke and Mirrors* later defended the policy of trying drug offenders twice for the same crime: "The intent is to get the bad guys off the street with apologies to none."

"Under civil forfeiture statutes passed by Congress in the 1980s, the federal government now has the right to seize real estate, vehicles, cash, securities, jewelry, and any other property connected to a marijuana offense. The government need not prove that the property was bought with the proceeds of illegal drug sales, only that it was used—or was intended to be used—in a crime. A yacht can be seized if a single joint is discovered on it. A farm can be seized if a single marijuana plant is found growing there. According to Steven B. Duke, a professor at Yale Law School, in some cases a house can be seized if it contains books on marijuana cultivation. The U.S. Supreme Court ruled last year that the government can seize property even when its owner had no involvement in, or knowledge of, the crime that was committed. When property is seized, its legal title passes instantly to the government. The burden of proving its "innocence" falls upon the original owner. In 1994 assets worth roughly $1.5 billion were forfeited under state and federal laws. In perhaps 80 percent of those cases the owner was never charged with a crime. The forfeiture statutes have deepened the injustice of the war on drugs by enabling wealthy defendants to surrender property in return for shorter sentences; plea-bargain negotiations often turn into haggling sessions worthy of a Middle Eastern souk.

The proceeds from an asset forfeiture are divided among the law-enforcement agencies involved in the case, a policy that invites the abuse of power. Former Justice Department officials have admitted in newspaper interviews that many forfeitures are driven by the need to meet budget projections. The guilt or innocence of a defendant has at times been less important than the availability of his or her assets. In California thirty-one state and federal drug agents raided Donald P. Scott's 200-acre Malibu ranch on the pretext that marijuana was growing there. Scott was inadvertently killed during the raid. No evidence of marijuana cultivation was discovered, and a subsequent investigation by the Ventura County District Attorney's Office found that the drug agents had been motivated partly by a desire to seize the $5 million ranch. They had obtained an appraisal of the property weeks before the raid. In New Jersey, Nicholas L. Bissell Jr., a local prosecutor known as the Forfeiture King, helped an associate to buy land seized in a marijuana case for a small fraction of its market value. In Connecticut, Leslie C. Ohta, a federal prosecutor known as the Queen of Forfeitures, seized the house of Paul and Ruth Derbacher when their twenty-two-year-old grandson was arrested for keeping marijuana there. Although the Derbachers were in their eighties, had owned the house for almost forty years, and had no idea that their grandson kept pot in his room, Ohta insisted upon forfeiture of the house. People should know, she argued, what goes on in their own home. Not long after, Ohta's eighteen-year-old son was arrested for selling LSD from her Chevrolet Blazer. Allegedly, he had also sold marijuana from her house in Glastonbury. Ohta was quickly transferred out of the U.S. attorney's forfeiture unit—but neither her car nor her house was seized by the government.

The only way a defendant can be sure of avoiding a mandatory-minimum sentence under federal law is to plead guilty and give "substantial assistance" in the prosecution of someone else. The willingness to turn informer has become more important to a drug offender's fate than his or her role in a crime. The U.S. attorney, not the judge, decides whether the defendant's cooperation is sufficient to warrant a reduction of the sentence. Although this system helps to avoid expensive trials and provides evidence for future indictments, it also leads to longer prison terms for the minor participants in a drug case. Kingpins have a great deal of information to provide, whereas drug couriers often have none.

A little-known provision of the forfeiture laws rewards confidential informers with up to 25 percent of the assets seized as a result of their testimony. During the 1980s the United States developed a wealthy and industrious class of professional informers. In 1985 the federal government spent $25 million on informers. Last year it spent more than $100 million.

Informing on others has become not just a way to avoid punishment but a way of life. In major drug cases an informer can earn a million dollars or more. A recent investigation by the National Law Journal found that the proportion of federal search warrants relying exclusively on unidentified informers nearly tripled from 1980 to 1993, increasing from 24 percent to 71 percent. The growing reliance on informers has given an unprecedented degree of influence to criminals who have a direct financial interest in gaining convictions. Informers have been caught framing innocent people. Law-enforcement agents have been caught using nonexistent informers to justify search warrants.

"Criminals are likely to say and do almost anything to get what they want," Stephen S. Trott, a federal judge who was the chief of the Justice Department's Criminal Division during the Reagan years, says in the National Law Journal. "This willingness to do anything includes not only truthfully spilling the beans on friends and relatives but also lying, committing perjury, manufacturing evidence, soliciting others to corroborate their lies with more lies, and double-crossing anyone with whom they come into contact, including—and especially—the prosecutor."

The legal and monetary rewards for informing on others have even spawned a whole new business: the buying and selling of drug leads. Defendants who hope to avoid a lengthy mandatory-minimum sentence but who have no valuable information to give prosecutors can now secretly buy information from vendors on the black market. According to Tom Dawson, a prominent Kansas defense attorney, some professional informers now offer their services to defendants in drug cases for fees of up to $250,000.

Most of the people being imprisoned for marijuana offenses are ordinary Americans without important information to provide, large assets to trade, or the income to pay for high-priced attorneys. Allen St. Pierre, the deputy director of the National Organization for the Reform of Marijuana Laws, has spoken to literally thousands of people who have been arrested for pot-related offenses. He receives about a hundred phone calls each week from people who are losing their jobs, losing their houses, feeling desperate for advice. They tend to be working people: house painters, clerks, carpenters, and mechanics. Their cases tend to be handled, or mishandled, by family attorneys with little knowledge of the marijuana laws. America's prisons are full of poor and working-class marijuana offenders.

Children of the upper middle class are rarely sent to prison for marijuana offenses today. Their parents usually enroll them in private drug-treatment programs before trial and hire attorneys who specialize in drug cases. Privileged young men and women are usually treated more leniently in court. The daughter of Judge Rudolph Slate, the man who sentenced Douglas Lamar Gray to life for buying a pound of marijuana, was later arrested for selling the drug. She was granted youthful-offender status. The records in her case have been sealed; most likely she received probation. The son of Indiana Congressman Dan Burton, an outspoken proponent of life sentences for some marijuana-related crimes, was arrested for transporting nearly eight pounds of pot from Louisiana to Indiana in the trunk of his car. Six months later Danny L. Burton II was arrested again, this time at his Indianapolis apartment, where police found thirty marijuana plants and a shotgun with six shells. Federal prosecutors declined to press charges against Burton's son; Indiana prosecutors gained dismissal of the charges against him; and a Louisiana judge sentenced him to community service, probation, and house arrest. As chairman of the House Government Reform and Oversight Committee, Burton is now leading the investigation of ethical lapses in the Clinton Administration. He will not comment on his son's case.

The harshest punishments are given to people who won't cooperate with the government. The pressure to inform on others is immense—as is the cost of resisting it. In 1993 Jodie Israel was arrested for marijuana possession and balked at testifying against her husband, a Rastafarian marijuana trafficker. Federal prosecutors in Montana threatened her with a long prison sentence. Although Israel possessed only eight ounces of marijuana at the time of her arrest, under the broad federal conspiracy laws she could be held liable for many of her husband's crimes. Israel was thirty-one years old, the mother of four young children. She had never before been charged with any crime. Judge Jack Shanstrom warned her in court that without a promise of cooperation "you are not going to see your children for ten plus years." Nevertheless, Israel refused to testify against her husband. She was sentenced to eleven years in federal prison without parole. Her husband was sentenced to twenty-nine years without parole. Her children were scattered among various relatives.

"A Matter of Practicality"

I N 1988 State Senator Stewart J. Greenleaf wrote the bill that made tough mandatory-minimum drug sentences part of Pennsylvania law. Greenleaf, a Republican from rural Montgomery County, is now the chairman of the Senate Judiciary Committee in Pennsylvania—and an outspoken critic of mandatory-minimum sentences. "These laws just haven't worked as we planned," he now admits. Politicians are refusing to acknowledge

the true cost of the nation's drug laws. "We're not being honest," Greenleaf says, "to the public or to ourselves."

In adopting mandatory-minimum sentences, Pennsylvania had simply followed the federal government's lead, aiming to give long prison terms to major drug dealers. Instead the state's prisons have been flooded with low-level drug offenders who cannot be paroled. Over the past decade the state's prison population has doubled. Its prison system is now operating at 54 percent above capacity. In order to keep pace with the current rate of incarceration, Pennsylvania will have to open a new prison every ninety days. Each new prison cell costs about $110,000 to build and about $25,000 a year to main-

POT DEALERS ARE BEING GIVEN LIFE

SENTENCES WHILE VIOLENT OFFENDERS ARE BEING RELEASED EARLY. IN 1980 THERE WERE ALMOST TWICE AS MANY VIOLENT OFFENDERS IN FEDERAL PRISON AS DRUG OFFENDERS. TODAY THERE ARE FAR MORE PEOPLE IN FEDERAL PRISON FOR MARIJUANA CRIMES THAN FOR VIOLENT CRIMES. MORE PEOPLE ARE NOW INCARCERATED FOR MARIJUANA THAN FOR MANSLAUGHTER OR RAPE.

tain. At the moment nearly 70 percent of the inmates in Pennsylvania's prisons are nonviolent offenders. Convicted murderers granted early release have gone on a number of well-publicized killing sprees. "Expensive prison space must be held for those who are truly violent or career criminals," Greenleaf has come to believe. "This problem has transcended party lines and social ideologies; it is a matter of practicality and fiscal responsibility."

As prisons become more and more overcrowded, state legislators across the country are exploring a wide range of alternative sentences. At least half a dozen states now allow low-level drug offenders to avoid prison terms by entering drug-treatment programs. In Pennsylvania, where perhaps 80 percent of all crimes are being committed by either alcohol or drug abusers, the state District Attorneys Association and the local chapter of the American Civil Liberties Union both advocate emphasizing substance-abuse treatment rather than imprisonment. Greenleaf favors treatment programs, intensive probation, and ninety-day "shock incarceration" in jail or boot camps for most drug offenders—alternatives that are far less expensive than sending people to prison. Although he worries about the political fallout from his stance, he will not budge. "We have to be smart about whom we incarcerate," Greenleaf says, "and not waste taxpayers' money."

The trend toward alternative sentences for drug offenders has lately gained support in some unexpected quarters. Arizona's recently passed Proposition 200 not only allows the medicinal use of marijuana but also has reformed the state's approach to drug control. Since the early 1980s Arizona had aggressively pursued a drug strategy of "zero tolerance," administering harsh punishments for illegal drug use, not just for drug trafficking and possession. Failing a urine test was grounds for prosecution in Arizona: a person could face criminal charges in Phoenix for a joint smoked in Philadelphia days or even weeks before. Arizona's prisons grew overcrowded, and tent cities rose in the desert to house inmates. Proposition 200 declared that "drug abuse is a public health problem" and vowed to "medicalize" the state's drug-control policy. In order to free up prison cells for violent offenders, the initiative called for the immediate release of all nonviolent prisoners who had been convicted of drug possession or use. It called for drug treatment, drug education, and community service instead of prison terms for nonviolent minor drug offenders. And it called for the creation of a state Drug Treatment and Education Fund through an increased tax on alcohol and tobacco. Proposition 200 was endorsed by aging hippies, former members of the Reagan Administration, the retired Democratic senator Dennis DeConcini, and the retired Republican senator Barry Goldwater, among others. On Election Day, Arizona voters backed the initiative by a margin of two to one. But the Clinton Administration attacked Proposition 200 as though it were a dangerous heresy, threatening to block its implementation and to prosecute any physicians who recommend marijuana to their patients. Clinton's drug czar, Barry McCaffrey, called the Arizona initiative a subterfuge, part of "a national strategy to legalize drugs."

While the Administration escalates the war on marijuana, law-enforcement officers on the front lines are beginning to question some of its tactics. Steve White served with the Drug Enforcement Administration and its predecessor, the Bureau of Narcotics and Dangerous Drugs, for twenty-eight years before his retirement, last year. Twenty-three of those years were spent working undercover in Indiana, mainly tracking down marijuana growers. Under White's leadership the Cannabis Eradication Program arrested more pot growers every year in Indiana than were arrested in just about any other state. White strongly condemns marijuana use and gives anti-drug lectures at high schools. But he opposes the long prison terms that first-time marijuana growers now receive. "I'm a big advocate of alternative sentencing," he says. "For most pot growers, prison isn't the answer. These aren't violent people. They usually have jobs, and homes, and children. Why make their families a burden to the community?" White has learned over the years that marijuana growers come from all sorts of backgrounds and possess a variety of skills. "Put them to work, make them do community service," he suggests. "Prison terms only strengthen their anti-establishment views." Most commercial marijuana growers will quit the business after being caught once or twice. White feels little sympathy, however, for the unrepentant growers who are motivated by big money and the thrill of breaking the law. After a third conviction for large-scale marijuana cultivation, he thinks, alternative sentences should no longer apply. "Make prison a real pleasant place," White says, "and keep those guys in there forever."

The long prison sentences now given to marijuana offenders have turned marijuana—a hardy weed that grows wild in all fifty states—into a precious commodity. Some marijuana is currently worth more per ounce than gold. A decade ago the policy analysts Peter Reuter and Mark A. R. Kleiman observed that the price of an illegal drug is determined not only by its supply, demand, and production costs but also by the legal risks of selling it. As the risks increase, so does the profit. This theory has been supported by the huge rise in marijuana prices since the latest war on drugs began. In 1982 the street price for an ounce (adjusted for inflation) was about $75. By 1992 it had reached about $325. Although the costs of cultivating marijuana rose somewhat during that period, most of the 333 percent price increase represented sheer profit—the reward for evading punishment. The legal risks of cultivation have encouraged growers to produce much more potent strains of the drug, which bring a higher price and require a lower volume of sales. Growers have also found another means of reducing their risk: bribery. Throughout the nation's rural heartland local sheriffs are being paid to look the other way during the marijuana harvest. Even local prosecutors and judges are being corrupted by drug money. The large profit margins transformed U.S. marijuana cultivation in the 1980s from a fringe economic activity into a multibillion-dollar industry—despite the fact that marijuana use was falling at the time. In Indiana the value of the annual marijuana crop now rivals that of corn. In Alabama it rivals that of cotton. The threat of long prison sentences has succeeded in making some marijuana growers rich, but it has hardly affected the availability of pot. In 1982, when President Reagan declared his war on drugs, 88.5 percent of America's high school seniors said that it was "fairly easy" or "very easy" for them to obtain marijuana. In 1994 the proportion of seniors who said they could easily obtain it was 85.5 percent.

The Benefits of Decriminalization

HARRY J. Anslinger headed the Federal Bureau of Narcotics during the 1930s and supervised the campaign to make marijuana illegal under state and federal laws. In "Marijuana: Assassin of Youth" and similar articles Anslinger led readers to believe that the drug rendered its users homicidal, suicidal, and insane. Amid the anxieties of the Great Depression, marijuana use was linked to poor Mexicans and blacks, "inferior" races whose alleged sexual promiscuity and violence stemmed partly from smoking pot. "The dominant race and most enlightened countries are alcoholic," one opponent of marijuana use claimed, expressing a widely held belief, "whilst the races and nations addicted to hemp ... have deteriorated both mentally and physically." Marijuana was the "killer weed," a foreign influence on American life that was capable of transforming healthy teenagers into sex-crazed maniacs. Anslinger later admitted to the historian David F. Musto that the FBN had somewhat exaggerated the dangers of marijuana. Anslinger had hoped to make marijuana seem so awful and so terrifying that young people would be afraid to try it even once.

Marijuana's "un-American" reputation has made it immensely appealing to rebellious, disaffected youth. Lurid propaganda films like *Reefer Madness*, *Devil's Harvest*, and *Marijuana: Weed With Roots in Hell*, which promised a glimpse of not only the horrors but also the "weird orgies" caused by the drug, no doubt encouraged more than one brave soul to take a puff. The huge difference between the alleged and the actual effects of marijuana has long provided young people with grounds for distrusting authority. Praised by rebels and artists as diverse as Cab Calloway, Jack Kerouac, Arlo Guthrie, and Snoop Doggie Dog, marijuana has attained a lofty symbolic importance. A distinct culture has evolved around marijuana, one championed by proud outcasts. The laws aimed at that culture have only perpetuated it, enshrining the cannabis leaf as a symbol of adolescent protest.

In 1970 President Richard Nixon appointed a commission to study the health effects, legal status, and social impact of marijuana use. After more than a year of research the National Commission on Marijuana and Drug Abuse concluded that marijuana should be decriminalized under state and federal laws. The commission unanimously agreed that the possession of small amounts of marijuana in the home should no longer be a crime. "Recognizing the extensive degree of misinformation about marijuana as a drug, we have tried to *demythologize* it," the commission explained. "Viewing the use of marijuana in its wider social context, we have tried to *desymbolize* it." The commission argued that society should strongly discourage marijuana use while devoting more resources to preventing and treating heavy use. "Considering the range of social concerns in contemporary America," it said, "marijuana does not, in our considered judgment, rank very high."

"President Nixon felt betrayed by the commission and rejected its findings. A decade later the National Academy of Sciences studied the health effects of marijuana and concluded that it should be decriminalized, a finding that President Reagan rejected. Nevertheless, ten states

have largely decriminalized marijuana possession, thereby saving billions of dollars in court and prison costs—without experiencing an increase in marijuana use. Ohio currently has the most liberal marijuana laws in the nation: possession of up to three ounces is a misdemeanor punishable by a $100 fine. In July of last year, with little fanfare, Ohio decriminalized the cultivation of small amounts of marijuana for personal use. The change in the laws was backed by the state's conservative Republican governor, George V. Voinovich.

There seems to be little correlation between the severity of a nation's marijuana laws and the rate of use among its teenagers. In the United Kingdom, where drug penalties are harshly enforced, the rate of marijuana use among fifteen-and sixteen-year-olds is the highest in Western Europe—one and a half times the rate in Spain and the Netherlands, where the drug has been decriminalized. The UK rate is six times as high as the rate in Sweden, a nation that has single-mindedly pursued a public-health approach to drug control. Sweden now has the lowest rate of marijuana use in Western Europe. Under Swedish law the maximum punishment for most marijuana traffickers is a prison term of three years.

Cultural factors exert far more influence on a country's rate of marijuana use than any changes in the law. The Netherlands decriminalized marijuana in 1976—and yet teenage use there declined by as much as 40 percent over the next decade. The rate of use among American teenagers peaked in 1979 and had already fallen by 40 percent when Congress passed the Anti-Drug Abuse Act, in 1986. As young Americans became more health conscious, their use of alcohol and tobacco also declined. Since 1979 the rate of alcohol use among American teenagers has fallen by 52 percent—without any life sentences for selling beer.

The conclusions of the National Commission on Marijuana and Drug Abuse are as valid today as they were twenty-five years ago: the United States should decriminalize marijuana for personal use; possessing small amounts of it should no longer be a crime; growing or selling it commercially, using it in public, distributing it to young people, and driving under its influence should remain strictly forbidden. The decriminalization of marijuana—including, as in the Ohio model, the cultivation of small amounts—could be the first step toward a rational and sensible drug-control policy. The benefits would be felt immediately. Law-enforcement resources would be diverted from the apprehension and imprisonment of marijuana offenders to the prevention of much more serious crimes. The roughly $2.4 billion the United States spends annually just to process its marijuana arrests would be available to fund more-useful endeavors, such as treatment for drug education and substance abuse. Thousands of prison cells would become available to house violent criminals. The profits from growing and selling marijuana commercially would fall, as would the incentive to bribe public officials. But the decriminalization of marijuana is only a partial solution to the havoc caused by the war on drugs. Mandatory-minimum sentences for drug offenders should be repealed, allowing judges to regain their time-honored powers and ensuring that an individual's punishment fits the crime. The asset-forfeiture laws should be amended so that criminal investigations are not motivated by greed—so that assets can be forfeited only after a conviction, in amounts proportionate to the illegal activity. The use of professional informers should be limited and carefully monitored. The message sent to the nation's teenagers by these steps would be that our society will no longer pursue a failed policy and needlessly ruin lives in order to appear tough.

Decriminalizing marijuana would also help to resolve the current dispute over its medicinal use. Seriously ill patients would no longer risk criminal prosecution while trying to obtain their medicine. Although heavy marijuana use may exacerbate underlying psychological problems and may harm the respiratory system through the inhalation of smoke, marijuana is one of the least toxic therapeutically active substances known. No fatal dose of the drug has been established, despite more than 5,000 years of recorded use. Marijuana is less toxic than many common foods. Denying cancer patients, AIDS patients, and paraplegics access to a potentially useful medicine that is safer than most legally prescribed drugs is inhumane. Some of the claims made in the 1970s and 1980s about the effects of marijuana—that it causes brain damage, chromosome damage, sterility, infertility, and even homosexuality—have never been proved. Marijuana use may pose dangers that are still unknown. And yet the British medical journal *The Lancet*, in a recent editorial calling for the decriminalization of marijuana, felt confident enough to declare, "The smoking of cannabis, even long-term, is not harmful to health."

Although marijuana does not turn teenagers into serial killers or irreversibly destroy their brains, it should not be smoked by young people. Marijuana is a powerful intoxicant, and its use can diminish academic and athletic performance. Adolescents experience enough social and emotional confusion without the added handicap of being stoned. If marijuana use does indeed exert subtly harmful effects on the reproductive and immune systems, young people could be at greatest risk. Lying to teenagers about marijuana's effects, however, only encourages them to doubt official warnings about much more dangerous drugs, such as heroin, cocaine, and amphetamines. The drug culture of the 1960s arose in the midst of tough anti-drug laws and simplistic anti-drug propaganda. In a nation where both major political parties accept millions of dollars from alcohol and tobacco lobbyists, demands for "zero tolerance" and moral condemnations of marijuana have a hollow ring. According to Michael D. Newcomb, a substance-abuse expert at the University of Southern California, "Tobacco and alcohol are the most widely used, abused, and deadly drugs ingested by teenagers." Eighth-graders in America today drink alcohol three times as often as they use marijuana. Drug-education programs should respect the intelligence of young people by promoting drug-free lives without scare tactics, lies, and hypocrisy. And drug abuse should be treated like alcoholism or nicotine addiction. These are health problems suffered by Americans of every race, creed, and political affiliation, not grounds for imprisonment or the denial of property rights.

At the Alabama penitentiary where Douglas Lamar Gray is imprisoned, perhaps half a dozen inmates are

THE CONCLUSIONS OF THE NATIONAL COMMISSION ON MARIJUANA AND DRUG ABUSE ARE AS VALID TODAY AS TWENTY-FIVE YEARS AGO: THE UNITED STATES SHOULD DECRIMINALIZE MARIJUANA FOR PERSONAL USE AND THE POSSESSION OF SMALL AMOUNTS OF IT; GROWING OR SELLING IT COMMERCIALLY, USING IT IN PUBLIC, DISTRIBUTING IT TO YOUNG PEOPLE, AND DRIVING UNDER ITS INFLUENCE SHOULD REMAIN STRICTLY FORBIDDEN.

serving life without parole for marijuana offenses. One was given a life sentence for loading his pickup truck with ditchweed, a form of wild marijuana that is not psychoactive. Another was given a life sentence for possessing a single joint. Hundreds of inmates may be serving life sentences for marijuana-related offenses in prisons across the United States. The pointless misery extends from these inmates to their families and to the victims of every crime committed by violent offenders who might otherwise occupy those prison cells. A society that punishes marijuana crimes more severely than violent crimes is caught in the grip of a deep psychosis. For too long the laws regarding marijuana have been based on racial prejudice, irrational fears, metaphors, symbolism, and political expediency. The time has come for a marijuana policy calmly based on the facts.

IT'S TIME FOR REALISM

BEYOND LEGALIZATION
NEW IDEAS FOR ENDING THE WAR ON DRUGS

by MICHAEL MASSING

Among readers of *The Nation* who follow the drug issue, it's an article of faith that the war on drugs has failed miserably. The clogging of our prisons with low-level drug offenders, the widespread curtailment of civil liberties in the name of drug enforcement, the strained relations with drug-producing nations to our south, the whole puritanical mindset associated with Just Say No—all have contributed to a consensus on the urgent need for change.

As to what the change should be, there are some clear areas of agreement. Virtually all liberals, for instance, would like to see the police stop making so many drug arrests, which currently number more than 1.5 million a year. Everyone, too, would like to see an overhaul of the nation's harsh and discriminatory drug-sentencing laws—a step that would, among other things, reverse the relentless flow of black and Latino men into prison.

Beyond that, though, the consensus breaks down. And this has helped stall the movement for reform. Despite growing dissatisfaction with the drug war among the general public, progress toward change has been minimal, and the inability of liberals to propose a persuasive alternative helps explain why.

On the left, three schools of drug reform prevail. Each has something to offer but, by itself, is an inadequate guide to change. The most sensational is the CIA-trafficking school. Actually, this is less a school than a tendency, limited to certain sectors of the left, but it has absorbed much intellectual energy over the years, beginning with Alfred McCoy's 1972 study *The Politics of Heroin in Southeast Asia* and extending through Senator John Kerry's Congressional investigation in the eighties and, more recently, Gary Webb's book *Dark Alliance*. According to this perspective, America's drug problem cannot be fully understood without examining the CIA's periodic alliances with drug-running groups abroad, from the Hmong tribesmen in Laos to the *mujahedeen* in Afghanistan to the *contras* in Nicaragua. By teaming up with and providing cover

to these forces, it is alleged, the CIA has facilitated the flow of drugs into the United States at critical moments. In the most eye-popping version of this theory, advanced by Gary Webb, traffickers linked to the CIA-backed *contras* are said to have supplied cocaine to major dealers in South Central Los Angeles, thus helping to set off the nation's crack epidemic. Though well aware of this activity, the CIA did nothing to intervene. (This theory was seized upon by some leaders of the black community, including Congresswoman Maxine Waters, who wrote a glowing foreword to Webb's book.)

With its chronicling of the CIA's ties to drug-tainted groups, the CIA-trafficking school deserves credit for exposing the hypocrisy of the drug war. It also raises important questions about the types of alliances the United States sometimes make abroad. As a guide to drug reform, though, it's a dead end. However much the *contras* were involved in drug trafficking (and the evidence strongly suggests they were), they were clearly no more than bit players in the overall cocaine trade. If any one group was primarily responsible for the flow of cocaine into the United States, it was the Colombian traffickers, and no one has accused the CIA of abetting them. On the contrary, the US government has for the past fifteen years been waging all-out war on the Colombian narcos, with little to show for it.

Adherence to the CIA-trafficking school leads one into some strange policy terrain. In focusing so strongly on the intelligence agency, this school seems implicitly to accept the idea that Washington could actually do something about the flow of drugs into the United States if it really wanted to. If only the CIA would fight the traffickers, rather than shield them, it's implied, we could reduce the availability, and abuse, of drugs in this country. Yet, after thirty years of waging war on drugs, it should be apparent that with or without the CIA's help, the United States is incapable of stemming the flow of drugs into this country. The CIA-trafficking school unwittingly bolsters the idea that the true source of America's drug problem lies outside our borders, and that the solution consists in cracking down on producers, processors and smugglers. In an odd way, then, this school actually reinforces the logic underlying the drug war.

Michael Massing's The Fix (Simon & Schuster) *won* The Washington Monthly's *Political Book Award for 1998. He is an adjunct professor at the Columbia School of Journalism.*

By now, it should be clear that America's drug problem is home-grown, and that any effort to combat it must be centered here. In particular, we must confront the real source of our problem—the demand for drugs. On this point, many liberals subscribe to the "root causes" school. This holds that the problem of drug abuse in America reflects deeper ills in our society, such as poverty, unemployment, racial discrimination and urban neglect. To combat abuse, we must first address these underlying causes—though policies to promote full employment, increase the minimum wage, provide universal health insurance, end housing segregation and create opportunities for disadvantaged youths.

In focusing attention on the link between poverty and drug abuse, the root-causes school provides a valuable service. Studies indicate that drug addiction in the United States is disproportionately concentrated among the unemployed and undereducated. And certainly most liberals would endorse measures to improve their lot. This, however, takes us far beyond the realm of drug policy. To maintain that we must end poverty and discrimination in order to combat drug abuse seems a prescription for paralysis. The key is to find a strategy that is humane, affordable and sellable—to find a strategy, in short, that could actually work.

Certainly such a standard would seem to rule out the third main school of left/liberal drug reform—legalization. On the surface, drug legalization has undeniable appeal. If drugs were legalized, the vast criminal networks that distribute them, and that generate so much violence, would disappear. Prison space would be reserved for the truly dangerous, black motorists would no longer be stopped routinely on the New Jersey Turnpike, relations with countries like Mexico and Colombia would improve and Americans would no longer be hounded for the substances they decide to consume—a matter of personal choice.

Yet legalizing drugs would entail some serious risks, the most obvious being an increase in abuse. While legalizers tend to cite drug prohibition as the source of all evil when it comes to drugs, drugs themselves can cause extensive harm. Heroin, cocaine, crack and methamphetamine are highly toxic substances, and those addicted to them engage in all kinds of destructive behavior, from preying on family members to assaulting strangers to abusing children. In all, there are an estimated 4 million hard-core drug users in the United States. Though making up only 20 percent of all drug users nationwide (the rest being occasional users), this group accounts for two-thirds to three-quarters of all the drugs consumed here. They also account for most of the crime, medical emergencies and other harmful consequences associated with drugs. If drugs were legalized, the number of chronic users could well increase.

History is full of cautionary examples. In the early seventies, for instance, doctors routinely began prescribing Valium (a minor tranquilizer) for everyday cases of anxiety. As the number of prescriptions increased, so did the incidence of abuse; by the late seventies Valium was sending more people to hospital emergency rooms than any other drug, heroin and cocaine included. As physicians became aware of Valium's dangers, they began writing fewer prescriptions for it, and the number of emergency cases began dropping as well. Clearly, making drugs easier to get can increase the extent to which they are abused, and one can only imagine what would happen if such potent intoxicants as heroin and crack suddenly became available by prescription or were sold openly. Under the regimes favored by some libertarians and free-marketeers, legalized drugs would be sold commercially and marketed aggressively, with potentially disastrous results for addicts and kids.

From a political standpoint, the liabilities of legalization are no less obvious. According to opinion polls, most Americans strongly oppose legalizing drugs. While the unpopularity of an idea should not automatically disqualify it, legalization seems a long-term loser. Indeed, the fact that legalization has so often been presented as the sole alternative to the drug war has hindered the movement for reform.

By now, the risks of legalization have become so evident that even onetime supporters no longer advocate it. Instead, they have embraced a variant of legalization called harm reduction. Not always easy to define, harm reduction generally holds that the primary goal of drug policy should not be to eliminate drug use but rather to reduce the harm that drugs cause. Those who can be persuaded to stop using drugs should be; those who can't should be encouraged to use their drugs more safely. To that end, harm reductionists favor expanding the availability of methadone, setting up needle-exchange programs, opening safe-injection rooms for heroin users and establishing heroin-maintenance programs that provide addicts with a daily dose of the drug.

There is much to admire in harm reduction. Its encouragement of tolerance for drug addicts provides a welcome alternative to the narrow moralism of the drug war. At times, though, harm reductionists take tolerance too far. In their eagerness to condemn the drug war, they sometimes fail to acknowledge the damage that drug addiction itself can inflict. While rightly condemning the political hysteria surrounding "crack babies," for instance, harm reductionists tend to overlook the havoc crack has wrought on inner-city families. And, while commendably calling for more needle-exchange programs, they rarely acknowledge that syringes are often handed out indiscriminately at these exchanges, with little effort to intervene with addicts and get them to address their habits.

Nonetheless, harm reduction—by recognizing that chronic users are at the core of the nation's drug problem and that they constitute a public-health rather than law-enforcement problem—can help point the way toward a more rational drug policy. The key is to develop a policy that is as tough on drug abuse as it is on the drug war.

In formulating such a policy, a good starting point is a 1994 RAND study that sought to compare the effectiveness of four different types of drug control: source-control programs (attacking the drug trade abroad), interdiction (stopping drugs at the border), domestic law enforcement (arresting and imprisoning buyers and sellers) and drug treatment. How much additional money, RAND asked, would the government have to spend on each approach to reduce national cocaine consumption 1 percent? RAND devised a model of the national cocaine market, then fed into it more than seventy variables, from seizure data to survey responses. The results were striking: Treatment was found to be seven times more cost-effective than law enforcement, ten times more effective than interdiction and twenty-three times more effective than attacking drugs at their source.

The RAND study has generated much debate in drug-research circles, but its general conclusion has been confirmed in study after study. Yes, relapse is common, but, as RAND found, treatment is so inexpensive that it more than pays for itself while an individual is actually in a program, in the form of reduced crime, medical costs and the like; all gains that occur after an individual leaves a program are a bonus. And it doesn't matter what form of treatment one considers: methadone maintenance, long-term residential, intensive outpatient and twelve-step programs all produce impressive outcomes (though some programs work better for certain addicts than for others).

To be effective, though, treatment must be available immediately. Telling addicts who want help to come back the next day or week is a sure way to lose them. Unfortunately, in most communities, help is rarely available immediately; long waiting lists are the rule. In New York State alone, it is estimated that every year 100,000 people who would take advantage of drug or alcohol treatment if it were available are unable to get into a program.

Such numbers reflect the government's spending priorities. Of the $18 billion Washington spends annually to fight drugs, fully two-thirds goes to reduce the supply of drugs and just one-third to reduce the demand. In all, less than 10 percent of federal funds go to treat the hard-core users, who constitute the real heart of the problem. Closing the nation's treatment gap should be a top priority for the government.

How can we make this happen? According to federal estimates, the government would have to spend about $3.4 billion a year on top of current treatment expenditures to make help available to all who want it; the states would have to spend roughly an equivalent amount. If the current 67/33 percent split in the federal drug budget between the supply and demand sides were equalized, this would free up close to the sum in question at the federal level. Actually, a strong case could be made for reversing these proportions and allocating two-thirds to the demand side, but a 50/50 split seems as much as can be hoped for in the current political climate.

Finding a more effective means of preventing drug use among young people is another urgent need. Today, prevention consists mainly of Just Say No messages broadcast on TV or preached in the classroom. Unfortunately, research shows that such messages by themselves do not work. To succeed, prevention, like treatment, needs to focus on those most at risk. The problem is not so much with kids who smoke an occasional joint but with those who regularly use drugs and/or alcohol. For youths living in poor neighborhoods, effective prevention would mean more recreational programs, after-school activities and summer job opportunities (a key plank of the root-causes school). For more privileged students, prevention might take the form of early-warning systems in which teachers, counselors and parents work together to intervene with youths who show signs of getting into trouble with drugs, legal or otherwise.

As for the nation's drug laws, the goal should not be abolishing them—keeping drugs illegal can help contain abuse—but making them more rational so that small-time offenders are not hit with excessive penalties. And, whenever possible, nonviolent addicts and sellers who are arrested should be offered treatment as an alternative to incarceration. More generally, arresting low-level offenders should be society's last, not first, line of defense.

A word on marijuana. At present, almost 700,000 people a year are arrested for the sale or possession of pot. This is madness. Marijuana is far less toxic than heroin, cocaine or even alcohol, and the idea of putting people in jail for possessing it seems absurd. At the same time, marijuana is not innocuous, especially for young people, and we do not want to do anything that would make it even more available than it is now. Legalizing marijuana would certainly risk that. A far more rational approach would be to decriminalize the drug; people caught using pot in public would be subject to a civil penalty punishable by a fine, much as a traffic violation is. The production, importation and sale of marijuana, however, would remain illegal (though not subject to the ridiculously harsh penalties now in place). Decriminalization offers a realistic middle ground between the excesses of our current approach and the potential perils of legalization.

In my recent book *The Fix,* I argue that a public-health approach to the drug problem can work based on the one time we actually tried it—during the Nixon Administration. Nixon, a staunch law-and-order advocate, is remembered for having launched the war on drugs, but, drawing on his pragmatic instincts, he in fact made treatment his main weapon in that war. Confronting a national heroin epidemic, the White House created a special action office headed by physicians and addiction specialists, who spent hundreds of millions of dollars to set up a national network of clinics that offered help to all those who wanted it. The result was a marked decline in heroin-related crime, overdose deaths and hospital emergency-room visits. The national heroin epidemic was thus stanched.

Unfortunately, that network largely disintegrated during the Reagan years, so that by the time crack struck, treatment clinics were completely overwhelmed. Today, our drug problem is far larger and more complex than it was under Nixon. But the research confirming treatment's effectiveness has grown, too, and in light of the ongoing failure of the drug war, a public-health approach stressing treatment over prosecution, counseling over incarceration, would seem to offer our most humane, practical and politically viable alternative.

Unit 6

Unit Selections

Key Points to Consider

❖ Using the four perspectives for defining deviance, how would you define different sexual behaviors as deviant?

❖ Should schools be involved in sex education? Why or why not?

❖ Is sexual addiction a problem in American society? Defend your answer.

❖ Should prostitution and the sex industry be legalized and regulated? Explain.

❖ Should sadomasochism be forbidden by law? Why or why not?

❖ Discuss whether homosexuals can be converted into heterosexuals.

 **Links** | **www.dushkin.com/online/**

These sites are annotated on pages 4 and 5.

Alexander Liazos in "The Poverty of the Sociology of Deviance" (*Social Problems, 20,* 1972), refers to the sociology of deviance as the study of "nuts, sluts, and perverts." While that phrase would eliminate many of the types of deviance dealt with earlier, it is perhaps the best expression of what most people think of when they think of deviance. Sex is a very popular topic in our society. We are exposed to it in many ways. For example, advertising is heavily sex-oriented. Automobile advertisements often picture sexy men and women driving their vehicles. A recent Coca Cola television commercial depicts female office workers admiring a handsome bare-chested construction worker drinking a Diet Coke. Perfumes and colognes are sold with the suggestion that the wearer will be more attractive to members of the opposite sex. Many popular magazines discuss topics such as how to sexually turn on one's mate, how to perform better sexually, and how to meet the mate of one's dreams. News shows and talk shows on television often have explicit discussions of sexual topics. In addition, many people spend many hours per day in front of a computer talking about sex with people they do not know outside the computer world. Many of them discuss their deepest sexual needs and desires, as well as trading sexually explicit pictures of themselves, their spouses, and others. Others attempt to meet sexual partners on the Internet, and some adult pedophiles try to identify and meet with possible victims. Sex is no longer a private matter between lovers and friends; it is now a part of the public world.

Sex is an excellent example of how behaviors may come to be socially defined as deviance. Each of the four perspectives of deviance, and the five variations of the social definition of deviance, is important in determining whether or not a sexual act is deviant. For example, a deeply religious person may consider any form of sexual intercourse other than the "missionary position" to be deviant from the absolutist perspective. Some people consider disrobing for money to be immoral; others find stripping to be a good and honest means of earning a living. Prostitution is most often defined as deviant behavior. Sexual deviance is also a good example of how social definitions of deviance serve a boundary-setting function. For example, various surveys of sexual behavior have found that many people are open to such things as new positions for

sexual intercourse and oral sex, but they would draw the line at engaging in anal sex. Others may go further and find it pleasurable and stimulating to give and receive pain as part of sex. Likewise, what is or is not considered to be pornographic or obscene is socially defined. For example, the U.S. Supreme Court has ruled that obscenity is defined by community standards of acceptability. That is, what is socially defined as obscenity in one community may be acceptable in another community. The lesson to be learned is that sexual deviance, like beauty, is socially defined.

Homosexuality is often socially defined as deviance. In our society, the norm is that a woman will be sexually attracted to a man, and that a man will be sexually attracted to a woman. Sexual attraction to people of the same sex is often viewed as being outside of socially acceptable boundaries. People who think they are homosexual often find themselves trying to understand who they are versus who society says they should be. Many realistically fear rejection by their friends and family should their sexual preference become publicly known. Although homosexuals comprise somewhere between 1 and 10 percent of the U.S. population, misconceptions about them abound. Often, homosexual teachers face dismissal from their jobs because parents and administrators fear that they will coerce the children into homosexual behavior, or that they will molest the children. Religious leaders tend to condemn them as sinners. Many landlords will not rent properties to homosexual couples. Most health insurance companies will not recognize a homosexual companion as they would a spouse, even when a similar relationship exists. Many states ban homosexual sex under sodomy statutes. Most states do not recognize homosexual marriages (often referred to as a commitment, rather than a marriage), and homosexuals who apply for marriage licenses may be prosecuted. The Defense of Marriage Act (1996) is designed to guarantee the right of a state to not accept as legally binding a homosexual marriage that was legally performed in another state. In other countries, such as Denmark, Sweden, and Norway, such marriages are legal, and homosexuals are not as extremely viewed as being deviants as they are in the United States.

This unit deals with a number of sexual behaviors that may be socially defined as deviant.

WHERE'D YOU LEARN THAT?

American kids are in the midst of their own sexual revolution, one leaving many parents feeling confused and virtually powerless

By RON STODGHILL II

THE CUTE LITTLE COUPLE LOOKED AS if they should be sauntering through Great Adventure or waiting in line for tokens at the local arcade. Instead, the 14-year-olds walked purposefully into the Teen Center in suburban Salt Lake City, Utah. They didn't mince words about their reason for stopping in. For quite some time, usually after school and on weekends, the boy and girl had tried to heighten their arousal during sex. Flustered yet determined, the pair wanted advice on the necessary steps that might lead them to a more fulfilling orgasm. His face showing all the desperation of a lost tourist, the boy spoke for both of them when he asked frankly, "How do we get to the G-spot?"

Whoa. Teen Center nurse Patti Towle admits she was taken aback by the inquiry. She couldn't exactly provide a road map. Even more, the destination was a bit scandalous for a couple of ninth-graders in the heart of Mormon country. But these kids had clearly already gone further sexually than many adults, so Towle didn't waste time preaching the gospel of abstinence. She gave her young adventurers some reading material on the subject, including the classic women's health book *Our Bodies, Ourselves,* to help bring

them closer in bed. She also brought up the question of whether a G-spot even exists. As her visitors were leaving, Towle offered them more freebies: "I sent them out the door with a billion condoms."

G-spots. Orgasms. Condoms. We all know kids say and do the darndest things, but how they have changed! One teacher recalls a 10-year-old raising his hand to ask her to define oral sex. He was quickly followed by an 8-year-old girl behind him who asked, "Oh, yeah, and what's anal sex?" These are the easy questions. Rhonda Sheared, who teaches sex education in Pinellas County, Fla., was asked by middle school students about the sound kweif, which the kids say is the noise a vagina makes during or after sex. "And how do you keep it from making this noise?"

There is more troubling behavior in Denver. School officials were forced to institute a sexual-harassment policy owing to a sharp rise in lewd language, groping, pinching and bra-snapping incidents among sixth-, seventh- and eighth-graders. Sex among kids in Pensacola, Fla., became so pervasive that students of a private Christian junior high school are now asked to sign cards vowing not to have sex until they marry. But the cards don't mean anything, says a

14-year-old boy at the school. "It's broken promises."

It's easy enough to blame everything on television and entertainment, even the news. At a Denver middle school, boys rationalize their actions this way: "If the President can do it, why can't we?" White House sex scandals are one thing, but how can anyone avoid Viagra and virility? Or public discussions of sexually transmitted diseases like AIDS and herpes? Young girls have lip-synched often enough to Alanis Morissette's big hit of a couple of years ago, *You Oughta Know,* to have found the sex nestled in the lyric. But it's more than just movies and television and news. Adolescent curiosity about sex is fed by a pandemic openness about it—in the schoolyard, on the bus, at home when no adult is watching. Just eavesdrop at the mall one afternoon, and you'll hear enough pubescent sexcapades to pen the next few episodes of *Dawson's Creek,* the most explicit show on teen sexuality, on the WB network. Parents, always the last to keep up, are now almost totally pre-empted. Chris (not his real name), 13, says his parents talked to him about sex when he was 12 but he had been indoctrinated earlier by a 17-year-old cousin. In any case, he gets his full share of information from the tube. "You name the show,

"If you're feeling steamy and hot, there's only one thing you want to do."

—STEPHANIE, WHO LOST HER VIRGINITY AT 14

From *Time,* June 15, 1998, pp. 52-59. © 1998 by Time Inc. Magazine Company. Reprinted by permission.

and I've heard about it, *Jerry Springer,* MTV, *Dawson's Creek,* HBO *After Midnight . . .*" Stephanie (not her real name), 16, of North Lauderdale, Fla., who first had sex when she was 14, claims to have slept with five boyfriends and is considered a sex expert by her friends. She says, "You can learn a lot about sex from cable. It's all mad-sex stuff." She sees nothing to condemn. "If you're feeling steamy and hot, there's only one thing you want to do. As long as you're using a condom, what's wrong with it? Kids have hormones too."

In these steamy times, it is becoming largely irrelevant whether adults approve of kids' sowing their oats—or knowing so much about the technicalities of the dissemination. American adolescents are in the midst of their own kind of sexual revolution—one that has left many parents feeling confused, frightened and almost powerless. Parents can search all they want for common ground with today's kids, trying to draw parallels between contemporary carnal knowledge and an earlier generation's free-love crusades, but the two movements are quite different. A desire to break out of the old-fashioned strictures fueled the '60s movement, and its participants made sexual freedom a kind of new religion. That sort of reverence has been replaced by a more consumerist attitude. In a 1972 cover story, TIME declared, "Teenagers generally are woefully ignorant about sex." Ignorance is no longer the rule. As a weary junior high counselor in Salt Lake City puts it, "Teens today are almost nonchalant about sex. It's like we've been to the moon too many times."

The good news about their precocious knowledge of the mechanics of sex is that a growing number of teens know how to protect themselves, at least physically. But what about their emotional health and social behavior? That's a more troublesome picture. Many parents and teachers—as well as some thoughtful teenagers—worry about the desecration of love and the subversion of mature relationships. Says Debra Haffner, president of the Sexuality Information and Education Council of the United States: "We should not confuse kids' pseudo-sophistication about sexuality and their ability to use the language with their understanding of who they are as sexual young people or their ability to make good decisions."

One ugly side effect is a presumption among many adolescent boys that sex is an entitlement—an attitude that fosters a breakdown of respect for oneself and others. Says a seventh-grade girl: "The guy will ask you up front. If you turn him down, you're a bitch. But if you do it, you're a ho. The guys

From what sources do teenagers today mainly learn about sex?		
	1986	1998
Friends	43%	45%
Television	11%	29%
Parents	8%	7%
Sex Ed	18%	3%

From a telephone poll of 1,011 adult Americans taken for TIME/CNN on April 8–9 by Yankelovich Partners Inc. Sampling error is 3.1%

are after us all the time, in the halls, everywhere. You scream, 'Don't touch me!' but it doesn't do any good." A Rhode Island Rape Center study of 1,700 sixth- and ninth-graders found 65% of boys and 57% of girls believing it acceptable for a male to force a female to have sex if they've been dating for six months.

Parents who are aware of this cultural revolution seem mostly torn between two approaches: preaching abstinence or suggesting prophylactics—and thus condoning sex. Says Cory Hollis, 37, a father of three in the Salt Lake City area: "I don't want to see my teenage son ruin his life. But if he's going to do it, I told him that I'd go out and get him the condoms myself." Most parents seem too squeamish to get into the subtleties of instilling sexual ethics. Nor are schools up to the job of moralizing. Kids say they accept their teachers' admonitions to have safe sex but tune out other stuff. "The personal-development classes are a joke," says Sarah, 16, of Pensacola. "Even the teacher looks uncomfortable. There is no way anybody is going to ask a serious question." Says Shana, a 13-year-old from Denver: "A lot of it is old and boring. They'll talk about not having sex before marriage, but no one listens. I use that class for study hall."

Shana says she is glad "sex isn't so taboo now, I mean with all the teenage pregnancies." But she also says that "it's creepy and kind of scary that it seems to be happening so early, and all this talk about it." She adds, "Girls are jumping too quickly. They figure if they can fall in love in a month, then they can have sex in a month too." When she tried discouraging a classmate from having sex for the first time, the friend turned to her and said, "My God, Shana. It's just sex."

Three powerful forces have shaped today's child prodigies: a prosperous informa-

tion age that increasingly promotes products and entertains audiences by titillation; aggressive public-policy initiatives that loudly preach sexual responsibility, further desensitizing kids to the subject; and the decline of two-parent households, which leaves adolescents with little supervision. Thus kids are not only bombarded with messages about sex—many of them contradictory—but also have more private time to engage in it than did previous generations. Today more than half of the females and three-quarters of the males ages 15 to 19 have experienced sexual intercourse, according to the Commission on Adolescent Sexual Health. And while the average age at first intercourse has come down only a year since 1970 (currently it's 17 for girls and 16 for boys), speed is of the essence for the new generation. Says Haffner: "If kids today are going to do more than kiss, they tend to move very quickly toward sexual intercourse."

The remarkable—and in ways lamentable—product of youthful promiscuity and higher sexual IQ is the degree to which kids learn to navigate the complex hypersexual world that reaches out seductively to them at every turn. One of the most positive results: the incidence of sexually transmitted diseases and of teenage pregnancy is declining. Over the past few years, kids have managed to chip away at the teenage birthrate, which in 1991 peaked at 62.1 births per 1,000 females. Since then the birthrate has dropped 12% to 54.7. Surveys suggest that as many as two-thirds of teenagers now use condoms, a proportion that is three times as high as reported in the 1970s. "We're clearly starting to make progress," says Dr. John Santelli, a physician with the Centers for Disease Control and Prevention's division of adolescent and school health. "And the key statistics bear that out." Even if they've had sex, many kids are learning to put off having more till later; they are also making condom use during intercourse nonnegotiable; and, remarkably, the fleeting pleasures of lust may even be wising up some of them to a greater appreciation of love.

For better or worse, sex-filled television helps shape your opinion. In Chicago, Ryan, an 11-year-old girl, intently watches a scene from one of her favorite TV dramas, *Dawson's Creek.* She listens as the character Jen, who lost her virginity at 12 while drunk, confesses to her new love, Dawson, "Sex doesn't equal happiness. I can't apologize for my past." Ryan is quick to defend Jen. "I think she was young, but if I were Dawson, I would believe she had changed. She acts totally different now." But Ryan is shocked by an episode of her other favorite

"If the President can do it, why can't we?"

—A MALE STUDENT, REASONING AT A DENVER MIDDLE SCHOOL

show, *Buffy the Vampire Slayer,* in which Angel, a male vampire, "turned bad" after having sex with the 17-year-old Buffy. "That kinda annoyed me," says Ryan. "What would have happened if she had had a baby? Her whole life would have been thrown out the window." As for the fallen Angel: "I am so mad! I'm going to take all my pictures of him down now."

Pressed by critics and lobbies, television has begun to include more realistic story lines about sex and its possible consequences. TV writers and producers are turning to groups like the Kaiser Family Foundation, an independent health-policy think tank, for help in adding more depth and accuracy to stories involving sex. Kaiser has consulted on daytime soaps *General Hospital* and *One Life to Live* as well as the prime-time drama *ER* on subjects ranging from teen pregnancy to coming to terms with a gay high school athlete. Says Matt James, a Kaiser senior vice president: "We're trying to work with them to improve the public-health content of their shows."

And then there's real-life television. MTV's *Loveline,* an hour-long Q.-and-A. show featuring sex guru Drew Pinsky (*see accompanying story*), is drawing raves among teens for its informative sexual content. Pinsky seems to be almost idolized by some youths. "Dr. Drew has some excellent advice," says Keri, an eighth-grader in Denver. "It's not just sex, it's real life. Society makes you say you've got to look at shows like *Baywatch,* but I'm sick of blond bimbos. They're so fake. Screenwriters ought to get a life."

With so much talk of sex in the air, the extinction of the hapless, sexually naive kid seems an inevitability. Indeed, kids today as young as seven to 10 are picking up the first details of sex even in Saturday-morning cartoons. Brett, a 14-year-old in Denver, says it doesn't matter to him whether his parents chat with him about sex or not because he gets so much from TV. Whenever he's curious about something sexual, he channel-surfs his way to certainty. "If you watch TV, they've got everything you want to know," he says. "That's how I learned to kiss, when I was eight. And the girl told me, 'Oh, you sure know how to do it.' "

Even if kids don't watch certain television shows, they know the programs exist and are bedazzled by the forbidden. From schoolyard word of mouth, eight-year-old Jeff in Chicago has heard all about the foul-mouthed kids in the raunchily plotted *South Park,* and even though he has never seen the show, he can describe certain episodes in detail. (He is also familiar with the AIDS theme

of the musical *Rent* because he's heard the CD over and over.) Argentina, 16, in Detroit, says, "TV makes sex look like this big game." Her friend Michael, 17, adds, "They make sex look like Monopoly or something. You have to do it in order to get to the next level."

Child experts say that by the time many kids hit adolescence, they have reached a point where they aren't particularly obsessed with sex but have grown to accept the notion that solid courtships—or at least strong physical attractions—potentially lead to sexual intercourse. Instead of denying it, they get an early start preparing for it—and playing and perceiving the roles prescribed for them. In Nashville, 10-year-old Brantley whispers about a classmate, "There's this girl I know, she's nine years old, and she already shaves her legs and plucks her eyebrows, and I've heard she's had sex. She even has bigger boobs than my mom!"

The playacting can eventually lead to discipline problems at school. Alan Skriloff, assistant superintendent of personnel and curriculum for New Jersey's North Brunswick school system, notes that there has been an increase in mock-sexual behavior in buses carrying students to school. He insists there have been no incidents of sexual assault but, he says, "we've dealt with kids simulating sexual intercourse and simulating masturbation. It's very disturbing to the other children and to the parents, obviously." Though Skriloff says that girls are often the initiators of such conduct, in most school districts the aggressors are usually boys.

Nan Stein, a senior researcher at the Wesley College Center for Research on Women, believes sexual violence and harassment is on the rise in schools, and she says, "It's happening between kids who are dating or want to be dating or used to date." Linda Osmundson, executive director of the Center Against Spouse Abuse in St. Petersburg, Fla., notes that "it seems to be coming down to younger and younger girls who feel that if they don't pair up with these guys, they'll have no position in their lives. They are pressured into lots of sexual activity." In this process of socialization, "no" is becoming less and less an option.

In such a world, schools focus on teaching scientific realism rather than virginity. Sex-ed teachers tread lightly on the moral questions of sexual intimacy while going heavy on the risk of pregnancy or a sexually transmitted disease. Indeed, health educators in some school districts complain that teaching abstinence to kids today is getting to be a futile exercise. Using less final terms like "postpone" or "delay" helps draw some kids

in, but semantics often isn't the problem. In a Florida survey, the state found that 75% of kids had experienced sexual intercourse by the time they reached 12th grade, with some 20% of the kids having had six or more sexual partners. Rick Colonno, father of a 16-year-old son and 14-year-old daughter in Arvada, Colo., views sex ed in schools as a necessary evil to fill the void that exists in many homes. Still, he's bothered by what he sees as a subliminal endorsement of sex by authorities. "What they're doing," he says, "is preparing you for sex and then saying, 'But don't have it.' "

With breathtaking pragmatism, kids look for ways to pursue their sex life while avoiding pregnancy or disease. Rhonda Sheared, the Florida sex-ed teacher, says a growing number of kids are asking questions about oral and anal sex because they've discovered that it allows them to be sexually active without risking pregnancy. As part of the Pinellas County program, students in middle and high school write questions anonymously, and, as Sheared says, "they're always looking for the loophole."

A verbatim sampling of some questions:

- "Can you get AIDS from fingering a girl if you have no cuts? Through your fingernails?"
- "Can you get AIDS from '69'?"
- "If you shave your vagina or penis, can that get rid of crabs?"
- "If yellowish stuff comes out of a girl, does it mean you have herpes, or can it just happen if your period is due, along with abdominal pains?"
- "When sperm hits the air, does it die or stay alive for 10 days?"

Ideally, most kids say, they would prefer their parents do the tutoring, but they realize that's unlikely. For years psychologists and sociologists have warned about a new generation gap, one created not so much by different morals and social outlooks as by career-driven parents, the economic necessity of two incomes leaving parents little time for talks with their children. Recent studies indicate that many teens think parents are the most accurate source of information and would like to talk to them more about sex and sexual ethics but can't get their attention long enough. Shana sees the conundrum this way: "Parents haven't set boundaries, but they are expecting them."

Yet some parents are working harder to counsel their kids on sex. Cathy Wolf, 29, of North Wales, Pa., says she grew up learning about sex largely from her friends and from reading controversial books. Open-

"Teens today are almost nonchalant about sex."

—JUNIOR HIGH SCHOOL COUNSELOR IN SALT LAKE CITY, UTAH

minded and proactive, she says she has returned to a book she once sought out for advice, Judy Blume's novel *Are You There God? It's Me, Margaret,* and is reading it to her two boys, 8 and 11. The novel discusses the awkwardness of adolescence, including sexual stirrings. "That book was forbidden to me as a kid," Wolf says. "I'm hoping to give them a different perspective about sex, to expose them to this kind of subject matter before they find out about it themselves." Movies and television are a prod and a challenge to Wolf. In *Grease,* which is rated PG and was recently re-released, the character Rizzo "says something about 'sloppy seconds,' you know, the fact that a guy wouldn't want to do it with a girl who had just done it with another guy. There's also another point where they talk about condoms. Both Jacob and Joel wanted an explanation, so I provided it for them."

Most kids, though, lament that their parents aren't much help at all on sexual matters. They either avoid the subject, miss the mark by starting the discussion too long before or after the sexual encounter, or just plain stonewall them. "I was nine when I asked my mother the Big Question," says Michael, in Detroit. "I'll never forget. She took out her driver's license and pointed to the line about male or female. 'That is sex,' she said." Laurel, a 17-year-old in Murfreesboro, Tenn., wishes her parents had taken more time with her to shed light on the subject. When she was six and her sister was nine, "my mom sat us down, and we had the sex talk," Laurel says. "But when I was 10, we moved in with my dad, and he never talked about it. He would leave the room if a commercial for a feminine product came on TV." And when her sister finally had sex, at 16, even her mother's vaunted openness crumbled. "She talked to my mom about it and ended up feeling like a whore because even though my mom always said we could talk to her about anything, she didn't want to hear that her daughter had slept with a boy."

Part of the problem for many adults is that they aren't quite sure how they feel about teenage sex. A third of adults think adolescent sexual activity is wrong, while a majority of adults think it's O.K. and, under certain conditions, normal, healthy behavior, according to the Alan Guttmacher Institute, a nonprofit, reproductive-health research group. In one breath, parents say they perceive it as a public-health issue and want more information about sexual behavior and its consequences, easier access to contraceptives and more material in the media about responsible human and sexual interaction.

LISTENING IN ON *BOY TALK*

THE THREE BOYS, ALL 12, HAVE REQUESTED THAT THEIR MOMS NOT BE ALLOWED IN THE room. W. takes pains to close all the doors to the dining room where the discussion is going to take place. At one point, he gets up to chase away his little brother. W.'s friends H. and P. are twins, but H. quickly points out, "Trust us. We have completely different views on the subject." The subject is sex.

Do the boys think about sex?

"Do we ever," giggles W.

"Yes is the short answer," says H. "We think about when we will have sex and who it will be with. We've seen nudity—on TV, in *Playboys.*"

"He took them from my dad last year," P. interrupts. "My dad is a writer, and he was using them to research an article."

Why did H. take the *Playboys*? "Put yourself in our shoes," he explains. "You're 12 years old, and you're alone in the house. What would you do?"

The three boys have checked out *Beverly Hills 90210,* which, says H., "definitely had enough sex going down." The Internet is tempting and accessible but, says W., "you never really use it because it takes so much time and money." They say the movie that really got their juices flowing was the vintage frat-boy flick *Animal House.* W. saw it at a sleepover, and the twins say their older brother brought it home one night. Says W.: "It really opened me up to sex."

Do the three hang out with girls much?

"I have no shortage of time with girls," says H.

"He certainly doesn't," says his twin.

"What I mean is, I have a lot of friends who are girls," says H., stressing that the conversations don't get much into sex. "I'm really careful how I talk to girls. You have to have personal limits. Sex is not something I go around blabbing about." But girls are enough on their minds so that P. taped a phone conversation his brother was having with a classmate about girls.

The three have attended school dances where they've seen people "grinding" and getting "frisky and stuff." At the ice-skating rink, P. saw a seventh-grade couple tightly embracing and passionately kissing. "It was pretty scary," he says.

The subject turns to other classmates. "I think he likes boys," says H. about one. He and W. start to imitate the classmate, talking in high voices and with their hands. What makes them so suspicious? "He went out for five months with a girl and didn't kiss," says H. "I went out with someone for five days, and we did kiss."

"Maybe he's bisexual," says W.

"The vibe here is overhomophobic," says P. with a look of disapproval.

"We really try not to be homophobes," says his chastened brother.

How much sex goes on among the other kids in their grade? Says H. "There are some who do make out; they do hang out on the couch at parties. I think they go as far as kids our age should. They can't go beyond the makeout stage because somebody will find out."

But, says W., "the only reason they don't go further is because they're afraid rumors will be spread."

The three devise a makeshift formula to measure appropriate sixth-grade sexual activity. On a scale of 1 to 10, level 2 is hand holding, 4 is hugging, 6 is kissing and 7 is tongue-kissing. "If they're feeling each other up with their clothes on," says H., "then one thing leads to another. They're 12 years old. You know what I mean? Before you know it, you'll have kids our age having sex." Says W.: "The frenching thing is the edge." For now.
                                                                —*By Charlotte Faltermayer*

And in the next breath, they claim it's a moral issue to be resolved through preaching abstinence and the virtues of virginity and getting the trash off TV. "You start out talk-

"If you watch TV, they've got everything you want to know."

—BRETT, 14, IN DENVER

Since 1991, the teenage birth rate has dropped 12%

ing about condoms in this country, and you end up fighting about the future of the American family," says Sarah Brown, director of the Campaign Against Teen Pregnancy. "Teens just end up frozen like a deer in headlights."

Not all kids are happy with television's usurping the role of village griot. Many say they've become bored by—and even resent—sexual themes that seem pointless and even a distraction from the information or entertainment they're seeking. "It's like everywhere," says Ryan, a 13-year-old seventh-grader in Denver, "even in *Skateboarding* [magazine]. It's become so normal it doesn't even affect you. On TV, out of nowhere, they'll begin talking about masturbation." Another Ryan, 13, in the eighth grade at the same school, agrees: "There's sex in the cartoons and messed-up people on the talk shows—'My lover sleeping with my best friend.' I can remember the jumping-condom ads. There's just too much of it all."

Many kids are torn between living up to a moral code espoused by their church and parents and trying to stay true to the swirling laissez-faire. Experience is making many sadder but wiser. The shame, anger or even indifference stirred by early sex can lead to prolonged abstinence. Chandra, a 17-year-old in Detroit, says she had sex with a boyfriend of two years for the first time at 15 despite her mother's constant pleas against it. She says she wishes she had heeded her mother's advice. "One day I just decided to do it," she says. "Afterward, I was kind of mad that I let it happen. And I was sad because I knew my mother wouldn't have approved." Chandra stopped dating the boy more than a year ago and hasn't had sex since. "It would have to be someone I really cared about," she says. "I've had sex before, but I'm not a slut."

With little guidance from grownups, teens have had to discover for themselves that the ubiquitous sexual messages must be tempered with caution and responsibility. It is quite clear, even to the most sexually experienced youngsters, just how dangerous a little information can be. Stephanie in North Lauderdale, who lost her virginity two years

DR. DREW, *AFTER-HOURS* GURU

KIDS AREN'T SUPPOSED TO BE TUNING IN TO DR. DREW PINSKY ON *Loveline,* MTV's popular nightly call-in show on relationships. The program is aimed at young adults, and, Pinsky says, younger teens shouldn't watch it without a parent nearby. But they manage to. Sometimes because of a technicality: the show airs at 10 p.m. in the Central time zone instead of 11 p.m., as it does on the East and West coasts. But mainly because the subject is sex. And if sex is on the tube, adolescents are sure to find a way of getting to it—and talking about it.

And what do kids see? This scene, for example: Dr. Drew listening closely to an embarrassed 21-year-old whose girlfriend has been joking to his friends about the size of his penis. Pinsky handles this painful subject with a quick, matter-of-fact suggestion: Take a closer, more informed look at your abusive girlfriend. After a crass joke from Pinsky's partner, comedian Adam Carolla—there to provide levity—*Loveline*'s newest co-host, Diane Farr, affirms that size, despite what the ads for *Godzilla* say, is not all it's cracked up to be. Pinsky's message, both educational and reassuring, is one that permeates his show: Respect yourself.

"I suppose I'm a healthier role model than, say, Slash of *Guns N' Roses,*" concedes the practicing internist of his idol status among the scores of adolescents and young adults comforted by his gently informative, utterly genuine approach. But what motivates him is his ability to reach a population in desperate need of information—a skill he first discovered 15 years ago as a medical student in California. When two disc-jockey acquaintances were starting a new show on relationships, they asked him to be the medical consultant. Pinsky, now a happily married parent of triplets, had sensed that young people were not receiving much sex education from their parents—a result of what he calls the 1970s "abdication of parenting" ethos. But he was stunned by the response to the first few shows. "It was an epiphany. The most important health issues for younger people were being presented to FM disc jockeys!"

A full-fledged convert, Pinsky signed on as "Dr. Drew" to what quickly became *Loveline,* the hit Los Angeles-based radio show he still plays host on (and which MTV's version is based on). His growing medical practice confirmed his suspicions about kids: "Behind closed doors, they wouldn't talk at all. In my white coat, I was an authority figure. I was Dad, their worst nightmare." In a medium in which kids were comfortable, he could "demystify" difficult issues surrounding sexuality and "maybe make adolescence less painful."

What may make *Loveline* a particularly compelling alternative to, say, daytime TV's *Jerry Springer,* is its underlying "mission." Pinsky is obsessed with changing what he views as a culture of "broken-down interpersonal relationships" that lack intimacy. He calls the show a "sheep in wolf's clothing that discourages sexual activity and encourages responsibility and connection in a hip, relatable context. Of particular concern to him is the rest of the media, which often portray sex as a simple physical act with no emotional consequences. Is he troubled about young teens having sex? Pinsky says a significant percentage may be reacting to having been sexually abused. He also suggests, though, that as a whole this group tends to be healthier, more inquisitive and "more realistic" than the older generation. That bodes well for Pinsky's aim to change the world. "We're not glamourizing sex; we are confronting behavior," he says emphatically. "The idea is to climb into their culture. I'll take any punch. I'm just grateful I'm welcomed."

—*By Harriet Barovick*

ago, watches with concern as her seven-year-old sister moves beyond fuzzy thoughts of romance inspired by *Cinderella* or *Aladdin* into sexual curiosity. "She's always talking about pee-pees, and she sees somebody on TV kissing and hugging or something, and she says, 'Oh, they had sex.' I think she's

going to find out about this stuff before I did." She pauses. "We don't tell my sister anything," she says, "but she's not a naive child." —*With reporting by Julie Grace/Salt Lake City, Richard Woodbury/Denver, Charlotte Faltermayer/New York, Timothy Roche/Fort Lauderdale and other bureaus*

THE SEX INDUSTRY

Giving the customer what he wants

To its buyers and sellers, the sex trade is just another business

AT THE Vegas striptease joint in Kiel, in northern Germany, business is flat. So is the champagne. Dancers sit listlessly at the bar, waiting for a customer to buy them an overpriced "cocktail" in exchange for a few minutes of sympathetic conversation. "Too much sex on television," explains the manager grumpily. "Why should people pay here when they can get it for free just sitting at home?" Ten years ago, he says, business was so much better.

Next door, in Kiel's Eros Centre (one of Germany's big licensed brothels), scores of prostitutes stand waiting at the doors of their rooms, ogled by a trickle of men traipsing along the red-lit corridors. Business is bad here too. The standard price, DM50 (about $30), is unchanged since 1992—in other words, it has dropped by nearly a third in real terms.

Welcome to the international sex industry, turnover at least $20 billion a year and probably many times that, of which Kiel's struggling little red-light district is a corner. It is the black sheep of the entertainment industry, in parts hugely lucrative, in parts pitifully poorly paid. Riddled with malpractice and sleaze, it unites one of the world's oldest businesses, prostitution, and one of its newest, Internet sex. Just possibly, respectability beckons.

To start with, some categories. There are what may be called services: prostitution, striptease and telephone sex. And there are products: pornography and sex aids. In both parts of the industry, a handful of well-run and imaginative businesses are making money as never before—through upmarket escort agencies, for instance, or over the Internet, or by intelligently exploiting market niches. Traditional businesses, especially the many small and amateurish ones, are threatened with extinction.

What is going on? The biggest change, as in so many industries, is globalisation. In many poor countries, international tourism and business travel have made prostitution spectacularly rewarding. In Riga's luxury Hotel de Rome, a designer-dressed Latvian woman working the night bar, at $200 a time, confides that she nets an average $5,000 a month, in a country where the average wage is one-twentieth of that. "I meet some useful people too," she says; she is planning to set up a marketing agency soon. In the Hotel Gellert, in Budapest, a Hungarian woman proudly shows off one of the world's most coveted passports: her earnings have financed a marriage of convenience with a Swiss. Naturalisation is imminent—enabling her to work, she says, "anywhere I want in the world."

Hundreds of thousands of women from poor countries dream of something similar. For most, a tourist visa suffices. At the bottom of the market, few language or other skills are required. Increasingly, western providers of sexual services are finding it difficult to compete with foreigners. As in other industries, these new competitors work longer hours, for less money, and with less concern for safety and comfort than their western counterparts.

Much the same is happening on the product side of the business. Sex aids these days are produced almost exclusively in China. Most West European producers of sex videos use East European actors wherever possible. "They cost less and do more," an executive at Germany's Silwa production company explains, bluntly. In only eight years, Budapest has become probably the biggest centre for pornography production in Europe, eclipsing rivals such as Amsterdam and Copenhagen. Stars' fees have dropped sharply. Even excruciating or humiliating acts usually cost the producer only two or three hundred dollars, roughly a third of the fees paid ten years ago.

Hand in hand with globalisation goes another business trend—commoditisation. The downmarket end of the industry, be it run-of-the-mill pornography or street prostitution, is a buyers' market, where prices are ratcheted downwards and only the cheapest supplier survives. A lorry driver going from Prague to Berlin sees hundreds if not thousands of prostitutes lining the E55 highway offering their services. The cheapest, typically Gypsies or Ukrainians, charge a pitiful $10, or less.

Where does this leave the entrepreneur? For the ruthless ones, the road to riches is clear and brutal: cut costs by treating your workers abominably. Women and girls can be enticed (or kidnapped) from poor countries, smuggled into rich ones and worked as sex slaves. If they complain, they are warned, not only they but their families back home will suffer. Russian pimps in Western Europe have a reputation for astonishing violence and cruelty. There is still plenty of money to be made in this line of business. But in the longer term the future of cut-price prostitution looks bleak. Bruised, terrorised prostitutes in ugly surroundings attract only the least choosy, and worst-paying, customers.

Even for the non-criminal parts of the industry, the main response to the last ten years has been to keep churning out cheap material. "A lot of people in the sex industry don't know very much about sex—they're just ignorant chauvinist men," says Tuppy Owens, Britain's best-known campaigner for freer sex laws, and a fierce critic of the standards in the commercial sex industry. But, she says, customers get what they deserve: "The people doing the good things aren't the ones making the money. People actually want the bad stuff." Many customers of the sex industry, it seems, find that a sordid rip-off chimes nicely with their need for a touch of degradation.

A more intelligent response to price pressure and global competition, in the sex industry as in any other, is to go upmarket. Prostitutes in hotel bars and nightclubs charge five or six times as much as their sisters on the streets. One well-known call girl in London specialises in investment bankers and charges £1,000 a night. Upscale prostitution is safer: customers may be nicer; hotels offer more protection than a pimp (they have a reputation to protect, after all) and take a smaller cut.

Perhaps the best example of specialisation comes among prostitutes working in the Gulf states, where aristocratic Arabs are the best-paying customers. Tastes are clear: local women are prized most highly (at up to $2,000, according to an insider); other Arab women come sec-ond. Europeans and then Thai and Filipino women cost the least. The result? Moroccan prostitutes have been learning colloquial Gulf Arabic, so that they can pass as locals and collect a higher fee; Russians lucky enough to have Middle Eastern complexions and features have been studying Arabic to increase their earning power. For their part, classy London call-girls have been learning Russian: globalisation, after all, creates lots of new customers, as well as new competition.

Pornucopia

The same applies to pornography. The bottom of the market is hopelessly oversupplied. Watching every one of the many tens of thousands of pornographic videos made in the past 20 years would take most of an adult life-time. Staying awake would be a big problem: most are barely distinguishable, with feeble plots and dialogue. Demand for basic porn is all but saturated. This has yet to sink in. "There are still people who think that putting any old sex scene on screen will make them a fortune. All it really does is drive down prices," sniffs the Silwa executive.

As in any business threatened with commoditisation, what really makes money is building a brand or finding a niche. Consumers will pay a premium for a familiar face—such as Teresa Orlowski, the Hanover-based porn star who now runs one of Germany's biggest sex-video businesses. Offering customers something new or different works too. Videos on subjects which would have been considered odd, or even kinky, a few years ago, such as tickling, or foot fetishes, can now be found occupying a shelf or two in the "adult" section of any well-stocked video store. American porn barons such as Steven Hirsch of Vivid Video have made a fortune by producing (slightly) more upmarket fare, featuring such innovations as connected dialogue and intimations of a plot.

Vivid is the most powerful studio in America's porn-film industry. Na-tionally, adult videos bring in $2½ billion a year, according to *Adult Video News,* and account for more than a quarter of all sales and rentals at the typical video store. Most of the industry resides in the San Fernando Valley, on the north side of LA's Santa Monica mountains, and especially in two centres of activity. Van Nuys, once a middle-class suburb ("the town that started right", says its motto), is home to both Vivid and Doc Johnson's, a maker of sex toys. Chatsworth, an area of industrial warehouses on the Valley's northern rim, has so many porn studios that it is known locally as Silicone Valley. One of its biggest studios, Trac Tech, is a gigantic affair, with permanent sets made up to look like a hospital, a bar and a restaurant—also bedrooms, obviously.

As in many another industrial cluster, the Valley's porn business has drawn other firms towards it. There are talent agencies, such as Pretty Girls International; strip clubs such as Bob's Classy Lady, which allow women to show their talents and earn money between films; and sex-aid factories, one of which does a nice line in casts of porn stars' genitalia. Great Western Litho, which prints the covers of hard-core videos, is one of the Valley's leading employers, along with Hewlett-Packard and Anheuser-Busch.

Perhaps with a view to improving its reputation, or to developing distinctive brands, or maybe just because its principals have a sense of humour, the adult-film business loves to imitate the pretensions of mainstream Hollywood. The industry has its own Oscars, complete with stretch limousines and gushing acceptance speeches, as well as its own fan clubs and film critics. Vivid Video has revived the Hollywood studio system, signing actors on exclusive contracts and promoting its actresses as "Vivid girls", a cut above the regular porno crowd. Mr Hirsch spends most of his time on the phone talking about distribution and licensing.

Just now mainstream Hollywood is returning the compliment. Apart from "Boogie Nights", an affectionate study of the rise and fall of a young porn star, four other new mainstream films take porn as their subject—including "Merchants of Venus", by Len Richmond (the son of a sex-toy entrepreneur), and "Some Nudity Required", a hit at the recent Sundance Film Festival." Hollywood could learn some valuable business lessons from its embarrassing sibling in the Valley. Unlike the regular studios, plagued by rising costs (particularly for stars' salaries) and dismal profits, the porn business has been excellent at controlling costs. Only a handful of leading actresses earn up to $100,000 a year; most are paid say $300 for a girl-girl scene and $400 for a boy-girl scene.

One fast-growing part of the American porn business has ever lower costs: the "home-video" industry. Home-made videos, typically shot with cheap handheld camcorders, and with actors working for love (or something) more than money, now account for between a fifth and a third of all adult videos made in America. As part of the industry moves upmarket, seeking higher prices to cover its higher costs, the rest may be heading even further downmarket, with costs as close to zero as may be, with prices and quality to match.

The advent of the home-video camera is by no means the only change in technology affecting the industry. But the porn business is a keen innovator—again unlike mainstream Hollywood. Most leading porno stars have their own web sites, some of them interactive. New tapes allow you to watch up to eight films simultaneously, while some CD-ROMS allow you a measure of control over what happens on the screen.

The Internet is the most important of all the changes, technological or otherwise, affecting the global sex industry. Among other things, it has removed the biggest obstacles to selling pornography and sexual services: shame and ignorance. The "World Sex Guide", for instance, is an Internet site that gives detailed

(anonymous) reviews of brothels, escort agencies and nightclubs in hundreds of cities around the world. In the past, a dissatisfied customer of the sex industry had almost no recourse. Furtive buyers are seldom hard bargainers, or loud complainers. The Internet is changing this. If a $50 "private show" in a striptease bar proves to be nothing more than a bored wiggle behind a curtain, a dissatisfied customer has the chance to warn future ones to take their money elsewhere.

For escort agencies, for example, the Internet cuts out the trouble and expense of sending colour catalogues, or videos, to prospective clients. Previously restricted to marketing their services through small advertisements in newspapers and telephone directories, prostitutes can tempt their customers much more effectively in cyberspace. Well-run pornographic websites are the most profitable places on the Internet (which, for the moment, admittedly, is not saying much).

At the same time, however, the Internet removes a large chunk of the sex industry's potential market by creating a vast new source of free or nearly free material. Online communication means that the exhibitionist and the voyeur, the person who likes writing smutty stories and the person who likes reading them, can get together for the price of a local telephone call. One wellknown meeting place on the Internet is www.bianca.com; it says it has more than a million visits a day.

Another technological development —cheap colour printing, and the consequent increase in magazine titles—has created a further problem for the industry. Readership for most mainstream soft-porn magazines, such as *Penthouse*, has plummeted over the past 20 years. New magazines, such as Britain's *GQ* or *Loaded*, offer much of the titillation with almost none of the embarrassment. Barriers between pornography and entertainment are also being blurred by the liberalisation of broadcasting. Documentary pro-

grammes on such challenging themes as the problems *ménages à trois* face when trying to book hotel rooms are standard fare on late-night private television stations in much of continental Europe.

What about standards?

Evidently the sex industry is exposed to many of the forces that normal businesses must content with. But will it ever become quite normal—an entirely respectable part of the entertainment industry? History suggests it might: a Victorian visiting any modern Western city, or picking up a newspaper or glancing up at many a billboard, might conclude that it already had. Public reserve is not set in stone. Tolerance of pornography has changed a good deal even in the past two decades. The subject matter of famous obscenity trials from the 1960s and 1970s seems almost comical in comparison with the material now shown in the late evening on, for example, Britain's Channel 4 or Germany's Pro 7.

But the industry has some way to go, judging by the alacrity with which many sex-industry tycoons still seek to establish themselves in other businesses once they have made some serious money. One of the Arab world's best-known pimps founded a bank. The current top Russian pimp in the Middle East is building a hotel. How long will it be before sex-entrepreneurs can marry their children to royalty, or even to legitimate tradespeople, without the bother of diversifying?

Presumably, it will happen faster if the industry's practitioners find a political voice, so that they can lobby legislators to remove or streamline the remaining legal restrictions on the industry. Surprisingly, this seems to be happening, particularly in America. California's pornography industry already wields considerable political clout—as well it might, given its scale. There is also a vocal lobby in Australia (it recently sent research to legislators showing an inverse correlation between numbers of legal brothels and the incidence of sex crimes). In Germany, by contrast, industry groups still concentrate on enforcing the law rather than changing it. The pornographic filmakers' association, the GüFA, upholds its members' copyright interests. Another body polices the country's draconian retailing laws—taking petrol stations to court, for example, if they dare to sell pornography.

The commercial interest in cleaning up the industry coincides with an important objective of social policy: ending trafficking in women. Campaigners on this issue, sponsored by the European Union and other international bodies, are increasingly sure that only legalisation gives a basis for tackling criminality. There are even flickers or organisation from the people who bear the brunt of the current hypocritical legal climate, the workers. Erotic dancers in America have formed a union, and even staged a strike last year. In Germany workers in the same occupation are already organized by the IG Medien trade union.

Prohibition of gambling and alcohol have both been tried in varying degrees in dozens of countries around the world, always with the result of stimulating illegality and sleaze. The sex industry appears to be no different. All developed economies have conceded that the business is impossible to stamp out. Tolerating prostitution while leaving it technically illegal or semi-legal encourages corruption: policemen are paid to turn a blind eye. It also renders the workers helpless against their employers. Until recently, sex slaves who escaped from brothels in most European countries were usually deported as illegal aliens, which hardly helped the authorities nail their oppressors. The inexorable trend, in both law and public morals, is towards legalisation of what is already tolerated.

That would free law-enforces to concentrate on what is not tolerated, such as the sexual exploitation of children. And it would put the greater part of the sex business where it ultimately belongs—as just another branch of the global entertainment industry.

Producers of pornography would compete for real Oscars. Street prostitution might be treated like any other outdoor entertainment, such as busking, regulated according to local taste and circumstance. Brothels and strip clubs would arouse no more comment than casinos and nightclubs. Some customers might find it all rather dull and clinical: a niche would remain for the authentic experience, complete with gorilla on the door, over-priced drinks and grubby red velvet sofas. Others might like the new professionalism. Frequent flyer miles? You read it here first.

Who Owns Prostitution—and Why?

Why decriminalizing prostitution is the right thing to do

Lacey Sloan

Prostitution is a crime—or is it a business? Its practitioners are victims—or are they entrepreneurs? They're oppressed—or are they rulers of their own destiny?

So it goes—and has gone for centuries—in the debate over the status of prostitutes and their maligned profession.

THE DEBATE

Nowadays, the verbal conflict exists primarily between some feminists and women escaping the sex-trade industry (all forms of sex work) on one side, and other feminists and women in the sex-trade industry who want to be considered legitimate workers on the other side. Although many people believe that all feminists recognize sex work (sexual activity performed for compensation) as victimization,[1] women who consider themselves feminists do not all speak with the same voice on this issue.[2]

Feminists and sex-trade workers claim sex-workers are businesswomen who should be granted the same freedom to work as any other worker.

Almost all feminists and sex workers who have written on the subject advocate that sex workers not be criminally liable for engaging in sex work. Almost all feminists and sex workers also acknowledge the abuse endured by sex workers and the poor social, political, and economic condition of women in general.[3] Beyond these similarities, two distinct points of view emerge. On one side are feminists and women escaping the sex-trade industry who believe that sex work is a form of victimization of women perpetrated by a patriarchal system that wants to maintain men's right to sexual access to women.[4] This group of women (frequently referred to as prostitution abolitionists) believes sex workers are victims and call for the abolition of the sex-trade industry (sex work would be legal,

Lacey Sloan is a professor in the Graduate School of Social Work at the University of Houston.

but procuring, pimping, and profiting from the wages of a sex worker would not).[5] On the other side of the debate, other feminists and sex-trade workers (frequently referred to as sex-workers' rights groups) claim sex workers are businesswomen who should be granted the same freedom to work as any other worker.[6] These sex-workers' rights groups claim sex workers are not victims, except of puritanical mores and oppressive laws; they want sex work legalized or decriminalized.

A LABOR MOVEMENT BLOSSOMS

Prior to 1973, sex workers were not acknowledged as being capable of speaking for themselves.[7] In 1973, Margo St. James organized a sex-workers' rights organization called COYOTE (Call Off Your Old Tired Ethics).[8] Together with a variety of professionals, including social workers, sex workers have tried to raise awareness about the abuse of sex workers by the state and police, and to effect changes in laws.[9]

By the mid-1970s, sex-workers' rights organizations began to form across the United States and around the world (for example, in The Netherlands, the Red Thread; in Atlanta Georgia, Hooking is Real Employment [HIRE]; and, in England, Prostitution Laws Are Nonsense [PLAN]). Sex-workers' rights groups believe that "most women who work as prostitutes have made a conscious decision to do so, having looked at a number of work alternatives."[10] These organizations, along with the American Civil Liberties Union (ACLU) and the National Organization for Women (NOW), want sex work decriminalized or legalized. These groups believe that the illegal status of most sex-trade workers leaves these women unprotected from acts of violence, rape, and exploitation.

The advent of the sex-workers' rights movement of the 1970s finally provided a forum for the sex worker to speak for herself. The sex-workers' rights movement was founded on three general tenets, all of which are based on the right to self-determination. First, members of the movement do not believe that all sex work is forced, and, in fact, believe that many women freely choose this work.[11] Second, they believe that sex work should be viewed and respected as legitimate work.[12] And third, they believe it is a violation of a woman's civil rights to be denied the opportunity to work as a sex worker.[13]

These women "demand recognition as workers" as well as "freedom to financial autonomy . . . occupational choice . . . sexual self-determination . . . (and) worker's rights and protections."[14]

Contrary to the abolitionists' plan to support sex workers while working to eliminate the institution of sex work, sex-workers' rights groups and many sex workers reject "support which requires them to leave the profession."[15] They also "object to being treated as symbols of oppression,"[16] an image placed on them by some authors.[17] Sex-workers' rights groups claim there is no difference in work in which a woman sells her hands, such as a typist, and work in which a woman sells her vagina, as in sex work.[18]

Sex workers and sex-workers' rights groups are concerned about the sexual violence, physical violence, and/or exploitation that prostitutes suffer at the hands of customers, pimps, and the police. As sex workers spoke out at the World Whores Congresses, many told of heinous acts of abuse that had been perpetrated against them and other prostitutes.[19] They acknowledged that sex workers have been kidnapped, tortured, raped, and forced into sex work. Yet, unlike those who rally for the abolition of sex work, those in favor of decriminalization (which would make all aspects of sex work legal, but perhaps subject to standard business regulations) want these abuses stopped by the enforcement of existing laws that prohibit kidnapping, assault, rape, and fraud. Those who support the decriminalization of prostitution and other forms of sex work

Sex workers have tried to raise awareness about the abuse of sex workers by the state and police, and to effect changes in laws.

point to the illegality of most sex work as one of the primary factors that leaves them vulnerable to abuse, rape, and exploitation.[20]

In countries where sex work is regulated, sex workers are stigmatized and placed under scrutiny not required of any other legal worker. Other forms of control enforced in regulated systems include registration of sex workers and "imprisonment" in brothels or within certain zones.[21] In countries and states where sex work is illegal and/or tolerated (authorities ignore or loosely enforce the laws), sex workers are unable to demand rights and benefits as workers and are generally denied police protection.[22] This leaves sex workers vulnerable to exploitation, poor working conditions, physical abuse, arrest, and incarceration.[23] Immigrant women who prostitute may be deported; mothers who prostitute can lose custody of their children.[24] These are but a few examples of the reasons sex workers want prostitution (sexual activity involving direct contact with customers for compensation) and sex work decriminalized, not regulated or prohibited (complete criminalization).

Controlling the Oldest Profession: From Ancient Rome to Nevada

From at least 600 B.C.E. through the early 1600s, government taxation and regulation of sex workers waxed and waned as societal attitudes for and against prostitution changed. In sixth-century Europe, earlier restrictions that had been placed on sex workers were eliminated and replaced with harsh penalties for procurers. In fact this action, taken by the Roman leader Justinian, was coupled with what may have been the first program designed to rehabilitate the sex worker. General consensus on the importance of regulating sex work does not seem to have occurred until the Reformation of the sixteenth century. At this time, the serious health threat of venereal disease seems to have been the major motivation for the regulation of prostitution. Sixteenth-century Europe was characterized by the widespread regulation and prohibition of sex work.

In the frontier West in the United States, sex work grew during the 1800s. Many women who traveled west have been described as adventurers who were not happy with life on the farm, and "did not find prostitution so reprehensible that they wouldn't engage in it." As in the East, sex work in the West was generally prohibited, but tolerated by law enforcement. Some western communities regulated sex workers by segregating brothels and conducting medical exams on the prostitutes.

Josephine Butler is frequently credited with leading the movement to abolish regulation of sex work. Viewing forced medical exams as a form of rape, and regulation as a means of maintaining

women in a life of sex work, she worked successfully to repeal the Contagious Disease Acts of 1864, 1866, and 1869, which had required registration and forced medical exams of prostitutes. Butler believed that sex workers were victims of economic injustice and a sexual double standard. Although Butler did not support the institution of prostitution, she felt that prohibition and regulation of sex workers served to further victimize prostitute women. Butler eventually distanced herself from the abolition movement, which had become more repressive to women as the focus changed from the abolition of regulation to the abolition of sex work itself.

In 1908, the United States joined the 1904 International Agreement for the Suppression of White Slave Traffic, in which countries agreed to take action against international prostitution. In 1910, the United States passed the White Slave Traffic Act, also known as the Mann Act, which prohibited interstate or international travel for the purpose of prostitution. By 1925, all states had enacted legislation directed at stopping white slavery and prostitution. Although these laws stopped regulated prostitution, and temporarily impacted tolerated prostitution, illegal prostitution continued. Although prostitution is prohibited in all states except Nevada, it is tolerated in varying degrees across the country. Most forms of sex work that do not involve intimate physical contact with a customer, such as telephone sex, peep shows, topless dancing, and nude dancing, are legal, though regulated.

—*Lacey Sloan*

EMPOWERMENT FOR ALL WOMEN

Sex workers and sex workers' rights groups reject the notion that female heterosexuality perpetuates male privilege and men's dominance of women.[25] Many sex workers believe that it empowers all women for sex workers to charge men for what men expect all women to provide for free.[26] This conflicts with the view that the sex-trade industry perpetuates men's belief in their right to sexual access to all women.[27] It has been stated that,

> [Blinded] by their own experiences as middle-class women, the social purity feminists were entirely unable to perceive the ways in which other women—their own working class sisters—could act as sexual agents rather than as victims, using sex to further their own purposes and pleasures.[28]

Sex workers, prostitutes' rights groups, social workers, and others working for decriminalization point to the history of control of prostitution to reveal that most methods adopted to protect and support prostitutes, such as regulation (legalizing but licensing, taxing, and imposing rules for operation), have failed. Initiatives to prohibit sex work or prostitution have resulted in the isolation, increased vulnerability, abuse, and exploitation of sex work. Programs to regulate sex work have resulted in the control and further stigmatization of sex workers. And, finally, efforts to abolish sex work have denied sex workers their rights to autonomy and self-determination.

Notes

1. C. A. MacKinnon, *Feminism Unmodified: Discourses on Law and Life* (Cambridge, Mass.: Harvard University Press, 1987).

2. L. Bell, ed., *Good Girls, Bad Girls* (Seattle: The Seal Press, 1987). F. Delacoste and P. Alexander, *Sex Work: Writings by Women in the Sex Industry* (Pittsburgh: Cleis Press, 1987), V. Jenness, *Making It Work: The Prostitutes' Rights Movement in Perspective* (New York: Aldine De Gruyter, 1993); G. Pheterson, ed., *A Vindication of the Rights of Whores* (Seattle: The Seal Press, 1989).

3. S. K. Hunter, "Prostitution Is Cruelty and Abuse to Women and Children," *Michigan Journal of Gender and Law,* 1, 1–14.

4. A. Dworkin, *Intercourse* (New York: The Free Press, 1987); MacKinnon op. cit.

5. K. Barry, C. Bunch, S. Castley, eds., *International Feminism: Networking Against Female Sexual Slavery* (New York: The International Women's Tribune Centre, Inc., 1984); MacKinnon, op. cit.

6. Bell; Delacoste and Alexander; Jenness; Pheterson, op. cit.

7. Pheterson, op. cit.

8. Jenness, Pheterson, op. cit.

9. Pheterson, op. cit.

10. Coyote Howls, 1988, cited in Jenness op. cit.

11. Jenness, Pheterson, op. cit.

12. Ibid.

13. Jenness, op. cit.

14. International Committee on Prostitutes' Rights, cited in Pheterson, op. cit. pp. 192–97.

15. Ibid., p. 192.

16. Ibid.

17. Barry, Bunch, and Castley, op. cit.; Brownmiller; Dworkin; MacKinnon, op. cit.

18. Jenness, Pheterson, op. cit.

19. Pheterson, op. cit.

20. Ibid.

21. Ibid.

22. Ibid.

23. Ibid.

24. Ibid.

25. Jenness, op. cit.

26. Jenness, op. cit., National Coalition Against Sexual Assault, *Support for Sex Trade Workers* (1991a).

27. Barry, Bunch, and Castley; Dworkin; MacKinnon, op. cit.

28. A. Snitow, C. Stansell, and S. Thompson, eds., *Powers of Desire: The Politics of Sexuality* (New York: Monthly Review Press, 1983).

The PLEASURE of the PAIN

Why Some People Need S & M

By Marianne Apostolides

Bind my ankles with your white cotton rope so I cannot walk. Bind my wrists so I cannot push you away. Place me on the bed and wrap your rope tighter around my skin so it grips my flesh. Now I know that struggle is useless, that I must lie here and submit to your mouth and tongue and teeth, your hands and words and whims. I exist only as your object. Exposed.

Of every 10 people who reads these words, one or more has experimented with sadomasochism (S & M), which is most popular among educated, middle- and upper-middle-class men and women, according to psychologists and ethnographers who have studied the phenomenon. Charles Moser, Ph.D., M.D., of the Institute for Advanced Study of Human Sexuality in San Francisco, has researched S & M to learn the motivation behind it—to understand why in the world people would ask to be bound, whipped and flogged. The reasons are as surprising as they are varied.

For James, the desire became apparent when he was a child playing war games—he always hoped to be captured. "I was frightened that I was sick," he says. But now, he adds, as a well-seasoned player on the scene, "I thank the leather gods I found this community."

At first the scene found him. When he was at a party in college, a professor chose him. She brought him home and tied him up, told him how bad he was for having these desires, even as she fulfilled them. For the first time he felt what he had only imagined, what he had read about in every S & M book he could find.

James, a father and manager, has a Type A personality—in-control, hard-working, intelligent, demanding. His intensity is evident on his face, in his posture, in his voice. But when he plays, his eyes drift and a peaceful energy flows through him as though he had injected heroin. With each addition of pain or restraint, he stiffens slightly, then falls into a deeper calm, a deeper peace, waiting to obey his mistress. "Some people have to be tied up to be free," he says.

As James' experience illustrates, sadomasochism involves a highly unbalanced power relationship established through role-playing, bondage, and/or the infliction of pain. The essential component is not the pain or bondage itself, but rather the knowledge that one person has complete control over the other, deciding what that person will hear, do, taste, touch, smell and feel. We hear about men pretending to be little girls, women being bound in a leather corset, people screaming in pain with each strike of a flogger or drip of hot wax. We hear about it because it is happening in bedrooms and dungeons across the country.

For over a century, people who engaged in bondage, beatings and humiliation for sexual pleasure were considered mentally ill. But in the 1980s, the American Psychiatric Association removed S & M as a category in its *Diagnostic and Statistical Manual of Mental Disorders*. This decision—like the decision to remove homosexuality as a category in 1973—was a big step toward the societal acceptance of people whose sexual desires aren't traditional, or vanilla, as it's called in S & M circles.

What's new is that such desires are increasingly being considered normal, even healthy, as experts begin to recognize their potential psychological value. S & M, they are beginning to understand, offers a release of sexual and emotional energy that some people cannot get from traditional sex. "The satisfaction gained from S & M is something far more than sex," explains Roy Baumeister, Ph.D., a social psychologist at Case Western Reserve University. "It can be a total emotional release."

Although people report that they have better-than-usual sex immediately after a scene, the goal of S & M itself is not intercourse: "A good scene doesn't end in orgasm, it ends in catharsis."

S & M: No Longer A Pathology

"If children at [an] early age witness sexual intercourse between adults . . . they inevitably regard the sexual act as a sort of ill-treatment or act of subjugation: they view it, that is, in a sadistic sense."—Sigmund Freud, 1905

Freud was one of the first to discuss S & M on a psychological level. During the 20 years he explored the topic, his theories crossed each other to create a maze of contradictions. But he maintained one constant: S & M was pathological.

> *People become masochistic, Freud said, as a way of regulating their desire to sexually dominate others.*

People become masochistic, Freud said, as a way of regulating their desire to sexually dominate others. The desire to submit, on the other hand, he said, arises from guilt feelings over the desire to dominate. He also argued that the desire for S & M can arise on its own when a man wants to assume the passive female role, with bondage and beating signifying being "castrated or copulated with, or giving birth."

The view that S & M is pathological has been dismissed by the psychological community. Sexual sadism is a real problem, but it is a different phenomenon from S & M. Luc Granger, Ph.D., head of the department of psychology at the University of Montreal, created an intensive treatment program for sexual aggressors in La Macaza Prison in Quebec; he has also conducted research on the S & M community. "They are very separate populations," he says. While S & M is the regulated exchange of power among consensual participants, sexual sadism is the derivation of pleasure from either inflicting pain or completely controlling an unwilling person.

Lily Fine, a professional dominatrix who teaches S & M workshops across North America, explains: "I may hurt you, but I will not harm you: I will not hit you too hard, take you further than you want to go or give you an infection."

Despite the research indicating that S & M does no real harm and is not associated with pathology, Freud's successors in psychoanalysis continue to use mental illness overtones when discussing S & M. Sheldon Bach, Ph.D., clinical professor of psychology at New York University and supervising analyst at the New York Freudian Society,

maintains that people are addicted to S & M. They feel compelled to be "anally abused or crawl on their knees and lick a boot or a penis or who knows what else. The problem," he continues, "is that they can't love. They are searching for love, and S & M is the only way they can try to find it because they are locked into sadomasochistic interactions they had with a parent."

Linking Childhood Memories And Adult Sex

"I can explore aspects of myself that I don't get a chance to explore otherwise. So even though I'm playing a role, I feel more connected with myself."—Leanne Custer, M.S.W., AIDS counselor

Meredith Reynolds, Ph.D., the Sexuality Research Fellow of the Social Science Research Council, confirms that childhood experiences may shape a person's sexual outlook.

"Sexuality doesn't just arise at puberty," she says. "Like other parts of someone's personality, sexuality develops at birth and takes a developmental course through a person's life span."

In her work on sexual exploration among children, Reynolds has shown that while childhood experiences can indeed influence adult sexuality, the effects usually "wash out" as a person gains more sexual experience. But they can linger in some people, causing a connection between childhood memories and adult sexual play. In that case, Reynolds says, "the childhood experiences have affected something in the personality, and that in turn affects adult experiences."

Reynolds' theory helps us develop a greater understanding of the desire to be a whip-bearing mistress or a bootlicking slave. For example, if a child has been taught to feel shame about her body and desires, she may learn to disconnect herself from them. Even as she gets older and gains more experience with sex, her personality may retain some part of that need for separation. S & M play may act as a bridge: Lying naked on a bed bound to the bedposts with leather restraints, she is forced to be completely sexual. The restraint, the futility of struggle, the pain, the master's words telling her she is such a lovely slave—these cues enable her body to fully connect with her sexual self in a way that has been difficult during traditional sex.

Marina is a prime example. She knew from the time she was 6 years old that she was expected to succeed in school and sports. She learned to focus on achievement as a way to dismiss emotions and desires. "I learned very young that desires are dangerous," she says. She heard that message in the behavior of her parents: a depressive mother who let her emotions overtake her, and an obsessively health-conscious father

She says it slowly, making her slave wait for every second, forcing him to focus only on her, to float in anticipation of the sensations she will create inside him.

who compulsively controlled his diet. When Marina began to have sexual desires, her instinct, cultivated by her upbringing, was to consider them too frightening, too dangerous. "So I became anorexic," she says. "And when you're anorexic, you don't feel desire; all you feel in your body is panic."

Marina didn't feel the desire for S & M until she was an adult and had outgrown her eating disorder. "One night I asked my partner to put his hands around my neck and choke me. I was so surprised when those words came out of my mouth," she says. If she gave her partner total control over her body, she felt, she could allow herself to feel like a completely sexual being, with none of the hesitation and disconnection she sometimes felt during sex. "He wasn't into it, but now I'm with someone who is," Marina says. "S & M makes our vanilla sex better, too, because we trust each other more sexually, and we can communicate what we want."

Escaping the Modern Western Ego

"Like alcohol abuse binge eating and meditation, sadomasochism is a way people can forget themselves." Roy Baumeister, Ph.D., professor of psychology, Case Western Reserve University

It is human nature to try to maximize esteem and control: Those are two general principles governing the study of the self. Masochism runs contrary to both, and was therefore an intriguing psychological puzzle for Baumeister, whose career has focused on the study of self and identity.

Through an analysis of S & M-related letters to the sex magazine *Variations.* Baumeister came to believe that "masochism is a set of techniques for helping people temporarily lose their normal identity." He reasoned that the modern Western ego is an incredibly elaborate structure, with our culture placing more demands on the self than any other culture in history. Such high de-

---

Whip Smart: Beyond the Boundaries of Safe Play

While S & M can be a psychologically healthy activity—its motto is "safe, sane and consensual"—sometimes things do get out of hand:

Abuse It is rare, but some "Tops" get too involved in power and forget to monitor their treatment of the "Bottom." "I call them 'Natural Born Tops,'" says dominatrix Lily Fine, "and I don't have time for them." Also, some bottoms want to be beaten because they have low self-esteem and think they deserve it. They are forlorn, absent and unresponsive during and after a scene, in this case, S & M ceases to be play and becomes pathological.

Boundaries A small percentage of people inappropriately bring S & M power play into other facets of their life. "Most people in S & M circles are dominant or submissive in very specific situations, while in their everyday life they can play a whole range of roles," says psychology Professor Luc Granger. But, he continues, if the only way a person can relate to someone else is through a kind of sadomasochistic game, then there is probably a deeper psychological problem.

The Use of S & M as Therapy People often confuse the fact that they feel good after S & M with the idea that S & M is therapy, says psychology Professor Roy Baumeister. "But to prove that something is therapeutic, you have to prove that it has lasting beneficial effects on mental health . . . and it's hard to prove even that therapy is therapeutic." In mental health terms, S & M doesn't make you better and it doesn't make you worse.

---

mands increase the stress associated with living up to expectations and existing as the person you want to be. "That stress makes forgetting who you are an appealing escape," Baumeister says. That is the essence of "escape" theory, one of the main reasons people turn to S & M.

"Nothing matters except you, me and the sound of my voice," Lily Fine tells the tied-up and exposed businessman who begged to be spanked before breakfast. She says it slowly, making her slave wait for every sound, forcing him to focus only on her, to float in anticipation of the sensations she will create inside him. Anxieties about mortgages and taxes, stresses about business partners and job deadlines are vanquished each time the flogger hits the flesh. The businessman is reduced to a physical creature existing only in the here and now, feeling the pain and pleasure.

"I'm interested in manipulating what's in the mind," Lily says. "The brain is the greatest erogenous zone."

In another S & M scene, Lily tells a woman to take off her clothes, then dresses her only with a blindfold. She commands the woman not to move. Lily then takes a tissue and begins moving it over the woman's body in different patterns and at varying speeds and angles. Sometimes she lets the edge of the tissue just barely brush the woman's stomach and breasts; sometimes she bunches

---

the tissue and creates swirls on her back and all the way down. "The woman was quivering. She didn't know what I was doing to her, but she was liking it," Lily remembers with a smile.

One night I asked my partner to put his hands around my neck and choke me.

Escape theory is further supported by an idea called "frame analysis," developed by the late Irving Goffman, Ph.D. According to Goffman, despite its popular conception as darkly wild and orgiastic, S & M play has complex rules, rituals, roles and dynamics that create a "frame" around the experience.

"Frames suspend reality. They create expectations, norms and values that set this situation apart from other parts of life," confirms Thomas Weinberg, Ph.D., a sociologist at Buffalo State College in New York and the editor of *S & M: Studies in Dominance & Submission* (Prometheus Books, 1995).

Excerpts from an S & M Glossary

Sadomasochism (S & M): An activity involving the temporary creation of highly unbalanced power dynamics between two or more people for erotic or semi-erotic purposes.

Bondage and Discipline (B & D): A subset of S & M not involving physical pain.

Top: The dominant person in a scene; synonyms: dominant, dom, master/mistress.

Bottom: The submissive person in a scene; synonyms: submissive, sub, slave.

Switch: A person who enjoys being a Top in some scenes and a Bottom in others.

Sadist: A person who derives sexual pleasure from inflicting pain on others.

Masochist: A person who derives sexual pleasure from being abused by others. Sadist and masochist are sometimes used playfully in the S & M community, but are generally avoided because of psychiatric denotation.

Scene: An episode of S & M activity; the S & M community.

Negotiating a Scene: The process of loosely outlining what the players want to experience before they begin a scene.

Play: Participation in a scene.

Toy: Any implement used to enhance S & M play.

Safe Word: A prearranged word or phrase that may be used to end or renegotiate a scene. This is a clear signal meaning "Stop, this is too much for me."

Dungeon: A place designated for S & M play.

Dominatrix (pl. Dominatrices): A female Top, usually a professional.

Lifestyle Dominant/Submissive: A person involved in a relationship in which S & M is a defining dynamic.

Fetish: An object that is granted special powers, one of which is the ability to sexually gratify. It is often wrongly confused with S & M.

Vanilla Sex: Conventional heterosexual sex.

Once inside the frame, people are free to act and feel in ways they couldn't at other times.

S & M: Part of the Sexual Continuum

S & M has inspired the creation of many psychological theories in addition to the ones discussed here. Do we need so many? Perhaps not. According to Stephanie Saunders, Ph.D., associate director of the Kinsey Institute for Research in Sex, Gender and Reproduction at Indiana University, "a lot of behaviors that are scrutinized because they are seen to be marginal are really a part of the continuum of sexuality and sexual behavior."

After all, the ingredients in good S & M play—communication, respect and trust— are the same ingredients in good traditional sex. The outcome is the same, too—a feeling of connection to the body and the self.

Laura Antoniou, a writer whose work on S & M has been published by Masquerade Books in New York City, puts it another way: "When I was a child, I had nothing but S & M fantasies. I punished Barbie for being dirty. I did Bondage Barbie, dominance with GI Joe. S & M is simply what turns me on."

Marianne Apostolides is author of Inner Hunger: A Young Women's Struggle through Anorexia and Bulimia *(W..W. Norton, 1996). Her last article for* PSYCHOLOGY TODAY, *"How To Quit the Holistic Way," was published in October 1996.*

READ MORE ABOUT IT

Screw the Roses, Send Me the Thorns: The Romance and Sexual Sorcery of Sadomasochism, Philip Miller and Molly Devon (Mystic Rose Books, 1995)

S & M: Studies In Dominance and Submission, Thomas S. Weinberg, editor (Prometheus Books, 1995)

Dark Eros: The Imagination of Sadism, Thomas Moore (Spring Publications, 1996)

GAY NO MORE?

A **breakaway** group of
Christian and **secular** therapists claims
to be able to **convert** homosexuals into
heterosexuals—if they'll just **get with the
program. So what exactly** *is* the **program?**
And does it work? BY BARRY YEOMAN

IT'S A SUNDAY MORNING in Lecanto, Florida, and Faith
Chapel is filled with the Holy Spirit. Tambourines shaking,
guitar jamming, the storefront church is awash in praise.
"Dance with all your might," sing Pentecostal Christians in
khakis and lightweight dresses. "The time's drawing near."
Church members filter down the aisles, and knots of people
form, hands touching shoulders, hands touching faces. A
woman faints and is covered by a white blanket. Another
lifts her arms as her fellow worshippers crowd around her,
encouraging her ecstasy until she, too, faints. "Thank you
Jesus, thank you Jesus," people intone, while the pianist
plays a running melody.

Steve Simmons is in his element. A pale-eyed 38-year-old
with cowboy boots and a goatee, he runs here and there,
his long curly hair slicked back and cascading past his collar.
He sings in the ensemble, prays with people, lays on hands.
His wife Shawn is never far away.

Simmons' old life, by contrast, seems very far away. Earlier in his marriage, he was a closeted homosexual, sneaking off on lunch breaks to find quick release with other men at a lakefront park.

The **KEY** was an "accountability group," **SIX** to **EIGHT** men to whom **he** was **REQUIRED** to **report** every **homosexual** contact, every SAME-SEX *fantasy,* every trip to a **gay bar.**

"Any chance I could get to get away from the house, I was out," he says. He eventually settled into a relationship with a co-worker, and the two men planned to move in together as soon as Simmons could ditch Shawn and their two-year-old daughter.

It took him most of an evening to break the news to Shawn. He brought her to a restaurant but couldn't tell her there; at home, he fumbled for a half-hour before blurting out that he was gay. "What can I do to help?" Shawn asked her husband. Taken aback by his wife's good will and dogged by his religious beliefs, Simmons realized he couldn't leave his marriage. "I know about this ministry," he told her. "I'm willing to go through it if you're willing to stick it out."

She was. So Simmons split up with his male partner and started attending the Orlando-based Eleutheros, one of more than 100 Christian organizations in the United States dedicated to helping people forego gay sex.

There, at a ministry that believes homosexuality stems from family dysfunction, Simmons talked about growing up with a father who was a military medic and would disappear for six-month tours aboard a Coast Guard cutter. He discussed his "domineering and controlling" mother. And he recalled the male teenage cousin who lured him, at nine years old, into unreciprocated sexual service. "I remember feeling that I had made him happy," Simmons now recalls. "I could please a guy, and maybe in some respects, I was trying to please my father." With the help of

Eleutheros, Simmons came to believe that his same-sex urges were an unhealthy mutation of a natural desire to receive the affirmation of other men.

At the same time, he started learning how to avoid temptation. The key was an "accountability group," six to eight men to whom he was required to report every homosexual contact, every same-sex fantasy, every trip to a gay bar. All of a sudden, it was like, 'Do I really want to do this?' To be honest with these guys, that means I've got to stop. And it's not easy."

Though Simmons no longer was sexually intimate with men, he remained attracted to them. "There were times when driving down the road and just looking at a guy in the next car was enough to keep my fantasy life going," he says. "And I could keep myself going on fantasy for a long time."

Other would-be converts dropped out of the ministry, but Simmons persisted, attending meetings up to three times a week. Eventually, he began thinking of homosexuality as an addiction, something he could never get rid of but could keep in check. "The accountability groups give you a chance to sober up," he says. "They give you the time to get away from the sex long enough to start thinking a little more clearly. That was a big part of the recovery process for me, because I finally had a chance to stop and see exactly what my actions were doing, who I was hurting."

Now, four years after leaving Eleutheros, Simmons considers himself one of the ministry's successes. He and his wife have worked on their relationship, and he feels more physically engaged with her. "She still probably wants more sex than we have," he says. "But it's nothing like it was before. Before, we'd have sex maybe once a month. Now it's six to eight times a month. We've come a long way in that respect." Simmons occasionally finds other women attractive, too. "I work outside delivering mail, and I see women, and I think, 'Wow, that looks good.' But I wouldn't say I'm all the way there.

"I don't feel like a stereotypical straight guy, the beer-drinking 'Hey buddy, let's shoot some deer, '" Simmons adds. But neither does he feel consumed by his same-sex desires. "There's still some attraction to men. But it doesn't set off the same bells and whistles it used to. Now I'm a little freer; I can say, 'Wow, that's a very attractive-looking man' and leave it at that. If a guy looked at me and winked, there might be a little sexual flush. But if he's just sitting there, and I look over and he's very handsome—it's not a big deal."

Simmons' is one of the real-life stories behind the "ex-gay" movement, a loose alliance of secular counselors, renegade psychoanalysts and Christian ministries that believe homosexuality is a pathology that can be overcome. Though no statistics exist on the number of men and women who have tried to change their orientations, Exodus International, the Christian ex-gay umbrella-organization, estimates it has fielded 200,000 inquiries from homosexuals and their families since the 1970s, according to director Bob Davies. Exodus and its member ministries now draw more than 400 inquiries a month.

Operating quietly for many years, the movement suddenly burst into notoriety last summer, when 15 conservative organizations began a $400,000 advertising blitz in the *New York Times,* the *Washington Post, USA Today* and other major newspapers. The ads feature photos of men and women who have struggled with same-sex attraction and have a text that reads, "Thousands of ex-gays like these have walked away from their homosexual identities. While the paths each took into homosexuality may vary, their stories of hope and healing through the transforming love of Jesus Christ are the same."

The ads have sparked a firestorm of controversy, with lesbian and gay activists accusing the sponsors, including the Christian Coalition, of exploiting sexually confused individuals to promote an ideological agenda. It has been a made-for-media issue, and the press has focused on the political debate.

Lost among the coverage have been the more personal issues: What is the nature of sexual orientation, and is it mutable? Who are the thousands of people seeking to change their sexualities? What life experiences drive someone to seek a "conversion" to heterosexuality? And what does it mean to convert? Are homosexuals truly shedding their same-sex attractions? Or do they continue to struggle against their natural impulses, accepting celibacy or marriage as a socially sanctioned substitute? In other words, can one really "learn" to be straight?

Moreover, is it healthy to try? For people within the ex-gay movement, this last is an easy question to answer. They believe that homosexuality is sick or immoral, and anything that frees someone from having gay sex is inherently health-

ful. "We're not free from the opportunity, but we're free from the power of sin," says Greg Wallace, an ex-gay who now runs the Living Waters ministry in Beech Grove, Indiana. "The word 'recovery' means the ability to live a productive and enjoyable life, beyond the control of life-dominating sexual behavior and impulse."

The vast majority of mental-health professionals, however, view reorientation programs with skepticism and alarm. In December, the American Psychiatric Association's board voted unanimously to oppose conversion therapy, saying that it could "reinforce self-hatred already experienced by the patient." Even the American Psychoanalytic Association, once in favor of attempts to "cure" homosexuality, has moved away from endorsing such efforts. Marvin Margolis, M.D., Ph.D., past president of the association, calls same-sex attraction "a variant of normal sexuality."

Most psychologists say that conversion ministries and therapists are trying to force lesbians and gay men into a mold that doesn't really fit, and the results could lead to depression, addiction, even suicide. "When people repress their orientation, in order to make all that work, they hide under layers and layers of incredibly destructive behavior," says Terry Norman, D. Min., a professional counselor in Kansas City. "Ultimately, it kills."

Sexual orientation is one of the great mysteries of the human mind. For decades, researchers have tried to figure out what makes someone attracted to a particular sex, and the question is far from settled. Most scientists now believe that there isn't a single cause; rather, our desires spring from the complex interplay of biology and environment.

"Our understanding of why people have the sexual orientation they do is still very poor," says Stephen John Clark, Ph.D., an assistant professor of psychology at Vassar College. "There is growing evidence that events that happen very early in life, genetic influences, the environment in the womb and experiences in the first years of life play a large role in determining one's sexual orientation. The evidence is not conclusive, however, and workers in the field are far from a consensus." It's not even clear, he adds, whether everyone's sexuality is shaped by the same forces. "People are diverse. They fall in love with all sorts of different people. Should it surprise us if it turns out that who they fall in love with is determined by a variety of factors?"

In recent years, scientists have intensified the search for biological causes of homosexuality. Best known is the controversial work of molecular geneticist Dean Hamer, Ph.D., of the National Cancer Institute, who is focusing on finding a so-called "gay gene." Looking at families with more than one gay member, Hamer and his colleagues have used inheritance patterns to theorize that the X chromosome contains a gene that predisposes some men toward homosexuality. In one study, Hamer examined 40 pairs of gay brothers and found that 33 of the pairs had five identical strips of DNA on their X chromosomes. Hamer and his colleagues are now searching for a specific gene within these DNA strips, and are also looking for other chromosomes that might have a connection to sexual orientation.

Researchers have also been examining whether brain structure correlates with sexual orientation. At San Diego's Salk Institute, Simon LeVay, Ph.D., a neuroscientist, has noted in autopsy studies that a cer-

> "I do not believe that any man can ever be truly at peace in living out a homosexual orientation.

tain nucleus—or cell cluster—in the hypothalamus is between two and three times larger in straight men than in gay men. He has also observed that this nucleus is generally smaller in deceased women, leading him to hypothesize that smaller structures are somehow correlated with sexual attraction toward men. (LeVay did not know the orientation of the deceased women whose brains he was studying.) LeVay's findings are open to challenge; for example, some critics note that the "gay brains" belonged to men who died of AIDS, whose nuclei might have been shrunk by their medications.

While many psychologists day are convinced that biological factors will ultimately prove to play a strong role in determining sexual orientation, a breakaway group of therapists believe that this entire body of science is off the mark. Known as "reparative therapists," they hew to an alternative theory of homosexuality, which has been adopted by both the secular and religious arms of the ex-gay movement. Their theory harks back to old notions of

homosexuality as a mental disorder—notions repudiated by the American Psychiatric Association a quarter-century ago.

The current leader of this movement is Joseph Nicolosi, Ph.D., director of the National Association for Research and Therapy of Homosexuality. A life-long heterosexual, Nicolosi makes no pretense of hiding his biases. "Nature made man complementary to woman, and to cling to the sameness of one's own sex is to look at the world with one eye," he writes in his book *Reparative Therapy of Male Homosexuality* (Jason Aronson, 1991). "I do not believe that any man can ever be truly at peace in living out a homosexual orientation."

To Nicolosi and his followers, gay male sexuality stems directly from a poor relationship between a boy and his father. If a father isn't a strong influence on the family, and if he doesn't provide emotional support and physical affection, then the child won't learn to identify with adult men. As he grows older, the boy will start looking for the maleness he never acquired, and his search will take on sexual overtones.

"People are gendered. We are naturally gendered into male and female. So the male homosexual is trying to find his unfulfilled masculinity," Nicolosi declares. "His homosexual attractions are a symptom of his desire to find his masculine identification and same-sex emotional needs."

Critics consider this a deeply flawed argument. Andrew Sullivan, former editor of *The New Republic* and a gay man, notes that if distant fathers were the cause, "then most of the generations born between 1930 and 1980 would be homosexual. There might also, perhaps, be a startling rise in homosexuality among African-Americans in the last 20 years, when absent fathers have become the norm, rather than the exception."

But Nicolosi presses on, maintaining that homosexuals can never be truly happy. He describes gay sex as "isolated and narcissistic," because partners experience orgasm separately and must negotiate their sexual roles in the acts they perform. And he claims "sexual sameness" causes partners to lose interest and look for other contacts. Nicolosi ignores the fact that lesbians are famously monogamous and dismisses two respected studies saying the majority of gay men have 20 or fewer partners in their lifetimes. "I just don't believe it," he says.

In Nicolosi's therapy, clients discuss their relationship with their parents, their sense of maleness, and new ways to interpret their sexual attractions. They're encouraged to form platonic friendships with handsome straight men in order to demystify and desexualize those men. And they are prevailed on to reclaim their masculinity by playing sports, getting angry and expressing their relationship needs directly.

The result is not instant heterosexuality. A successful client "doesn't immediately walk down a street and get a sexual charge from looking at a woman," Nicolosi says. "But he will begin to notice women. He will begin to feel a desire to get married and have a family." He will still be attracted to men, Nicolosi says, "but that sexual desire is greatly diminished. If the attraction is intense, it becomes a signal to him that there's something amiss in his life. 'Wow, what is going on that I'm having a feeling like this? Have I been honestly connected to my wife? Have I been keeping connections with my friends?' "

Using such techniques, Christian ministries and reparative therapists claim to successfully convert about 30% of homosexuals in their programs. But are those really successes?

Nicolosi and his adherents don't track former clients, and mainstream psychologists have their doubts that these transformations are long-lasting. "I have yet to see a conversion hold," says Michael Picucci, Ph.D., a psychologist in New York City. More troubling, however, is the fact that these programs do not, as Nicolosi acknowledges, change basic sexual orientation. "The danger is that some individuals are going to end up feeling that in some important way their life is a lie and a sham," observes Christopher Wallis, M.D., a member of the American Psychoanalytic Association's committee on issues of homosexuality.

The consequences can be devastating. Terry Norman, the St. Louis counselor, says "orientational repression" sometimes leads to drug and alcohol abuse, workaholism and compulsive sex. There also have been reports of people killing themselves, or attempting to, after failing to convert. "After hearing the categorical promises that these programs work, what do people conclude when they do these things and it doesn't work for them?" asks Norman. "That God doesn't bless them, that they really are pieces of trash that pollute the Earth."

Just who tries to change? Not the average gay man or woman. Would-be converts, say psychologists, typically me from deeply authoritarian backgrounds where homosexuality is branded immoral or a sin, while others are married and cannot reconcile their family commitments with their erotic desires.

Many also are facing tremendous problems, including alcoholism, drug abuse, sexual abuse and parental violence or rejection. Mike Jones, 44, remembers that his first sexual contact in adolescence involved mutual masturbation with his father. "That was the first time that my reaching out to my father was received by him," says Jones, who runs the Corduroy Stone ministry in Lansing, Michigan. Through his involvement in Exodus International, says Jones, he has learned how to live a celibate life, though he continues to fantasize about men when he masturbates. He finds himself attracted to about a quarter of the men who pass through his ministry. (When those feelings surface, he says, he channels them into platonic friendship.)

Dena Westcott of Orlando, an Eleutheros graduate who grappled with suicidal tendencies and her own explosive temper, voices a similar experience. The ministry has helped her confront childhood sexual abuse and her relationship with a hateful mother. It also taught her to cultivate close platonic friendships with other women, particularly when she feels her lesbian attractions intensifying.

It should come as no surprise, then, when ex-gays express satisfaction about getting their homosexuality "under control." Faced with a panoply of problems, many have acted out sexually, seeking encounters to ease their pain. By dealing with core issues, conversion programs put the brakes on destructive sexual and social behavior. But, as psychologists point out, this has nothing inherently to do with homosexuality.

For every person who claims a conversion to heterosexuality, there are several others who fail in their efforts. Two of the founders of Exodus International, Michael Bussee and Gary Cooper, left the organization after falling in love, and more than a dozen Christian ministries have closed down after their leaders reverted back to homosexuality. There is now an informal network of "ex-ex-gays," people who tried unsuccessfully to change their orientations, and instead have learned to live as gay men and lesbians. "Sexuality is an incredible part of life. But it's not *the* aspect, and I needed to get on with living," says Jallen Rix, a Christian music singer.

The product of a strict Southern Baptist upbringing, Rix wanted badly to be accepted by his family and community, but found that men excited him sexually. There were "doctor" games with male cousins, encounters with strangers in the woods near his home, and at the Christian college he attended, a physical friendship with a male student. To ward off suspicions, Rix became a "semi-compulsive liar," adept at deflecting any query that would reveal his homosexuality.

When the dissonance became too great, Rix began attending the California-based ministry Desert Stream where worship and pep talks were allied with "dives into our past," he recalls. "They'd have all this outdated therapy that because of an absent or passive father, I have identified more with my mother and I'm attracted to men." Rix became suspicious of the ministry's techniques. Young men and older male mentors, who were supposed to serve as surrogate fathers, sometimes began living together in relationships that were essentially gay, except that there was no sex.

More important, the program didn't work for Rix. "I went home and I was still horny for men." After a year and half and still desperate for help, Rix drove to another charismatic church where a woman promised to exorcise his homosexuality. She laid hands on his head, anointed his forehead with oil and started praying. "I wanted this to work so bad," he recalls. "I grunted and squeezed and tried to shove this homosexuality out of me. I remember afterwards, going out for fast food and trying to coach myself, 'It's gone. Yeah, it's gone.' But it wasn't."

Disillusioned, Rix started coming to terms with being gay. He continued to perform Christian music for conservative churches and private schools, but by his early 30s realized he couldn't hide his sexual orientation. Now 35, he still performs, but generally for liberal and gay churches. Rix doesn't regret his time in the ministry. But he worries that others are being pressured into conformity and denial, rather than learning how to lead authentic lives. "When people say they're happy being married, they're really saying, 'I am acceptable to myself and to the people around me.' I don't think they'll feel that way in the long run."

Unit 7

Key Points to Consider

❖ How would you define mental illness?

❖ What images or stereotypes of mental illness and the mentally ill do you have?

❖ How would you feel knowing that a friend has been treated for mental illness? How about a neighbor, a potential spouse, or a baby-sitter for your children?

❖ What, if any, limits would you want placed on the lives of people who have been treated for mental illness?

❖ What should be done for people who are diagnosed as mentally ill?

❖ Should we assume that people who are diagnosed as mentally ill will always be mentally ill? Why or why not?

 **Links**   **www.dushkin.com/online/**

These sites are annotated on pages 4 and 5.

Some years ago, a friend was studying to be a physician. As part of his training, he rotated through internships in a number of subjects. While in his psychiatric rotation, the police brought a man to the hospital. The man, totally nude, had been directing rush-hour traffic at a nearby intersection. Although he had very little training in psychiatry, my friend concluded that the man was dangerously mentally ill—a conclusion that was based primarily on his social definition of mental illness. Identifying what we mean by physical illness is easy. If people have an ear infection, the flu, or a cold, we know that they are physically ill. When it comes to mental illness, however, a precise definition is difficult. In 1991 Harold Kaplan and Benjamin Sadock defined mental disorder as a clinically significant behavioral or psychological syndrome that is associated with distress or disability, and not merely an expected response to a particular event. This is consistent with the definition of mental disorder given in the *Diagnostic and Statistical Manual of Mental Disorders* (DSM-IV). The DSM-IV is a set of basic diagnostic criteria used by mental health professionals, along with clinical judgment, to

also repulsed by them. Common misconceptions include the belief that mentally ill people can never recover their mental health and that they engage in bizarre or unpredictable behavior and are dangerous. Such stereotypes may lead to discrimination against the mentally ill. For example, a mentally ill person may have trouble being hired or finding an apartment to rent. Generally, these stereotypes are false.

Stereotypes of the mentally ill and social definitions of mental illness as deviance may be based on a number of factors. One of these factors involves what we hear and see in the media. For example, we sometimes hear about a mentally ill person who shoots up a post office. This tells us that mentally ill people are dangerous. Many large, corporate-owned psychiatric hospitals advertise in the media about suicide and depression and the need for treatment. One mental health company's television ad implies that if teenagers spend much time talking on the phone, they must be suffering from an unspecified type of mental illness. Stereotypes of mental illness may also be formed from observations of a few persons whom we know

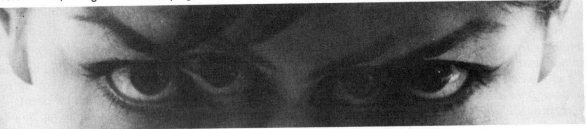

determine whether or not a person is suffering from a mental illness and what class of disorder it may be. However, since the first edition of the DSM, several behaviors have been added to the manual and several behaviors have been removed from it. This would suggest that what is, or is not, a mental disorder is socially defined. For example, an earlier edition of the DSM listed homosexuality as a disorder, while the DSM-IV does not. David Rosenhan (1973), in his classic study, "Being Sane in Insane Places," firmly established that psychiatric professionals are often unable to identify distinct behavioral symptoms. Consequently, they rely on stereotypes and social definitions of mental illness and the mentally ill. Thus, it may reasonably be concluded that mental illness is a socially defined form of deviance.

All of us hold stereotypes about different types of people and behaviors. Stereotypes may be thought of as a set of socially defined ideas or beliefs that characterize groups of people or behaviors. From personal experience, it seems that many of us are apprehensive of people who have been diagnosed as mentally ill. For example, in several surveys conducted over the past 50 years, Americans have indicated that they would not want to have a mentally ill neighbor, friend, or babysitter. Many people are not only frightened of the mentally ill but

to have been diagnosed as mentally ill. When observing other people who act strangely, we may choose to define their behavior as mental illness. Periodic behavioral fads may also influence stereotypes of mental illness and the mentally ill. For example, a few years ago, several entertainers claimed that they suffered from multiple personality disorder (MPD). One result of these claims was the publication of popular magazine articles and books on the topic, which popularized the disorder even more. MPD is a response to traumatic victimization in early childhood, the result of which is the death of the individual's personality and the subsequent development of two or more substitute personalities. It is unlikely that many of these well-known people actually have MPD, as it is an extremely rare disorder.

The unit begins with an article by Thomas Szasz, "Idleness and Lawlessness in the Therapeutic State," in which the author discusses his criticisms of the psychiatric establishment and the concept of mental illness. Other articles focus on such topics as social anxiety or phobias and eating disorders like anorexia nervosa and bulimia among college students. Other articles deal with explaining why mental illness occurs, the treatment of mental disorders, and how society needs to reform how it views mental illness and the mentally ill.

Idleness and Lawlessness in the Therapeutic State

Thomas Szasz

Thomas Szasz is professor of psychiatry emeritus at the State University of New York Health Sciences Center in Syracuse, and adjunct scholar at the Cato Institute, Washington, D.C. He is the author of twenty-two books (which have been translated into fifteen languages), including the classic Myth of Mental Illness *and, most recently,* Our Right to Drugs: The Case for a Free Market.*

From an economic point of view, persons may be divided into two groups, producers and parasites. Producers provide for their own needs by their labor or capital. Parasites do not. Some, for example infants and indigents, are unable to support themselves; called dependents, they receive food and shelter from parents, family, or the state, or perish. Others, for example criminals, are unwilling to support themselves lawfully; called predators, they use force or the threat of force to extract from producers the goods and services they want. Unless a person is able and willing to be a producer, he must become a dependent or a predator or perish. Thus, any circumstance—biological, cultural, economic, or political—that discourages or prevents peaceful market relations among productive adults encourages dependency, predation, or both.

How does the chronic mental patient (in this essay, I use certain terms and phrases—such as mental illness, mental patient, schizophrenia, psychiatric treatment—whose customary implications and conventional meanings I reject, but to avoid defacing the text, I have refrained from placing such prejudging expressions between quotation marks each time they appear; also, I use the masculine pronoun to refer to both men and women and the terms "psychiatrist" and "mental patient" to refer to all mental health professionals and their clients)—who is homeless, often breaks the law, begs for money and scavenges for food, and receives disability payments from the Social Security system for schizophrenia—fit into this scheme? Is he a dependent or a predator or both? Before we can answer this question, we must reject the facile but fallacious assumption that there is an intrinsic connection between illness and idleness or between illness and lawlessness. Most chronically ill persons—for example, diabetics—are not idle, are not economically dependent, and are not inclined (because of their illness) to lawlessness. In contrast, most chronic mental patients—especially schizophrenics—are idle, economically dependent, and inclined (allegedly because of their illness) to lawlessness.

Evidence—and Lack of Evidence

Prior to this century, there was no schizophrenia. The diagnosis of dementia praecox—modeled after the grand old cause of madness, dementia paralytica (a form of tertiary syphilis affecting the brain)—was invented by Emil Kraepelin in 1889. In 1911 Eugen Bleuler replaced the term "dementia praecox" with "schizophrenia." Although there was no evidence that these diagnoses identified genuine diseases, each term was eagerly accepted as the name of a brain disease (or a group of brain diseases). In fact, both Kraepelin's and Bleuler's original accounts show that they were aware that while their patients' idleness was a reality, their illness was not. Kraepelin wrote:

> Gentlemen,—You have before you today a strongly-built and well-nourished man, aged twenty-one.... The patient gives us a correct account of his past experiences. His knowledge speaks for the high degree of his education; indeed, he was ready to enter the University a year ago.... No physical disturbances can be definitely made out, except exaggerated knee-jerks.... [I]n spite of his good education, he lies in bed for weeks and months, or sits about without feeling the slightest need of occupation.... [H]e declares that he is ready to remain in the hospital for the present.... As the illness developed quite gradually, it is hardly possible to fix on any particular point of time as the beginning.

Although this person exhibited no evidence of being ill, Kraepelin called him a "patient" and attributed his behavior to a devastating brain disease. Bleuler's account of schizophrenia resembles Kraepelin's. He wrote:

> Idleness facilitates the predomination by the complexes over the personality; whereas regulated work maintains the activity of normal thinking. These recommendations cannot always be fulfilled since we are often dealing with *patients who are dependent on their parents and on others....* Many schizophrenic Italians are quite willing to remain in the hospital and be fed, clothed, and cared for.

Similar descriptions of chronic mental patients abound in the modern psychiatric literature. Here are a few examples: "A working-class unemployed schizophrenic, recently discharged from hospital, sat at home all day, brewing tea and smoking, and playing records, and proving himself a great aggravation to his mother." The language is misleading. This man did not sit "at home." He sat in a house that was another person's home, to the maintenance of which he did not contribute, and where he was not welcome. In another case, a mother describes her schizophrenic daughter's presence in the parental home thus: "Whenever Ruth is at home, he [her father] feels continually irritated by her lack of purpose and idleness." A report in a psychiatric trade journal begins as follows: "John S. has chronic schizophrenia. For most of his 40 years he has lived at home with devoted parents.... John has frequent bouts of bizarre and uncontrollable behavior." Finally, a typical newspaper article recounts the odyssey of a physically healthy fifty-year-old man who, after having spent virtually all of his adult life in mental hospitals, now "spends most of his time painting acrylic portraits, ocean scenes, and images with Oriental hummingbirds.... [He] takes long walks around the city, attends [baseball] games, and borrows mysteries from the main library."

Today, after a century of intensive research, there is still no evidence that schizophrenia is an illness. It is clear, however, that many persons called schizophrenic are idle and lawless. Which is cause, and which is consequence? Does schizophrenia cause individuals to be idle and lawless, or are individuals called "schizophrenic" because they are idle and lawless? I submit that the incentive for inventing this diagnosis/disease was to establish, by medico-legal fiat, that certain dependent and disorderly persons are sick and that their unwanted and unlawful behaviors are the unintended symptoms of their disease. At any rate, that is still the most conspicuous social function of the diagnosis of schizophrenia.

The facts stare us in the face. "Lack of money," as Lord Bauer pithily put it, "is not the *cause* of poverty, it *is* poverty." Similarly, schizophrenia is not the *cause* of idleness and lawlessness, it is the *name* of the fictitious disease that we attribute to certain persons exhibiting such behaviors.

If we define deviance down, we increase the number of socially disruptive persons in society. By the same token, if we define competence up, we increase the number

Today, after a century of intensive research, there is still no evidence that schizophrenia is an illness.

of unemployable persons in society. The *Wall Street Journal* (1 March 1994) quotes a French psychiatrist complaining that "to prescribe an anti-depressant to a jobless person whose benefits are running out may seem normal. But when the practice is repeated hundreds of thousands of times, it amounts to a sort of society-wide medical treatment of unemployment." This "treatment" is as fictitious as the alleged disease it supposedly combats. The truth is that, in the nineteenth century, Western societies began to use psychiatric diagnoses to validate idleness as illness, and then used the pretext of an incurable psychosis to justify psychiatric indoor relief—that is, maintaining certain adult dependents as (involuntary) patients in mental hospitals. In the 1950s, psychiatrists began to administer neuroleptic drugs to mental hospital patients to validate the claim that formerly incurable mental diseases were treatable, and Western societies then used the pretext of drug-induced remission of schizophrenia to justify psychiatric outdoor relief—that is, maintaining certain adult dependents on drugs and disability checks.

Behavior as Illness

Bleuler's original account of the behavior of schizophrenic patients is also replete with remarks about their lawlessness, which, without any evidence, he also attributes to their alleged illness. He wrote:

> A large part of the so-called impulsive behavior is automatic.... [The patient] suddenly breaks loose, strikes out, destroys in the wildest fury and anger.... Regrets after such releases are rare, of course, in schizophrenia. The patients feel their behavior is justified.... Often they assert that it was the "voice" that drove them to fury.

Not surprisingly, the relatives of schizophrenic patients welcome the view that their kinfolks' criminality is a symptom of their malady. This letter, from the mother of a mentally ill son, is typical:

> Our adult son ... is currently in jail as a result of extremely violent behavior caused by his illness. Because of his illness, he is dangerous to his family and others. The dangerous symptoms of our son's illness are not unique to him. In fact, through our contacts with the Massachusetts AMI and NAMI, we have found many, many families who have suffered the same fear and terror we have experienced *because* of behavior *caused* by the mental illnesses of family members.

To support her argument, the writer cites newspaper reports about "mentally ill individuals who ... killed a parent [and] broke into parents' home and assaulted them." Another patient's sister writes: "The way I look at it, he is one of the most unfortunate individuals. He suffers from paranoid schizophrenia, and during a very psychotic episode, seventeen years ago ... he caused a terrible tragedy. It ended in the loss of life to two people he was very close to ... he suffers from a no-fault neurobiological disorder."

Psychiatrists insist that schizophrenia is a brain disease like Parkinsonism, but it is also unlike Parkinsonism (and other neurological diseases) because it causes the patient to display disorderly behavior. This alleged fact imparts unique status to mental illnesses as moral and legal justifications for depriving innocent persons of liberty (civil commitment) and for excusing guilty persons of responsibility for their crimes (the insanity defense). Moreover, science, medicine, law, and public opinion alike now accept the patently absurd claim that psychiatrists can distinguish brain diseases that cause idleness and lawlessness from those that do not.

The psychiatric perspective on behavior thus commits us to attributing a lawless and unproductive lifestyle to mental illness (as a "no-fault brain disease") and a law-abiding and productive lifestyle to the free will of a responsible moral agent (for which he deserves credit).

The Socially Competent Self

One of the greatest social problems facing American society today is that it produces an ever-increasing number of able-bodied young adults who are unproductive,

idle, and lawless. Many are said to suffer from schizophrenia. According to the *Psychiatric Times* of November 1993, individuals diagnosed as schizophrenic "use 25 percent of all U.S. hospital beds, 40 percent of all long-term care days, and 20 percent of all Social Security days. The total economic costs associated with schizophrenia are estimated at $33 billion."

Until relatively recently, many common behaviors—such as idleness (vagrancy), homosexuality (perversion), masturbation (self-abuse), and suicide (self-murder)—were considered to be crimes, sins, or both. In this century, all of these behaviors have become medicalized. Some—for example, masturbation and homosexuality—were first transformed into mental diseases and were then accepted as normal behaviors; others—for example, idleness and suicide—still tend to be viewed as illnesses or the manifestations of illnesses.

Why does one young person become a productive adult, and another an unproductive schizophrenic? To answer this question, we must begin with the plain fact that, to take his place in modern society, a person must achieve a certain level of social competence and economic usefulness, and that to do so, children and adolescents must develop self-discipline and acquire

Today it is psychiatric doctrine that mental illness is a virtually universal affliction.

marketable skills. In short, young people must prepare themselves to be productive by being useful to others, as others define usefulness.

Although the development of a socially competent self is clearly of paramount importance for the fate of both the individual and the society of which he is a member, this subject receives little or no attention in the psychiatric literature. Instead, that literature is replete with accounts that exaggerate the significance of the individual's experiences during early childhood, to which many experts attribute a destiny-determining role in the life of the adult. While the early years of life are important, the remaining years of childhood and youth—from, say, five to twenty-five—are even more important. It is during that period that the young person—nurtured or neglected by family, church, school, and society—must design, build, perfect, and test himself, as a future adult.

Notwithstanding the contemporary American delusion that a good parent loves his child unconditionally, such tolerance has limits and imposes deadlines. The limits depend largely on the parents' expectations. The deadlines, for the most part, are set by society and comprise the various stages of the passage from childhood to adulthood. This passage begins with the child's expulsion from home to attend school, continues with his development from childhood to adolescence, and is completed with his transition from adolescence to adulthood. The entire process is expected to end during the third decade, at the latest. In short, between his teens and twenties, the young person must learn to become useful to others and stand on his own feet. If he fails to accomplish this task, he and his family are destined to face serious difficulties, nowadays often conceptualized in psychiatric terms, typically as the manifestations of schizophrenia.

If this process of maturation goes awry, the adolescent begins to envy his peers and to feel inferior to them. To dull the pain of this experience, he often protects himself by means of a self-destructive psychological defense. He tells himself he is better than others, becomes arrogant and conceited—psychiatrists call it "narcissistic"—and embraces the logic of hostile entitlement: "I am not a useless person. Others are unworthy of my doing anything for them. They have more than I do and ought to feel guilty and help me." (There are important similarities between the antiproductive mentality of the chronic mental patient and the anti-capitalist mentality of the socialist/communist, who, as it were, tells himself, "Everything the producers have, they have gained by exploiting others. I have a right to rob them of their possessions." I realize, of course, that sometimes psychiatrists also call productive persons—for example, James Joyce and Ludwig Wittgenstein—"schizophrenic.")

If parents and peers respond to the adolescent's failing struggle by treating him as an individual with "special problems," which they often do, they compound the problem. Gradually, parents and teachers expect less and less of the "problem child," and he does less and less for them and himself. Once past adolescence, he is likely to slide into continued dependence—on parents, as long as they support him, then on relatives or social and welfare agencies. Somewhere down this path, the young adult may commit or threaten to commit a violent act—against himself or others—which his family can no longer ignore. He is then brought into the presence of a psychiatrist, who diagnoses him as schizophrenic and launches him on the career of the chronic mental patient.

The point I want to emphasize is that an adolescent is not yet a functioning member of adult society. It is an error, therefore, to speak of his "dropping out." First, he must "drop in." If he fails to do so, he is likely to find himself in a situation similar to Holden Caulfield's predicament in J. D. Salinger's *The Catcher in the Rye*.

Management of Madness

Individual liberty is contingent on a social system that guarantees respect for private property and market relations. In turn, the game of market relations is contingent on players who understand the rules, possess the capacity to adhere to them, and can be held accountable for violating them. These requirements exclude children (persons under the age of consent). Does this mean that all chronological adults are able to participate in the market? If not, how do we separate those who are able from those who are not?

The inability or unwillingness of infants, idiots, and the insane to participate in the reciprocal human relations characteristic of the market has always been recognized. Since the Middle Ages, English law treated these three classes of persons as if they comprised a homogeneous group, characterized by the absence of the capacity for reasoning and self-control, rendering them unfit to participate in political society. Accordingly, they were deprived of the benefits of liberty and the burdens of responsibility were lifted from their shoulders.

Infancy and idiocy pose relatively few problems of definition and identification. As for insanity, for a long time it was a rare condition, because only individuals who behaved like the proverbial rampaging "wild beast" were categorized as mad. As long as there were few such persons in society, their management presented no special political problem. However, with the establishment of the trade in lunacy toward the end of the seventeenth century, the criteria for madness began to expand and the stage was quickly set for the development of the psychiatric problems that bedevil us today. Public madhouses soon became the rage and the plague of insanity descended on the Western world. Today it is psychiatric doctrine that mental illness is a virtually universal affliction. Nevertheless, the bracketing of the insane with infants has remained the operative justification for the legal control of the mentally ill. "Freedom," writes Milton Friedman, "is a tenable objective only for responsible individuals." He is right. But then he adds: "We do not believe in freedom for madmen or children." Let us examine in what ways madmen are like, and unlike, children.

The sole similarity between infants and insane persons is that both are treated paternalistically. The differences between them, however, could hardly be greater. Infants cannot live as homeless street persons, commit crimes, or kill themselves; insane adults can, and often do, all these things. Finally, even if we grant the claim that some mental patients are immature (childlike) and that it is therefore appropriate to treat them paternalistically, it does not follow that they are sick (in any meaningful sense of that term). Immaturity is not a disease. A childish adult needs to grow up, not to be involuntary drugged. Clearly, the analogy between children and madmen is strategic, not descriptive. G. K. Chesterton had it right when he observed that "the madman is not the man who has lost his reason. The madman is the man who has lost everything except his reason."

The ostensibly altruistic coercion of protesting adults should always arouse our suspicion. Adults—even immature, irrational, or insane adults—are not children. "There is," wrote René Descartes, "no soul so weak that it cannot, properly directed, acquire full control of its passions." Indeed, responsibility is not merely a personal trait of the Other; it is also an expectation We have of him. Thus, we hold young children and even dogs responsible (for controlling their urges to urinate in their pants and to bite people).

The modern management of madness has obscured the basic differences between children and adults and the rules appropriate for controlling the conduct of each group. Children are not small adults, and schizophrenics are not children in adult bodies. The criteria for the misbehavior of children are laid down and enforced by parents and teachers, whereas the criteria for the misbehavior of adults are laid down by legislators and enforced by judges, juries, and prison guards. It is morally desirable that parents discipline their children, but it is morally undesirable that the state discipline adults. Instead, adults ought to be punished for their crimes (which may or may not have the effect of disciplining them). Both the aim and the effect of psychiatrizing the nature and control of the misbehaving adult is to obscure and abolish these fundamental distinctions. In our misguided effort to combine treating the sick with punishing the criminal, we have all but destroyed our fundamental ideas about moral agency, individual liberty, and personal responsibility.

The State as Therapist, as Tyrant

Individuals and institutions that enforce the law must have power. In theocracies, the sovereign is answering only to God, who is above man-made law. Hence, the historic threat to personal liberty has been unlimited government, and the history of liberty, especially in the English-speaking world, has been the history of efforts to limit the sovereign's sovereignty.

In the democratic West today, however, the principal danger to liberty lies not so much in the state's naked power to oppress by lawlessness as in its subtle power to seduce and infantilize by offering to protect people from the vicissitudes of life, especially illness. Historically, this is a recent threat. Hence, political philosophy lacks a tradition of opposing the State as Therapist comparable to its tradition of opposing the State as Tyrant. Even Ludwig von Mises was blind to this threat. He wrote: "Even if we admit that every sane adult is endowed with the faculty of realizing the good of social cooperation and of acting accordingly, there still remains the problem of infants, the aged, and the insane. We may agree that he who acts antisocially should be considered mentally sick and in need of care." Although Mises recognized that "psychiatrists are vague in drawing a line between sanity and insanity," he stated: "It would be pre-

posterous for laymen to interfere with this fundamental issue of psychiatry." But precisely because the psychiatrist's authority to "draw a line between sanity and insanity" forms the basis of his power to deprive persons of liberty and because laymen bear the ultimate responsibility for delegating that power to him, laymen *must* address the twin issues of insanity and psychiatric power.

I have long maintained that we should reject psychiatric paternalism and accord the same rights to and impose the same responsibilities on mental patients as we accord to and impose on persons with bodily illness or no illness. The principle of *parents patriae* suffices and is the sole appropriate mechanism for the care and control of incompetents, that is, of adults who are severely mentally retarded or have been rendered temporarily or permanently unconscious or demented by injury or illness. Such persons, exemplified by the comatose patient, can neither seek nor reject medical help.

Since the modern liberal sees the state as a protector, he welcomes therapeutic paternalism as enlightened scientific-humanitarian progress replacing archaic religious-judicial punitiveness. It is therefore especially noteworthy, and unfortunate, that classical liberals and conservatives—who tend to see the state as a threat—also welcome its coercive-therapeutic interventions, exemplified by its treatment of the mental patient as a childlike person who cannot be held responsible for his conduct. George F. Will declares: "Most [solitary homeless persons who live on the streets] are mentally ill." James Q. Wilson states: "Take back the streets. Begin by reinstitutionalizing the mentally ill." Charles Krauthammer agrees: "Getting the homeless mentally ill off the streets is an exercise in morality, not aesthetics. . . . Most of the homeless mentally ill . . . are grateful for a safe and warm hospital bed." But if they are grateful, why must they be coerced?

I agree with the tacit premises of these commentators. Public places belong primarily to the productive members of society. Regardless of whether we call individuals indigents or insane, homeless or mentally ill, persons who enjoy the benefits of liberty have no right to treat public places as their domiciles or otherwise interfere with the public order. However, I reject as hypocrisy calling troublesome persons "troubled," and punishing them under the guise of giving them medical treatment.

The history of psychiatry is eloquent testimony to the failure of coercion masquerading as care and cure. However, as soon as ostensibly altruistic interventions (political or psychiatric) result in so-called unintended consequences, plainly harmful to their denominated beneficiaries, the cry goes up that the interventionists had only good intentions. It is a singularly hollow claim. We cannot know another person's intentions; the coercive interventionist can justify his use of force only by proclaiming good intentions; and coercive interventions result in harmful consequences for their denominated beneficiaries so regularly and indeed predictably that I believe we should conclude that these consequences are not unintended.

Because the self-correcting mechanism of the market is absent from both statist-economic and statist-psychiatric interventions, each diminishes the ostensible beneficiaries' freedom and self-defined best interests. Foreign aid increases the power and prestige of the political authorities who receive and administer it and impoverishes the people it is supposed to help. Psychiatric aid similarly increases the power and prestige of the psychiatric authorities who receive and administer it and diminishes the dignity and liberty of the people it is supposed to help; and by disjoining rights and responsibilities, it also places society at the mercy of a class of predators endowed with inalienable psychiatric excuses.

SUGGESTED FURTHER READING

Peter T. Bauer. *Dissent on Development: Studies and Debates in Development.* London: Weidenfeld and Nicolson, 1971.

Peter T. Bauer. *Reality and Rhetoric: Studies in Economic Development.* London: Weidenfeld and Nicolson, 10984.

Eugen Bleuler. *Dementia Praecox or the Group of Schizophrenias* [1911], trans. by Joseph Zinkin. New York: International University Press, 1950.

Milton Friedman. *Capitalism and Freedom.* Chicago: University of Chicago Press, 1962.

Emil Kraepelin. *Lectures on Clinical Psychiatry* [1894], in *The Faber Book of Madness,* ed. Roy Porter. London: Faber and Faber, 1991.

Ludwig von Mises. *Human Action: A Treatise on Economics.* New Haven: Yale University Press, 1949.

Thomas S. Szasz. *Schizophrenia: The Sacred Symbol of Psychiatry* [1976]. Syracuse: Syracuse University Press, 1988.

Thomas S. Szasz. *Insanity: The Idea and Its Consequences.* New York: Wiley, 1987.

Thomas S. Szasz. *Cruel Compassion: Psychiatric Control of Society's Unwanted.* New York: Wiley, 1994.

Social Anxiety

For millions of Americans, every day is a struggle with debilitating shyness

BY JOANNIE M. SCHROF AND STACEY SCHULTZ

It is something of a miracle that Grace Dailey is sitting in a restaurant in a coastal New Jersey town having an ordinary lunch, at ease with her world. Her careful, tiny bites of a tuna sandwich may seem unremarkable, but they are in fact a milestone. Back in her grade school cafeteria, she could only sip a bit to drink each day, unable to eat while she imagined her classmates' eyes boring into her. (Her high school teachers mistook her anxiety about eating for anorexia.) Only in her 20s, when panic attacks began to hit, did Dailey learn about the condition called social anxiety disorder, also known as "social phobia." But despite some success with behavioral therapy and anxiety-reducing medication, the 32-year-old still struggles. "I would be a different person in a different place if I didn't have to deal with this on a daily basis," she says, frustration apparent in her furrowed brow.

Shyness is a nearly universal human trait. Most everyone has bouts of it, and half of those surveyed describe themselves as shy. Perhaps because it's so widespread, and because it suggests vulnerability, shyness is often an endearing trait: Princess Diana, for example, won millions of admirers with her "Shy Di" manner. The human species might not even exist if not for an instinctive wariness of other creatures. In fact, the ability to sense a threat and a desire to flee are lodged in the most primitive regions of the brain.

But at some life juncture, roughly 1 out of every 8 people becomes so timid that encounters with others turn into a source of overwhelming dread. The heart races, palms sweat, mouth goes dry, words vanish, thoughts become cluttered, and an urge to escape takes over.

This is the face of social phobia, the third most common mental disorder in the United States, behind depression and alcoholism. Like Woody Allen in the film *Annie Hall*, some social phobics can barely utter a sentence without obsessing over the impression they are making. Others refuse to use public restrooms or talk on the telephone. Sometimes they go mute in front of the boss or a member of the opposite sex. At the extreme, they build a hermitic life, avoiding contact with others (think of young Laura in Tennessee Williams's *Glass Menagerie* or the ghostly Boo in *To Kill a Mockingbird*).

Though social anxiety's symptoms have been noted since the time of Hip-

SUCCESS STORY. In high school, cheerleaders made a sport of saying "hello" to Steve Fox just to watch him blush. Now he is married to one of the girls who used to tease him.

From *U.S. News & World Report*, June 21, 1999, pp. 50–57. © 1999 by U.S. News & World Report. Reprinted by permission.

Coming to you direct

Public service ads—or just a sales pitch?

By Brendan I. Koerner

Pasted on bus shelters nationwide, the posters ask passersby to imagine being allergic to people. The picture is of a handsome young man, despondently staring at a coffee cup as an apparently happy couple sits at the other end of his table. "Over 10 million Americans suffer from social anxiety disorder," the text reads. "The good news is that this disorder is treatable." A toll-free number and a Web site are listed.

The ads bear the seals of three nonprofit advocacy groups: the American Psychiatric Association, the Anxiety Disorders Association of America, and Freedom From Fear, a trio that together make up the Social Anxiety Disorder Coalition. But funding for their public awareness campaign comes from a far less visible partner: SmithKline Beecham, the pharmaceutical giant whose flagship antidepressant, Paxil, was recently approved by the Food and Drug Administration for the treatment of debilitating shyness, formally known as social anxiety disorder.

Top of the pack. The move made Paxil the first selective serotonin reuptake inhibitor (SSRI) to win that designation. In the crowded SSRI marketplace, which rang up sales of near $7 billion last year, companies are constantly on the lookout for new ways in which their brands can be used—for social phobia, panic disorder, obsessive-compulsive disorder, bulimia. "You really need to keep your brand on the top of the pack," says Sergio Traversa of Mehta Partners, which does investment research on pharmaceutical companies. When you have multiple users, then "it's a relatively cheap alternative to developing new drugs. . . . On one side, it's cheaper, and it also helps keep the brand popular." Not surprisingly, some critics see profit, rather than altruism, as the motive behind SmithKline's financial backing of the "Imagine being allergic to people" campaign, and they question whether the statistics put forward in such advertising are accurate.

Blurring the line between public service and marketing is common practice in the industry. Back in 1996, when Paxil was cleared for the treatment of panic disorder, SmithKline sponsored the "Paxil Report on Panic," in which one third of those surveyed said either they or someone they knew had suffered from a panic attack—a sudden rush of terror or extreme fear. Bristol-Myers Squibb, which sells the antidepressants Serzone and Desyrel, sponsors the popular Depression.com Web site, which includes an "Are You Depressed?" quiz. And Eli Lilly, the maker of Prozac, the top-selling SSRI, launched an "educational television campaign" last month, featuring a 30-minute program chronicling the tales of 10 depression sufferers—all recovered, thanks to its brand.

SmithKline insists that helping the afflicted, not boosting sales, is the goal of

ALLERGIC TO PEOPLE?. A drug company funds this "education campaign" designed to raise awareness of social phobia and to promote treatments such as therapy and medication.

the poster blitz. "We find that less than 5 percent of patients are really treated today," says Barry Brand, product director for Paxil. "There's tremendous need out there." The company, he adds, is adamant about deterring frivolous use. "We don't want this to be a pill that you take for shyness," continues Brand. "We don't want you to think, 'Oh, I'll take a Paxil and I'll feel good.'"

Market forces. Hollow words, says Elliot Valenstein, professor of psychology and neuroscience at the University of Michigan and author of *Blaming the Brain*. "[Drug companies] can anticipate criticism very well. But at the same time, their marketing will assume there are many more people out there" whom they will attract. Indeed, the track records of other "lifestyle drugs" show that many are used to achieve modest goals such as shedding a few pounds or becoming more productive at work. "When Prozac came on the market, it was just approved for severe depression," says Sidney Wolfe, director of the Health Research Group of Public Citizen, a consumer advocacy group. "But it was used for all kinds of depression." Just as Prozac became a $3 billion-a-year seller thanks in part to those users, Paxil will bolster its sales by targeting the merely meek, predicts Valenstein. "Shyness can't be marketed because most people recognize it as a normal variation on personality," he says. "But 'social phobia' sounds like a disease. I'm sure a lot of thought was given to pushing that particular terminology."

The coalition's brochure is careful to highlight the tag line "It's not just shyness," and the campaign's literature never directly mentions Paxil. But some of the symptoms described are familiar to virtually anyone who has faced pressure: blushing, sweating, dry mouth, pounding heart. And SSRIs are praised as vital to the recovery process. In the campaign's video, a sufferer gives testimony to the healing role of her medication: "I wouldn't have been able to concentrate on therapy and the coping skills" without the drug's ability to "take the edge off." Valenstein says that since Paxil is the only FDA-approved SSRI for the disorder, it will become the prescription of choice for general practitioners, who prescribe the majority of antidepressants.

Alec Pollard, director of the anxiety disorders center at the St. Louis Behavioral Medicine Institute, says the cynicism surrounding Paxil clouds its positive effects, which can be remarkable. "I can't say to you that people won't be given Paxil that don't need it," says Pollard. "But we wouldn't want to judge a treatment based on the fact that sometimes it will be inappropriately applied. That's inevitable. That's why particularly primary-care physicians need to be educated on proper use."

But Wolfe is concerned that the direct-to-consumer marketing approach will drive some patients to demand the medication without proper evaluation. "People are going to ask for it, and they're going to get it," he says. In the realms of managed care, doctors may be only too willing to acquiesce to those demands. "It is possible to give people careful diagnosis," says Erik Parens, an associate at the Hastings Center, a bioethics think tank. "But diagnosis takes time, and it costs money. Therefore, it is cheaper to give people the drug they ask for."

pocrates, the disorder was a nameless affliction until the late 1960s and didn't make its way into psychiatry manuals until 1980. As it became better known, patients previously thought to suffer panic disorder were recognized as being anxious only in social settings. A decade ago, 40 percent of people said they were shy, but in today's "nation of strangers"—in which computers and ATMs make face-to-face relations less and less common—that number is nearing 50 percent. Some psychologists are convinced that the Internet culture, often favored by those who fear human interaction, greases the slope from shyness down to social anxiety. "If people were slightly shy to begin with, they can now interact less and less," says Lynne Henderson, a Stanford University researcher and director of the Shyness Clinic in Menlo Park, Calif. "And that will make the shyness much worse."

Much worse—and, for drug companies, far more lucrative: Recently, SmithKline Beecham won FDA approval to market the antidepressant Paxil for social phobia, leading to a raft of "public education campaigns"—on top of those already put out by the National Institute of Mental Health and the Anxiety Disorders Association of America. This media blitz has raised concerns that normally shy people will conclude they're social phobics and seek medications for what is a complex, emotional problem, or opt for such drugs merely as "lifestyle" aids to win friends and influence people (story, "Coming to You Direct").

Hard-hitting. Social phobia hit Steve Fox so hard in high school that girls made a sport of saying "hello" just to watch him turn beet red. He refused to speak in class and never dated; even walking in front of other people left him with sweaty palms and gasping for air. By the time Fox was 19, his father was concerned enough to find a doctor, and a combination of medication and therapy has helped him recover. Fox, now 23, recently gave a speech in front of

UNABLE TO DRIVE. Roland Bardon had to rely on his mother to chauffeur him when he was overwhelmed by anxiety about what others thought of his driving.

1,700 people, and he is married to one of the cheerleaders who used to tease him.

Normal shyness and serious social phobia are clearly different, but they are related. Emanuel Maidenberg, associate director of UCLA's Social Phobia and Performance Anxiety Clinic, says that shyness is to social phobia what a fair complexion is to skin cancer. "It's a predisposing factor but will only translate into disease under certain circumstances," he says. "For pale people, that might be 10,000 hours in the sun. For shy people, it might be a string of embarrassing events."

Even though some people are born with a tendency toward extreme shyness, biology is by no means destiny. Harvard researcher Jerome Kagan has shown that by 8 weeks of age, babies display innate shyness or boldness. Roughly 1 in 5 will consistently be frightened of and avoid anything or anyone new, while the others welcome the unknown, reaching out to touch strangers or to grab new objects. Yet, many shy babies become gregarious 10-year-olds, and some outgoing babies become shy, even socially phobic, adults.

Life experiences can mold the brain to become more or less shy over time. Through a process psychologists call "contextual conditioning," the brain attaches a fear "marker" to the details of a situation that causes trauma (place, time of day, background music). So when a child gets a disparaging tongue-lashing from a teacher, the student will feel at least a bit nervous the next few times he or she steps into that class-

room. But sometimes the brain is too good at making those associations, says Maidenberg, and the anxiety grows like a cancer, attaching itself to the act of entering any classroom or talking to any teacher.

The classic behavior of a child who does not know how to handle these "daggers to the heart," says University of Pennsylvania psychiatrist Moira Rynn, is to avoid any attention at all. In fact, social phobia used to be known as avoidant personality disorder. First, avoidant kids may stop inviting friends over. Some will only speak to certain people, usually their parents, a condition known as "selective mutism" (box, "Suffering in Silence"). Others develop "school refusal." By avoiding the very situations they need to learn the social skills of adulthood, these children end up diminishing their ability to cope. Not only can a parent who is highly critical train a child to cower, but even the gentlest parent can raise a fearful child. "If parents avoid social situations or worry excessively about what the neighbors think of them," says Richard Heimberg, director of the Adult Anxiety Clinic at Temple University in Philadelphia, "the message to a child is that the world is full of danger, humiliation, and embarrassment."

Social phobia affects about half of its victims by age 8, and many others during adolescence, when social fears are more pronounced. Others live with an undetected problem that surfaces when facing a new public arena (college, a new job) that overwhelms them. Grace Dailey, who had managed to suffer qui-

---

A spectrum of shyness

A touch of timidity is human, but too much shyness can be debilitating

NORMAL SHYNESS

■ You are jittery beginning a public speech, but afterward you are glad you did it.

■ Your mind goes blank on a first date, but eventually you relax and find things to talk about.

■ Your palms sweat in a job interview, but you ask and answer thoughtful questions.

EXTREME SHYNESS

■ You clam up and your heart races when you know people are looking at you.

■ You tremble when speaking up at a meeting, even if it is only to say your name.

etly through high school, was seized with sudden panic attacks in her college classes. The episodes were so distressing that she would race out of lecture halls, and she considered dropping out. She did graduate, with the help of thoughtful professors who let her take tests by herself and who kept classroom doors open so that she didn't feel so trapped.

More women than men are thought to suffer social anxiety, but because shyness and demureness are smiled upon in females and less acceptable in males, more men turn to professionals for help. Roland Bardon, 27, knew he needed to see a psychologist after becoming too anxious to drive a car. "I worry about making other drivers mad," he says. "When people honk, that kind of criticism drives me crazy." He still avoids taking the wheel whenever he can.

Talking to strangers. It's Friday night at the Shyness Clinic in Menlo Park, Calif., time for this week's social phobia information session. But in the tiny room decorated haphazardly with fake flowers, only one man has shown up. The very nature of their disorder often causes social phobics to hide, and revealing themselves to a stranger is the last thing they want to do. Tonight's newcomer put off coming for two months. Clinic patients attend group meetings once a week, but some cannot even bring themselves to show up at all.

When the socially anxious do make it into clinics, they usually start with a few months of cognitive behavioral therapy. The cognitive element fights what psychiatrist Isaac Tylim of the Maimonides Medical Center in Brooklyn calls the intellectual core of social phobia: the belief that others will pass negative judgments on you and that unbearable humiliation will result. "I turn down invitations to go to lunch with people I really admire, even though I desperately want to go," says a Kentucky housewife and mother of two girls who exhibit a similar timidity. "I assume that as soon

as we get together, they'll regret having asked and want to get away from me as soon as possible." These distortions cause an emotional reaction that sends social phobics running away from even the most promising friendships. Through cognitive restructuring—a fancy term for replacing faulty thoughts with realistic ones—many social phobics learn to question the insidious fears that, no matter how irrational, paralyze them in their everyday lives.

Perhaps the most salient feature of social anxiety is what is known as flooding: the sensation of being so overwhelmed that panic sets in. Almost everyone feels mild flooding at the podium during the first minute or so of an important speech, but for most people the discomfort soon subsides. A social phobic can suffer such agony for more than an hour. But even in social phobics, flooding will eventually subside, if only because of sheer exhaustion. That is why behavioral therapists coach social phobics to remain in terrifying situations until the symptoms abate and it becomes clear that nothing bad is going to happen.

The first place that Melinda Stanley, professor of behavioral sciences at the University of Texas-Houston Health Sci-

in front of Stanley and an audience of graduate-student volunteers. Other therapists take social phobics through practice runs of embarrassing situations, like walking through a hotel lobby with toilet paper on their shoes or spilling a drink. It's not unlike physical training, says Henderson. "Just as our gym workouts get easier as time goes by, to stay socially fit we must push ourselves to engage with others until it is second nature."

When a case is so severe that patients cannot even ride an elevator with a therapist, drugs can enable the social phobic to endure behavioral therapy. The perfect medication has yet to be found. Antidepressants known as monoamine oxidase inhibitors (MAOs) have been used for over a decade, but they can cause side effects such as fainting spells, heart palpitations, and blurred vision, and users must follow strict diets excluding everything from coffee to cheese to red wine. Researchers have experimented with Xanax, Valium, and other tranquilizers but have had mixed success, not least because those drugs can cause physical dependence. Some sufferers try beta blockers, which are helpful for surviving a speech or a party but use less as a long-term therapeutic tool.

IN HIDING. Mark Goomishian dropped out of high school and has spent decades in virtual seclusion.

ence Center, takes many patients is the elevator. Riding up and down, the patient practices greeting and making small talk with fellow passengers. "Sometimes it takes 10 or 15 rides, and sometimes it takes all day," says Stanley, "but the phobic's heart will eventually stop racing for fear of what the newcomer might think of him or her." Eventually, the patients progress to giving speeches

Most popular now are the antidepressants known as selective serotonin reuptake inhibitors (SSRIs), which have fewer side effects than the old anxiety drugs. "[Patients treated for depression] were spontaneously reporting that they were losing their social anxiety," explains Murray Stein, director of the anxiety clinic at the University of California-San Diego. Studies of the SSRIs Paxil and

SOCIAL ANXIETY			
■ You avoid starting conversations for fear of saying something awkward.	■ You will do anything, even skip work, to avoid being introduced to new people.	■ You have trouble swallowing in public, making it hard to dine out or go to parties.	■ You feel you never make a good impression and that you are a social failure.

SEVERE SOCIAL ANXIETY		
■ You are free of nervousness only when alone and you can barely leave the house.	■ You constantly worry about being embarrassed or humiliated by others.	■ You have panic attacks and often leave the room rather than hold a conversation.

THE SHY CHILD
Suffering in silence

Samantha Williams seems like a typical 11-year-old, enchanted with the prospect of teenage life as she begins to lose interest in childish activities. But at the end-of-the-year cookout she's planning for the girls in her fifth-grade class, Samantha will stand out in one particular way: Most of Samantha's friends have never heard the sound of her voice. Since kindergarten, she has never spoken to any of her teachers or uttered a single word in class, and until very recently, she hasn't made so much as a peep on the playground.

Samantha has a form of childhood social anxiety known as selective mutism. She can comprehend spoken language and she is able to speak, but because she is very shy and anxious around even familiar people, she is unable to talk in public. About 1 percent of kids are like Samantha and have extreme trouble talking to strangers. These children almost always converse easily with their parents—one or both of whom are likely to suffer themselves from some form of social phobia.

Selective mutism has been mistakenly associated in the past with childhood abuse or trauma, charges that researchers say are not supported by scientific evidence. Until recently, it was called "elective mutism," but doctors changed the name because it implied a willful stubbornness of the child that "we've found is really not the case," says Anne Marie Albano, director of the anxiety disorders program at the New York University Child Study Center.

A child's inability to speak in public is not only frustrating for parents, it can also be frightening. When Samantha missed the bus home from school one day, she was unable to tell school officials that she needed to call home for a ride. Instead, she began the 2½-mile trek home, until her mother, in a fran-

WITHOUT A SOUND. Samantha Williams, 11, has not spoken in school since kindergarten. She is being treated for "selective mutism."

tic search of the neighborhood, spotted her. "I worry about her safety," her mother says. "I especially worry that she won't be able to ask for help if she needs it."

Fortunately, behavioral therapy can be effective. Parents, teachers, and friends can play a role, too, says NYU's Albano. "Everyone must maintain the expectation that the child will speak," she says. "We offer rewards and privileges when kids do talk, and we let them experience the consequences when they don't speak," such as earning a poor grade if they miss an oral report in class.

For some children, medication such as Prozac is helpful, but it can take months before the drugs take effect. "One third of the kids we treat get a great deal of benefit from the medication," says Bruce Black, assistant professor of psychiatry at Tufts University School of Medicine. Another third see some benefit, and the rest don't respond at all, he says. Samantha Williams has been taking Paxil, a drug similar to Prozac, for a few months. Her parents hope she will respond as well as 10-year-old Jenna, a selective mute from Maine. After six months of Prozac, Jenna silently decided one day last November that she would talk in school. When she did, her classmates cheered— and her teachers cried.

—S.S.

Luvox show great improvement in about half of social phobics, and studies now underway of other new antidepressants, like Effexor and Serzone, are also showing promise. But Henderson urges caution amid the current hoopla over drugs, which she worries are too often used as temporary crutches. "People tend to relapse as soon as they get off the medication," she warns, adding that research indicates that over the long run, therapy might keep a person in better stead. Just as troubling, says Tylim, is the message that only a drug can save them. "These are people whose very problem is a feeling of inadequacy, and the use of drugs can exacerbate that."

Because some social phobics have been out of the habit of talking with others for so long, therapists often have to help patients brush up on the most basic of social skills. For example, it never dawns on many of the most shy that they should introduce themselves to the person standing in front of them. And they often are stuck in the conversation-killing habit of answering questions with one-word answers. "I had to learn that if someone doesn't seem interested in the first sentence out of my mouth, I should not just turn and walk away cold," says Rick Robbins, a 31-year-old who was voted most shy of his Indiana high school class and whose social anxiety led him to drop out of college.

Perhaps the most common thing social phobics have to learn for the first time is to listen. "All kinds of alarm bells and sirens are distracting to social phobics," says Maidenberg. "So it is nearly impossible to hear what a person standing 4 inches away is saying." In fact, it is sometimes difficult for an extremely shy person to even feign interest in a companion's words. "Social pho-

bics don't realize that most people in a room are not taking much notice of them," says Tylim, who says that social phobics in some ways crave the spotlight but fear that humiliation will come from it.

That's why Bernardo Carducci, author of *Shyness* and director of the Shyness Research Institute at Indiana University Southeast, is convinced that shifting the focus away from the self is the most therapeutic thing a shy person can do. "They desperately want to connect with others," he says; otherwise, they would merely be contented introverts or recluses who simply prefer their own company. Carducci sends patients to soup kitchens, hospitals, and nursing homes as a way of escaping the tyranny of self-centeredness. "It works because you get out there and start to see how shy other people can be," says Rick Robbins. "And then you don't feel so all alone, so different from everyone else." At first, he tried to pry himself out of his problem with alcohol, what therapists dub "liquid extroversion." Then he forced himself to go to social occasions, where he would sit—miserable, silent, and sick to his stomach. If anything, these kinds of efforts at beating shyness will only aggravate the condition, because they are negative experiences that reinforce the fear.

Learning to cope. And because shyness is at least partially genetic, researchers unanimously agree that it is a mistake to try to become "unshy." Rather, the goal is to take steps to function despite the pounding heart and sweaty palms. Some do advance work for the tough moments. "Before I go out, I come up with four or five topics I would like to talk about," says Robbins. "Usually by the third one I bring up, I find something in common and forget about my nerves." Mark Goomishian, who has trouble even signing a check in public, looks for social arenas where he can be more himself, such as the local coffee shop, where he meets others for regular games of chess. "Because you don't have to talk during the game," he says, "it's a socially anxious person's sport."

In fact, many therapists say that if the socially phobic could rein in their anxiety enough to function, they would help make the world a better place. Many beloved figures in history have suffered shyness, including Eleanor Roosevelt, Robert Frost, and Albert Einstein. Shyness in its milder forms is associated with traits such as greater empathy, more acute perceptiveness, canny intuition, and beneficent sensitivity. All qualities that are nothing to be shy about.

With Brendan I. Koerner and Danielle Svetcov in Menlo Park, Calif.

PANIC ON THE PODIUM

Why everyone gets stage fright

From behind the counter of his Louisville, Ky., smoke shop, Gayle Sallee says he could chat forever with customers who wander through. But when the cigar boom hit in the early 1990s, and requests poured in for him to give lectures, seminars,

TERRORS OF FAME. The cigar craze shoved smoke shop owner Gayle Sallee into the spotlight, where he was forced to overcome his dread of public speaking.

and radio and TV interviews, Sallee says he was petrified: "Even if I was only asked to speak to 10 old slobs who like to smoke, I would get sick just thinking about it."

The fear of public speaking is by far the most prevalent social anxiety, affecting many people who are not the least bit shy in other settings. That makes perfect sense to researchers, who say that stage fright is the same ancient anxiety that hits all creatures when they are in full view of potential predators. But many of us freeze up even before a group of trusted friends. *Shyness* author Bernardo Carducci says this is because of the psychological rule of "salient objects." It is human nature, according to this principle, to scrutinize the most noticeable person in a room (i.e., the professor, the work-

shop leader, the soloist, the only African-American, the only woman) far more critically than those who blend into the background. And standing in front of a crowd makes us the "salient object," so that we become only too conscious of each gesture and phrase.

Hang in there. Speech coaches say that the self-consciousness fades if nervous speakers don't give up too soon. Many speakers mistakenly assume their cottony mouths and shaking hands mean they are failing miserably. "Those sensations are merely signals that you are trying to do something meaningful and important," says Brooklyn psychiatrist Isaac Tylim. That knowledge was small comfort to Sallee as he struggled through months of stammering and stuttering on the cigar circuit. "None of the stuff about picturing people in their underwear worked at all," he recalls. But after six months of weekly presentations, Sallee suddenly realized halfway through a radio interview one Saturday morning that he was relaxed. "Once the fear died down, the fun began," he says. "Now it's to the point where when I'm in an audience, I really wish it was me up there on the stage."

—J.M.S.

Dying to be Thin

Eating disorders cripple—literally—millions
of young women, in large part because
treatments are not always effective or accessible

by Kristin Leutwyler

I don't own a scale. I don't trust myself to have one in the house—maybe in the same
way that recovered alcoholics rightfully clear their cabinets of cold medicines and
mouthwash. At 5'7", I know that I usually weigh 118 pounds, and I know that is considered normal for my frame. But 13 years ago, when I was 15 years old and and the
same height, I weighed 67 pounds, and I thought I was grossly, repulsively obese.

My own bout with anorexia nervosa—the
eating disorder that made me starve myself
into malnutrition—was severe but short-lived.
I had a wonderful physician who worked
hard to earn my trust and safeguard my
health. And I had one great friend who slowly,
over many months, proved to me that one ice
cream cone wouldn't make me fat nor would
being fat make me unlovable. A year later I
was back up to 95 pounds. I was still scrawny,
but at least I knew it.

I was—am—lucky. Eating disorders are
often chronic and startlingly common. One
percent of all teenage girls suffer from anorexia nervosa at some point. Two to 3 percent
develop bulimia nervosa, a condition in
which sufferers consume large amounts of
food only to then "purge" away the excess
calories by making themselves vomit, by
abusing laxatives and diuretics, or by exercising obsessively. And binge eaters—who overeat until they are uncomfortably full—make
up another 2 percent of the population.

In addition to the mental pain these illnesses cause sufferers and their families and
friends, they also have devastating physical

consequences. In the most serious cases, binge
eating can rupture the stomach or esophagus.
Purging can flush the body of vital minerals,
causing cardiac arrest. Self-starvation can also
lead to heart failure. Among anorexics, who
undergo by far the worst complications, the
mortality rate after 10 years is 7.7 percent, reports Katherine A. Halmi, a professor of psychiatry at Cornell University and director of
the Eating Disorders Clinic at New York Hospital in Westchester. After 30 years of struggling with the condition, one fifth die.

Because studies clearly show that people
who recover sooner are less likely to relapse,
the push continues to discover better treatments. Eating disorders are exceedingly complex diseases, brought on by a mix of
environmental, social and biological factors.
But in recent years, scientists have made some
small advances. Various forms of therapy are
proving beneficial, and some medications—
particularly a class of antidepressants known
as selective serotonin reuptake inhibitors
(SSRIs)—are helping certain patients. "SSRIs
are not wonder drugs for eating disorders,"
says Robert I. Berkowitz of the University of

Pennsylvania. "But treatments have become more successful, and so we're feeling hopeful, even though we have a long way to go to understand these diseases."

Weighing the Risks

When I began working on this article, I phoned my former physician, a specialist in adolescent medicine, and I was a little surprised that she remembered my name but not my diagnosis. In all fairness, my illness was a textbook case. I had faced many common risk factors, starting with a "fat list" on the bulletin board at my ballet school. The list named girls who needed to lose weight and by how much. I was never on it. But the possibility filled me with so much dread that at the start of the summer, I decided I had to get into better shape. I did sit-ups and ran every day before and after ballet classes. I stopped eating sweets, fats and meat. And when I turned 15 in September, I was as lean and strong as I've ever been.

Scientists know that environment contributes heavily to the development of eating disorders. Many anorexic and bulimic women are involved in ballet, modeling or some other activity that values low body weight. Men with eating disorders often practice sports that emphasize dieting and fasting, such as wrestling and track. And waiflike figures in fashion and the media clearly hold considerable sway. "The cultural ideal for beauty for women has become increasingly thin over the years," Berkowitz notes. In keeping, among the millions now affected by eating disorders every year, more than 90 percent are female.

Like me, most young women first develop an eating disorder as they near puberty. "Girls start to plump up at puberty," Estherann M. Grace of Children's Hospital in Boston says. "And this is also when they start looking at magazines and thinking, 'What's wrong with me?'" Recognizing that anorexia nervosa often arises as girls begin to mature physically, psychiatrists recently revised the diagnostic standards. "It used to be that one of the criteria was that you had to have missed a period or suffered from amenorrhea for three months," says Marcie B. Schneider of North Shore University Hospital. "And so we missed all those kids with eating disorders who had not yet reached puberty or had delayed it." Now the criteria include a failure to

meet expected growth stages, and more 10, 11- and 12-year-olds are being diagnosed.

Puberty is a stressful time—and stressful events typically precede the onset of psychiatric conditions, including eating disorders. Maybe I would have stopped dieting had my parents not separated in the summer, or my grandmother had not died that fall, or I hadn't spent my entire winter vacation dancing 30-odd performances of the *Nutcracker*. Maybe. I do know that as my life spun out of control around me, my diet became the one thing I felt I could still rein in. "Anorexics are terribly fearful of a loss of control," Grace says, "and eating gives them one area in which they feel they have it."

Most people under stress will overeat or undereat, Grace adds, but biology and personality types make some more vulnerable to extremes. Anorexics tend to be good students, dedicated athletes and perfectionists—and so it makes some sense that in dieting, too, they are highly disciplined. In contrast, bulimics and binge eaters are typically outgoing and adventurous, prone to impulsive behaviors. And all three illnesses frequently arise in conjunction with depression, anxiety and obsessive-compulsive disorder—conditions that tend to run in families and are related to malfunctions in the system regulating the neurotransmitter serotonin.

I most definitely became obsessed. I read gourmet magazines cover to cover, trying to imagine the taste of foods I would not let myself have—ever. I cut my calories back to 800 a day. I counted them down to the singles in a diet soda. I measured and weighed my food to make my tally more accurate. And I ate everything I dished, to make sure I knew the precise number of calories I had eaten. By November, none of my clothes fit. When I sat, I got bruises where my hip bones jutted out in the back. My hair thinned, and my nails became brittle. I was continuously exhausted, incredibly depressed and had no intention of quitting. It felt like a success.

Sitting Down for Treatment

The first barrier to treating eating disorders is getting people to admit that they have one. Because bulimics are often a normal weight and hide their strange eating rituals, they can be very hard to identify. Similarly, binge eaters are extremely secretive about their practices. And even though seriously ill anorexics are quite noticeably emaciated, they are the least willing of all patients with eating disorders to get help. "Anorectics are not motivated for treatment in the same way as bulimics are," Halmi comments. "Because anorexia gives patients a sense of control, it is seen as a positive thing in their lives, and they're terrified to give that up."

I certainly was—and a large part of getting better involved changing that way of thinking. To that end, cognitive behavioral therapy (CBT) has had fair success in treating people with anorexia, bulimia and binge eating disorder. "There are three main components," explains Halmi, who views CBT as one of the most effective treatments. Patients keep diaries of what they eat, how they feel when they eat and what events, if any, prompt them to eat. I used to feel guilty before meals and would ask my mother for permission before I ate. She never would have denied me, but asking somehow lessened my guilt.

CBT also helps patients identify flawed perceptions (such as thinking they are fat) and, with the aid of a therapist, list evidence for and against these ideas and then try to correct them. This process let me eventually see the lack of reason in my belief that, say, a single cookie would lure me into a lifetime bender of reckless eating and obesity. And CBT patients work through strategies for handling situations that reinforce their abnormal perceptions. I got rid of my scale and avoided mirrors.

Working in collaboration with researchers at Stanford University, the University of Minnesota and the University of North Dakota, Halmi is now comparing relapse rates in anorexics who have been randomly assigned to treatment with CBT or the SSRI drug Prozac, or a combination of both. Unfortunately, the dropout rate has been high. But earlier evidence has suggested that Prozac—which had not yet been approved when I was sick—may benefit some patients, helping them to at least stop losing weight. "Essentially every young woman with anorexia is also dealing with depression, and so SSRIs help alleviate some of the somatic symptoms associated with that," Grace says.

Not everyone believes SSRIs do much for anorexics, particularly those who are not desperately ill. But SSRIs have proved effective in people with bulimia. In conjunction with James Mitchell, director of neuroscience at the University of North Dakota, and Scott J. Crow, professor of psychiatry at the University of

Minnesota, Halmi has just completed collecting data on 100 bulimics who received cognitive behavioral therapy for four months. Those who still did not improve underwent further therapy and drug treatment with Prozac. "When it comes to bulimia," Berkowitz tells me, "it is clear that both psychotherapy and pharmacology are helpful."

Swallowing the Truth

New treatments for eating disorders could benefit millions of adolescents—if they can get them. Most face a greater challenge getting help today than I did 13 years ago. "One of the big topics now is how to survive in this era of managed care," Schneider tells me. "You have to be at death's door to get into a psychiatric hospital," Berkowitz says, "and once a patient is stabilized, the reimbursements often stop. This is not an inexpensive disease to have." I went through a year of weekly therapy before I reached a stable, if not wholly healthy, weight. In comparison, Berkowitz notes that the insurance policies he has encountered recently often pay for only 20 sessions, with the patient responsible for a 50 percent co-payment.

"It's absolutely sinful," Halmi says. "It is a disaster for eating-disorder patients, particularly anorexics." She points out that relapse rates are much lower in adolescents who receive treatment long enough to get back up to 90 percent of their ideal weight; those who gain less typically fare worse. But insurance rarely lasts long enough. "It used to be you could hospitalize a kid for three or four months," Schneider says. "Now you can at most get a month or so, and it's on a case-by-case basis. You're fighting with the insurance company every three days." The fact that it may be cheaper to treat these patients right the first time seems to make little difference to insurance companies, she adds: "Their attitude is that these kids will probably have a different carrier down the road."

Down the road, the consequences of inadequate treatment are chilling. Debra K. Katzman of the Hospital for Sick Children in Toronto recently took magnetic resonance imaging (MRI) scans of young women with anorexia nervosa before and after recovery and found that the volume of cerebral gray matter in their brains seemed to have decreased—permanently. "The health of these kids does rapidly improve when they gain back some weight," Schneider says, "but the changes on the MRIs do not appear to go away."

In addition, those who do not receive sufficient nutrition during their teen years seriously damage their skeletal growth. "The bones are completed in the second decade, right when this disease hits, so it sets people up for long-term problems," Grace asserts. These problems range from frequent fractures to thinning bones and premature osteoporosis. "I talked to one girl today who is 16. She hasn't been underweight for that long, but already she is lacking 25 percent of the bone density normal for kids her age," Schneider says. "And I have to explain to her why she has to do what no inch in her wants to—eat—so that she won't be in a wheelchair at age 50."

Because drugs used to treat bone loss in adults do nothing in teens, researchers are looking for ways to remedy this particular symptom. "[Loss of bone is] related to their not menstruating and not having estrogen," Grace explains. "But whereas estrogen does protect older women against bone loss, it doesn't seem to help younger ones." She and a coworker are now testing the protective effects of another hormone in young girls. Halmi also emphasizes that estrogen treatment for patients with eating disorders is a waste of time. Instead "you want to get them back up to a normal weight," she states, "and let the body start building bone itself."

All of which brings us back to the concept of normal weight—something many women simply don't want to be. A recent study found that even centerfold models felt the need to lie about their heights and weights. Christopher P. Szabo of the Tara Hospital in Johannesburg reviewed the reported measurements of women in South African editions of *Playboy* between February 1994 and February 1995 and calculated their apparent body mass indices. Even though these models all looked healthy, 72 percent had claimed heights and weights that gave them a body mass index below 18—the medical cutoff for malnourishment. "Maybe 5 percent of the population could achieve an 'ideal' figure, with surgical help," Grace jokes. "I'm sorry, but Barbie couldn't stand upright if she weren't plastic."

I remember all too well thinking that I would look fat at a normal weight. Sometimes I still do worry that I look fat. But I take my perceptions with a grain of salt. After all, I haven't exactly proved myself to be a good judge in that regard. Somehow I've come to a point when I don't need to measure my self-worth in pounds—or the lack thereof—provided I'm happy and well. I gave up a lot—ballet, friendships, a sense of community and security. But in return, I got my health back.

The Infection Connection

PSYCHOLOGY HAS LONG HELD THAT MENTAL ILLNESS IS BORN OF ADVERSE EXPERIENCES. MORE RECENTLY, RESEARCH HAS POINTED THE FINGER AT FLAWED GENES. NOW A THIRD CULPRIT MAY BE EMERGING: INVASION BY BACTERIA AND VIRUSES.

BY HARRIET WASHINGTON

Eight-year-old Seth broke from the grasp of Jane, his harried mother, for the third time in 10 minutes. Tearing across the emergency room, he stopped short, transfixed by a piece of paper lying on the floor. His red-rimmed eyes seemed to bulge from their sockets and his mouth twitched violently, as if he were in pain. Indifferent to Jane's pleas to stop, he proceeded to pick up from the floor every piece of paper, no matter how filthy, with hands that were reddened and raw. It was the state of his hands that had precipitated the trip to the hospital: Seth had spent most of the night in the bathroom, washing them over and over.

With his head jerking spasmodically and his fingers pecking at pieces of paper and cigarette butts, the boy resembled some strange overgrown bird. Then, suddenly terrified, he flew back to Jane and began pulling on her arm. "Mommy, Mommy let's leave!" he whimpered. "They're going to kill us. They're coming!"

Jane tried her best to calm him, but she too was beginning to panic. Two days before, Seth had been a perfectly normal little boy whose most serious health problems were the occasional cold or sore throat. He had become mentally ill overnight.

What caused Seth's anxiety, his tics, his obsessive-compulsive behavior? Astonishingly it was probably that minor sore throat, his doctors concluded. Today scientists are increasingly coming to recognize that the bacteria and viruses that frequently invade our bodies and cause sore throats and other minor ailments may also unleash a host of major mental and emotional illnesses, including anorexia, schizophrenia and obsessive-compulsive disorder.

It is a theory sharply at odds with earlier views of the genesis of psychological illness. Followers of Freud long held that mental and emotional trouble is primarily the result of poor parenting, especially by mothers. Indeed, until about 30 years ago, psychoanalysts frequently placed the blame for schizophrenia on "schizophrenogenic" mothers. Obsessive-compulsive disorder, also, was put at Mom's door. "It was thought to be the result of harsh toilet training," observes Susan Swedo, M.D., chief of pediatrics and developmental neuropsychiatry at the National Institutes of Mental Health. But such theories, which added immeasurable guilt to the burdens of parents with mentally ill offspring, have turned out to have little evidence to back them up, most experts now agree.

Instead, in recent years, the focus has shifted to genes as the main source of mental illness. Faulty DNA is thought to be at least partly responsible for, among other problems, anxiety and panic disorders, schizophrenia, manic depression and antisocial personality disorder, which is characterized by impulsive, excessively emotional and erratic patterns of interpersonal behavior.

Yet genetics doesn't appear to wholly account for the occurrence of major psychiatric ailments. If heredity alone were to blame, identical twins would develop schizophrenia with a high degree of concordance, but in fact in only 40% of cases in which one identical twin has the disease does the other twin have it as well. Autism, though it has been observed to run in families, also strikes five of every 10,000 children apparently arbitrarily. Nor can depression and other affective disorders be completely explained by damaged DNA. Says Ian Lipkin, Ph.D., a neuroscientist and microbiologist at the University of California at Irvine: "Genetics doesn't hold the key to understanding how to fit these square pegs into round holes."

Bacteria and viruses may be that key, but scientists have been slow to grasp the idea. Consider the case of syphilis, which is caused by the bacterium *Treponema pallidum*. In its final, or tertiary,

stage, the disease can precipitate psychiatric problems like dementia, mania, depression, delusions and Tourette's-like tics. Though some scientists suspected a connection between infection with the bacterium and the mental disturbances that may take three to five decades to emerge, the link became widely accepted only in the 1940s after the introduction of the antibiotic penicillin as a treatment for syphilis. In the interim, patients with syphilis who later developed psychiatric problems were often institutionalized as crazy. But

WHAT YOU CAN DO

Since we know so little about the viruses and bacteria that cause some types of mental illness, it makes sense to avoid them when you can. Here, advice on preventing infection from leading scientists (much of which sounds uncannily like Mom's):

- Eat a healthy diet.
- Get plenty of sleep.
- Reduce stress.
- Get a flu shot each fall.
- Be aware that sex with multiple partners raises your risk of infection.
- Wash your hands frequently. (Though you might be tempted to use one of the many antibacterial soaps on the market, such cleansers may promote the growth of drug-resistant "superbugs.")
- Don't eat meat that isn't well-cooked, or if you have any questions about how it was stored or prepared.
- Find out whether you have any physical conditions that increase your risk of infection, and discuss preventive steps with your doctor. If, for example, you have a prolapsed mitral valve (a valve in the heart that doesn't close properly, increasing risk of infection), your doctor may recommend that you take antibiotics before having dental work done.
- Pay attention to your body. Even minor symptoms—fever, chills, a sore neck—can mean you're doing battle with an infection, and you should discuss them with your doctor. Pay special attention to your children's symptoms.
- If you are prescribed antibiotics, finish the entire course of therapy.
- If you work in a medical setting—even as a technician or clerk—be sure to seek vaccinations against hepatitis and other pathogens you may acquire from patients.
- If you're pregnant, take special care to avoid respiratory ailments such as influenza. Avoid contact with cat litter, which can harbor *Toxoplasma*, a microbe that can cause birth defects or even spontaneous abortion.

even with the link established, Freud's theories were in ascendance and few scientists were willing to consider that microbes might be a common source of other mental illness.

Now, decades later, infection has emerged as a prime suspect in psychological illnesses. The inadequacy of genetic and experiential explanations has prompted scientists to look elsewhere—and their gaze has come to rest on physical ailments, such as heart disease, cancers and ulcers, that in some cases have an infectious origin. Could the same be true, they wonder, for mental and emotional ills?

Improved technology has made it easier to find out. Since active only when inside other living creatures, microbes are notoriously hard to grow, and therefore study in the lab, but scientists' ability to do so has increased steadily over the last few decades. Other tools have allowed researchers to see their quarry more clearly. For about a decade, microbiologists have used a technique called polymerase chain reaction, or PCR, to replicate a small piece of genetic material over and over until it forms a quantity large enough to study—and large enough to show the lingering traces of an infection. A new variant of PCR, called representational difference analysis, introduced in 1994, allows scientists to go one step further and compare the differences between two separate pieces of DNA (including healthy and diseased segments, for instance). And the refinement of electron microscopes has permitted researchers to follow the "footprints" left by infection in patients' cerebrospinal fluid.

The introduction of CAT scans in the early 1970s has been another leap forward. Before then, only an X-ray—or an autopsy—could reveal damage to the brain, and then only in its grossest form. CAT scans show subtle changes that can be tracked over time, giving researchers a more accurate sense of a microbe's impact. MRI, developed in the early 1980s, has added three-dimensionality to pictures of the brain, and PET scans, invented soon after, have added motion. Now bacteria and viruses can be caught red-handed.

Still, teasing out the tie between microbes and psychological problems has proved a difficult task, in no small part because of the cunning and guile of the pathogens themselves, which have many ways of attacking our bodies and brains.

T. pallidum, syphilis' causative bacterium, proceeds in straightforward fashion: it attacks and kills brain cells. After entering the body—usually through sexual intercourse, or through the mother's placenta into her fetus—the bacterium travels along the lymph system until it arrives at the brain. Once it lodges there, it spares few structures, inflaming some neurons and stripping the myelin, or insulation, from others. (Without myelin, nerve impulses are slowed or stopped altogether.)

Other microbes are more devious. The human immunodeficiency virus, for example, which can cause anxiety, delirium, psychosis and suicidal impulses, uses a Trojan horse strategy. Instead of directly attacking brain cells, it infects macrophages, the immune-system enforcers that roam the bloodstream, engulfing foreign cells that may pose a threat to the body. After hitching a macrophage ride into the brain, HIV cranks out cytokines, protein peptides that kill off neurons. The virus *Chlamydia pneumoniae* may use a similar trick—slipping into the brain and manufacturing cytokines—to cause Alzheimer's disease.

Streptococcal bacteria, like those that cause strep throat, take yet a different tack. As they invade the body, they automatically trip the body's defense alarm, calling up the immune system's antibody soldiers. But once the skirmish begins, the bacteria camouflage themselves within that very immune system. Like a wolf in sheep's clothing, they disguise themselves through molecular mimicry, cloaking themselves in proteins that imitate the body's own proteins, and thereby elude attack. For reasons scientists don't yet understand, the antibodies of some people—perhaps those with a genetic predisposition—then turn on their bodies' own tissues, assailing neurons in the basal ganglia. These structures, located between the more primitive lower brain and the higher cortical centers, help interpret information from the senses and are key to healthy emotions and behavior.

The self-destruction instigated by streptococcal bacteria can be particularly dangerous to young children. Because their immune systems are "naive," or underdeveloped, "their bodies mount a vigorous response to streptococci, but it is not terribly effective, and their antibodies wind up injuring their own neurons instead of the bacteria," explains Swedo. She believes that such self-induced damage leads some children to develop obsessive-compulsive disorder.

In an experiment conducted earlier this year, Swedo replaced the blood plasma of 28 children who suffered from OCD (and who had elevated levels of streptococcus antibodies) with healthy donor plasma, reasoning that such a switch would remove the trouble-making antibodies. Within a month, the incidence of tics declined by half, and their other OCD symptoms were reduced by 60%. "That was really gratifying," says Swedo. "It means that OCD is a medical illness, and if you catch it before there is scarring in the brain, you can cure it."

OCD isn't the only mental illness associated with streptococcus. Though anorexia nervosa has been tied to a distorted body image, societal pressure to be thin, discomfort with developing sexuality and other emotional and cultural factors, doctors have also noted that the eating disorder sometimes appears or worsens after a case of strep throat. Streptococcus has been implicated as well in Tourette's syndrome and in Sydenham's chorea, which makes the arms and legs of those afflicted jerk in a manner often likened to dancing.

Researchers think that the seeds of yet other mental illnesses may be planted while a fetus is still in the womb, when the pregnant mother-to-be becomes infected. Flu epidemics have been followed a generation later by waves of schizophrenia in England, Wales, Denmark, Finland and other countries, and a recent study published in the New England Journal of Medicine reports higher rates of schizophrenia among children born in crowded areas in cold weather—conditions hospitable to respiratory ailments.

Scientists suspect that in such cases a virus, such as the one that causes influenza or a newer candidate, the Borna virus, may insinuate itself into the fetal brain at a crucial stage of development. The microbe then subtly deranges the brain's neural connections in a process that becomes apparent only as the brain reaches full maturity, in early adulthood. In people with schizophrenia, parts of the brain—the cortex, thalamus, limbic system and basal ganglia—shrink, while crevices and fluid-filled spaces enlarge by as much as half, and the brain's chemical balance shifts. Such changes might well be the terrible legacy of a prenatal virus.

Microbes that cause mental illness can also enter the body another way—on one's fork. In the mid-1990s, an outbreak of Creutzfeldt-Jakob disease struck fear into meat-eaters, especially in England, where 35 people died after eating infected beef. While alive, the victims of what was dubbed "mad cow disease" exhibited bizarre symptoms such as continual screaming, inappropriate laughter, failure to bathe and compulsive walking.

Scientists theorized that the "mad cows" became infected because they were fed on sheep afflicted with the disease known as scrapie, but a similar infection endemic to cows may be to blame. (Scrapie in sheep, bovine spongiform encephalitis in cows and Creutzfeldt-Jakob disease in humans are all believed to be caused by what's known as a prion, or infectious protein, which acts in a manner similar to a virus.) Contaminated human growth hormone, corneal transplants and surgical instruments have also been suspected of communicating the disease to humans. Earlier this year, the British medical journal The Lancet reported that multiple surgeries and living on a farm are risk factors for CJD. Though the disease is considered rare, Yale neuropathologist Laura Manueldis, M.D., who thinks that the causative agent is actually a small virus rather than a prion, suspects that CJD is more common than we believe, and is often misdiagnosed as Alzheimer's.

Why doesn't every child with a strep throat develop an anxiety disorder? Or dementia strike every adult with syphilis? Our bodies protect us from most invasions by unfriendly microbes, but the vulnerable—those with poor health, weakened immune systems or, perhaps, genetic susceptibility—are less equipped to fend off the viruses and bacteria that may eventually cause mental illness.

Continuing research is likely to bring more effective vaccines and antibiotics, but prevention and treatment will have to be every bit as shrewd as the infectious agents themselves, which spread and reproduce in seemingly countless ways. More worrisome is the fact that illness-causing organisms may be outwitting our antimicrobial strategies. With the development of antibiotics and antivirals, researchers had hoped to vanquish viruses and bacteria once and for all. But they underestimated the wily ingenuity of these microbes, which soon produced strains resistant to the new miracle medicines.

Likewise, scientists at one time believed that infectious agents evolved to become less potent, if only to ensure their own survival: the longer an infected host stays alive, after all, the greater the number of people who can be exposed to the pathogen, and the more likely the microbe is to reproduce itself. But recent research has turned up a less reassuring reality: under some conditions, microbes can flourish with increased virulence in crowded modern cities. These densely populated areas can maintain dangerous pathogens that otherwise might whip through a community and then have nowhere else to go.

To fight these pathogens successfully doctors will have to tailor the treatments to the specific disease. Sometimes, for example, they may want to relieve an infected patient's fever and inflammation; at other times, fever must be left alone to kill off heat-sensitive viruses. Syphilis can be cured with penicillin, and doctors have had some success in prescribing antibiotics to people with anorexia. Other illnesses require more involved treatment, such as Swedo's plasma replacement for children with OCD, and some ailments cannot be helped much at all. The only way to treat HIV dementia, for example, is to try to slow the replication of the virus itself. No current therapy does this permanently and many HIV-positive patients still suffer psychiatric symptoms. (In fact, suicide is a leading cause of death among the HIV-infected.) There's no treatment for Creutzfeldt-Jakob disease beyond palliative care, and by the time influenza-induced schizophrenia becomes apparent, the neurological damage is already done.

Still, science continues to offer hope that one day such infectious agents will be controlled or even eliminated. That day can't come too soon for Swedo, a pediatrician by training. "When I practiced medicine at Memorial Hospital in Chicago, I saw parents suffer horribly when they lost their children to leukemia," she says. "When I came to the NIMH, I began to see parents lose their children to OCD and schizophrenia. These parents' grief is so much more profound. The fact that their children's illnesses are socially unacceptable makes their pain almost unbearable." Now that we know many psychiatric ills begin with a microbe, rather than a suffocating mother or remote father, "we can start treating mentally ill people without the shame and blame. We can treat them medically."

MENTAL HEALTH REFORM

WHAT IT WOULD REALLY TAKE

Tipper Gore has brought a welcome focus on the problem. But millions of mentally ill Americans aren't getting the treatment they need. And there's no easy fix

BY JOHN CLOUD LOS ANGELES

GERALD MINSK USED TO DROP ACID and smoke pot to help quell paranoid delusions that Boston's North End mafiosi were conspiring against him. Yes, it's crazy to take hallucinogens to soothe your hallucinations. But that's what untreated mental illness does to you. It can also leave you jobless and sleeping under the Boston University bridge. That's what happened to Minsk, anyway, in the 1970s. For years, his bipolar disorder was virtually ignored as he cycled in and out of jails, mental hospitals and community centers, none of which took the time, or had the resources, to treat him properly.

Millions of Americans are treated the same way. As a rule, mentally ill people are no more likely than their neighbors to be violent. But untreated mental illness can have horrific results. Andrew Goldstein asked to be hospitalized in New York because he was terrified of phantom voices.

Instead, budget-conscious officials most often referred him to short-term emergency care. Last year, in a psychotic state, he shoved a woman from a subway platform to her death under the wheels of a train.

Though tragedies like this one make headlines, the real shock is what happens to the vast majority of mentally ill people. Most Americans with mental illness simply aren't treated. Of the 2 million who suffer from schizophrenia, for instance, more than half receive substandard care. Only a third of those with serious depression receive *any* treatment. Reformers have tried to call attention to these problems for years—former First Lady Rosalynn Carter has been an advocate since the '60s—but the mentally ill have a powerful new ally.

Tipper Gore, wife of the Vice President, has organized a first-ever White House conference on mental health, which takes place next week. Gore, who disclosed in the run-up to the conference that she was treated for depression in the early '90s, has prodded her husband's boss to ask Congress to spend more money to treat the mentally ill. President Clinton backs a bill in Congress to force employers to help too by providing equal insurance coverage for mental and physical health. (Currently, insurance plans can charge higher co-payments for psychiatric visits than for other medical care.) Clinton aims to set an example by announcing at the conference that the Federal Government will begin providing its employees equal benefits for mental and nonmental ailments.

Even if all the proposals become law, they will represent only the first steps in solving the crisis of the mentally ill. There's not much political benefit to pushing the cause of people with mental disorders, and over the past 30 years governments have done little to fulfill a promise made by President John F. Kennedy in 1963 to subsidize mental-health services in every community.

Instead, communities have hired a lot of police, and today cops are the primary care givers for most of the unemployed mentally ill. That's because 200,000 of them are homeless, according to the National Alliance for the Mentally Ill, an advocacy group. Another 200,000 are incarcerated, usually as a result of petty crimes. Fewer than 70,000, on the other hand, live in state mental hospitals. And according to a study by Maryland researchers, less than 10% of Americans with schizophrenia are treated in the smaller community programs envisioned by Kennedy-era reformers.

Attacking this problem all at once is impossible. It would take billions of dollars. The state of Virginia alone would have to spend $500 million to begin providing adequate community treatment, according to a 1998 report prepared for it by consultants. Virginia's Governor, Jim Gilmore, has proposed spending $41 million instead. The Clinton plan would increase the mental-health grants that go to all states by just $70 million next year, to $358 million in all.

In Congress, two Senators who have seen family members with mental illness benefit from modern treatments are trying to improve access to care for others. Republican Pete Domenici of New Mexico and Democrat Paul Wellstone of Minnesota have introduced a bill that would force employers to provide the same level of coverage for mental and physical illnesses. Although the bill would represent the most meager of advances—it would help only those well enough to work—its passage will still require a monumental lobbying effort. Business groups are already working against it, saying it's part of a liberal package of insurance reforms that would raise their costs.

Domenici and Wellstone point out that the legislation is a solid long-term investment, since it would help people get treated before their illnesses become so severe that they lose their jobs or hurt themselves. Even business lobbyists admit that the cost increases for mental-health insurance will be small (maybe 1%). But they fear it will open the door to other mandates as well. "You have to remember that the Patient's Bill of Rights is being considered too," says Kate Sullivan of the U.S. Chamber of Commerce, referring to the proposal in Congress to make it easier for people to get around the cost restrictions of managed care. "So you're talking about 1% here and 1.5% there, but in the aggregate, you're looking at a 6% increase, which is huge."

Prospects for the mental-health bill look even weaker in the House than in the Senate, where Domenici chairs the influential budget committee. House majority whip Tom DeLay of Texas, who has close ties to business groups, was 1 of just 17 members of the House to vote against a very weak 1996 version of the Domenici-Wellstone proposal; he also seems to have a deep suspicion of psychology in general. Just last month, he accused the American Psychological Association of trying to "normalize pedophilia" after the association published a study suggesting that not all childhood victims of sexual abuse necessarily suffer mental illness as a result.

If DeLay's views on psychology are a bit harsh, many Americans have only in the past decade begun to see mental disorders as illnesses, not moral shortcomings. Though we still whisper about it, we all know a Tipper Gore at work today. Indeed, in addition to pushing her policy goals, Gore is hoping her own story will nourish this cultural shift. She and other reformers want to convince the nation that mental illness doesn't result from bad parenting or lax churchgoing but from chemical imbalances. In Gore's case, she says there was a problem with her brain's "gas gauge."

This is canny p.r. Americans would probably feel much better about meeting the enormous costs of reform if they thought mental illness is as fixable as, say, "a game knee," as Dr. Peter Whybrow puts it. He hosted a May forum with Gore at the University of California, Los Angeles, where he chairs the psychiatry department. One of the reformers' favorite statistics is that 60% of those who have schizophrenia can be successfully treated, while just 41% of those who have angioplasty (to open up clogged blood vessels) can recover fully. Medical comparisons are often used by those coming out as mentally ill. In 1995, when Alma Powell, wife of retired General Colin Powell, said she had suffered depression, her husband said it was "very easily controlled with proper medication, just as my blood pressure is."

But this is where the p.r.—and the quick-fix politics—begin to collide with reality. To be sure, people with mental illness can get better. Advances of the past decade have given independent lives to some who thought they would never have them. But there are no cures for mental illness—only lifelong management—and treatment is highly unpredictable. At the UCLA forum and at similar events, Gore cites seemingly simple "success stories"—cases like that of Minsk, the man who had been homeless in Boston in the '70s. "We're proud of you," she told him. But those real-life cases tend to be much more complicated than fixing a game knee. Minsk's salvation wasn't medication—or it wasn't only that. By the mid-'80s, he had moved to Los Angeles and met an advocate for the mentally ill who won his trust. He helped Minsk sign up for benefits, find housing, and, yes, stay in treatment—therapy *and* medication.

Today, at 47, Minsk has a wife, a home and an e-mail account. He has become an

advocate himself, canvassing dirty streets of downtown L.A. to tell mentally ill people about Lamp, a center he helps run for them. But the people Lamp serves "need many different solutions," Minsk says. Some need food and a bed before they can consider getting well. Others have medicated themselves with illegal drugs for so long they have become addicts. Some want to take prescription medication for their illnesses, but some don't, because of side effects or for other reasons. Many Lamp folks have all these problems, each crisis ricocheting off the others until their lives seem hopeless. For everyone, Minsk says—including himself—"there is no beginning and no end" to mental illness. It is a profoundly individual experience.

Americans may not have recognized that reality the last time they tried to reform the system. Back then, in the 1960s, there were also new wonder drugs. Chlorpromazine and its cousins composed patients enough that reformers could suggest closing the institutions that had often done no more than chain the ill to their beds. President Kennedy signed the landmark bill in 1963 that was to create as many as 2,000 community mental-health centers, compassionate places that would dispense the drugs and ease the ill into society.

Psychiatrists started to notice that the drugs brought some awful side effects—facial contortions, blurred vision—and many patients began to refuse them. But "deinstitutionalization," as the reform movement was called, was well under way. Nearly half a million patients were returned to their communities between the mid-'50s and the mid-'80s. The Federal Government never built all the centers Kennedy promised—there are just 740 today—and states didn't make up the slack.

Each state blundered differently. Washington State tied community mental-health spending to the size of welfare rolls, a sign of stigma itself. In Illinois, the state often paid nursing homes to take many of its patients. But old people and mentally ill people don't have the same needs, and few nursing homes hired the staff needed to treat the different set of patients. A bill before the Illinois legislature would require those hirings, but the efforts come too late for Russell Weston Jr. In 1996 he became an outpatient at an underfunded community mental-health center in Waterloo, Ill. The staff there can't closely monitor every patient, and Weston disappeared—until last July, when he shot and killed two U.S. Capitol police officers.

Such crimes have had political consequences. Some New York legislators, for instance, want to make it easier to force people into treatment. Such measures have a law-and-order feel, and politicians like New York Attorney General Eliot Spitzer—a Democrat who barely won his race last year—have embraced them. But most advocates for the mentally ill point out that even if the potentially violent mentally ill could be committed more easily, there are still few places to take them.

If Tipper Gore and the reformers are to educate Americans about mental illness and hence reduce its stigma, they will have to be honest about such complexities. But openness about mental illness isn't easy. Gore has at times even seemed reluctant to share her saga. She refuses to name the medication she took, and she gives few details about the nature of her depression, saying mainly that it emerged after a car accident that nearly killed her son.

Such pressures affect those who work daily to fight stigma. Consider Michael Faenza. "If I didn't take medication for depression, I would drink a quart of Jack Daniels every week to slow my thoughts enough to go to sleep," he said recently. At first he asked that the comment not be printed. But then he reconsidered: he is, after all, president of the National Mental Health Association, a 90-year-old advocacy group. "That's one of the pieces in this puzzle, to remove the shame," Faenza says. "It takes some courage to do that."

TIME/CNN POLL

■ **Do you know anyone who has had a mental illness that required treatment?**

Yes	35%
No	63%

■ **Should government spend more, less or the same amount of money to treat people with mental illness who can't afford to pay?**

More	67%
Less	4%
Same amount	23%

■ **Should employers be required to offer insurance for mental illness at the same level as insurance for physical illness?**

Yes	77%
No	18%

■ **Tipper Gore recently said she had suffered from depression and was successfully treated with medication. Would this make her less qualified to perform the duties of First Lady if her husband were elected president?**

Yes	13%
No	81%

From a telephone poll of 1,017 adult Americans taken for TIME/CNN on May 26-27 by Yankelovich Partners Inc. Sampling error is ±3.1%. "Not sures" omitted.

Unit 8

Unit Selections

Key Points to Consider

❖ What examples of societal deviance can you think of in your own experience and observation of society?

❖ Why do psychologists today believe that everyone is prone to stereotyping? Give some personal examples of stereotypical behavior and bias. Do you think that society can influence how people think? If so, how?

❖ Give some examples of "corporate welfare." What accounts for its continued growth? How does corporate welfare affect the private citizen? Explain how some companies have used welfare recipients to create a labor force.

❖ Describe the arguments for and against jury nullification, and explain your own position.

❖ What do you think can be done, and by whom, to lessen the "food insecurity" that some members of the elderly population experience?

 **Links** | **www.dushkin.com/online/**

These sites are annotated on pages 4 and 5.

Societal Deviance and Social Inequality is a new unit in this fourth edition of the anthology. It reflects a belief that deviance is not merely deviant personal behavior, but also behavior that is committed against other persons or society. Social inequality involves the belief that some persons are socially defined as disadvantaged due to their life circumstances. Social inequality can be applied to a number of life circumstances, such as poverty, race, gender, health, and many other phenomena. Central to a discussion of social inequality and societal deviance are status and stereotypes. There are two types of status, achieved and ascribed. Status that is earned—for example, college graduate, parent, corporate president—is labeled achieved status. Status that we are born with and have no control over, on the other hand, is called ascribed status. Gender and race are two examples of ascribed status. Stereotypes are standardized mental pictures that are held in common by members of a group. They often represent oversimplified opinions, prejudiced attitudes, and uncritical or derogatory judgments about people in a society. An example of a stereotype would be the statement, "So many black persons are poor because blacks are lazy." As this example suggests, stereotypes do not have to be accurate in order to exist. Social inequality is dependent on the meanings that people attach to status and stereotypes, which can lead to victims of social inequality being labeled as deviant, not because of the actions they themselves take, but because of the negative labels that are attached to them by the dominant powers in a society. To this extent, social inequality defines what is deviance and what is not, and allows for *societal deviance* that treats others as social unequals.

The articles in this unit deal with social inequality and make the point that deviance can occur even when the individuals or their societies are the victims of social deviance rather than being the perpetrators of deviant acts.

Currently, welfare reform is a major issue in many states. Historically, it has been the case that many middle- and upper-class individuals looked down upon the poor because they had to depend on public assistance to live. While quick to condemn the less fortunate in society, to the point of calling the poor lazy and deadbeats, corporate America was always first in line to pick up the check for corporate welfare. Political entities around the nation have been only too happy to build new factories for major corporations, to let the companies out of paying taxes, and to give companies all they want in exchange for the companies' providing jobs to those who have been on welfare. Imagine if you went to the governor of your state and asked her or him to provide you with a home and that you not be required to pay taxes because you would hire 10 people to maintain your garden. Chances are that your governor would laugh you out of her or his office. That would not happen to a major corporation. The poor are often used as the tools of corporations and the state who benefit themselves at the expense of the poor. In recent years, the states, in conjunction with the federal government, have initiated welfare-to-work programs. Under these programs, poor people are told that they will only receive cash benefits for a limited number of years in their lifetimes and that they must find employment. Welfare recipients who fail to look for a job are dropped from welfare. Other recipients are placed in poor paying dead-end jobs designed to produce failure. For example, in the article "Plucking Workers," the author describes how the state of Missouri conspired with meat-packing companies to force welfare recipients to take on hard but low-paying jobs plucking chickens, with the threat of losing all benefits if they did not comply. Workers who left the chicken plants would then be denied benefits because they quit their jobs. This is how social inequality works. But the deviant behavior belongs to society in the form of the unsavory relationship between the state and the corporation.

Other articles in this unit deal with such things as the high rate of AIDS among Latinos and how America is letting millions of our elderly starve in the land of plenty. Both of these are forms of societal deviance inflicted upon vulnerable members of our society by forces often beyond their control. For example, Rafael Campo tries to make the point that 20 percent of new AIDS cases are reported among young Latinos, who make up less than 10 percent of the United States' population. He suggests that Latinos are disenfranchised from the rest of society, and that due to strong religious values and a culture that condemns homosexuality as well as discussions about sex and birth control, they lack access to the kind of information that would be helpful in preventing the spread of AIDS. Like Latinos, elderly people of all races in our society seem to be disenfranchised due to their achieved status of elderly. The stereotype is that older people, because they often are debt-free, have a lot of disposable income, and consequently cannot suffer from hunger. The reality is that many older people, although debt-free, live on limited incomes that support high medical costs and a few other expenses. The result is that they may not have enough money for food and are therefore malnourished. Furthermore, as Trudy Lieberman points out, corporate and governmental America fails the elderly by being more concerned with other groups and profits, and do not contribute significantly to feeding programs for the elderly.

Jury nullification deals with the issue of whether juries have a social responsibility to acquit obviously guilty defendants because of an unjust legal system. Proponents claim that jurors have a moral duty to acquit guilty defendants who belong to minority populations because of past and present perceived injustices perpetrated against those populations by society. For example, a proponent of jury nullification might argue that a jury should acquit a black man who obviously killed a white man, because in the past, blacks were wrongfully convicted and executed on false charges that they had killed white men and raped white women. Opponents of jury nullification argue that while it was historically the case that black men were falsely convicted and executed for crimes that they did not commit, it would be an equal travesty of justice to now acquit guilty persons and allow them to kill again, with impunity. That is, they argue, two wrongs not making a right. At the same time, the last article in the unit deals with men who were wrongly condemned to die for crimes that they did not commit. It is pointed out that certain states have far worse records for this type of societal deviance than do other states. The article also points out the nature of the police and prosecutors who avidly pursued convictions against innocent people in the name of justice, even when justice was truly injustice.

WHERE BIAS BEGINS: THE TRUTH ABOUT STEREOTYPES

Psychologists once believed that only bigoted people used stereotypes. Now the study of unconscious bias is revealing the unsettling truth: We all use stereotypes, all the time, without knowing it. We have met the enemy of equality, and the enemy is us.

By Annie Murphy Paul

Mahzarin Banaji doesn't fit anybody's idea of a racist. A psychology professor at Yale University, she studies stereotypes for a living. And as a woman and a member of a minority ethnic group, she has felt firsthand the sting of discrimination. Yet when she took one of her own tests of unconscious bias, "I showed very strong prejudices," she says. "It was truly a disconcerting experience." And an illuminating one. When Banaji was in graduate school in the early 1980s, theories about stereotypes were concerned only with their explicit expression: outright and unabashed racism, sexism, anti-Semitism. But in the years since, a new approach to stereotypes has shattered that simple notion. The bias Banaji and her colleagues are studying is something far more subtle, and more insidious: what's known as automatic or implicit stereotyping, which, they find, we do all the time without knowing it. Though out-and-out bigotry may be on the decline, says Banaji, "if anything, stereotyping is a bigger problem than we ever imagined."

Previously researchers who studied stereotyping had simply asked people to record their feelings about minority groups and had used their answers as an index of their attitudes. Psychologists now understand that these conscious replies are only half the story. How progressive a person seems to be on the surface bears little or no relation to how prejudiced he or she is on an unconscious level—so that a bleeding-heart liberal might harbor just as many biases as a neo-Nazi skinhead.

As surprising as these findings are, they confirmed the hunches of many students of human behavior. "Twenty years ago, we hypothesized that there were people who said they were not prejudiced but who really did have unconscious negative stereotypes and beliefs," says psychologist Jack Dovidio, Ph.D., of Colgate University. "It was like theorizing about the existence of a virus, and then one day seeing it under a microscope."

The test that exposed Banaji's hidden biases—and that this writer took as well, with equally dismaying results—is typical of the ones used by automatic stereotype researchers. It presents the subject with a series of positive or negative adjectives, each paired with a characteristically "white" or "black" name. As the name and word appear together on a computer screen, the person taking the test presses a key, indicating whether the word is good or bad. Meanwhile, the computer records the speed of each response.

A glance at subjects' response times reveals a startling phenomenon: Most people who participate in the experiment—even some African-Americans—respond more quickly when a positive word is paired with a white name or a negative word with a black name. Because our minds are more accustomed to making these associations, says Banaji, they process them more rapidly. Though the words and names aren't subliminal, they are presented so quickly that a subject's ability to make deliberate choices is diminished—allowing his or her underlying assumptions to show through. The same technique can be used to measure stereotypes about many different social groups, such as homosexuals, women, and the elderly.

THE UNCONSCIOUS COMES INTO FOCUS

From these tiny differences in reaction speed—a matter of a few hundred milliseconds—the study of automatic stereotyping was born. Its immediate ancestor was the cognitive revolution of the 1970s, an explosion of psychological research into the way people think. After decades dominated by the study of observable behavior, scientists wanted a closer look at the more mysterious operation of the human brain. And the development of computers—which enabled scientists to display information

LIKE THE CULTURE, OUR MINDS ARE SPLIT ON THE SUBJECTS OF RACE, GENDER, SEXUAL ORIENTATION.

very quickly and to measure minute discrepancies in reaction time—permitted a peek into the unconscious.

At the same time, the study of cognition was also illuminating the nature of stereotypes themselves. Research done after World War II—mostly by European émigrés struggling to understand how the Holocaust had happened—concluded that stereotypes were used only by a particular type of person: rigid, repressed, authoritarian. Borrowing from the psychoanalytic perspective then in vogue, these theorists suggested that biased behavior emerged out of internal conflicts caused by inadequate parenting.

The cognitive approach refused to let the rest of us off the hook. It made the simple but profound point that we all use categories—of people, places, things—to make sense of the world around us. "Our ability to categorize and evaluate is an important part of human intelligence," says Banaji. "Without it, we couldn't survive." But stereotypes are too much of a good thing. In the course of stereotyping, a useful category—say women—becomes freighted with additional associations, usually negative. "Stereotypes are categories that have gone too far," says John Bargh, Ph.D., of New York University. "When we use stereotypes, we take in the gender, the age, the color of the skin of the person before us, and our minds respond with messages that say hostile, stupid, slow, weak. Those qualities aren't out there in the environment. They don't reflect reality."

Bargh thinks that stereotypes may emerge from what social psychologists call in-group/out-group dynamics. Humans, like other species, need to feel that they are part of a group, and as villages, clans, and other traditional groupings have broken down, our identities have attached themselves to more ambiguous classifications, such as race and class. We want to feel good about the group we belong to—and one way of doing so is to denigrate all those who aren't in it. And while we tend to see members of our own group as individuals, we view those in out-groups as an undifferentiated—stereotyped—mass. The categories we use have changed, but it seems that stereotyping itself is bred in the bone.

Though a small minority of scientists argues that stereotypes are usually accurate and can be relied upon without reservations, most disagree—and vehemently. "Even if there is a kernel of truth in the stereotype, you're still applying a generalization about a group to an individual, which is always incorrect," says Bargh. Accuracy aside, some believe that the use of stereotypes is simply unjust. "In a democratic society people should be judged as individuals and not as members of a group," Banaji argues. "Stereotyping flies in the face of that ideal."

PREDISPOSED TO PREJUDICE

The problem, as Banaji's own research shows, is that people can't seem to help it. A recent experiment provides a good illustration. Banaji and her colleague, Anthony Greenwald, Ph.D., showed people a list of names—some famous, some not. The next day the subjects returned to the lab and were shown a second list, which mixed names from the first list with new ones. Asked to identify which were famous, they picked out the Margaret Meads and the Miles Davises—but they also chose some of the names on the first list, which retained a lingering familiarity that they mistook for fame. (Psychologists call this the "famous overnight-effect.") By a margin of two-to-one, these suddenly "famous" people were male.

Participants weren't aware that they were preferring male names to female names, Banaji stresses. They were simply drawing on an unconscious stereotype of men as more important and influential than women. Something similar happened when she showed subjects a list of people who might be criminals: without knowing they were doing so, participants picked out an overwhelming number of African-American names. Banaji calls this kind of stereotyping *implicit,* because people know they are making a judgment—but just aren't aware of the basis upon which they are making it.

Even further below awareness is something that psychologists call automatic processing, in which stereotypes are trig-

gered by the slightest interaction or encounter. An experiment conducted by Bargh required a group of white participants to perform a tedious computer task. While performing the task, some of the participants were subliminally exposed to pictures of African-Americans with neutral expressions. When the subjects were then asked to do the task over again, the ones who had been exposed to the faces reacted with more hostility to the request—because, Bargh believes, they were responding in kind to the hostility which is part of the African-American stereotype. Bargh calls this the "immediate hostile reaction," which he believes can have a real effect on race relations. When African-Americans accurately perceive the hostile expressions that their white counterparts are unaware of, they may respond with hostility of their own—thereby perpetuating the stereotype.

Of course, we aren't completely under the sway of our unconscious. Scientists think that the automatic activation of a stereotype is immediately followed by a conscious check on unacceptable thoughts—at least in people who think that they are not prejudiced. This internal censor successfully restrains overtly biased responses. But there's still the danger of leakage, which often shows up in nonverbal behavior: our expressions, our stance, how far away we stand, how much eye contact we make.

The gap between what we say and what we do can lead African-Americans and whites to come away with very different impressions of the same encounter, says Jack Dovidio. "If I'm a white person talking to an African-American, I'm probably monitoring my conscious beliefs very carefully and making sure everything I say agrees with all the positive things I want to express," he says. "And I usually believe I'm pretty successful because I hear the right words coming out of my mouth." The listener who is paying attention to non-verbal behavior, however, may be getting quite the opposite message. An African-American student of Dovidio's recently told him that when she was growing up, her mother had taught her to observe how white people moved to gauge their true feelings toward blacks. "Her mother was a very astute ama-

THE CATEGORIES WE USE HAVE CHANGED, BUT STEREOTYPING ITSELF SEEMS TO BE BRED IN THE BONE.

WE HAVE TO CHANGE HOW WE THINK WE CAN INFLUENCE PEOPLE'S BEHAVIORS. IT WOULD BE NAIVE TO THINK THAT EXHORTATION IS ENOUGH.

teur psychologist—and about 20 years ahead of me," he remarks.

WHERE DOES BIAS BEGIN?

So where exactly do these stealth stereotypes come from? Though automatic-stereotype researchers often refer to the unconscious, they don't mean the Freudian notion of a seething mass of thoughts and desires, only some of which are deemed presentable enough to be admitted to the conscious mind. In fact, the cognitive model holds that information flows in exactly the opposite direction: connections made often enough in the conscious mind eventually become unconscious. Says Bargh: "If conscious choice and decision making are not needed, they go away. Ideas recede from consciousness into the unconscious over time."

Much of what enters our consciousness, of course, comes from the culture around us. And like the culture, it seems that our minds are split on the subjects of race, gender, class, sexual orientation. "We not only mirror the ambivalence we see in society, but also mirror it in precisely the same way," says Dovidio. Our society talks out loud about justice, equality, and egalitarianism, and most Americans accept these values as their own. At the same time, such equality exists only as an ideal, and that fact is not lost on our unconscious. Images of women as sex objects, footage of African-American criminals on the six o'clock news,—"this is knowledge we cannot escape," explains Banaji. "We didn't choose to know it, but it still affects our behavior."

We learn the subtext of our culture's messages early. By five years of age, says Margo Monteith, Ph.D., many children have definite and entrenched stereotypes about blacks, women, and other social groups. Adds Monteith, professor of psychology at the University of Kentucky: "Children don't have a choice about accepting or rejecting these conceptions, since they're acquired well before they have the cognitive abilities or experiences to form their own beliefs." And no matter how progressive the parents, they must compete with all the forces that would promote and perpetuate these stereotypes: peer pressure, mass media, the actual balance of power in society. In fact, prejudice may be as much a result as a cause of this imbalance. We

create stereotypes—African-Americans are lazy, women are emotional—to explain why things are the way they are. As Dovidio notes, "Stereotypes don't have to be true to serve a purpose."

WHY CAN'T WE ALL GET ALONG?

The idea of unconscious bias does clear up some nettlesome contradictions. "It accounts for a lot of people's ambivalence toward others who are different, a lot of their inconsistencies in behavior," says Dovidio. "It helps explain how good people can do bad things." But it also prompts some uncomfortable realizations. Because our conscious and unconscious beliefs may be very different—and because behavior often follows the lead of the latter—"good intentions aren't enough," as John Bargh puts it. In fact, he believes that they count for very little. "I don't think free will exists," he says, bluntly—because what feels like the exercise of free will may be only the application of unconscious assumptions.

Not only may we be unable to control our biased responses, we may not even be aware that we have them. "We have to rely on our memories and our awareness of what we're doing to have a connection to reality," says Bargh. "But when it comes to automatic processing, those cues can be deceptive." Likewise, we can't always be sure how biased others are. "We all have this belief that the important thing about prejudice is the external expression of it," says Banaji. "That's going to be hard to give up."

One thing is certain: We can't claim that we've eradicated prejudice just because its outright expression has waned. What's more, the strategies that were so effective in reducing that sort of bias won't work on unconscious beliefs. "What this research is saying is that we are going to have to change dramatically the way we think we can influence people's behaviors," says Banaji. "It would be naive to think that exhortation is enough." Exhortation, education, political protest—all of these hammer away at our conscious beliefs while leaving the bedrock below untouched. Banaji notes, however, that one traditional remedy for discrimination—affirmative action—may still be effective since it bypasses our unconsciously compromised judgment.

But some stereotype researchers think that the solution to automatic stereotyping lies in the process itself. Through practice, they say people can weaken the mental links that connect minorities to negative stereotypes and strengthen the ones that connect them to positive conscious beliefs. Margo Monteith explains how it might work. "Suppose you're at a party and someone tells a racist joke—and you laugh," she says. "Then you realize that you shouldn't have laughed at the joke. You feel guilty and become focused on your thought processes. Also, all sorts of cues become associated with laughing at the racist joke: the person who told the joke, the act of telling jokes, being at a party drinking." The next time you encounter these cues, "a warning signal of sorts should go off—'wait, didn't you mess up in this situation before?'—and your responses will be slowed and executed with greater restraint."

That slight pause in the processing of a stereotype gives conscious, unprejudiced beliefs a chance to take over. With time, the tendency to prevent automatic stereotyping may itself become automatic. Monteith's research suggests that, given enough motivation, people may be able to teach themselves to inhibit prejudice so well that even their tests of implicit bias come clean.

The success of this process of "de-automatization" comes with a few caveats, however. First, even its proponents concede that it works only for people disturbed by the discrepancy between their conscious and unconscious beliefs, since unapologetic racists or sexists have no motivation to change. Second, some studies have shown that attempts to suppress stereotypes may actually cause them to return later, stronger than ever. And finally, the results that Monteith and other researchers have achieved in the laboratory may not stick in the real world, where people must struggle to maintain their commitment to equality under less-than-ideal conditions.

Challenging though that task might be, it is not as daunting as the alternative researchers suggest: changing society itself. Bargh, who likens de-automatization to closing the barn door once the horses have escaped, says that "it's clear that the way to get rid of stereotypes is by the roots, by where they come from in the first place." The study of culture may someday tell us where the seeds of prejudice originated; for now the study of the unconscious shows us just how deeply they're planted.

CORPORATE WELFARE

A TIME investigation uncovers how hundreds of companies get on the dole—and why it costs every working American the equivalent of two weeks' pay every year

By Donald L. Barlett and James B. Steele

HOW WOULD YOU LIKE TO PAY ONLY A QUARTER OF THE REAL ESTATE TAXES you owe on your home? And buy everything for the next 10 years without spending a single penny in sales tax? Keep a chunk of your paycheck free of income taxes? Have the city in which

which governments large and small subsidize corporations large and small, usually at the expense of another state or town and almost always at the expense of individual and other corporate taxpayers.

Two years after Congress reduced welfare for individuals and families, this other

ment service. It can also be a tax break—a credit, exemption, deferral or deduction, or a tax rate lower than the one others pay.

The rationale to curtail traditional welfare programs, such as Aid to Families with Dependent Children and food stamps, and to impose a lifetime limit on the amount of aid

---

During one of the most robust economic periods in our nation's history, the Federal Government has shelled out $125 billion in corporate welfare, equivalent to all the income tax paid by 60 million individuals and families.

---

you live lend you money at rates cheaper than any bank charges? Then have the same city install free water and sewer lines to your house, offer you a perpetual discount on utility bills—and top it all off by landscaping your front yard at no charge?

Fat chance. You can't get any of that, of course. But if you live almost anywhere in America, all around you are taxpayers getting deals like this. These taxpayers are called corporations, and their deals are usually trumpeted as "economic development" or "public-private partnerships." But a better name is corporate welfare. It's a game in

kind of welfare continues to expand, penetrating every corner of the American economy. It has turned politicians into bribery specialists, and smart business people into con artists. And most surprising of all, it has rarely created any new jobs.

While corporate welfare has attracted critics from both the left and the right, there is no uniform definition. By TIME's definition, it is this: any action by local, state or federal government that gives a corporation or an entire industry a benefit not offered to others. It can be an outright subsidy, a grant, real estate, a low-interest loan or a govern-

received, was compelling: the old system didn't work. It was unfair, destroyed incentive, perpetuated dependence and distorted the economy. An 18-month TIME investigation has found that the same indictment, almost to the word, applies to corporate welfare. In some ways, it represents pork-barrel legislation of the worst order. The difference, of course, is that instead of rewarding the poor, it rewards the powerful.

And it rewards them handsomely. The Federal Government alone shells out $125 billion a year in corporate welfare, this in the midst of one of the more robust economic periods in the nation's history. Indeed, thus far in the 1990s, corporate profits have totaled $4.5 trillion—a sum equal to the cumulative paychecks of 50 million working Americans who earned less than $25,000 a year, for those eight years.

That makes the Federal Government America's biggest sugar daddy, dispensing a range of giveaways from tax abatements to price supports for sugar itself. Companies get government money to advertise their products; to help build new plants, offices and stores; and to train their workers. They sell their goods to foreign buyers that make the acquisitions with tax dollars supplied by the U.S. government; engage in foreign transactions that are insured by the government; and are excused from paying a portion of their income tax if they sell products overseas. They pocket lucrative government contracts to carry out ordinary business operations, and government grants to conduct research that will improve their profit margins. They are extended partial tax immunity if they locate in certain geographical areas, and they may write off as business expenses some of the perks enjoyed by their top executives.

The justification for much of this welfare is that the U.S. government is creating jobs. Over the past six years, Congress appropriated $5 billion to run the Export-Import Bank of the United States, which subsidizes companies that sell goods abroad. James A. Harmon, president and chairman, puts it this way: "American workers... have higher-quality, better-paying jobs, thanks to Eximbank's financing." But the numbers at the bank's five biggest beneficiaries—AT&T, Bechtel, Boeing, General Electric and McDonnell Douglas (now a part of Boeing)—tell another story. At these companies, which have accounted for about 40% of all loans, grants and long-term guarantees in this decade, overall employment has fallen 38%, as more than a third of a million jobs have disappeared.

The picture is much the same at the state and local level, where a different kind of feeding frenzy is taking place. Politicians stumble over one another in the rush to arrange special deals for select corporations, fueling a growing economic war among the states. The result is that states keep throwing money at companies that in many cases are not serious about moving anyway. The companies are certainly not reluctant to take the money, though, which is available if they simply utter the word relocation. And why not? Corporate executives, after all, have a fiduciary duty to squeeze every dollar they can from every locality waving blandishments in their face.

State and local governments now give corporations money to move from one city to another—even from one building to another—and tax credits for hiring new employees. They supply funds to train workers or pay part of their wages while they are in training, and provide scientific and engineering assistance to solve workplace technical problems. They repave existing roads and build new ones. They lend money at bargain-basement interest rates to erect plants or buy equipment. They excuse corporations from paying sales and property taxes and relieve them from taxes on investment income.

There are no reasonably accurate estimates on the amount of money states shovel out. That's because few want you to know. Some say they maintain no records. Some say they don't know where the files are. Some say the information is not public. All that's certain is that the figure is in the many billions of dollars each year—and it is growing, when measured against the subsidy per job.

In 1989 Illinois gave $240 million in economic incentives to Sears, Roebuck & Co. to keep its corporate headquarters and 5,400 workers in the state by moving from Chicago to suburban Hoffman Estates. That amounted to a subsidy of $44,000 for each job.

In 1991 Indiana gave $451 million in economic incentives to United Airlines to build an aircraft-maintenance facility that would employ as many as 6,300 people. Subsidy: $72,000 for each job.

In 1993 Alabama gave $253 million in economic incentives to Mercedes-Benz to build an automobile-assembly plant near Tuscaloosa and employ 1,500 workers. Subsidy: $169,000 for each job.

And in 1997 Pennsylvania gave $307 million in economic incentives to Kvaerner ASA, a Norwegian global engineering and construction company, to open a shipyard at the former Philadelphia Naval Shipyard and employ 950 people. Subsidy: $323,000 for each job.

This kind of arithmetic seldom adds up. Let's say the Philadelphia job pays $50,000. And each new worker pays $6,700 in local and state taxes. That means it will take nearly a half-century of tax collections from each individual to earn back the money granted to create his or her job. And that assumes all 950 workers will be recruited from outside Philadelphia and will relocate in the city, rather than move from existing jobs within the city, where they are already paying taxes.

All this is in service of a system that may produce jobs in one city or state, thus fostering the illusion of an uptick in employment. But it does not create more jobs in the

nation as a whole. Market forces do that, and that's why 10 million jobs have been created since 1990. But most of those jobs have been created by small- and medium-size companies, from high-tech start-ups to franchised cleaning services. FORTUNE 500 companies, on the other hand, have erased more jobs than they have created this past decade, and yet they are the biggest beneficiaries of corporate welfare.

To be sure, some economic incentives are handed out for a seemingly worthwhile public purpose. The tax breaks that companies receive to locate in inner cities come to mind. Without them, companies might not invest in those neighborhoods. However well intended, these subsidies rarely produce lasting results. They may provide short-term jobs but not long-term employment. And in the end, the costs outweigh any benefits.

And what are those costs? The equivalent of nearly two weekly paychecks from every working man and woman in America—extra money that would stay in their pockets if it didn't go to support some business venture or another.

If corporate welfare is an unproductive end game, why does it keep growing in a period of intensive government cost cutting? For starters, it has good p.r. and an army of bureaucrats working to expand it. A corporate-welfare bureaucracy of an estimated 11,000 organizations and agencies has grown up, with access to city halls, statehouses, the Capitol and the White House. They conduct seminars, conferences and training sessions. They have their own trade associations. They publish their own journals and newsletters. They create attractive websites on the Internet. And they never call it "welfare." They call it "economic incentives" or "empowerment zones" or "enterprise zones."

Whatever the name, the result is the same. Some companies receive public services at reduced rates, while all others pay the full cost. Some companies are excused from paying all or a portion of their taxes due, while all others must pay the full amount imposed by law. Some companies receive grants, low-interest loans and other subsidies, while all others must fend for themselves.

In the end, that's corporate welfare's greatest flaw. It's unfair. One role of government is to help ensure a level playing field for people and businesses. Corporate welfare does just the opposite. It tilts the playing field in favor of the largest or the most politically influential or most aggressive businesses....

Plucking Workers

Tyson Foods looks to the welfare rolls for a captive labor force

BY CHRISTOPHER D. COOK

Government and business officials in Missouri have developed an efficient way to slash the welfare rolls: order recipients to gut chickens or pigs for Tyson Foods, ConAgra, or Premium Standard Farms, or else lose their benefits. Under an initiative called Direct Job Placement, the companies have hired hundreds of former welfare recipients. But turnover has been high, and many—balking at the prospect of gutting fifty chickens per minute—have disappeared or been dropped from the welfare rolls by the state.

As one woman on welfare discovered, even having a newborn baby and no means of transportation is no excuse. When the thirty-year-old mother, whose name was withheld for confidentiality, informed her case managers of these extenuating circumstances, they were not sympathetic.

"They told her she had to work at Tyson's even if she had to walk to get there [a six-mile trek]," says Helen Chewning, a former family advocate with the Missouri Valley Human Resource Center in Sedalia. "They sanctioned her while she was pregnant" and then ordered her to work at Tyson when her baby was just eleven days old, Chewning recalls. "She hasn't had any income for six months. How are they supposed to live?"

Christopher D. Cook is an investigative journalist based in San Francisco.

The single mother is one of more than 110,000 Missourians who have left welfare since January 1993, a stunning 43 percent decline in caseload. Under Direct Job Placement, since May 1995, the state has placed more than 5,400 people in jobs, if temporarily.

But in Missouri and nationwide, these plummeting caseloads are deceptive. According to *The Washington Post,* nearly 40 percent of those who left welfare during a three-month period last year were cut off for breaking the rules—not because they landed jobs.

In the cold calculus of welfare reform, a closed case means success, regardless of what happens to the recipient. As President Clinton celebrates the nation's lowest welfare count since 1969, evidence is piling up across the country that thousands are being coerced into hazardous, short-term jobs or simply kicked off welfare.

Missouri has cut caseloads with such zeal that Clinton used the state as a backdrop last August to announce that 1.4 million people have left welfare since 1996. "We now know that welfare reform works," he proclaimed in a speech to business executives in St. Louis. Clinton touted Missouri's Direct Job Placement approach as a national model. "Thirty-five other states have allowed Missouri to show them that this is a good reform, and they are also doing it," he said.

But state records tell a different story. Missouri is on a sanctioning binge of astounding proportions, pushing thousands off welfare without getting them into jobs. "Since January 1993, the monthly number of welfare recipients who have had their TANF [Temporary Assistance for Needy Families] grant reduced for not looking for work or accepting a job has increased from twenty-seven to 7,345—saving taxpayers over $3 million," according to the state Department of Social Services. The records show soaring numbers of people are being sanctioned by the state: They've been cut off welfare for refusing a job or missing an interview. The caseload has plummeted from 5,228 per month in 1993 to just 265 this May, but much of the caseload decline is simply due to sanctions.

One impetus behind the sanctions, critics assert and state officials acknowledge, is the threat of working in poultry plants or in hog slaughterhouses, where assembly-line jobs involve processing animal parts at a feverish pace in a dirty and dangerous environment.

"It's the same as slavery," says Jerry Helmick, business agent for the United Food and Commercial Workers in Kansas City. "The government sends you there for an interview. If you can stand up and walk, Tyson is going to offer you a job, and you either take it or you're out of the system altogether."

Tyson and other meat-processing companies with high rates of injury and constant employee turnover are corralling the new captive labor force created by welfare reform. In a welfare-to-work program begun by the state in 1995, Missouri welfare agencies send recipients directly to labor-starved, low-wage employers. State documents describe the Direct Job Placement program as "a cooperative effort between local employers and the Division of Family Services," in which "employers experiencing labor-market shortages fill vacancies with recipients."

It's the ultimate public-private partnership, supplying business with a steady reserve of cheap labor while enabling social-service agencies to meet intense caseload-reduction targets set by federal and state officials.

The program includes several Tyson plants, ConAgra chicken processors, Premium Standard's hog-raising and processing plants, and numerous temp agencies and nursing homes. In rural areas with tight labor markets, large companies have near-monopoly control over job placement—and they have transformed county welfare offices into their own private hiring halls.

In the north-central Missouri town of Milan near the Iowa border, a Premium Standard pork-processing plant and a ConAgra chicken-processing factory are the main beneficiaries of the new welfare-to-work regime.

"We have been lucky in Milan because Premium Standard Farms opened up here," says Karen Fay, the Division of Family Services caseload manager for the area. "If we have a person that applies for food stamps who is eligible to work, we send them to Premium Standard Farms. Their job is to cut apart whatever part they get. At Premium Standard Farms, the pigs are fastened on a belt, and they cut the same part of each pig."

Fay recognizes that people in the welfare-to-work program have few other options. "All we have is PSF [Premium Standard Farms] and ConAgra," she says.

Lisa Garison, human-resources director for Premium Standard's plant in Milan, says the welfare pool has aided the company's expansion. "We continue to try to grow, and any resource that is here in this area, our goal is to tap it." The welfare supply, she says, "has been a key in helping us staff.... We hire as many of them as we can. They [case managers at the Division of Family Services] give us as many as they can."

Garison says recipients' work experiences have been mixed: "Some people we've had wonderful success with, and then others find it's a real challenge to enter the work world at the pace that we work at."

Roger Allison, executive director of the Missouri Rural Crisis Center, says Premium Standard's vast hog-raising houses spew noxious methane and hydrogen sulfite gases that reek from fifteen miles away. "These are people who are captive in a workplace that is abusive and environmentally unhealthy," he says. But since the pig farms are classified as agricultural operations, they are not subject to inspections or regulation by the Occupational Safety and Health Administration. (Premium Standard's processing plants do fall under OSHA jurisdiction.)

Garison rejects the charge that it's captive labor. "I don't see those folks as only having one way out of that situation," she says. "There should be plenty of opportunity for people to find the kind of work they want to do; they may have to do something they don't like for a while."

People who accept a Tyson job are in for a rude awakening. "The first job they get is the puller job—pulling the internal organs out," says Tim Barchak, Missouri political director for the Service Employees International Union. "A lot of these workers will lose their fingernails in two or three weeks from the bacteria and chicken fat." Nearly one-third of Missouri's 103,000 poultry workers suffered an injury or illness in 1995, according to the Bureau of Labor Statistics.

Former Tyson worker Jason Wolfe, twenty-three, toiled for a year and a half on the "thighing line," hanging dead birds on metal shackles for $6.75 an hour. "They want you to hang forty or fifty of these birds in a minute for four to six hours straight, without a break," he says. "If you miss any, they threaten to fire you." The work is so stressful, Wolfe says, that at times, "I'd wake up in the middle of the night and catch my arms rehanging chickens."

Adding insult to injury, Tyson fires people who have too many "occurrences," the company's term for sick days. According to Wolfe, Tyson terminates workers who miss more than five days in a year for any reason. "I was fired because of an occurrence problem because I had to go to the doctor a couple of times," Wolfe says.

"Tyson is very bad about firing people if they are sick or their children are sick," says Chewning. "It's happening all the time. I have people coming in who can't pay their rent because of that. If you have a sick child, you have to take them to the doctor. If you don't, social services will come after you for neglect."

Ed Nicholson, a top spokesman at Tyson headquarters in Springdale, Arkansas, confirms this policy. "If there are six occurrences, a person can be terminated," he says. "If a person is out for three days with an ailment and they have a doctor's note, that would be one occurrence." But each time an employee misses work due to a new ailment, according to Nicholson, it counts as another occurrence.

The grueling and hazardous work means an annual turnover rate of roughly 75 percent, according to Greg Denier of the United Food and Commercial Workers in Washington, D.C. Many stay on the job for just a few months before succumbing to injury or sheer exhaustion. The harsh conditions and high turnover create a constant need for new workers. And as unemployment rates dipped well below 5 percent across the Midwest in the mid-1990s, the industry saw its supply of available workers begin to dry up.

Rather than improve conditions to attract employees, the pig and poultry industries have resorted to importing workers from Mexico and housing them in temporary mobile-home facilities. At Premium Standard, "they're actually having to ship Mexicans into and out of housing to fill these jobs, because they can't get enough people to work there," says Brenda Proctor, a consumer economist with the University of Missouri.

According to numerous union officials and former Tyson worker Jason Wolfe, Tyson advertises for Mexican workers to come to its Midwestern plants and even transports them to Missouri. "Sometimes [Tyson's recruiters] get a freezer truck and load them up and take them up here," says Wolfe, who talked with Mexican workers at the plant.

Ed Nicholson denies that the firm recruits or imports Mexican workers. "We have not transported anyone across the border," he says. Instead, Tyson offers bonuses for employees who bring in new workers, he says. "Some of that literature got passed along to people down there [in Mexico], and it gave the impression that we were advertising down there. The word gets out that jobs are available and people show up from Mexico, Texas, or Guatemala."

If low-wage, immigrant workers are good for Tyson and other companies, the idea of a captive labor force provided directly by the state is even more appealing. In 1995, as welfare reform swept the nation, Tyson lobbied to gain easy access to the abundance of cheap workers thrust onto the labor market.

The Direct Job Placement program "was born out of Tyson's need for additional workers," says Linda Messenger, welfare director for Pettis County, where the program began.

When Tyson opened shop six miles west of Sedalia, "It couldn't find enough folks to fill these jobs because the work is messy, and there's lots of carpal tunnel," says Proctor. The company, lured there by Sedalia's powerful state senator, James Mathewson, spent six months advertising in area newspapers and job centers, with little success. "Tyson had trouble with the labor supply and was getting upset."

So Tyson "began doing some informal visiting with Senator Mathewson about their need for more workers," recalls Messenger.

According to Proctor, "Mathewson sponsored a bill after this erupted and got D.F.S. [the Division of Family Services] to try a pilot where, if somebody applied for benefits, they were sent directly to Tyson. If they declined, they were refused benefits for sixty days."

Tyson personnel manager Jennifer Cave says Senator Mathewson was "the driving force" helping the company link up with the welfare department, but she doesn't recall who initiated the discussions.

The program is tailor-made for Tyson. "They have pretty much a constant need for employees because there's a high turnover there. So our offices keep in touch with their employment needs," says Deb Hendricks, information officer for the Missouri Division of Family Services.

Before the Direct Job Placement program, adds welfare director Messenger, "we had clients who were job-ready, who for one reason or another had not responded to Tyson's job advertisements on their own. They have a reputation. It's hard work, sometimes cold and dirty. It's not a glamorous job, and some people were turned off by that."

But once the program was in place, the agency—and Tyson—had leverage. Members of Messenger's staff visited the Tyson plant and "were able to get [clients] to the point of agreeing to an interview," she says. "We would set them up with an appointment, and if they failed to keep the interview we sanctioned them, and that meant they lost their food stamps. Actually, some of them did choose to lose their benefits instead of going to Tyson's."

In fact, the program has driven far more people off welfare than into jobs. Of the 195 recipients sent to one Tyson plant in Pettis County this year for mandatory interviews, just twenty-two accepted entry-level, assembly-line jobs paying $6.70 an hour. Meanwhile, thirty-nine were sanctioned. Local welfare administrators concede they have no idea what happened to the other 134 recipients, who have disappeared from the county rolls.

While the state regards these disappearances as success stories, officials acknowledge that it's a case of out of sight, out of mind. "If they just generally leave welfare, we don't know what they are doing," says Division of Family Services spokeswoman Christine Grobe. Caseload manager Karen Fay acknowledges that she doesn't have data on how many recipients are still working at the jobs where the state placed them. "We have not had to collect those, so we don't have them," she says.

> '**W**e would set them up with an appointment, and if they failed to keep the interview that meant they lost their food stamps. Actually, some of them did choose to lose their benefits instead of going to Tyson's.'

Federal law doesn't require states to ensure that the people who are cut off welfare get jobs, says Mark Greenberg of the Center for Law and Social Policy in Washington, D.C. Instead, the government offers "caseload-reduction credits" to states that trim their rolls sufficiently. It's possible, says Greenberg, for a state to "fully satisfy federal participation rates without getting anybody a single job."

Job retention is virtually nonexistent. Since 1995, the Tyson plant in Pettis County has hired seventy-five people from the welfare offices in Sedalia and neighboring Johnson and Henry counties, according to plant personnel manager Jennifer Cave. But, she says, just "five or less" are still working at the plant, which employs a total of 1,360.

"The processing industry just has high turnover," Cave says breezily. "It's repetitive-motion, unskilled labor."

Union officials say that's precisely the problem. "These are not jobs that give people a career," says Barchak of the Service Employees union. "Jobs in poultry-processing plants are temporary because people burn out quickly. Nobody who burns out in six months is taking with them any skill they can apply to the rest of the American work force."

Crystal Wolfe, Jason's brother, a nineteen-year-old former Tyson lineworker with two children, puts it more bluntly: "If you're just coming off welfare and you haven't worked in a while, that place will make you never want to work again."

DOES SILENCIO = MUERTE?

Notes on translating the AIDS epidemic

BY DR. RAFAEL CAMPO

Palomita chatters in one of my clinic exam rooms in Boston, her strongly accented voice filling the chilly institutional chrome-and-vinyl space with Puerto Rican warmth. She's off on another dramatic monologue, telling me about her new boyfriend.

"Edgar, he loves me, you know, he call me *mamacita*. He want me to be the mother of his children someday, OK? I ain't no slut. *Mira,* I don't need to use no condom with him."

Even the way she dresses is a form of urgent communication—the plunging neckline of her tropically patterned blouse, whose tails knotted above her waist also expose her flat stomach, the skin-tight denim jeans, the gold, four-inch hoop earrings, and the necklace with her name spelled out in cursive with tiny sparkling stones. Her black hair is pulled back tightly, except for a small squiggle greased flat against her forehead in the shape of an upside-down question mark.

"People think bad of him 'cause they say he dealing drugs. I tell them, 'No way, you shut your stupid mouths. He good to me and beside, he cleaner than you is.' Sure, he got his other girls now and then, but he pick them out *bien* carefully, you know what I mean. That his right as man of the house. No way he gonna give me *la SIDA*. We too smart for none of that shit. We trust each other. We communicate. We gonna buy us a house somewhere *bien bonita.* Someday we gonna make it."

She is seventeen years old, hasn't finished high school, and cannot read English. I have just diagnosed her with herpes, and I am trying to talk to her about AIDS and "safer sex." Her Edgar, who is also a patient of mine, tested HIV-positive last week. It's clear they have not discussed it.

Latinos are dying at an alarming rate from AIDS. And for all our glorious presence on the world's stage—in music, literature, art, from MacArthur grants to MTV to *Sports Illustrated*—this is one superlative no one can re-

ally boast about. Few Latinos dare even to mention the epidemic. The frenetic beat of salsa in our dance clubs seems to drown out the terrifying statistics, while the bright murals in our barrios cover up the ugly blood-red graffiti, and that "magical realism" of our fictions imagines a world where we can lose our accents and live in Vermont, where secret family recipes conjure up idealized heterosexual love in an ultimately just universe unblemished by plague.

Here, loud and clear, for once, are some of the more stark, sobering facts: In the U.S., Latinos accounted for one-fifth of all AIDS cases reported to the Centers for Disease Control last year, while making up only one-tenth of the U.S. population; AIDS has been the leading cause of death since 1991 for young Latino men in this country; in areas with especially high numbers of Latinos, such as Fort Lauderdale, Miami, Los Angeles, and New York, AIDS deaths among Latina women were four times the national average since 1995. While the infection rate among whites continues to decline, today, and every day, 100 people of color are newly diagnosed with HIV infection. Behold our isolated and desperate substance users, the most marginalized of the marginalized, our forsaken impoverished, and our irreplaceable young people.

I do not have to wonder at the reasons for the silence among Latinos about the burgeoning AIDS epidemic that is decimating us. Though I stare into its face every day in the clinic where I work, there are times when even I want to forget, to pretend it is not happening, to believe my people are invincible and can never be put down again. I want to believe Palomita is HIV-negative, that Edgar will stop shooting drugs and someday return to get on the right triple combination of anti-viral medications. I fervently hope that César, a twenty-year-old Colombian man who keeps missing his appointments, is taking his protease

inhibitors so that his viral load remains undetectable. I do not really know who pays for his drugs, since he is uninsured, but my thoughts do not dwell on it. In the end, I want to go home and rest after a long day in the clinic, to make love to my partner of fourteen years and feel that I'll never have to confront another epidemic. I want to look into his dark, Puerto Rican eyes and never have to speak of AIDS again.

But I know better. I know we must speak out—about the ongoing disenfranchisement of Latinos despite our much-touted successes, about the vicious homophobia of a *machista* Latino culture that especially fears and hates gay people whom it believes "deserve" AIDS, about the antipathy of the Catholic Church so many Latinos pray to for guidance they don't receive, about the unfulfilled dream of total and untainted assimilation for so many Mexicans, Dominicans, Cubans, and Puerto Ricans who came to America with nothing.

To break any of these silences is especially tempting, since together they allow me to blame most of the usual targets of my rage and frustration. Others are more difficult to penetrate, such as the persistent lack of access in Latino communities to lifesaving information about AIDS. Still others make almost no sense to me at all. Rosa, another patient of mine, tells me she knows she should not have sex without condoms, but continues to do so anyway because she is afraid her drug-dealing boyfriend would think she no longer loves him. Yet she hardly imagines that he might be using drugs, or wonders whether he has other sexual partners.

Our silence, in all its forms, is killing us. I wince at the familiar ring of this realization. I can't help but remember my patient Ernesto in his hospital bed with his partner Jesús sitting quietly at his side, a tiny statue of the Virgin of Guadalupe keeping its mute vigil, no other family or friends around. Ernesto died years ago of AIDS. It is not passé or trite or irrelevant to ask why we remain silent. It is absolutely imperative. We must understand the causes of our *silencio*.

Most of the Spanish-speaking patients who come to my clinic do not much resemble Ricky Martin or Daisy Fuentes or Antonio Sabato Jr. They are "the working poor," janitors or delivery boys or hotel laundry workers or high school dropouts or dishwashers—people with jobs that pay subsistence wages and provide no health benefits. Still, they consider themselves fortunate because so many have no jobs at all.

Many of them are illiterate, and many more speak no English. They have come to Boston mostly from Puerto Rico, but some are from Cuba, the Dominican Republic, Mexico, Colombia, Guatemala, El Salvador, and Nicaragua. Some sleep on park benches when the weather is warm enough and in shelters during the winter. Some live in crowded apartments. Some are undocumented immigrants. Some have lost their welfare benefits, some are trying to apply for temporary assistance, and almost none have enough to feed themselves and their families.

Older couples too often have lost children to drugs, street violence, and AIDS. Young people too often blame their parents and their teachers for their problems. Some know very little about AIDS and fault homosexuals, injection drug users, and prostitutes for poisoning the community. Some view *la SIDA* with resignation and see it as inevitable, part of the price some must pay for a chance at a better life.

But the vast majority of Latinos in the U.S. remain shortchanged, despite the glittering success of a few. For every Federico Peña, many more anonymous "illegals" are deported to Mexico each day, never given the chance to contribute to our society at all. For every Sammy Sosa, a makeshift boat full of Dominicans is lost at sea. And even more noxious than the large-scale efforts to dismantle affirmative action or to deny basic social services (including health care) to undocumented immigrants are the daily insults and obstacles that prevent Latinos from sharing fully in our nation's life. Lack of economic opportunities pushes Latinos toward criminal activities as a means to survive. Discrimination and rejection breed the kind of despair that drug use and unsafe sex only temporarily ameliorate. The despair and the apathy, heightened by what the very few who are successful have achieved, numb the soul.

It's a common litany, yet I can't help but see how this imposed demoralization is manifest in the behavior of so many of my patients. Why leave an abusive relationship, they say, when all that awaits is the cold streets? Why insist on a condom when it's so much easier not to and the reasons to go on living are not so clear anyway? It doesn't seem farfetched to me that this cumulative hopelessness is fueling the AIDS epidemic.

But these causes, the subject of so many lefty social work dissertations, do not get at the entire problem. We remain ourselves a culture in which men treat women as icons—or as powerless objects of our legendary sexual passions. Our wives must be as pure as we believe our own mothers to be, and yet we pursue our mistresses with the zeal of matadors about to make the kill. Brute force is excused as a necessary means by which Latino men must exert control over weak-willed women, and it is by no means secret that in the shadow of the AIDS epidemic lurks another senseless killer, the domestic violence that too often goes unreported.

Could Palomita and Rosa fear more than just losing the financial support of their boyfriends? For Yolanda, another patient of mine with HIV infection, it was the beatings from her husband that finally drove her onto the streets, where prostitution soon became her only means of making a living. Now she is dying.

Sexism's virulent *hermano* is homophobia. AIDS has long been considered a disease exclusively of homosexuals—especially in Spanish-speaking communities, where not only is HIV strongly associated with gayness, it is further stigmatized as having been imported from the decadent white world. Since we cannot speak calmly and rationally of homosexuality, we certainly cannot bring up AIDS, perhaps the only affliction that could be worse.

Latinos are allowed to be gay only outside the confines of their families and old neighborhoods. Indeed, many Latino men who have sex with men would never even consider themselves "gay" at all, a derogatory term that they would apply only to those whom they consider to be their "passive" partners. Even those who take pride in their homosexuality are not immune to this hatred. I have many gay Latino friends whose parents will not allow their partners to visit during holidays, friends who go to great lengths to (literally) "straighten out" their homes when family is coming to visit by creating fictitious separate bedrooms and removing anything sugges-

tive of homosexuality (which can get difficult, when one gets down to the joint Andy Garcia fan club application, the Frida Kahlo shrine, or the autographed and framed Gigi Fernandez poster).

Hand in hand with both sexism and homophobia goes Catholicism. Latinos are overwhelmingly Catholic, and the Catholic hierarchy remains overwhelmingly not only anti-gay, but also opposed to the use of condoms as a means to prevent HIV transmission. (The only time I have ever heard AIDS mentioned in a Catholic church was at a wedding service, when it was invoked as a reminder of what punishments lay in store for the fornicators and homosexuals who scorned marriage.) While on the one hand preaching about the sanctity of life, our religious leaders have abetted the deaths of countless Latinos by refusing to endorse the use of condoms as a means to prevent AIDS transmission.

No one disagrees with the monotonous message that abstinence is the safest sex of all. Yet in today's ascendant moment, when young Latinos must party—we drink our Cuba libres followed by café con leche, dance the merengue provocatively with shiny crucifixes dangling around our necks, and later engage in sultry, unsafe sex, even if always (supposedly) with partners of the opposite sex—such teaching is utterly impractical.

Then there are the people like me, the Cuban doctors and Chicano lawyers, the Nuyorican politicians and the displaced Argentine activists—those who mean well but who have allowed the silence to engulf us, too. The thick warm blanket of our insularity and relative power comforts us. We are a small, tightly knit group; we work hard and hope to send our children to Harvard or Stanford or Yale, praying that they stay out of trouble. We increasingly vote Republican, elated that George W. Bush tosses out a few words in a halting Spanish, and fearing that a liberal government might take away too much of what we have struggled to make for ourselves—and might allow too many others in for a share of our pie. We would hardly acknowledge Palomita and Edgar if we passed them in the street, and we might even regret their very existence, the way they bring all of us down by their ignorance and poverty. Full of our quiet self-righteousness, gripping our briefcases just a bit more tightly, we might not even feel sorry for them if we knew they were being afflicted with AIDS.

Mario Cooper, a former deputy chief of staff for the Democratic National Committee, knows firsthand about a community's indifference to AIDS. Black, gay, and HIV-positive, he spearheaded an initiative sponsored by the Harvard AIDS Institute called Leading for Life. The summit brought together prominent members of the African American community to talk frankly about their own AIDS epidemic—just as uncontrolled, just as deadly, and until last year's summit, just as silent as the one ravaging Latinos.

The key is to make people understand this is about all of us," Cooper says, as we brainstorm a list of possible invitees to another meeting, to be called *Unidos para la Vida.* Inspired by his past success in Boston, where the likes of Marian Wright Edelman, Henry Louis Gates Jr., and Dr. Alvin Poussaint eventually heeded his call to action, Cooper is now intent on tackling the same issue for Latinos.

"What came out of the Leading for Life meeting was incredible," he says. "Suddenly, everyone was paying attention, and things started happening for young African Americans. They started to learn more about AIDS." He is beaming, and we add Oscar de la Renta, Cristina, and Edward James Olmos to the list. "We have the chance to do the same thing here."

But after a few weeks of working on the project with him and others at the Harvard AIDS Institute, it became clear to us that we might be facing even greater obstacles than those he encountered in the black community. We had hardly even gotten started when conflicts over terminology almost sank the entire effort. "Latino" competed with "Hispanic," while all of us felt that neither term fully articulated the rich diversity and numerous points of origin of those who undeniably formed some kind of a community. Some of us secretly questioned whether a shared vulnerability to AIDS was itself enough to try to unify us. Was a Puerto Rican injection drug user in Hartford, Connecticut, really facing the same issues as a Salvadoran undocumented immigrant selling sex in El Paso, Texas? Was loyalty to the Venezuelan community, or Nicaraguan community, imperiled by joining this larger group? At times, we saw evidence of the kind of pecking-order mentality (in which certain nationalities consider themselves superior to others) that has since the days of Bolívar interfered with efforts to unify Spain's colonies in the New World.

If these mostly suppressed internal divisions were not enough to surmount, we also battled the general lack of interest in AIDS—yesterday's news, no matter how loudly we shouted the latest statistics, no matter how emphatically we pointed out the lack of access for Latinos to the new treatments.

"Don't they have a cure for that now?" remarked one person I called, exemplifying precisely the sort of misinformation we were working to correct, her breathy laugh further revealing both the kind of distancing from—and absence of comfort with—the entire issue that surely reinforced her lack of knowledge.

Others were simply fatalistic. "You can't change the way these kids think and behave," said one person who declined the invitation to attend the summit, "so why bother?"

"Tell them to stop having sex," came one memorably blunt response, before the phone crashed down on the other end.

"I pray for them," said another pious woman. "I pray that they will renounce their wicked ways and find peace in Christ." She then regretted to inform me that she would be unable to attend the summit.

The special insight I thought I could bring to the effort, as a gay Latino poet doctor who writes both poems and prescriptions, seemed to be of less and less use, as more and more "no" answers, accompanied by their usually polite excuses, filtered back to us. Weeks later, when the situation grew bleakest, Cooper only urged us to redouble our efforts. "We're dealing with a situation that is almost unfathomable to most of these people," he said. "It's an epidemic no one wants to believe exists. Latinos are supposed to be the rising stars of the next millennium, not the carriers of a disease that could wipe out humanity." What was on one level a glaring public health crisis had to be understood more radically. "We have to ask ourselves why this message isn't getting out. We're kidding ourselves if we think we're the magic solution. In fact, we may be part of the problem."

The work of Walt Odets, the Berkeley psychologist who shook up the safer sex establishment, immediately came to mind. Odets observed young gay men at the height of the AIDS epidemic in San Francisco, noting a pervasive hopelessness in the face of a belief that infection with HIV was inevitable. Behind the apathy and denial, might not the same thing exist in this second-wave epidemic among inner-city Latinos? The stupidity of our early efforts at sloganeering, which tried to encapsulate a myriad of complex issues un-

der a single bright banner, suddenly became utterly apparent to me. What faced us was not simply a matter of speaking out, of breaking a silence so many Latinos already living with HIV had already renounced. What we had to do was learn to speak their language, to incorporate in our every effort an entirely new mode of expression.

I knew right then that we had a lot more work to do.

Palomita's mood is decidedly less cheerful today. She is three-and-a-half-months pregnant, but that's not why she starts to cry. It's the end of January, and my office is just as cold as ever. A thin crust of ice is gradually forming on everything outside. Last week, while Palomita's HIV test was being run, a storm knocked out power to most of New England. My heart feels as empty and dark as one of the houses caught in the blackout now that I've read out her result.

"I don't believe you. You mean, I'm gonna die of AIDS?" A leading moment passes before the inevitable next question. "And what about my baby?"

Looking at Palomita, I wonder again at how AIDS does not get prevented, how it seems to have a terrible life of its own. I want to answer her questions, explain to her that AZT lowers the risk of maternal fetal transmission, that the new triple combination anti-retroviral regimens, if she takes them exactly as prescribed, could buy her many years with her child. But I can't. Instead I keep thinking about her name, which means "little dove," and trying to imagine the innocence her parents must have seen in her tiny face when they named her, trying to feel that boundless joy at the earliest moment of a new life. I am looking at Palomita as she cries, framed by a window from which she cannot fly. I am imagining peace. In her beautiful brown face, mirror of a million souls, I try to envision us all in a world without AIDS.

Dr. Rafael Campo teaches and practices internal medicine at Harvard Medical School and Beth Israel Deaconess Medical Center in Boston. He is the award-winning author of several books, including "The Poetry of Healing" (W.W. Norton, 1997) and [a] collection of poems "Diva" (Duke University Press, 1999). The "Unidos para la Vida" summit was held one year ago, sponsored by the Harvard AIDS Institute. None of the prominent Latinos mentioned in this article attended.

Five million elderly Americans have no food, or worry about getting enough to eat.

HUNGER IN AMERICA

BY TRUDY LIEBERMAN

Randall Mueck's job at San Francisco's meal clearinghouse is to decide who will get food and who will wait. In mid-January, 411 of the city's homebound elderly were on Mueck's waiting list, 100 more than a few months earlier. All qualify for a hot, home-delivered meal under the federal Older Americans Act, but there isn't enough money to feed everyone.

Seniors who move up the fastest are those in the custody of adult protective services, the dying and the very old. Twenty-five percent of the people asking for food are over 90. "I try to think of all 411 and fit someone in accordingly," Mueck explains. "Age is going to bump somebody way up."

That means Audrey Baker, 79, must wait. When she asked for help last September, Mueck assigned her 750 points out of the 900 or so she needed to qualify for a meal. In January, her score had reached 877. (Each day on the list adds a point.) Baker, a thin woman, is blind, falls a lot and is on the mend from a broken back. She also has hypertension and diabetes.

"I've outlived everybody else in my family," Baker says. "I don't have any friends." Her only help is an aide who comes for two hours on Fridays. Like many seniors, Baker is vague about what she eats. "It's whatever I can afford," she says. What will she eat this week? "I'll eat all right, but I don't know exactly what." Tonight it's an apple and some nuts.

Food isn't far from her mind, though. On the table beside the armchair in her tiny living room is a copy of the food magazine *Cooking Light,* in braille. "She's clearly struggling," says Frank Mitchell, a social worker with San Francisco's Meals on Wheels program. "How do you say, 'I know you're hungry. We'll serve you in three months'?"

But that's the reality all across the country. Thousands of elderly men and women too infirm to cook or even see the

flames of the stove are put on ration lists for food in the most bountiful country in the world. A 1993 study by the Urban Institute found that some 5 million elderly have no food in the house, or worry about getting enough to eat. They experience what the social service business calls "food insecurity." In Miami alone, 2,000 people are waiting. Says John Stokesberry, executive director of Miami's Alliance for Aging, "By the time we clean up the waiting list, some will be dead." Another study, done for the federal Administration on Aging, looked at food programs during the 1993–95 period and found that 41 percent of the country's 4,000 providers of home-delivered meals to the elderly had waiting lists. Malnutrition among the elderly is commonplace: Researchers at Florida International University estimate that 63 percent of all older people are at moderate or high nutritional risk. Some 88 percent of those receiving home-delivered meals are at similar risk, according to a study by Mathematica Policy Research.

In the face of shifting demographics, the picture isn't likely to improve. The number of people 60 and older has increased from 31 million in 1973 to 44 million today. And the number of the oldest old, those over 85 for whom assistance with meals is crucial, is growing even faster: Almost 1.5 million people were over 85 in 1970; in 2000, their number will exceed 4 million.

The homebound elderly are largely invisible. They aren't glamorous, and giving them food is not at the cutting edge of philanthropy. They are the antithesis of the "greedy geezer" who has come to represent all of the elderly in the public mind. They have no lobbyists—the interests of senior organizations lie elsewhere. Politicians neglect them; they don't vote or make campaign contributions. Often their children have moved far from home, leaving them without caregivers, a dilemma more keenly felt by women, who usually live longer than men. In 1970, 56 percent of the elderly over age 75 lived alone; by 1995, 76 percent were living by themselves.

For many, there are no meal lists to get on. In Big Springs, a speck on the Nebraska prairie, 134 of the town's 495 residents are eligible for a meal. But there's no money to start a

Trudy Lieberman is health policy editor at Consumer Reports *and a contributing editor of* Columbia Journalism Review. *This article represents her views, not those of* Consumer Reports. *Research support was provided by the Investigative Fund of* The Nation Institute.

food program. Vic Walker, director of the Aging Office of Western Nebraska, doesn't even have enough money to feed those living outside the city limits of Scottsbluff, the largest town in the area. One man living on a ranch three miles over the line "needed a meal so desperately," recalls Irma Walter, Walker's case manager. "He was so debilitated, but there was no access to food."

The Federal Commitment

More than thirty years ago, in 1965, Congress recognized the lengthening life span and the infirmities that come with it, and enacted the Older Americans Act to help seniors live out their last days at home with essential support: transportation, household

Some 63 percent of the elderly are at moderate or high nutritional risk—5 million experience what social workers call 'food insecurity.'

help and personal care. The act is not a welfare program; anyone over age 60 is eligible for services if there's room.

In his 1972 budget message, President Nixon noted that "a new commitment to the aging is long overdue," and two nutrition programs were added that year: centralized, or congregate, meal sites—now numbering about 16,000—where seniors could eat a hot lunch and socialize; and a delivery service to send a hot meal to the homebound elderly. Meals prepared by a cadre of local churches, social service agencies and nonprofit organizations, many with similar names, were meant to reach mobile seniors and the homebound in every nook and cranny of America.

The food programs were supposed to promote "better health" among the older population "through improved nutrition" and offer "older Americans an opportunity to live their remaining years in dignity." Nixon pledged that the federal commitment would "help make the last days of our older Americans their best days."

At the beginning, Nixon tried to make good on that promise. When the Office of Management and Budget thought the initial funding should be $40 million and Nixon's adviser on aging, Arthur Flemming, suggested $60 million, Nixon upped the amount to $100 million. Throughout the seventies the funding kept pace with need. After that, however, it did not. Adjusting for inflation, per capita appropriations for all Older Americans Act programs in 1995 should have been $39. Actual per capita funding was only $19. Although total annual spending for all services has gone from $200 million in 1973 to $865 million today, that money not only hasn't kept up with inflation but it also hasn't kept up with the number of people who need help. The 1995 federal appropriations were down by about 50 percent relative to what the government spent in 1973. Money spent for the two food programs has shrunk by a similar amount.

Though payment is not mandatory, three-quarters of the elderly who get a home-delivered meal and almost everyone who eats at the congregate sites contributes, sometimes as little as 50 cents, toward the roughly $5.30 it costs to provide a meal. Half of those receiving home-delivered meals and about one-third of participants eating at congregate meal sites have annual incomes of less than $7,900. "Those least able to pay won't eat unless they put something in," says Larry Ross, the chief fiscal officer for San Francisco's Commission on the Aging.

One Meal a Day

Most Americans eat three meals each day, or 1,095 meals a year. The elderly receiving home-delivered meals get only 250. Only 4 percent of food providers routinely offer more than one meal a day, five days a week, and few offer weekend meals. In San Francisco, 765 people lucky enough to receive their food from Meals on Wheels, one of the city's nine providers, get two meals seven days a week. The rest of the city's 1,660 food recipients get only one. If the city's Commission on the Aging paid for two meals per person, as many as 400 people now served would not get any meal. The trade-off is constant and stark: Do more people get fewer meals or do fewer people get more meals?

The Salvation Army, which serves the meals in San Francisco's Tenderloin district, resolves the question in favor of the former, but there is pain whichever way it's answered. Richard Bertolovzi lives in an S.R.O. He is a skinny, bearded man with greasy hair, missing front teeth and one red eye that looks infected. "You don't deliver tomorrow, do you?" "Bert" asks the young woman delivering his noon meal of fish, coleslaw, fruit cocktail, clam chowder, corn bread and milk. A curtain of disappointment falls over his face, and he looks away in disgust. "I'm hungry," he says. "I can eat anything. I have a loaf of bread, that's all. That's all I got. And I got some instant coffee." The Salvation Army is able to offer him only a can of Ensure, a nutritional drink, to get through the weekend.

The Limits of Philanthropy

Food providers have always had to look for donations to support their programs. Now they have to look even harder. "We're competing with more folks than ever," says Mary Podrabsky, president of the National Association of Nutrition and Aging Services Programs. The conventional wisdom these days is that philanthropy should do more and government as little as possible—or, as Heritage Foundation senior fellow Dan Mitchell puts it, "if it's worth doing, the private sector can do it."

When it comes to feeding the elderly, private-sector funding works a little bit in a few places, not at all in most others. San Francisco Meals on Wheels was able to raise $214,000 last year thanks in part to benefit dinners cooked by the city's top chefs. Its New York counterpart raised $8 million last year from direct-mail campaigns, social events, grants and corporate contributions to provide some weekend meals and to whittle down the city's waiting list, although some 700 people are still in the queue. This past November, New York Citymeals-on-Wheels fundraiser extraordinaire Marcia Stein raised $675,000 throwing a women's power luncheon at the Rainbow Room. Guests including Brooke Astor, Diane Sawyer and Lena Horne plunked down a minimum of $250 to dine on vegetable terrine and risotto with white truffles.

Towns like Ramona, California, population 30,000, high in the hills northeast of San Diego, have no such benefactors. Chuck Hunt, board president of the town's senior center, tells how he placed ads in the *Ramona Sentinel* and *North County Times* asking 1,000 people to pledge $100 or 2,000 people to give $50. He collected exactly $1,600—twelve people gave $100 and got on the center's "gold honor roll"; eight donated $50 for a place on the "silver honor roll." Hunt also wrote to Allied Signal Aerospace, where he had worked for twenty-six years, asking for $25,000 to pay down overdue food bills and repairs on the vans that deliver meals. He says he felt "let down" when his old employer said no.

Raising private money in places like Ramona or Big Springs, or even San Diego, is not easy. There are few large corporations and foundations to tap, and if there are any, they have little interest in feeding the elderly. "If you flat-out ask people for food for seniors, you don't get much of a response," says Daniel Laver, director of the Area Agency on Aging in San Diego. "Private foundations are looking at cutting-edge programs—new and innovative. Basic human needs programs are not as sexy."

In the new world of corporate giving, charity is often tied to the bottom line. During the holidays Kraft offered 600 meal providers $100 each if they placed a story about a Kraft promotion in their local media. Kraft said it would donate 25 cents to meal programs for each special coupon redeemed. To get the $100, however, providers had to submit press clippings showing they had fulfilled the deal's P.R. requirements. If they did, the $100 donation bought about twenty meals.

Such corporate "generosity" doesn't insure that seniors have enough to eat, nor can it build the necessary infrastructure of senior centers and food preparation sites; only adequate, continuing federal appropriations can do that. Says Bob Tisch, New York Citymeals-on-Wheels board president, feeding the elderly "is the government's responsibility."

State and Local Aid

States must contribute at least 15 percent of the total cost of the two federal meal programs. Some states go beyond that. Pennsylvania, for instance, contributes its lottery proceeds to services for the elderly. Local governments sometimes kick in money, and where they do, those funds help keep the food programs afloat. County funds including a dedicated portion of San Francisco's parking tax make up about 38 percent of the budget for home-delivered meals. The City of New York contributes 55 percent of the food-program budget. Voters in Cincinnati have twice approved a poverty-tax levy to support a variety of services for the elderly, most recently last fall by a margin of 65 percent to 35 percent. Eighty-three percent of the Council on Aging's $4.1 million budget for home-delivered meals is funded by the tax levy. "It's a myth that people don't want to help their elderly," says Bob Logan, director of the council, the agency serving the Cincinnati area. He says the levy "was overwhelmingly supported by the young, the old, Republicans, Democrats, minorities and non-minorities." But even a generous stream of local money can't stop waiting lists from mounting: In Cincinnati, local money just means those on the lists don't have to wait as long.

Furthermore, food programs in some localities are in jeopardy because of diminishing local tax revenues. Take, for instance, Saunders County in eastern Nebraska, a suburb of nearby Omaha. In the past few years the county has contributed around $68,000 a year for both congregate and home-delivered meals. Still, that money is inadequate, forcing some communities to serve the elderly only two or three days a week. (The law allows a program to provide food fewer than five days a week in rural areas.)

Service could be slashed even further, a result of reduced inheritance taxes, which have funded food programs for the elderly, and the state legislature's recent imposition of a limit on local property tax levies. "Some services are going to be cut or slimmed back," says Patti Lindgren, the County Clerk. "The ones that will be are those optional to the county, like senior services."

Penny-Wise and Pound-Foolish

The United States has no national policy on aging. Instead, an unwritten policy directs resources to the most expensive care in the last places the elderly stay—hospitals and nursing homes. When malnourished seniors go to the hospital, they may end up staying longer and costing more money. The Massachusetts Dietetic Association estimates that for every $1 spent on nutrition programs, $3.25 is saved in hospital costs. A study in Little Rock compared two groups of hospitalized seniors who were the same age and had the same diagnosis. One group had received home-delivered meals; the other group had not. Patients who got food stayed in the hospital half as long as those who didn't. Ronni Chernoff, associate director of geriatric research at the V.A. hospital in Little Rock, who supervised the research, figured that the cost of eight extra days in the hospital—some $4,800 at Little Rock rates—was the equivalent of providing someone with a meal a day for two and a half years.

An acute episode such as breaking a bone, healing a surgical incision or the flu makes demands that a poorly nourished body cannot accommodate. "The people I'm not serving but know in my heart of hearts I should are those just coming out of the hospital," says Gail Robillard, a nutritionist with the Jefferson Council on Aging in Metairie, Louisiana. Without such assistance, they often go back to the hospital, a vicious cycle that Robillard believes can be prevented with good nutrition. Medicare's home health care benefit covers the services of nurses, aides and a variety of therapies, but not food.

Without food, the elderly also go to nursing homes prematurely, adding to what is already a huge national expense. The United States spends about $80 billion a year on nursing-home care, nearly half paid by taxpayers through Medicaid. A year in a nursing home averages around $40,000; a year's worth of meals, $1,325.

Needed: A Champion

Despite the compelling statistics, no one in Congress seems willing to champion the cause of meals for the elderly. The closest these days is New York Senator Alfonse D'Amato, who pushed through a 3.5 percent increase in funds for congregate and home-delivered meals last year. In fact, says one Senate staffer, "there has been a general push to cut back on Older Americans Act appropriations for many years." Money from the Department of Agriculture, which also contributes to the programs, has been cut from about $150 million to $140 million, further limiting the number of meals providers can serve. A House staffer explains: "No one speaks ill of the program. On the other hand, no one gets excited about it." Lack of enthusiasm makes it an easy target to cut or ignore.

"The Older Americans Act has suffered because it is such a feel-good, sound-good act it doesn't translate into tangible things anyone can look at and champion so it gets the necessary increases," says Bob Blancato, director of the 1995 White House Conference on Aging. Food competes in the same spending bill with the National Institutes of Health, Head Start and bilingual education, more glamorous activities that are easier for members of Congress to embrace. Last year the N.I.H. got a $900 million increase, boosting its budget to more than $13 billion. This year the President has proposed another $1.1 billion. "There's a lot of exciting scientific stuff happening," says a House staffer. "Everybody knows someone who's sick, and that always gets people's interest." Sickness caused by hunger doesn't have the same cachet. Head Start and bilingual education have also fared better, thanks largely to the Clintons. Indeed, last year bilingual education got a 25 percent increase, one of the largest in the entire federal budget.

The President's budget calls for no increase in money for food programs for the elderly this year, although some fifty members of the House recently signed a letter to Clinton urging such an increase. One of those who signed is Frank LoBiondo, a New Jersey Republican who has also circulated a letter of his own asking his colleagues to oppose the President's spending freeze. "It's difficult when the President didn't recognize the importance [of the program] in his budget," he says.

In the end, it will come down to a question of priorities, especially those of Representative Bob Livingston, a Republican from Metairie who chairs the House Appropriations Committee. Meanwhile, the nutrition programs in his district struggle; some people wait as long as thirteen months for a meal. Gail Robillard says she, too, is "prioritizing on top of prioritizing," trying to allocate food to the neediest. "Livingston says he's interested in the elderly, but nothing specific ever comes from him," she says.

Ask what they eat and seniors say they manage, putting the best face on the most dehumanizing of predicaments. It's too demeaning to say otherwise. Confessing hunger is an admission that you can't provide for your most basic need. Pressed for what they really eat, seniors are apt to say tea and toast, cereal, cookies, a sandwich of peanut butter or baloney, even scraps foraged from the garbage.

"I'm not proud to say we lived out of dumpsters," says 74-year-old Helen McCleery, whose disabled son scoured garbage bins before McCleery got on the San Diego meal program. "We were eating whatever my son found—mostly vegetables. We washed the vegetables, sprayed them with Lysol and washed them again." They didn't touch meat, McCleery said; they were too afraid of E. coli and salmonella. Macular degeneration has taken her sight, and she is diabetic. She knows she wasn't eating right, but she and her son were living on $700 a month; their rent of $635 left little for food.

Unless there's renewed federal commitment to the elderly, their story will be repeated. It's the responsibility of everyone, says Michel Roux, president of Carillon Importers and board member of New York Citymeals-on-Wheels, "to think of these people as their parents."

Q: Should juries nullify laws they consider unjust or excessively punitive?

Yes: Juries can and should correct the overly broad use of criminal sanctions.

BY CLAY S. CONRAD

Conrad is an appellate attorney in Houston, on the board of the Fully Informed Jury Association and author of Jury Nullification: The Evolution of a Doctrine.

Jury nullification occurs when a criminal-trial jury refuses to convict a defendant despite proof of guilt because the jurors believe the law is unjust or is being unjustly applied. According to studies, 3 to 4 percent of jury criminal trials involve jury nullification. There is no way to prevent jury nullification because juries never can be ordered to convict or be punished for acquitting someone. A jury acquittal, under the Constitution, is final.

Juries rarely nullify irresponsibly. Consider the acquittal of Sam Skinner, a California AIDS patient prosecuted for using marijuana. The marijuana helped counteract the devastating side effects of the drug AZT and kept Skinner from wasting away. Although Skinner admitted to the facts, the jury found him not guilty because they believed the prosecution was fundamentally unjust.

Sometimes juries find defendants guilty only of lesser offenses when they believe the punishment for the charged offense is excessive. In earlier times, British law made theft of 40 shillings or more a capital offense. Juries often undervalued property so as to spare the life of the accused—including one case in which a jury found ten £10 notes to be worth 39 shillings. Jack Kevorkian's latest trial involved just that sort of amelioration. The jury found him guilty of second-degree murder despite the facts because they believed a conviction for first-degree murder would be too great.

Alternatively, it often is argued that race and prejudice lead to jury nullification more often than do considerations of justice. As common as that argument is, it doesn't hold water. During the 1960s in the trials of some who participated in crimes against civil-rights workers in the Deep South, it is true that juries returned "not guilty" verdicts. However, it also is true that sometimes prosecutors regularly refused to pursue those cases, police refused to investigate or testify honestly in them and judges eviscerated the cases through discretionary rulings. The juries rarely were given cases justifying conviction—and then were scapegoated for failings elsewhere in the system.

These contentions are proved by the fact that federal prosecutions for violations of civil-rights laws, involving the same cases, regularly ended in convictions—before juries selected from the same communities. Different judges, prosecutors and investigators—but the same jury pool. Obviously, any racist acquittals must be explained by something other than the juries.

A recent *National Law Journal* poll revealed that three in four Americans would nullify if they believed the court's instructions would lead to injustice. That only 3 to 4 percent of jury trials end in nullification verdicts shows that, in most cases, the law is just and justly applied. In exceptional, marginal or divisive cases, however, jurors often acquit in the interests of justice just as the Founders of this country intended.

The Founders on both sides of the ratification debate believed trial by jury was necessary to prevent governmental overreaching. Thomas Jefferson said it was the only way to anchor government to constitutional principles. Alexander Hamilton said it was the surest protection of the people's liberties. Theophilus Parsons, first chief justice of Massachusetts, said in the Constitutional Convention: "The people themselves have it in their power effectually to resist usurpation, without being driven to an appeal to arms. An act of usurpation is not obligatory; it is not law; and any man may be justified in his resistance. Let him be considered as a criminal by the general government, yet only his fellow-citizens can convict him; they are his jury, and if they pronounce him innocent, not all the powers of Congress can hurt him; and innocent they certainly will pronounce him, if the supposed law he resisted was an act of usurpation."

Many important colonial trials ended in nullification. American jurors knew they could refuse to enforce unjust laws. Early jurors routinely were informed by courts of their right to try the law as well as the fact, and lawyers regularly argued the merits of the law to the jury. The independent role of juries was well-accepted in early American law.

It was not until the mid-19th century that courts began to question the jury's independent voice. Judges attempted to bind juries to their instructions and began prohibiting lawyers from arguing law to the jury. The Supreme Court allowed such practices to stand, and today many judges wrongly believe they are forbidden to allow jury nullification to be discussed in court.

American courts have not always been so reluctant to trust the conscientious judgments of juries. In the early years of this country, the Supreme Court itself occasionally heard cases with a jury. In 1794, Justice John Jay, for a unanimous Supreme Court, instructed a jury: "It may not be amiss, here, gentlemen, to remind you of the good old rule, that on questions of fact, it is the province of the jury, on questions of law, it is the province of the court to decide. But it must be observed that by the same law, which recognizes this reasonable distribution of jurisdiction, you have nevertheless a right to take upon yourselves to judge of both, and to determine the law as well as the fact in controversy. On this, and on every other occasion, however, we have no doubt, you will pay that respect, which is due to the opinion of the court: For, as on the one hand, it is presumed, that juries are the best judges of fact; it is, on the other hand, presumable, that the courts are the best judges of the law. But still both objects are lawfully within your power of decision."

> **A just society has to have just rules. Juries, by refusing to enforce unjust rules, can help improve the law and the society that it governs.**

These instructions meticulously delineate the roles of bench and jury. The court instructed the jury on a general rule, which allowed for exceptions. They admonished the jury to take their instructions with respect, yet acknowledged that the jury could not be bound by them. These instructions fostered juror independence and responsibility, not jury lawlessness or wanton disregard for the rights of the parties. Similar instructions could assist jurors in delivering fair, just verdicts today—making sure the law is applied in a manner in which the citizens of this country approve and giving us a legal system of which again we could be proud. The Fully Informed Jury Association, a Section 501(c)(3) [tax-exempt] educational organization with a mission to inform potential jurors of their right to nullify unjust laws, has provided model initiatives to allow for just such instructions. These initiatives have been introduced by legislators in more than a dozen states.

What would be the result of informing jurors about their power to nullify the law in the interests of justice? Perhaps better questions would be: Is the criminal law applied more or less fairly in 1999 than it was in 1799? Is it more or less a source of social divisiveness and tension? Has the criminal sanction been wrested from providing social protection to become a tool for social engineering?

Criminal law often is a divisive factor in society. The nonsensical distinctions between powder and crack cocaine; enormous penalties for many minor crimes; unfair sentencing favoritism given to snitches (who serve a small fraction of the time given their underlings); criminalization of "wetlands" violations; regulatory, licensing and administrative infractions; and the often mechanical application of law favored by prosecutors have resulted in a hodgepodge of injustices strung together without rhyme or reason. Apologists who claim a society must have rules miss the point—a just society has to have just rules. Juries, by refusing to enforce unjust rules, can help improve the law and the society it governs.

Courts usually pretend injustices under law cannot occur. They can and too often do. As Judge Thomas Wiseman noted, "Congress is not yet an infallible body incapable of passing tyrannical laws." Occasionally, jurors follow their instructions, then leave court in tears, ashamed of their verdict.

This sort of thing is not supposed to happen in America. It isn't justice. If being a juror means anything, it should mean never having to say you're sorry. If the law is just and justly applied, jurors should be proud of their verdict and confident that any sentences meted out are well-deserved. Then we will engender respect for the law because, as Justice Louis Brandeis observed, for the law to be respected it first must be respectable.

What happens when a jury nullifies a law? One factually guilty person is acquitted in the interests of justice. If a particular law frequently is nullified, the legislature should bring the law into conformity with the judgment of the community. If the law is being misapplied, the legislature may make the law more specific or prosecutors may quit applying it over-broadly. The law is improved, and injustices are prevented.

Does jury nullification lead to anarchy—or is it democracy in action, allowing citizens to participate in the administration of justice? The concept that jury nullification is anarchy has been bandied about without analysis or justification in the face of juries being given nullification instructions for the first century of this country's existence without collapse into anarchy. Jury nullification does not eliminate law—it regulates it, allowing the people's perception of justice, not the government's, to prevail. It takes a true authoritarian to call such vital citizen participation in governmental decision-making "anarchy."

Trial by jury, according to the Supreme Court, exists to prevent oppression by government. It is easy to see that an occasionally oppressive government does not like to have its powers limited. However, those of us who someday may find ourselves on the other side of the equation should be grateful that the Founders of this country had the foresight and wisdom to install this safety valve, this elegant and time-tested mechanism to anchor our government to the principles of its Constitution. It would be a disgrace to those same Founders to be unwilling to utilize this safety valve today, when circumstances indicate it would be appropriate to do so.

No: Don't give society's mavericks another tool to subvert the will of the people.

By Nancy King

King teaches law at Vanderbilt University and is author of the article, "Silencing Nullification Advocacy Inside the Jury Room and Outside the Courtroom."

Inviting jurors to acquit regardless of what the law says is a tempting cure-all for the law's ills. But cultivating jury nullification is a mistake. Like the peddler's elixir, jury nullification is just as likely to produce unpleasant side effects as it is to bring relief. The most compelling reasons to be wary of the practice of jury nullification are the very arguments its advocates trot out in its defense—history, democracy, fairness, political change and the Constitution itself.

One does not have to look back far into history to find a good reason for discouraging jury nullification. True, the colonists embraced the jury's power as a weapon against the king's oppressive laws. And, we're reminded, juries bravely blocked prosecutions of those who resisted the Fugitive Slave Act, Prohibition and the Vietnam War draft. But jury nullification has not been neatly confined to the rejection of "bad" law or the release of "good" defendants. A much less appealing pattern of jury lawlessness is also prominent in our nation's history. For generations juries have refused to convict or punish those who clearly are guilty of violence against unpopular victims, particularly African-Americans. The Klan Act, barring Ku Klux Klan sympathizers from juries after the Civil War, was passed because juries were exercising their "independence" to ignore civil-rights statutes. In Texas after the Civil War, prosecutors had to strike from juries those who "believe, morally, socially, politically, or religiously, that it is not murder for a white man to take the life of a [N]egro with malice aforethought." This is not a proud legacy. We should not assume that refusal to punish those who harm members of less popular groups is entirely behind us just because some juries, in some places, are more racially diverse than they used to be.

Racism, of course, is not the only risk. To invite nullification is to invite jurors to devise their own defenses to a criminal charge. All three branches of government may have labored to eliminate similar considerations from the assessment of guilt. Juries have acquitted defendants in rape cases after concluding that the victims deserved to be raped because of the way they dressed or acted. Jurors may acquit protesters who trespass, damage property or harm others if they conclude the defendants were right to bypass lawful means of redress. Jurors may believe that reasonable doubt is not a strong-enough burden of proof and require fingerprints or eyewitnesses before convicting. They may decide that certain conduct by the police should be a complete defense, oblivious of efforts by legislators and judges to craft remedies and regulations for police misconduct. Now, as in the past, encouraging "good" nullification inevitably means encouraging "bad" nullification as well, because there is no way to second-guess a jury's acquittal once delivered.

It is not feasible to try to separate "good" nullification from "bad." Even nullification advocates cannot agree on what type of nullification is acceptable. One supporter would require nullification instructions only in cases involving nonviolent acts of civil disobedience where the defendant had "given serious thought" to legal means of accomplishing the same objective. Another would encourage jury pronouncements on the law only when the issue was the constitutionality of a criminal statute. A third insists that "true" nullification is limited to decisions "based on conscientious grounds." In a recent survey, college students were asked whether jury nullification included any combination of a set of possible reasons for acquittal, all of which the researchers believed were valid reasons for juries to nullify, such as, "The police wrongfully assaulted the defendant after he was arrested." When only 13 percent of those surveyed agreed that nullification included all of the reasons listed, the researchers concluded their subjects had a lot to learn about nullification. The response should suggest something else—that it is wishful thinking to assume that legislators or judges will be able to agree when jurors should ignore the law and when they should not.

One might support expanding the lawmaking role of the jury if one believes juries are an essential feature of our democracy, better at assessing whether a law is "just" or "unjust" than democratically elected legislators. But juries probably are much worse at this task. Unlike legislators or electors, jurors have no opportunity to investigate or research the merits of legislation. Carefully stripped of those who know anything about the type of case or conduct at stake, juries are insulated from the information they would need to make reliable judgments about the costs and benefits, the justice or the injustices, of a particular criminal prohibition. Nor can jurors seek out information during the case. The so-called "safety valve" of jury nullification, which exempts a defendant here and there from the reach of a controversial law, actually reduces the pressure for those opposed to a truly flawed statute to lobby for its repeal or amendment and deprives appellate courts of opportunities to declare its flaws.

Nullification's supporters point out that legislatures cannot anticipate unfair applications of the laws they enact, so jury nullification is needed for "fine-tuning." But jurors are not in any better position than judges or prosecutors to decide which defendants should be exempted from a law's reach. Again, jurors probably are much worse at this function because they lack critical information. Any juror who actually knows the defendant is excused from the jury. Jurors only can speculate on the penalty that would follow from their verdict. Unless the defendant testifies (and most defendants do not), the jury will never hear him explain his side of the story nor learn whether he has a prior record. They may never learn of evidence suppressed because it was illegally obtained or because of other errors

on the part of the prosecution. More importantly, because jurors decide only one case, they cannot compare the culpability of different defendants or assess the relative importance of enforcing a particular prohibition against a particular defendant. No doubt about it: Juries are excellent fact finders and lie detectors. But when facts are not in issue and guilt is clear, the ability of jurors to reach sound decisions about when the law should be suspended and when it should be applied is questionable at best.

Jury nullification sometimes is touted as an effective political tool for those who have failed at the voting booth and on the legislative floor. There are two problems with this argument. First, if a group is not influential enough to obtain favorable legislation, it is not likely to secure a majority in the jury box. At most, jurors with dissenting views succeed in hanging the jury. But hung juries are a political dead end. The defendant is not spared; he can be tried again and convicted. More importantly, as a recent recommendation in California demonstrates, rising hung-jury rates inevitably lead to proposals to eliminate the unanimity requirement, proposals that if adopted would shut down minority viewpoints more effectively than any instruction against nullification ever could.

Our democratic process should not be jettisoned so arbitrarily by an unelected group of citizens, who need never to explain themselves.

Even if a politically unsuccessful group finds strength in some local jury boxes, should we really be heartened by the prospect of being stuck with the decision of 12 people who have been encouraged to ignore the pronouncements of the state or nation's elected representatives? If there is a concentrated population of homophobes, racists or anti-Semites in my state, I, for one, do not want judges and lawyers encouraging jurors drawn from these communities to apply their own standards—standards that may vary with the victim's sexual orientation, race or religion. Local dissent, of course, is not limited to group-based views. People disagree strongly about a variety of laws—laws against possessing weapons, euthanasia, driving after a couple of drinks, the use of marijuana, slapping one's wife or children around or the dumping of paint or oil. There are places well-suited for resolving these disagreements: the legislature and the polling booth. Our democratic process should not be jettisoned arbitrarily by an unelected group of citizens who need never explain themselves.

Finally, the Constitution does not support an enhanced lawmaking role for juries. Jurors have no personal constitutional right to disregard the law—otherwise, they would not be required to take an oath to obey it. Nor do defendants have a constitutional right to insist that jurors be given the opportunity to disregard the law. True, judges cannot overturn a conviction or acquittal without the consent of the defendant (through appeal, motion or otherwise). But this rule is in place not because the Constitution considers the jury a superior lawmaker but because the Fifth Amendment prohibits the government from putting the defendant in jeopardy of life or limb more than once for the same offense. Judges also are barred from directing verdicts of guilt, but only because the Sixth Amendment guarantees to the defendant a jury's assessment of the facts.

Beyond what is necessary to protect these important interests of the accused, our refusal to tolerate jury nullification must not stray. Judges, for example, should continue to avoid seating jurors who cannot or will not promise to follow the judge's instructions; continue to prohibit argument and deny instructions concerning defenses not supported by the evidence; continue to instruct jurors about the law and require them to follow these instructions; and continue to prohibit nullification advocates from approaching jurors with nullification propaganda (just as

they bar prosecution sympathizers from lobbying the jury for conviction). Although each of these practices is designed to prevent jury nullification, each is constitutional because the Constitution does not protect jury nullification itself. It protects a defendant's right to fact-finding by a jury and to the finality of a verdict.

Legislators and judges so far steadfastly have rejected repeated proposals to lower barriers to jury nullification because they understand that the costs of such changes would far outweigh any benefits they may bring. Other fundamental changes in our jury system, such as the Supreme Court's decision to ban race-based peremptory challenges as a violation of the equal-protection rights of potential jurors, have been preceded by sustained social, political and legal critique of the status quo. A similar groundswell to cede more power to those who sit in jury boxes in criminal cases has never existed and, fortunately, probably never will.

The wrong men on Death Row

A growing number of bad convictions challenges the death penalty's fairness

BY JOSEPH P. SHAPIRO

Gary Gauger's voice was flat when he called 911 to report finding his father in a pool of blood. Police arrived at the Illinois farmhouse Gauger shared with his parents and discovered that his mother was dead, too. The 40-year-old son, a quirky ex-hippie organic farmer, became a murder suspect. After all, someone had slashed Ruth and Morrie Gauger's throats just 30 feet from where Gary slept. There were no signs of a struggle or robbery. But what most bothered the cops was the son's reaction: He quietly tended to his tomato plants as they investigated. Eventually, Gauger was sentenced to die by lethal injection—until it became clear police had the wrong guy. His case is not unusual.

After years of debate, most Americans now believe the death penalty is an appropriate punishment for the most repulsive murders. But that support is rooted in an underlying assumption: that the right person is being executed. The most recent list by an antideath-penalty group shows that Gary Gauger is one of 74 men exonerated and freed from death row over the past 25 years—a figure so stark it's causing even some supporters of capital punishment to rethink whether the death penalty can work fairly. Among them is Gerald Kogan, who recently stepped down as chief justice of Florida's Supreme Court. "If one innocent person is executed along the way, then we can no longer justify capital punishment," he says.

Mistaken convictions. For every 7 executions—486 since 1976—1 other prisoner on death row has been found innocent. And there's concern even more mistaken convictions will follow as record numbers of inmates fill death rows, pressure builds for speedy executions, and fewer attorneys defend prisoners facing execution. Next week,

Gauger and scores of others mistakenly condemned will gather at Northwestern University School of Law in Chicago for the National Conference on Wrongful Convictions & the Death Penalty. They are "the flesh and blood mistakes of the death penalty," says Richard Dieter of the Death Penalty Information Center.

Timeout sought. Executions have been rare since the death penalty was reinstated in 1976. But the pace is picking up. There are now 3,517 prisoners on death row in the 38 capital-punishment states—an all-time high and a tripling since 1982. The 74 executions in 1997—the most since 1955—represented a 60 percent spike from the year before. Citing bad lawyering and mistaken convictions, the American Bar Association last year called for a death-penalty moratorium. This month, Illinois legislators will vote on such a ban. That state, more than any other, is grappling with the problem: It has exonerated almost as many men (nine) on death row as it has executed (11).

It's tempting to view the reprieved as proof that the legal system eventually corrects its mistakes. But only one of the nine men released in Illinois got out through normal appeals. Most have outsiders to thank. Northwestern University journalism professor David Protess and four of his students followed leads missed by police and defense attorneys to tie four other men to the rape and murders that put four innocent men in prison. "Without them, I'd be in the graveyard," says Dennis Williams, who spent 16 years on death row. "The system didn't do anything."

Most damning of the current system would be proof that a guiltless person has been executed. Credible, but not clear-cut, claims of innocence have been raised in a handful of executions since

1976. Leonel Herrera died by lethal injection in Texas in 1993 even though another man confessed to the murder. The U.S. Supreme Court ruled that, with his court appeals exhausted, an extraordinary amount of proof was required to stop his execution. Governors, the court noted, can still grant clemency in such cases. But what was once common is now so politically risky that only about one death row inmate a year wins such freedom.

How wrongful convictions happen: Gary Gauger's calm gave a cop a hunch. But it was Gauger's trusting nature that gave police a murder tale that day in 1993. Gauger says that during 18 hours of nonstop interrogation, detectives insisted they had a "stack of evidence" against him. They didn't—but it never occurred to the laid-back farmer that his accusers might be lying. Instead, he worried he might have blacked out the way he sometimes did in the days when he drank heavily. So Gauger went along with police suggestions that, to jog his memory, he hypothetically describe the murders. After viewing photos of his mother's slit throat, Gauger explained how he could have walked into her rug shop next to the house ("she knows and trusts me"), pulled her hair, slashed her throat and then done the same to his dad as he worked in his nearby antique-motorcycle shop. To police, this was a chilling confession. Even Gauger, by this point suicidal, believed he must have committed the crimes.

False confessions. Though police failed to turn up any physical evidence during a 10-day search of the farm, prosecutors depicted Gauger as an oddball who could have turned on his mother and father. He was a pot-smoking ex-alcoholic who once lived on a commune and brought his organic farming ways back to Richmond, Ill. The

From *U.S. News & World Report*, November 9, 1998, pp. 22-24, 26. © 1998 by U.S. News & World Report. Reprinted by permission.

judge rolled his eyes during Gauger's testimony and, when defense attorneys objected, simply turned his back on Gauger. The jury took just three hours to reach a guilty verdict. "Nutty as a fruitcake," the jury foreman declared afterward.

A study by Profs. Hugo Bedau of Tufts University and Michael Radelet of the University of Florida found three factors common among wrongful capital convictions. One third involve perjured testimony, often from jailhouse snitches claiming to have heard a defendant's prison confession. (At Gauger's trial, a fellow inmate made a dubious claim to hearing Gauger confess. The man, contacted in jail by *U.S. News,* offered to tell a very different story if the magazine would pay for an interview.) One of every 7 cases, Bedau and Radelet found, involves faulty eyewitness identifications, and a seventh involve false confessions, like Gauger's.

False confessions occur with greater frequency than recognized even by law-enforcement professionals, argues Richard Leo of the University of California–Irvine. About a quarter, he estimates, involve people with mild mental retardation, who often try to hide limitations by guessing "right" answers to police questions. Children are vulnerable, too. Chicago police in September dropped murder charges against two boys, 7 and 8 years old, who confessed to killing 11-year-old Ryan Harris with a rock to steal her bicycle. After a crime laboratory found semen on the dead girl's clothes, police began looking for an older suspect. An educated innocent person, likely to trust police, may be especially prone to police trickery—which courts allow as often necessary to crack savvy criminals. "My parents had just been murdered and these were the good guys," Gauger says. "I know it sounds naive now, but when they told me they wouldn't lie to me, I believed them."

The falsely convicted is almost always an outsider—often from a minority group. In Illinois, six of the nine dismissed from death row were black or Hispanic men accused of murder, rape, or both of white victims. But the No. 1 reason people are falsely convicted is poor legal representation. Many states cap fees for court-appointed attorneys, which makes it tough for indigents to get competent lawyers. And it's been harder for inmates to find lawyers to handle appeals since Congress in 1996 stopped funding legal-aid centers in 20 states.

How wrongful convictions get discovered: Gary Gauger has a simple answer to how he won his freedom: "I got lucky." Of all the 74 released from death row, Gauger's stay was one of the briefest—just eight months. Shortly after his conviction, FBI agents listening in on a wiretap overheard members of a motorcycle gang discussing the murder of Ruth and Morrie Gauger. Last year, two members of the Outlaws Motorcycle Club, Randall "Madman" Miller and James "Preacher" Schneider, were indicted for the Gauger killings. But a federal judge last month ruled the wiretaps were unauthorized and dismissed all the charges. The U.S. Attorney says he is seeking to reinstate them.

Even when another person confesses, the legal system can be slow to respond. Rolando Cruz and Alejandro Hernandez spent 10 years each on death row in Illinois for the rape and murder of 10-year-old Jeanine Nicarico. Shortly after their convictions, police arrested a repeat sex offender and murderer named Brian Dugan who confessed to the crime, providing minute details unknown to the public. Prosecutors still insisted Cruz and Hernandez were the killers—even after DNA testing linked Dugan to the crime. At Cruz's third trial, a police officer admitted that he'd lied when he testified Cruz had confessed in a "vision" about the girl's murder. The judge then declared Cruz not guilty. In January, seven police officers and prosecutors go on trial charged with conspiracy to conceal and fabricate evidence against Cruz and Hernandez.

Discarded evidence. DNA profiling, perhaps more than any other development, has exposed the fallibility of the legal system. In the last decade, 56 wrongfully convicted people have won release because of DNA testing, 10 of them from death row. Attorneys Barry Scheck and Peter Neufeld, with the help of their students at New York's Cardozo School of Law, have freed 35 of those. But their Innocence Project has been hobbled by the fact that, in 70 percent of the cases they pursued police had already discarded semen, hair, or other evidence needed for testing.

Gauger had one other thing going for him that is key to overturning bogus convictions: outside advocates. Most important was his twin sister, Ginger, who convinced Northwestern Law School Prof. Lawrence Marshall (who also defended Cruz and organized next week's conference) to help her brother a week before the deadline for the final state appeal. In September 1994, Gauger's death sentence was reduced to life in prison. Two years later, he was freed. Marshall visited Gauger in prison with the surprise news. "That's good," he said with a smile and his customary calm.

How to prevent wrongful convictions: It's a fall afternoon and starlings are fluttering through the colorful maples that frame the Gauger farmhouse. Gary Gauger loads a dusty pickup with pumpkins, squash, and other vegetables. Inside, Ginger has taken up her mother's business of selling Asian kilims and American Indian pottery. A friend runs the vintage-motorcycle business, still called Morrie's Place, in an adjoining garage. For Gary Gauger, life seems normal again. Customers at his vegetable stand sort through bushels of squash. A hand-lettered sign advises: "Self Service: please place money in black box . . . thanks."

But there is pain, too, for his lost parents and for his 3½ lost years. And it's that part of his story Gauger will share at the upcoming conference in the hope of sparing others such pain. Other conferees at the Northwestern event are expected to endorse a moratorium on executions at least until safeguards are in place such as increased legal aid, certification of capital-trial attorneys, limits on use of jail-house snitches, access to post-conviction DNA testing, and the recording of all police interrogations. There will also be appeals for accreditation of forensic experts: The first Cruz trial turned on a bloody footprint identified by an expert who was later discredited when she claimed she could tell a person's class and race by shoe imprints.

Gauger says the worst part about being wrongfully convicted is knowing that the guilty person is free. The victim Gauger most thinks about is 7-year-old Melissa Ackerman. The little girl was grabbed from her bicycle, sodomized, and left in an irrigation ditch, her body so unrecognizable that she could be identified only by dental records. She was killed by Brian Dugan, while Rolando Cruz and Alejandro Hernandez sat behind bars—falsely convicted of another child's murder committed by Dugan.

Unit 9

Key Points to Consider

❖ How do the social definitions of deviance vary between cultures?

❖ Should we expect people in other cultures to conform to the norms and values of our culture?

❖ Should the United States government take a greater role in assisting custodial American parents in retrieving their kidnapped children from other countries?

❖ To what extent should we be involved in trying to change the norms and values of other cultures where the widespread transmission of HIV has reached pandemic proportions? Why?

 **Links** | **www.dushkin.com/online/**

These sites are annotated on pages 4 and 5.

The last unit in this anthology is also new to this edition. It deals with international perspectives on deviance. The articles in this unit could easily have been incorporated into other units in this book; however their international basis made them worthy of a unit of their own. Looking at deviance from an international perspective gives us the opportunity to better understand the relative nature of the social definition of deviance and how our norms and values may conflict with the norms and values of other cultures in the world.

The first article deals with genocide by Serbs against the Kosovars. Genocide involves the attempt by one ethnic group to destroy all of the members of another ethnic group. Genocide is a phenomenon that seems to repeat itself with horrific regularity. From the slaughter of Native Americans in the United States, to the holocaust of World War II that saw the murder of 6 million Jews, to the murder of Hutus and Tutus in Rwanda, and now the ethnic cleansing of the Kosovar Albananians by the Serbs, genocide repeats itself over and over again.

A form of deviance in Japan involves the organized criminals known as the Yakuza, descendants of medieval bands of gamblers. Financial regulators, both in Japan in the United States, believe that the Yakuza are responsible for a large part of the recent Asian financial crisis, including borrowing money from banks and corporations with no intention of ever paying it back.

In many undeveloped countries, AIDS has reached pandemic proportions with upwards of one-quarter of the populations of those countries being HIV-positive. The norms and values of the cultures in those countries are in part to blame for this trend. Those norms and values may hinder the ability of medical professionals to teach the population about ways to prevent the transmission of HIV, as well as preventing the distribution of medicines that can reduce the symptoms to those persons least able to afford the medicines.

The last two articles in this unit deal specifically with issues related to children as victims of the norms and values of Asian cultures. In Thailand, poor parents have made it a practice to sell their young daughters into prostitution. It is not unusual for girls as young as 6 years old to be rented out to men, often Americans or other Westerners, for the purpose of having sex. While Thailand ostensibly has laws prohibiting men from having sex with young children, in practice those laws are rarely enforced. In the past few years, both the United States and Canada have passed laws barring travel agencies in both countries from arranging pedophile tours to Thailand, as formerly had been the practice. The tours were arranged so that American and Canadian pedophiles could vacation in Thailand, and while there enjoy sexual activities with children. Such practices are believed to have led to a large increase in HIV infection among the young prostitutes of Thailand, as well as among the American and Canadian pedophiles who had sex with them.

The last article of this unit deals with an act of deviance that makes United States citizens victims of noncustodial parents who are foreign nationals. The foreign-national parents take the children from their custodial parent and then take the children back to their homeland. Often, the homeland is a country like Saudi Arabia, where the children are viewed as the property of their father, even if he does not have legal custody in this country. For example, a woman at my university married a Saudi man while he was at school in Jonesboro. They had a daughter together. After the parents divorced, the father came to Jonesboro for a visitation. He took the child back to Saudi Arabia without the permission of the mother, who has legal custody of the child. A Saudi court granted the father custody, and the child will probably never be able to leave Saudi Arabia again. The United States government shows no interest in protecting the interests of custodial American parents. The government refuses to become involved in such cases, perhaps taking the view that political accomodations are more important than the well-being of the youngest United States' citizens. It should be noted that while Saudi Arabia is used as an example above, other countries such as Austria, Germany, and Mexico similarly do not return kidnapped children to their custodial American parents. This is even true in those cases where the foreign courts have recognized the legal custody of the American custodial parent. According to the Reno task-force report, "The federal government has limited power to respond to internationl abductions once the abductor and child reach a foreign country." But victimized parents are convinced of cover-ups in these cases, feeling that the State Department is opposed to helping and is, indeed, caught up in an "international shell game."

KOSOVO CRISIS THE AWFUL TRUTH

CRIMES OF WAR

A team of TIME reporters discovers chilling evidence of Serbia's well-organized, vicious killing machine. It's even more horrific than you imagined

By JOHANNA MCGEARY PEC

THE HORROR STAYS LOCKED IN GENTIANA Gashi's mind. Her eyes are red-ringed holes in a pinched, exhausted face. She came home safely to Cuska last week, but she is still harrowed by the unspeakable memories of May 14, the day she left. Back then, she stood beside her weeping mother, too terrified to cry out, as she watched the Serbs march her father away with the other men, hands clasped behind his neck. He looked back once, tears streaming down his face. Gentiana's mother wept silently too as she watched her husband's retreating figure until laughing Serbs herded the women out of the village, elbowing them with sly smirks, singing obscene songs. That night when the women slipped back into Cuska, it was Gentiana who picked through the charred pieces of bodies inside three smoldering houses to find the remains of her father. She used to give him massages, she said. Ten men had died in that house, but when her fingers touched a familiar torso, "I knew his back, so he was my dad."

To save her mother from the hideous sight, Gentiana helped three women gather up the human debris of her father and 34 relatives and neighbors into little bags. They tagged each with a name and buried them in two communal graves. Then all those who had survived fled, some to the hills above the town of Pec, some to Albania, anywhere away from the Serbian brutality.

Gentiana Gashi is 11 years old.

Under a hot sun broken by violent summer showers, Kosovo is waking to a midsummer's nightmare. The sickly sweet smell of decaying flesh hangs in invisible clouds across the province, and the ground offers up body parts. Bits of ashen bone—a thigh, a rib cage—and chunks of roasted flesh litter the floors of burned-out houses. Corpses, left

where they fell, putrefy in fields and farmyards amid the buzzing of flies and the howling of stray dogs. As the first of Kosovo's Albanian refugees stream back across the borders or down from hiding in the hills, they are discovering just how pitiless a charnel house Serbian forces made of Kosovo.

But new life is blossoming. As the peacekeepers of KFOR steadily pushed their heavy tanks and APCs into the province last week, refugees from Albania and Macedonia followed right behind, heading home from rapidly emptying camps in cars crammed with family members, in tractor-drawn carts sagging under their loads, on foot, pushing wheelbarrows laden with bedding and babies. Uprooted Kosovars who had lived rough in the woods crept back to their villages through fields of blood-red poppies. Gun-toting soldiers of the Kosovo Liberation Army, smart in pressed camouflage, swaggered into cities and towns, posting guards along roads, securing villages house by house. And straggling before them along the roads leading north went the convoys of frightened Kosovar Serbs. They were heading into a bitter, unpromising exile along with the defiant Yugoslav troops in green or blue or black uniforms who had treated Kosovo to their savagery. Despite NATO promises of impartial safety, few Serbs wanted to test KFOR's protection against the reprisals they expected from vengeful Albanians.

What matters in Kosovo now is an accounting of what happened during the 78 days when Serbs rampaged through the province while NATO bombs were falling. Everyone has a tale of brutality to tell. The stories numb with their awful sameness. Yet as individual tales multiply, they form the shameful mosaic of a season of slaughter that spread across all Kosovo. The evidence before our own eyes is damning. So many

Albanians have lost husbands, brothers, wives or children. Nearly everyone has lost his or her home and most possessions. The scale of the terror that is emerging—possibly 10,000 killed, as many as 100 mass grave sites at latest NATO count—leaves little room right now for any emotion but horror.

The striking similarity of the accounts reinforces their credibility and confirms the calculated nature of the atrocities. And last week, as a team of TIME reporters spent days in and around Pec (prewar pop. 100,000), it was possible to discern method in the Serbs' awful madness. Kosovo, the evidence suggests, was razed by a killing machine on orders that stretched directly from Yugoslavia's commander in chief Slobodan Milosevic to the armed thug on the streets. The stories of Pec reveal in miniature how the entire plan worked.

One might be tempted to write off Kosovo as just another Balkan bloodletting. But if the U.S. is to take seriously its credo of humanitarian intervention, politicians and the public need to understand how and why people in the supposedly civilized world fall prey to animal violence. Kosovo has bred fresh hatreds that will lie unresolved beneath every political and social change the West tries to make in this corner of Europe. And we are faced once again this century with the tasks of assigning individual blame for horrors committed in the name of national policy, and determining how best to bring the guilty to justice.

The Killing Machine at Work

THE HUNTERS DROVE OUT OF KOSOVO AS THE people they once hunted drove in. Stuck in a 12-mile-long convoy, Marinko sat atop his

 From *Time*, June 28, 1999, pp. 24-32. © 1999 by Time Inc. Magazine Company. Reprinted by permission.

army tank surveying the exodus with the cold, dead eyes of a four-year veteran of the Yugoslav army. Marinko is a Kosovar Serb, and he concedes no defeat. "I will take my parents to Belgrade, relieve myself of military duties and return to my home in Pec," he said. "This is all I have. And if the Albanians want to come and take it from me, then let them make my day. I'll kill them. It will be guerrilla war." A ranking commander of the MUP—the Serbian special police—he seemed almost proud as he watched his men pack up for their inglorious retreat. "We worked closely here in March to clean up the terrorists [K.L.A.]," he bragged. And then he explained the awful tactics of destruction: "The paramilitary would go in first, the MUP would mop, and the VJ [Yugoslav army] would stand as the rear guard of the operation." There were different orders for all commands, he said as he took a pull on a cool orange Fanta. "We all worked in synchronicity. I alone killed 500 [alleged K.L.A. soldiers]." As for the killing of civilians, he added, "there are wacky members in every unit. And you just don't have the time to control them."

Pec revealed their handiwork. Except for a few shuttered apartment blocks and the main square around the Hotel Metohija, the city lay in silent ruin. Whole neighborhoods had been reduced to knee-deep rubble. Not a soul walked the streets. In Kapasnica, the section known as Little Albania, house after house, down every street in every direction, was a vacant husk, broken-walled and covered in soot. The only sound was the screech of jackdaws, the distant scurrying of a mangy dog and the drip, drip, drip of broken water pipes.

A gaunt figure stood outside No. 180 staring at what used to be the home of the 11-member Hasani family. Astrit, 21, one of five known survivors, had braved the empty city to find out how the family compound had fared. Scorch marks scarred the fresh white walls, renovated a year ago, that now rose only head high around debris. "Catastrophe," he said, afraid to enter for fear of booby traps.

Booby-trapping ruins. This was the nature of the Serbian killing machine, where one violent pass was not enough, where bodies could be found with 150 bullets in them. The cleansing of rich, urban centers like Pec was intended to rid the province permanently of large numbers of Kosovars and to destroy the Albanian intellectual and political culture. But Pec was also subject to a special fury. Going far beyond the brutal demands of military tactics or ethnic cleansing. Serbian forces swept through three times, wreaking destruction and expelling Albanians, including a final useless spasm of fury two weeks ago that razed most of the city and surrounding villages when Milosevic was about to surrender. "In Pec," said Astrit Hasani, "it was total vengeance."

The evidence is visible at house No. 19. The house spills its contents across the front porch, out the windows, across the garden. Broken glass mingles with an X ray, torn curtains and a pile of feces in the front hall. Across the long wall in the main room, letters are scrawled, 1 ft. high, in what appears to be blood: NATO AND KILLERS OF SERB BLOOD and YOU KILL SERB KIDS. The opposite wall is sprayed with blood, and dried puddles stain the floor beneath. Next to the lettering are bloody hand prints.

Serbs took over the neighborhood of Kapasnica as bases for the Yugoslav army and the dreaded paramilitary units known as the "Frenkijevci," or Frenki's Boys, after their reputed leader Franko Simatovic. The shadowy group, say numerous sources, operates under Belgrade's direct control, a kind of special-ops unit run by the secret police. Rumor has it most members are recruited from criminal circles. Frenki's Boys like to dress in black without formal insignia but with a preference for cowboy hats, pigtails and painted faces. In Pec, as in the rest of Kosovo, paramilitary units like Frenki's worked in concert with the VJ and the special-police units, as well as local Serbian civilians who joined in the savagery. All lines led straight back to Belgrade, and this time, unlike in Bosnia, there is no wiggle room for Milosevic to pin the blame for atrocities on "uncontrolled elements" and independent paramilitaries. Here's how Western diplomatic and Serbian sources say it worked:

Operation Horseshoe was a military plan designed and run under the auspices of Belgrade's general staff—as if the Joint Chiefs of Staff had planned and executed an operation to cleanse some ethnic population out of Texas. The job of actually bending the horseshoe fell to a special coordinating team that drew on both the MUP special police and Serbian paramilitaries. Many of these killers were visible in parts of Kosovo last week—sometimes stripped to the waist, heads shaved, making threatening gestures to anyone who challenged them.

The man charged with implementing these ideas in Kosovo was General Sreten Lukic, a high-ranking member of the state-security apparat and a personal friend of Milosevic's. Lukic boldly described Horseshoe last fall to Western diplomats as a massive clockwise sweep that would finally crush the K.L.A. Lukic told his visitors he hoped to finish the mission by mid-October. But that plan collapsed when it became apparent that the K.L.A., which had become expert at hiding and fighting in Kosovo's rough hills, wasn't going to cave in easily.

So Belgrade's military chiefs went back to the planning board. Instead of the massive "sweep" of the original attack, they developed a wickedly clever alternative: a series of smaller sweeps against the K.L.A. that would be combined with a wholesale assault on the civilian population. This two-punch would have the double purpose of depriving the K.L.A. of ground support and permanently altering Kosovo's demographics. Cities and towns would be emptied to depopulate the province. The VJ would shell villages so the police and paramilitaries could move in to put the population to flight, torch their houses and kill any residents who refused to go. While the West was trying to negotiate a diplomatic settlement at Rambouillet, Milosevic was positioning his forces. By the time NATO started bombing in late March, the VJ, police and paramilitaries were operating in concert across Kosovo—in Pec, Pristina, Podujevo. The tactics were always the same, and slaughtering civilians was the essential prod to the exodus.

It worked. After the first offensive in late March, Serbian forces rarely needed more than a corpse or two to force people from their homes. Idriz Xhemojli was one of the villagers from Ljesane, a few miles east of Pec, who ran to the hills two months ago when Serbian forces stormed in and gave residents an hour to leave. "The whole village went," he said, and they watched from the shelter of a hilly wood as the Serbs torched their houses. Two people who refused to turn over cash were shot; two others taken away. The rest, some 300 men, women and children, roamed the woods for two months.

Only Haxhi Kadria, 80, and his wife Rukije managed to stay behind. They survived a second attack on April 27, when every Albanian house was burned. But the Serbs came a third time, just two weeks ago, in a focused fury to obliterate the whole of Ljesane. In the yard of their shattered house last week lay Rukije's body; her skull was crushed, and maggots had made swift work of her body, leaving only bones, rags and hair. The brown, rotting corpse of Haxhi lay nearby in the garden.

In the hamlet of Ruhot, Istref Berisha, 43, found 10 bodies and buried them in a grave near a brook. The victims had been shot, knifed or burned. On a nearby gate, someone has spray-painted in Cyrillic WHITE EAGLES, the name of the paramilitaries associated with Serbian ultranationalist Vojislav Seselj. Nearly two miles away at Staradran, K.L.A. fighters are investigating a long stretch of freshly turned dirt, 8 ft. by 65 ft., believed to contain as many as 100 bodies. A leg clad in a black sock pokes out of one hole; a jawbone lies in another.

Gentiana Gashi's Story

DEATH CAME TO CUSKA—A TOWN ABOUT THREE miles east of Pec—fairly late in the war. Its villagers were especially peaceable, hoping to get along with two predominantly Serbian hamlets on either side. They had voluntarily given up their weapons, they say, on previous visits by the police. Residents were going about their normal business on the morning of May 14 when 30 or 40 men in masks appeared. Lirie Gashi, 28, was one of the women packed into a courtyard where police and VJ troops sat down to drink *raki*—a local form of grappa—from little black glasses before lining up the women to demand money. One soldier told Lirie to unfurl her bun to check if she had hidden cash in her hair. As they ordered the women to strip off their jewelry, they casually fired bullets at their feet. When they discovered the senile Aimone Gashi among the women, the Serbs pumped an automatic round into his back, killing him.

Over the next hour, 33 men were ordered into three separate houses by paramilitaries in red scarves and cowboy hats. Ahmet Gashi, the father of Gentiana, was one of them. Rexhe Kelmendi, 49, was another. "I was taken with the second group down here," he says, pointing to a low, wood-and-brick two-story house. "I was together with

eight others. When we entered the hallway of the house, one of the VJ gave us a lighter and told us to burn down the house. When I bent down to take the lighter, the shooting started. I started crawling, not lifting my head." He reached a window and tumbled out.

Others were less lucky; lined up against the walls in other houses, they died as one or two Serbs fired from left to right, execution style, then fired a second fusillade to make sure. The raiders forced Syle Gashi, 48 (the Gashis are a large extended family), to translate their commands into Albanian, promising to spare his life. When he jumped onto a tractor to leave with the women, a Serb grabbed him and thrust him alive inside a burning house. Caush Lushi, 52, was one of the wealthier men in Cuska. A Serb holding his son said he would free the youth if Lushi brought them all his cash. When he returned with the money, his son was already dead. The Serb frog-marched Lushi to the

nearest outhouse, stuffed him in and carved the Serbian national symbol of a cross with four *Cs* into his living chest. Then he kicked the door closed and fired round after round through the door.

"They came to kill,"said Sadir Gashi as he comforted his cousin Gentiana and her grieving mother Mexhide. The widow's eyes were red with weeping as she showed us the photographic remnants of a happy marriage. "I will always be happy to have these good images in my mind," she said softly, running her hand over Gentiana's hair, "and not his body in that horrible condition." She stopped a moment, then smiled sadly. "I hardly manage to sleep, and when I do, I dream of him. But not of what happened—of the good days we had together."

Other Albanians could not avoid the sight of Serb brutality. "I cannot tell you what it was like to see my father with bullets ripping him from head to toe," said Jusuf Tafili, who saw the corpse of his father 41 hours after

UNEARTHING THE FACTS

THE INTERNATIONAL CRIMINAL TRIBUNAL FOR THE FORMER YUGOSLAVIA recently charged Yugoslav leader Slobodan Milosevic with crimes against humanity. Now forensic experts from around the world are quickly converging on Kosovo to identify massacre sites. The sooner they begin, the better they can gather evidence, reconstruct events and uncover the extent of the atrocities so the prosecutor can argue that these were systematic abuses known or planned at the highest level. How the process works:

1 The tribunal receives information of potential crime scenes and dispatches investigators to the sites.

Last month's indictment of Milosevic and four top Yugoslav officials for their alleged roles in mass killings of civilians cited six Kosovo towns:

Crkolez/Padalishte March 27 · 20 dead
Izbica March 28 · 95 dead
Djakovica/Gjakove March 26 · 6 dead · April 2 · 20 dead
Racak Jan. 15 · 45 dead
KOSOVO Pristina
● Other mass graves
Velika Krusa/ Krushe e Mahde March 26 · 103 dead
Bela Crkva March 25 · 65 dead

Sources: The Graves: Srebrenica and Vukovar, Physicians for Human Rights, ICTFY

Information identifying a crime scene can come from a number of sources:

 EYEWITNESSES Interviews with refugees who've seen killings, or returning Kosovars and incoming soldiers who notice freshly dug graves

 AERIAL SURVEILLANCE Satellite images and aerial photographs can help to corroborate reports and pinpoint suspected sites

 COMMUNICATION INTERCEPTS Intercepted Serb military radio transmissions can place a particular unit in an area on the day of an atrocity

2 Each area is secured and checked for mines ...

24-HOUR GUARDS are posted to protect the site from tampering

A CORDON keeps out press, saboteurs and returning refugees

Pillaged building
Suspected grave
KFOR TROOPS sweep for mines using dogs and metal detectors

Threats to the Site
■ Small but powerful mines, like the PMA-2 at left, lurk inches beneath the surface
■ Weather and the passage of time can disturb evidence

he was executed by unknown Serbs. Among the killers, Jusuf believes, were some local Serbs. "I hope the Serbs who did that won't stay here," said Jusuf, "because I know who they are. If I find them, I will kill them."

Men like Jusuf Tafili scare the Serbs left in Kosovo. As tens of thousands of outraged Albanians rush home, tens of thousands of frantic Serbian civilians plod out. Standing on Thursday morning inside a ring of KFOR tanks idling in front of Pec's Hotel Metohija, Sasa Deletic eyed the empty streets and muttered, "If the Albanians control the city, then I will leave. They are animals." At least 50,000 Kosovar Serbs have joined the 40,000 troops trekking north to Serbia. Says Stojanka Markovic, piling her entire household on a rusty red Yugo: "This is it. We're in a state of panic." Markovic, her husband and her 76-year-old mother were the last Serbs to leave Podujevo, a metropolis in northern Kosovo, as their former Albanian neighbors moved back in. "They watched us leave," she said, shaking with fear, "as we watched them leave months ago."

A New Power in Kosovo

AND AS THE SERBS GO, THE POWER VACUUM in Kosovo is being filled not only by NATO but also by the K.L.A. So far, the rebels have left the retreating Serbs alone—though NATO commanders fear that won't last. But an armed K.L.A. certainly makes the province less friendly for any Serbs who dare remain. Under the military agreement, the K.L.A. is supposed to "demilitarize" and turn over its heavy weapons, but no piece of paper will make it give up its AK-47s. Or its dreams of independence—and revenge.

The K.L.A. forces immediately exploited NATO's victory to make themselves heroes to the refugees and grab a share of KFOR's authority. For an entire day, despite heavy cloudbursts, rebel units staged a massive victory parade that jammed downtown Prizren. They deployed everywhere around Pec, setting up checkpoints, patrolling the empty streets. "Tell KFOR the 131st Brigade of the [K.L.A.] is based at the publishing house," announced Commander Et'hem Ceku as he pulled up with troops in a minivan. "I am responsible for the civil and administrative matters of Pec." In the hills, K.L.A. units looked anything but ready to disperse. At an encampment near Ruhot, 30 fresh recruits in brand-new camouflage, some carrying expensive supersniper rifles, were being mustered into the unit.

Kosovo's Albanians set out from their refuges last week with such high hopes but arrived to such horror. The impact of those pit graves and decomposing bodies, incinerated villages and pulverized cities will haunt the Balkans for generations. In Washington the White House is busy searching for a leader to replace Milosevic if the defeated strongman falls. Clinton is expected this

3 ... then investigators examine the surface ...

100 EXPERTS, split into about 12 teams, will be assigned to crime scenes around Kosovo

CHANGES IN VEGETATION and fresh dirt suggest that bodies may be buried there

Finding the Evidence
- Investigators comb for clues, including bullet casings and bone fragments
- Each discovery is mapped, tagged and photographed

4 ... and finally the bodies are exhumed.

TIMETABLE Some sites will be exhumed by November, others will wait until spring

EXCAVATION done layer by layer, like an archaeological dig

Each stage is photographed

TIME Graphic by Ed Gabel and Joe Zeff

REUTERS (MILOSEVIC); THOMAS HALEY—SIPA FOR TIME (IDENTIFICATION)

How Bodies Are Identified
- Family members visually identify the corpse
- Medical records and other identification
- DNA analysis

5 A case is made to prosecute Milosevic.

Prosecutors will use the evidence to attempt to show that the crimes were systematic. They must also prove Milosevic was either involved or aware of the plans but did nothing to stop them. How they'll link him to the killings:

MASS GRAVES Many sites containing civilian Kosovar victims can help prove that massacres were systematic

PHYSICAL EVIDENCE Shell casings and other evidence at grave sites can link Serb soldiers directly to the atrocities

KOSOVARS Testimony from locals who saw others murdered can link whole Serb units to a massacre

CHAIN OF COMMAND If Serb soldiers are to blame, prosecutors can then trace the military chain of command to Milosevic himself

Paul Quinn-Judge/Moscow

Yeltsin's Fast-Break Generals

JUST WHEN IT SEEMED BORIS YELTSIN could not become more eccentric and unpredictable, the mad dash of some 200 Russian troops from Bosnia into Kosovo and their takeover of the Pristina airport has reduced political analysis of his regime to something very like chaos theory. The politics of presidential truculence and pique that has so long dominated decision making in Russia has now spilled into foreign relations. And the fact that the Russian military was able to bypass most of the country's top civilian decision makers shows that Yeltsin has a new set of favorites—Russian army generals with a bleak view of the outside world and its designs.

Even so, it is hard to pinpoint just how Yeltsin was involved in the NATO-trumping encampment at Pristina. Close aides insist that Yeltsin knew about—even ordered— the move. In fact, Russian military sources say, the raid was a spur-of-the-moment undertaking, devised by generals furious with NATO's stonewalling. The decision, say Russian sources, was taken no earlier than June 10, two days before the troops

moved in. At that point, U.S.-Russia talks on peacekeeping in Kosovo were going badly. Military representatives suspected that their main U.S. interlocutor, Deputy Secretary of State Strobe Talbott, was playing for time in Moscow, trying to keep negotiations bogged down until NATO had deployed. Yeltsin, meanwhile, was smarting at what he felt was Bill Clinton's condescension toward him. Sometime that day, Yeltsin was briefed on the talks, and he asked, as he often does, if anyone had any ideas. Chief of staff General Anatoli Kvashnin conferred with his aides and Lieutenant General Viktor Zavarzin, Russia's representative to NATO, and sketched out a surprise idea: a fast break out by Russian troops stationed in Bosnia. Yeltsin was shown the plan, military sources said, and grunted a comment that they construed to be approval. They were probably right: Yeltsin's ability to not leave fingerprints on risky decisions is a legend among his staff.

While only a few people in Moscow were privy to the plan, it seems to have been well known and warmly welcomed

in Belgrade. The Yugoslavs went out of their way to facilitate the convoy's movement, Russian military sources say. Serbian state officials secured the convoy's route through Serbia and ensured that a road into Kosovo was kept free of refugees and retreating troops. To allow the convoy to travel at top speed as much as possible, a Yugoslav military officer rode in every third vehicle, ready to navigate if the convoy was broken up in traffic.

The Pristina operation has given Russian military commanders a tremendous surge of confidence, and perhaps more important, it has helped the generals gain Yeltsin's ear. Russia's military hierarchy has little love for Yeltsin—one of his nicknames in the general staff is Pelmeni (a small dumpling), an apparent reference to his puffy features and tortured articulation. And the officers have little doubt that he will let them take the blame if the Pristina operation backfires. For the time being, though, an aggressive-sounding military has established a disturbingly close relationship with an ailing and mercurial president.

---

week to meet Milo Djukanovic, Montenegro's useful pro-Western President, and U.S. diplomats met secretly last week with Belgrade political opponents in hopes of promoting a homegrown challenge to Milosevic. Washington refuses to cooperate with Yugoslavia as long as he stays in power, but Clinton repeatedly emphasizes, "The U.S. and our European allies have no quarrel with the Serbian people."

The demise of Slobodan Milosevic alone would not suffice for Jusuf Tafili as he stood mourning his murdered father and the seven others buried together beneath simple wooden stakes reading A.T., S.T., R.T., I.A. . . . "All Serbian men had their hands in blood," he said. "If they were not directly involved

in crimes, they helped the criminals. They deserve no space in Kosovo anymore." Nor, he says, did Albanians "give all this blood to stay under Serbian hands." To repay their sacrifice and to exact justice, he says, the Kosovars deserve independence.

The horror in Kosovo has radicalized even those in the province who once considered themselves liberal. After a day in the ruins of Pec, his hometown, Dukagjin Gorani, a Kosovar journalist, said, "We have had enough of moderation here. The Serbs must go. Serbian will never be spoken here again."

For the Serbs and the Albanians, the fighting has stopped, but this war is not over. As his ancient, weathered face streamed with tears last week, Azem Mu-

caj placed roses on a dried puddle of blood at the entrance to Pec. The 72-year-old Albanian farmer had brought his 14-year-old son Gzim safely down from the hills after two months in hiding from the Serbs, reuniting the family of seven. On Wednesday, Gzim raced joyfully to the main road to cheer the KFOR tanks as they growled by. A car stopped in front of him. Five Serbs in black masks jumped out and, without saying a word, shot Gzim dead.

—With reporting by Dejan Anastasijevic/Vienna, Dusanka Anastasijevic/Podujevo, Massimo Calabresi/Cuska, Anthee Carassava/Pristina and Jan Stojaspal/Ljubenica

YAKUZA INC.

American investors are spending billions of dollars to snap up portfolios of bad loans from Japanese banks. That could put them on a collision course with notorious Japanese crime syndicates called 'yakuza'

BY DAVID E. KAPLAN

Last January, two Japanese private investigators were working a case in Akasaka, one of Tokyo's teeming entertainment districts, where building after building is honeycombed with bars and nightclubs. They had been sent by Kroll Associates, the U.S. security firm, to check on the ownership of a club-packed low-rise. The property was part of a portfolio of bad loans being offered to an American investor, who wanted to know who his borrowers might be.

After making discreet inquiries, the two investigators left the building. Outside, they were suddenly confronted by four young toughs, demanding to know who sent them. Before the PIs could finish answering, the thugs jumped them, smashing in the teeth of one PI and bloodying the other. The assailants were working for the Japanese breed of mobster known as *yakuza.*

Beset by bad debt, scandal, and a slumping economy, Japan's long-closed financial system is finally opening up to the world, but American investors may not like everything they find. Last week, Japanese authorities embarked on the first stage of a major reform of the nation's financial system, an initiative known locally as *kinyu biggu ban,* or financial big bang. The big bang is creating huge opportunities in Japan for American and other foreign financial institutions, which have responded by expanding operations and forming alliances with Japanese banks. Fidelity In-

vestments, Merrill Lynch, and other U.S. financial houses will introduce American money-management techniques in a bid to attract a portion of Japan's staggering $11 trillion pool of private savings.

> Descended from medieval bands of gamblers and peddlers, the Japanese *yakuza* are known for their striking full-body tattoos.

Yakuza recession. As part of the big bang, U.S. investors are spending billions of dollars to snap up huge portfolios of bad loans from Japanese banks. What the local banks aren't telling their new customers is that behind much of their economic woes stand Japan's wily crime syndicates. In the late 1980s, the *yakuza* became major players in the nation's wildly speculative real-estate market. Japanese crime experts now believe that as much as 40 percent of the banking industry's bad loans are tied to organized crime, representing a whopping $235 billion—an amount close to the combined GDP of Singapore and the

Philippines. The stakes are considerable not only for Japan and its foreign investors but also for the world economy. Policy makers in Washington are hoping that a financially stronger Japan will help push East Asia out of a deflationary spiral that could pose a serious threat to U.S. corporate profits and, therefore, American jobs. The problem is that until Japanese banks can clear away their mountain of bad debt, the nation's financial system is likely to remain wobbly and its economic recovery doubtful. The gangs have played such havoc with efforts to clean up the banking mess that one former top Tokyo cop calls his nation's economic crisis a "*yakuza* recession."

At the front lines of this crisis, suddenly, are American investors, among them a *Who's Who* of equity funds, investment banks, and real-estate trusts. Over the next few years, U.S. financial companies hope to spend more than $20 billion on the bad-loan portfolios, according to real-estate specialists at Ernst & Young. Goldman Sachs, Merrill Lynch, Morgan Stanley, and others are betting that their experience in liquidating property will pay off big in Japan. The firms are paying as little as 10 cents on the dollar for Japanese properties that range from downtown high-rises to abandoned golf-course developments.

But the risks for U.S. investors are substantial. *Yakuza* experts warn that Western capital has never before collided with Japanese organized crime in such a major way. "Foreign investors are

The 'yakuza' boast 80,000 members and associates.

moving into what's been exclusively a domestic concern," notes Kroll's Harry Godfrey, who for four years ran the U.S. Embassy's FBI office in Tokyo. "The *yakuza* aren't going to back away."

Risky business. Investors may be unprepared for what awaits them. "You've got inexperienced guys from New York coming here who don't know what they're getting into," says an investment banker with years of experience in Tokyo. "And when trouble starts, they're not going to advertise it back home." The trouble may already have begun. In November, a mysterious fire struck the home of a top executive at the Japan subsidiary of Cargill Inc., the U.S. agribusiness giant. Cargill was among the first foreign firms to buy portfolios of bad loans. When the fire occurred, Cargill executives were suspicious of foul play and called in police to investigate. No arrests have been made.

The majority of bad loans in Japan are tied to real estate, which U.S. investors hope to profit from in various ways. Most plan to cut new deals with the borrowers, gaining immediate cash flow and consent to sell the properties when the economy improves. Another option is to foreclose on the land and then redevelop or sell it off. Japanese authorities are also considering whether to allow securitization of the bad loans, a tool the United States used effectively in cleaning up the savings and loan industry. But the sale of securities based on *yakuza*-tied debt could make for unusual bedfellows. Conceivably, pension-fund holders in Sarasota or Sacramento could end up earning interest on mafia-run brothels in Osaka. Most investors know they are venturing into uncharted territory, pouring funds into what has been a closed market with little turnover. "No one has ever done this before," says an American investment banker based in Tokyo. "We're putting a grenade in the Japanese property market. Shrapnel will spread."

The wiser U.S. firms—like Morgan Stanley—are hiring high-powered investigators and law firms in Tokyo to go through the portfolios loan by loan. "They all see the potential for profit, and they all have the same questions," says

Godfrey of his firm's clients. "Who are we dealing with? Who's in the building?" One portfolio of 49 loans examined by Kroll found that 40 percent of the borrowers had ties to organized crime. Fully 25 percent of them had criminal records ranging from disrupting auctions to assault, extortion, and rape. *U.S. News* obtained a similar portfolio of 108 properties offered to Western investors by Mitsui Trust & Banking Co., one of Japan's largest banks. Thirteen of the properties—including condos, undeveloped land, and parking lots in Tokyo—are held by Azabu Building, a company that might not mean much to Americans but is quite familiar to Japanese police. In early March, Azabu's president, Kitaro Watanabe, received two years in prison for hiding some $18 million in assets from creditors. Azabu properties, moreover, are

HANDS-ON GANGSTERS.

In addition to their tattoos, Japanese gangsters often feature missing pinkies, cut to atone for a misdeed.

protected by groups tied to Tokyo's largest crime syndicate, according to police. One investigator who ventured onto one of Watanabe's properties was held hostage for an hour by its "tenants," until the gang's boss telephoned the hapless fellow, according to the man's associates. "Next time you come out here, come with the proper introductions!" shouted the godfather. "Go home, wash your face, and come visit us again."

The issue is sensitive enough that not one banker interviewed for this story—American or Japanese—would talk on the record. It's easy to understand why. "These guys are a nightmare to deal with," said a Tokyo banker responsible for collecting bad loans. Clearly, the risks are not for the faint-hearted. In 1993, Tomosaburo Koyama, a vice president of now bankrupt Hanwa Bank,

a regional lender outside Osaka, was gunned down outside his home. Koyama headed a section of the bank that collected problem loans, and police believe the murder is tied to a dispute with a local *yakuza* gang. A similar slaying occurred a year later, when the manager of a top branch of Sumitomo Bank was found shot through the head in his apartment building. Since 1991, assailants have committed dozens of violent acts against Japanese companies, including assaults, arson, and 21 shooting attacks on the homes of corporate executives. Much of the violence, police believe, is tied to business deals involving the *yakuza*. The crimes have left an atmosphere of fear within the banking industry. "It's impossible for the banks to collect the bad loans," says consultant Raisuke Miyawaki, former chief of the National Police Agency's organized-crime unit. "Their exposure to the *yakuza* is too strong." Bankers and Finance Ministry officials refer to the problem delicately as *moraru hazaado*—moral hazard.

The *yakuza* were not always so pervasive. For decades, Japanese gangsters were best known for their striking full-body tattoos and missing pinkies, cut to atone for an error or misdeed. Descended from medieval bands of gamblers and peddlers, the *yakuza* were largely local crime rings that controlled neighborhood card games and brothels. As Japan grew into the world's second-largest economy, the *yakuza*, too, grew increasingly sophisticated and business-minded. A handful of super syndicates expanded nationwide, gaining political access and influence over the entertainment and construction industries. Today, the *yakuza* comprise some 80,000 "made" members and associates—six times the size of the Italian-American Mafia. Despite their criminal behavior, the gangs are socially accepted in a way that shocks Western law enforcement. *Yakuza* members sport their own business cards and, until recently, ran offices with their gang names prominently displayed. This widespread tolerance has allowed the gangs to insert themselves into Japan's financial structure in far-reaching ways. It is not well understood

Attacks against Japanese companies are on the rise.

in the West that key portions of Japan's financial industry—debt collection, bankruptcy management, consumer finance—are heavily influenced by the *yakuza*. Most Japanese bankruptcies, for example, are traditionally handled off the books, largely by *yakuza*-backed fixers called *jiken-ya,* or "incident specialists." The gangs are also adept at crimes of extortion. Recent police crackdowns make it seem as if much of Japan Inc. is paying off the mob: In the past year, authorities have arrested nearly two dozen senior executives from 10 top companies—among them Hitachi, Nomura Securities, and Toshiba—for their alleged involvement with *yakuza*-tied racketeers.

What pushed the gangs so deeply into the financial world was Japan's Bubble Economy, the huge speculative boom that sent real-estate and stock prices soaring in the late 1980s. In terms of sheer market capitalization, the Tokyo Stock Exchange became the world's largest; the Osaka stock market bumped London's bourse to fourth place. The value of real estate in Tokyo, on paper, was said to exceed that of the entire United States. These overinflated assets became the collateral for a seemingly endless amount of credit extended to virtually any business in Japan—and the *yakuza* cashed in big. "The banks didn't check out their clients well," says a prominent Japanese banker with nearly 40 years' experience in the business. "Any business could get loans." In one famous case, Tokyo godfather Susumu Ishii received $2.3 billion in loans and loan guarantees from top brokerage houses, construction firms, and a delivery service. It is as if Federal Express, Merrill Lynch, and the Bechtel Corp. handed a multibillion-dollar line of credit to John Gotti's Gambino family. To Japanese who watched the gangs, it soon became clear that all this money was transforming the underworld. This new breed of criminal was dubbed the *keizai yakuza,* the economic gangster, and became the stuff of legend from Ginza nightclubs to Manhattan art auctions.

Dirty money. The Bubble popped in 1990, plunging Japanese property and stock markets to lows from which they

have yet to recover fully. Last January, the Ministry of Finance offered what analysts say is the first accurate accounting of the size of the bad loans left from the Bubble's collapse—nearly $600 billion, an amount larger than America's S&L debacle, in an economy less than half the size. Cleaning up the S&Ls, moreover, seems easy compared with what the Japanese face. The S&Ls were looted largely by white-collar crooks, not by violent crime syndicates. Much of the money lent to the gangs has simply disappeared, hidden away in mob investments, spent on fast living, or lost with deflating stock and property values.

The *yakuza* have fixed their keen eyes on what assets remain. As pressure mounts to foreclose and sell off the properties, the gangs are employing a black bag of enterprising tricks to profit from the cleanup. Their people are known in the business as *songiri-ya,* or "loss-cutting specialists"—a shadowy industry of *yakuza* squatters, extortionists, and investors. In one favorite loss-cutting technique, an indebted owner leases or sells the building to a gang, which then fills the property with mobsters. These underworld squatters use threats and violence to avoid foreclosure, gain a better settlement, or extract huge payoffs to move. Remarkably, some of these characters have occupied office buildings in major cities for as long as seven years. Police say there is even an active secondary market among the gangs, in which one group of loss-cutters sells to another. Another favorite mob tactic is to file false liens against the property and then demand payoffs to relinquish their claims. Still another technique is to scare off potential buyers, then come in at the last minute and buy the property at a rock-bottom price.

Where in all this are the police? To clean up the banking mess, Tokyo has set up a scaled-down version of America's Resolution Trust Corp., which liquidated the bulk of S&L properties in the United States. Officially, Japanese police are backing the new entity. But in practice, authorities are reluctant to intervene in what they see as civil matters—a reaction to the pre-World War II days when police seemed to intervene

everywhere. Disputes over contracts, liens, and tenants are best left to the private sector, they say. Missing, too, is the kind of legal assault on negligent lenders that the United States set up in the wake of the S&L failures. In cleaning up the S&L industry, prosecutors indicted more than 1,850 people, resulting in nearly 1,600 criminal convictions. In contrast, Japanese authorities have brought fewer than 100 indictments tied to the bad loans.

One who is trying to change the system is Kohei Nakabo, the crusading head of Japan's Housing Loan Administration. The HLA is charged with collecting the worst of the nation's bad loans—$50 billion of debt left by the collapse of Japan's housing lenders. In conformist Japan, Nakabo was an unusual choice for the job. The former head of the Japan Federation of Bar Associations, Nakabo was beaten by the *yakuza* while a young attorney and came out of retirement to take on the gangs again. His loan collectors have been threatened repeatedly by mobsters, and Nakabo himself receives round-the-clock protection from Japan's secret service. The outspoken attorney complains that penalties for the gangs are too light. Criminals can get 10 years in jail for assault, he notes, but they face less than two years for hiding assets or impeding loan collection. The bad-loan cases take time, too, and all this makes the payoff seem small to law enforcement. "The police are uninterested," he says. "Only the criminals think it's worthwhile." In the media, Nakabo rails against the "dark forces" behind the bad-loan crisis, and his tough stance has made him one of the most popular figures in Japan today.

One prominent Tokyo businessman, Ryuma Suzuki, is bullish on American investments in bad loans connected to the mob. "Japanese banks are acting like cowards," says Suzuki, who helps run a $1 billion organization with 7,000 employees. "I want to encourage U.S. banks to come to Japan. There's a huge business opportunity here, and it would help the trade deficit." Unfortunately, Suzuki's "company" is the Sumiyoshi-kai, Tokyo's largest crime syndicate.

'Yakuza' are tied to 40 percent of Japan's bad loans.

Suzuki disputes that the *yakuza* are the source of trouble and offers his services to help clear the properties for new investment. "We're not the problem," he argues. "The authorities are slow to clean up the mess, so they're looking for a scapegoat. But we can help. We would work our butts off because there's a commission." And what kind of commission does Suzuki charge? "I believe the going rate is 30 to 40 percent," he says.

Rising Sun. Other *yakuza*-related challenges may await U.S. investors. Because of the low turnover of real estate in Japan, few firms exist to manage and dispose of property. Among the handful of companies that do manage property, investigators warn, some work closely with the *yakuza*. Another danger, say police, comes from Japan's ultranationalists, right-wing gangs that are also tied closely to the mob. With their sound trucks and paramilitary uniforms, these thuggish bands are a common sight in Japan's largest cities. Crime experts warn that the rightists' sense of nationalism is being stirred by the high-profile foreign purchases, in a similar way that Japanese purchases of Rockefeller Center and other trophy properties once

bothered some Americans. For a mere $1,000 per day, one can hire a gang of the rightists, who arrive at a firm's headquarters with loudspeakered trucks that blast martial music and denunciations of the company inside. Occasionally, the harassment turns more serious: In January, a gun-toting ultranationalist took a Finance Ministry official hostage at the Tokyo Stock Exchange and demanded an end to plans for deregulating the financial industry. Some rightists also blame the United States for causing the Bubble's collapse and are thought to be behind bomb threats made to Morgan Stanley in 1992.

Faced with gangsters, ultranationalists, and unresponsive police, U.S. investors may find it hard to resist making handsome payoffs to the mob. "On the big discounted properties, you may have to cooperate with organizations like mine," advises godfather Suzuki. "Things can get a little rough out there." Privately, some U.S. investment bankers admit they may have to grease the wheels in order to clear their new properties. The profit potential is big enough, says one, that there's money to be made even after Suzuki's commission of 40 percent.

But such decisions will have repercussions on both sides of the Pacific, say *yakuza* watchers. If the gangs are paid off, it means a large infusion of American cash into the Japanese underworld, not a welcome thought for the United States, where *yakuza* practices have ranged from drug smuggling to extortion and money laundering. Nor does it help the small band of Japanese reformers like Nakabo, who are struggling to change their system. A more immediate threat, perhaps, is that posed to the investors themselves. As Japan's banking industry found, the gangs do not easily go away. Until now, the *yakuza* have largely left American business alone, but that may now change. "In the short term, you're getting an opportunity to make a profit," says former FBI man Godfrey. "But you're exposing yourself to paying off organized crime, and that could spill over to the rest of your business." As the Japanese like to say, dealing with the *yakuza* is like feeding a tiger. If you try to stop, the tiger will eat you.

With Steven Butler

Bitter Harvest

SPECIAL REPORT: How the sexual exploitation of girls has become big business in Thailand

BY BETTY ROGERS

THE PHOTOGRAPH DISPLAYED A TINY GOLD BUDDHA LODGED IN THE vagina of a 12-year-old. The image appeared in a roll of film dropped off at a photo shop in Bangkok. Outraged to see a holy object desecrated, the shop owner sent the picture to San-phasit Koompraphant, director of the Center to Protect Chil-dren's Rights, an advocacy group for abused children. "The owner did not anger because a child was treated so cruelly," Koompraphant says, "but because his Buddhist religion had been insulted. He probably would not notice another object used that way."

Koompraphant, a wiry man with a missionary intensity, tells the story as he climbs a wobbly ladder to reach for one of the many cardboard boxes that line his office. The Budaha incident began in Bangkok's Patpong district, famous for its tourist bars and sex clubs. A Thai man approached an Australian and of-fered him sex with two girls—the 12-year-old and her 6-year-old sister—who had been sold into prostitution by their relatives. The agent delivered the girls to the tourist's hotel room, where he abused and photographed them for months. He was eventually arrested and sentenced to jail—one of the few foreigners ever to be convicted in Thailand of sexually abusing children. The case involved all the classic players in the sex trade of young girls: family members, a recruiting agent, a male in pursuit of cut-rate pleasure, girls expected to trade sex for family income, and social workers struggling against government indifference.

Koompraphant opens a box and flips through bundles of photographs that document physical abuse suffered by young girls in Thailand's sex trade. He hands me a series of a Bur-mese girl covered with swollen bruises and slash marks formed into oozing scabs. Next he offers me a picture of a wasting young AIDS victim, reduced to a canvas of skin stretched across her skeletal frame. "This AIDS disease makes everything more crisis," he says. Finally he locates the pictures taken by the Australian. The children, tears streaming down their cheeks, per-form oral sex on the foreigner as he photographs them. In another photo, he has stuck a banknote in the younger girl's vagina. And

then there's one where her sister is face down with her arms handcuffed behind her back and her legs forced open.

I see the delicate beauty of the two moon-shaped faces with translucent skin. I see fear in their eyes. The 12-year-old has her hair pulled into a ponytail and wears a gingham dress with puffed sleeves. The 6-year-old stares out from underneath long bangs and straight black hair that curves below her chin. Her head reaches only as high as her older sister's thin shoulder.

KOOMPRAPHANT'S SPEECH IS RAPID AND DETERMINED AS HE DESCRIBES the exploitation he has witnessed. I ask whether he has chil-dren. His face relaxes and he almost smiles, "I have one boy. I feel bad when I think that my child, with a young beautiful body could be destroyed like this. I look at my son and think, yes, the family makes the first decision. The family can protect or abuse or destroy a child." But the family unit, the only social security in place for this nation of more than 60 million people, is pitted against the forces of a modern global economy that is consuming the lives of young females at an alarming rate. The economic policies embraced by the government, the military, business leaders, and international lenders have all played a major role in escalating this costly business.

Koompraphant's photos document the shadow side of a well-organized and profitable sex trade that, according to cal-culations by the Chulalongkorn University Political Economy Centre in Bangkok, generates annual revenues of around U.S. $4 billion. Several million people earn their living either di-rectly or indirectly from the activities of the prostitution in-dustry. In fact, a 1998 report by the International Labor Organization (ILO), entitled *The Sex Sector,* says Thai prosti-tution has grown so rapidly in recent decades that it has be-come a "commercial sector," one that contributes significant employment and national income. Yet the government's budget, statistics, and development plans do not recognize the trade, putting this lucrative business in an economic and legal twi-light zone. In addition, Thai commerce laws sanction prosti-

"Being poor, I had to leave home, hauling my virginity along." —Lyrics from a Thai folk song

tution as a "personal service," even though it is illegal under the penal code. The law thus recognizes the investment privileges of the sex trade while technically making its workers criminals.

The simple truth is that prostitution is a big business, well entrenched in Thailand's economy, and it is having a devastating effect on countless young girls—at least a third of all Thai sex workers are under the age of 18, the international legal standard for child labor. Teenagers are the most in demand with clients, and the majority of adult prostitutes entered the trade as children themselves. The ILO report concludes that children "are clearly more helpless against established structures and vested interests than adults" and much more likely to be "victims of debt bondage, trafficking, physical violence, or torture." As the industry has grown, so has the problem of trafficking, defined as the illegal movement of people into sex work through deceit, coercion, or force. Although it's primarily girls who are trafficked in Thailand, in recent years boys have also been forced into the tourist sex trade.

Thailand's sex industry is organized along two parallel tracks, with one market for Thai and immigrant workers who pay in local currency and a second for foreign tourists who bring with them badly needed foreign cash. Most researchers agree that Thailand's local sex trade employs far more people than the tourist trade. For centuries, Thai men have viewed visiting brothels as almost a national pastime. Prostitution is an accepted form of entertainment that men introduce their sons to and expect their wives to tolerate. A recent Ministry of Public Health study says that roughly three quarters of all Thai males regularly visit prostitutes and that prostitutes initiate almost half of all teenage boys into sexual activity.

> THE CUSTOMERS CAN CHOOSE A GIRL TO TAKE BACK TO THEIR HOTEL, OR HAVE A "BARFLY" —quick sex in a tiny back room monitored by a bouncer who pounds the door when it's time for the next customer.

The international sex market, however, is a more prestigious and intoxicating lure for families who expect to earn money through their daughters and for young girls desperately seeking a way out of poverty. Male tourists and business travelers from around the globe come to Thailand to indulge themselves at bargain prices in a freewheeling atmosphere, unconfined by taboos against sex with minors or the threat of arrest. The money they spend on sex, hotels, meals, gifts, transportation, and tourist extras is a major source of Thailand's foreign currency exchange.

HARD CURRENCY

AMONG THE FAVORED DESTINATIONS FOR FOREIGNERS WITH HARD CURrency is the Patpong district. In daytime, the main thoroughfare could be any crowded Asian street, choked with vehicles and

Sanphasit Koompraphant has helped to free children as young as six from forced sex work. "Some are in brothels sealed up so tight, they never have fresh air. The girls have sex with up to ten clients a day. During festivals and celebrations, they take even more."

dusty exhaust fumes. But around sunset, merchants transform the now barricaded roadway into a hawker's paradise lit by garish streetlights. Young men drift through the crowds, accosting pedestrians with photo albums that display girls and women for hire like choices in a fast-food restaurant.

On either side of this makeshift marketplace, Patpong's nightclubs open for the evening, offering drinks, dancing, and endless opportunities for sex. Bouncers and barkers entice gawking tourists and cruising men into bars sporting names like French Kiss, Pussy Galore, or the King's Love Boat. Young women dance a cancan in laced corsets and garters next door to a bar that features performers wearing schoolgirl uniforms.

In the Wheel of Love, the musty smell of human sweat and stale beer permeates the dimly lit room, which vibrates with flashing lights and loud rock music. I calculate that for every one male customer, ten females dance, greet, wait tables, or lounge about. The customers can choose a girl to take back to their hotel, or have a "barfly"—quick sex in a tiny back room monitored by a bouncer who pounds the door when it's time for the next customer. A petite teenager and an overweight American several times her size squeeze into the small table next to me. She orders drinks and soon tells him over the loud music, "You like me come with you? You pay at bar to buy me out to your room." I feel my translator nudge me to stop staring. An American colleague exclaims, "But he's going to crush her!" The couple embodies for me the imbalance of economic power that makes Thai and other Asian girls so vulnerable to the demands of foreign men.

At a nearby club, Super Scene, girls perform naked on a stage ringed with tall metal poles used as sex props. I arrive escorted by two former sex workers who talk our way past the grim bouncers and then go to clear our visit with the mamasan, the Japanese term used throughout Asia for a madam. They return with her approval, but I still keep my tape recorder hidden. The machine feels alien in this world of anonymous sex.

We wedge ourselves into a back table, practically the only fully clothed women in the bar. The music blares so loudly I twist earplugs from paper napkins and consider the permanent deafness that bar girls risk from this pounding on their eardrums. As soon as the dancers finish a set, a new group comes onstage so that all of them are eventually showcased for the customers. The performers pause at the bottom of the stage steps to slide off their thigh-length kimonos before stepping nude into the spotlight. The first two young women wrap the stage with colored streamers pulled slowly, with thrusting hip motions, from between their legs. The next two clasp their legs around each other and rock pubis to pubis to the beat of the music. Soon, two more girls dance out with a tall wooden cake with three phallic candles to celebrate a customer's birthday. They slowly ride the candles up and down as a third girl writes, *I love you, Howard,* on a piece of paper, using a pen clasped in her vagina. She squats down over firmly planted feet and swirls her hips to form the letters.

After sitting through several dance sets, I go in search of the mamasan, avoiding eye contact with the male clients. I feel like a banned antidote to their erotic arousal. Two young dancers waiting at the edge of the stage avert their eyes from me. The mamasan stands to the side dressed in a long silk sarong slit up one side and stiletto heels that make her tower over the naked girls. She is a gracious hostess who shows no sign of curiosity about my reason for being there. I learn that because her father deserted her family, she never attended school and can neither write nor read. "I only have a mum with nothing," she says. Poverty forced her into prostitution in the provinces when she was very young, and she eventually worked her way to Bangkok. It is a common story among Thai mamasans.

The mamasan maintains a personal network of recruiters who send her girls from all over the country, but she also tours some villages herself. "At first I go to the girl's home and tell her family, 'I see you don't have money. But you will if your daughter comes to Bangkok and works for me.' Sometimes at the beginning a girl is scared and fears it hurts. The first time she goes with a man, I don't let her stay all night. I go with her, wait in the hotel, and when she finish, I take her back to the bar. I negotiate how much a man pays and take the money. I say her the small things, like the man always leaves first the bed. I have to teach her everything that men love, from a blow job to when he wants her to go tomboy. You know, lady with lady." The mamasan and her recruiters constantly scout for young virgins, her top moneymaker. "I always save them for older men who give more money."

When I ask what her mother thinks about her profession, the mamasan shrugs. She just paid for two operations for her mother, "because," she says, "my mum, she don't want to die. She not really like me work here, but she wants to live a long time." Occasionally she still takes clients, but only for top money. "Four months ago I make a jackpot with this American man who not know Thai money." She derives her income from 16 sex workers, ages 14 to 24, who give her half their earnings from sex, drinks, and dancing, and who also cover the rental on the club. "When police do trouble, take girls away, I pay police and bring girls back. Then girls must work back money to me."

THE SEX ECONOMY

Statistics on the actual number of young girls working in either the international or the local sex trade are impossible to come by: prostitution exists in too many forms. Restaurant owners send their waitresses home with diners. Hotel maids are pimped by bellboys or men at the front desk. Salesclerks in department stores hire out as prostitutes. Female caddies will go home with golfers, for a price. Men can find quick relief in bars that specialize in blow jobs, where a bar girl will offer, "I smoke you," and take a man's penis into her mouth on the spot. In massage parlors, men can choose girls displayed in glass cages or behind one-way mirrors with numbers hung around their necks.

It is a trade that has grown steadily over the last three decades, the period when Thailand transformed itself at a rapid and often forced pace from an agricultural nation into an industrialized country. But the rewards of industrialization have not been equally distributed, and the gap between rich and poor has steadily widened. Two thirds of the population are in rural areas where they try to earn a living off a deteriorating land base. The explosion of the sex trade and the resulting trafficking of girls sold by their families or who sell themselves to survive goes to the heart of what has gone awry with Thailand's economic transformation. The current sex trade is not just an unexpected by-product of modernization. It is the result of a distinct strategy of development, one that has been supported by the U.S. and Thai militaries, the United Nations, the World Bank, the International Monetary Fund (IMF), and Western donor nations.

One of the key steps in turning the sex industry into a major commercial sector came in 1967, when Robert S. McNamara, as U.S. secretary of defense, oversaw the signing of a Recreation and Relaxation, or R&R, contract with the Thai government to provide vacation furloughs for soldiers fighting in Vietnam. A general in the Thai air force negotiated the treaty, and his wife ran Thailand's first sex-tour agency, Tommy Tours. The agreement shifted Thailand's long-established local prostitution industry into high gear, "upgrading" the extent and quality of services. The U.S. military invested considerable funds and expertise, making the sex industry more efficient in the process. The various agreements among the U.S. military, entrepreneurs, and the Thai government gradually strengthened the government's involvement in the sex trade, and the resulting job opportunities launched an exodus of rural youth from their homes into burgeoning urban centers. Although the U.S. did not introduce prostitution to Thailand, it certainly made the sex trade more visible, better organized, and more lucrative.

In 1971, McNamara returned to Thailand, this time as president of the World Bank, to discuss with government leaders their fears of economic collapse once the U.S. withdrew from Vietnam. At the time of his visit, the combination of sun, sand, and sex had turned the tourist industry into the nation's fifth largest earner of foreign exchange. A team of World Bank experts followed up McNamara's high-level mission with a 1975 report promoting mass tourism. The bank plan established airlines, tour operators, hotel owners, and the brokers of the sex industry as essential players in the national economy. Tourism became the equivalent of an export, central to the balance of payments, with the male orgasm as one of its mainstays.

Thailand's national and regional leaders implemented the bank's tourism formula, and they could hardly claim ignorance

***Chantawipa Noi Apisuk** works for Empower, which provides sex workers with a safe heaven, health education, counseling, and literacy classes. Women and girls can learn everything from office skills to how to get a client to use a condom.*

about the hidden purpose of the tourist industry. In a speech in 1980, Vice Premier Booncha Rajanasthian exhorted provincial governors "to consider the natural scenery in your provinces together with some forms of entertainment that some of you might consider disgusting and shameful, because we have to consider the jobs that will be created." By the mid-eighties, tourism had become the kingdom's top earner of foreign currency, overtaking even rice production. Travel guides and the government's own tourist literature explicitly encouraged male visitors to satisfy their sexual desires. One advertising campaign from Lauda Airlines, an Austria-based charter service, promoted its Bangkok route with a poster of a half-naked young girl and a postcard that ended with the signoff: "Got to close now. The tarts in the Bangkok Baby Club are waiting for us." In contrast, the Lauda poster advertising its charter to Australia pictured a kangaroo.

> THE SEX TRADE IS THE RESULT OF A DISTINCT STRATEGY OF DEVELOPMENT, ONE THAT HAS BEEN SUPPORTED BY THE U.S. MILITARY, the United Nations, the World Bank, the IMF, and Western donor nations.

Tourist profits and loans from the World Bank, the IMF, and private investors fueled the "economic miracle" that made Thailand dependent on foreign dollars and short on sustainable jobs. The rural population suffered as agriculture stagnated. The government's vigorous promotion of agribusiness diverted water from subsistence farmers and denied them access to credit. Deforestation schemes stripped hillsides of tree cover, causing erosion. The northern and northeast regions, home to many ethnic minorities, were particularly hard-hit by these economic policies—and became the largest supplier of sex workers.

Then in 1997, the economy collapsed under the weight of drastic currency devaluation, stock market plunges, and business failures. Growth slowed sharply, yet the ILO reported in 1998 that the sex industry showed no signs of slowing down: the devaluation of Thailand's currency has made sex tourism an even cheaper thrill for foreigners, and the sex workers who serve local men have simply lowered their prices to accommodate the new economic realities. Sex workers are now the primary breadwinners for many families: according to the ILO, urban prostitutes transfer U.S. $300 million in net income to rural families annually, a sum that exceeds the budget of many government development programs. It's not surprising that many experts believe Thailand cannot afford to give up or even curtail the sex trade without serious economic consequences.

One way to grasp the human implications of such a vast enterprise is to visit Empower, a sex-worker support organization with centers in Patpong and in the northern city of Chiang Mai. The group provides prostitutes with a safe haven, counseling, and courses in Thai literacy, English, office skills, and health education. On the day I visit the Bangkok center, I spy a bulletin board that offers a handy list of replies to the most common lines from clients who don't want to use a condom:

He: *I don't like condoms.* She: *Why don't you try them. I heard you stay hard longer with condoms.*

He: *I don't have a condom.* She: *I do. We can use mine.*

He: *No girl has ever asked me to use a condom, what sort of a girl are you?* She: *I'm a girl who cares about myself, my family, and my partner.*

In a corner of the office, a teenager sits alone, pecking at an old manual typewriter. I ask about her job. Her answer has my translator struggling to find the right word. "You know fire? She shows fire, uh, she's full of fire." I shake my head, not understanding, as I picture her dancing over a bed of flames with burning torches in her hand, rather like the fire baton routines of my high school majorette days. Everyone talks together in Thai. "Oh, sorry, she blows fire. She dances and smokes cigarettes out of her vagina."

When I ask her age, the girl, Bua, says 18, as do all the girls in Patpong now that the government has taken a stance against child prostitution. An Empower volunteer later tells me Bua just turned 15. She was recruited for sex work two years earlier by a woman who came to her village. Her mamasan kicked her out when she became pregnant, so she returned home to have her baby, who was stillborn. By then her father had taken a younger wife, leaving her mother destitute. Bua had no option but to find work fast. She and a friend caught a bus to Bangkok, where they arrived with no money but one essential asset: the name of a recruiter for a Patpong club. Bua has since brought two younger sisters and a cousin to work in Patpong. They sleep in shifts in her one-room apartment. "I speak with my mother about my work," she says. "Everybody in family knows what I do. I support them all. They unhappy if money not arrive every month."

GREEN HARVEST

WHEN A GIRL ENTERS SEX WORK, HER RELATIVES TYPICALLY RECEIVE a loan that can range from 6,000 Thai baht ($170) all the way to 90,000 baht ($2,600) for a virgin. (At press time, 35 baht equaled U.S. $1). Interest payments often double the loan, and employers usually charge for living expenses, makeup, clothing, medical care, and bribes to officials. The girl must pay back all the recruiting and transportation expenses. Until her debts are paid, she receives a weekly salary of approximately 10 percent of her earnings. Once she's paid off the debt, she will get to keep around half. With the average per capita income around 105,000 baht, ($3,000), and with rural families often earning much less, parents who once barely scraped a living out of the soil are financially comfortable on the advance and the earnings sent home. *Tok khiew,* or green harvest, is a term for the green rice paddy a farmer in sudden economic need pledges to a miller in exchange for only half the crop's market value. Selling prepubescent daughters has become so common that *tok khiew* now also refers to a farmer's offer of his daughter to the sex trade in exchange for cash.

The majority of the girls end up in local brothels that serve Thai men and migrant workers. These usually employ several dozen girls, each of whom takes six to ten clients a day for at least 25 days a month. Because the profits are smaller than in the international trade, the working conditions are bleaker and the abuse less visible.

> "OUR CULTURE OBLIGATES GIRLS TO LOOK AFTER THEIR PARENTS WHEN THEY GROW OLDER and for many, prostitution is the only way to do this."

Hoping to visit a local brothel, I travel north to Mae Sai, a town on the border with Burma. On my first evening there, I wander with a translator through the red-light district in a torrential downpour until a gust of wind destroys my umbrella. Two girls watching from the porch of an unmarked wooden house wave for us to come inside. In the parlor, four girls play cards around a table and shyly ignore us. They are dressed up, in full makeup, ready for customers. A photo calendar of Thailand's King Bhumibol and Queen Sirikit hangs above an elaborate red and gold altar to Buddha and his guardian deities. We learn that the mamasan, born to poor Chinese immigrants, makes daily offerings of incense, fruit, and tea at this altar to purify and protect her family business.

Several years ago, the government officially closed all brothels in response to an international outcry against child prostitution. Most quickly disguised themselves as "entertainment" businesses—restaurants, stores, and karaoke bars. This particular brothel masquerades as a shop. A kiosk has been installed like a stage set along a wall of the parlor. The store windows display two boxes of detergent and a few packages of dried noodles, potato chips, and candies.

We manage to talk with the girls right in front of the manasan because my translator shifts among English, Thai, Burmese, and minority dialects. Whenever the mamasan grows curious or suspicious, we talk with her about her early life of desperate poverty, her anger at her husband's new mistress, and her children, who attend Bangkok schools paid for by her brothel earnings. Our first conversation is with a young Chinese girl who bends over her spread fingernails in studious concentration, painting them red. Her shoulder-length black hair is held back by a barrette of smiling teddy bears. She describes how her father and an agent brought her across the Chinese and Burmese borders, dressed in traditional robes with

her hair twisted into tight rolls, to a job as a domestic helper. She was treated so badly that she fled to the brothel. When her parents finally learned where she worked, her father returned to Thailand, not to bring her home, but to take a load of 40,000 baht ($1,150) from the mamasan. "I have three younger sisters and I begged him not to bring them," she says.

The only customer to brave the storm during our visit roars up on a motorcycle and peels off a 150 baht note (approximately $4 at the time) for the mamasan. He points to the youngest girl, a 13-year-old from Burma, and follows her through a doorway. I time their encounter on a Felix-the-Cat clock ticking beside the calender with the Queen and King, and exactly 30 minutes later, he reappears, buckling his belt. The tiny girl beside him looks like an exquisite doll. Her first employer hired her as a maid for several months until he could sell her for a "virgin price" to a brothel in Chiang Rai. She ended up hooked on amphetamines and now works off a debt so heavy the mamasan won't let her out of her sight.

Brothels for local men traditionally display new arrivals in a *hong bud boree sut,* which translates as "the room to unveil virgins." Girls like the 13-year-old in this Mae Sai brothel could sometimes remain there for days or weeks while the owner haggled over a price with potential customers. Since the government passed the anti-child-prostitution act in 1996, owners and customers have handled the transactions more discreetly. "Virgins are usually ordered by customers willing to spend thousands of dollars for one night because the men want to reinvigorate themselves," says Sudarat Sereewwat, secretary-general of FACE (Coalition to Fight Against Child Exploitation), a nongovernmental organization (NGO) that monitors child trafficking and abuse.

Several hours into our visit, two policemen cruise by in a squad car and back up to stare at me. They yell out, "Got any girls in there?" Smiling and shaking her head no, the mamasan goes over to the window to banter with them. She roars with laughter at her own joke about how the policemen must think I'm one of the new girls in the brothel. We learn that all the girls who work for her are undocumented immigrants under the age of 18, but no one bothers to hide what is going on.

POVERTY PLUS

THE FIRST WHO PROFIT ARE PARENTS OR RELATIVES," SAYS SAISUREE Chutikul, a senator, former cabinet minister, and longtime advocate for the rights of women and children. She has spent years trying to understand the social forces that push girls to enter sex work at ever-earlier ages. "Second are agents. We have the pimps, the brothel owners, the managers, the procurers, the transporters. We have hotel owners and tour operators. And those police and officials earning bribes. So they all work together in a highly organized network that gets a big boost from our national policy to promote tourism."

But it's not poverty alone, Chutikul insists, that drives a girl into the sex industry. "The cause is poverty plus: plus no education, plus no vocational skill, plus discrimination against girls. We also have poverty plus *kah nam nom,* which translates to 'to pay back your mother's breast milk.' Our culture obligates girls to look after their parents when they grow older

Though she's a senator and an advisor to the office of the prime minister, **Saisuree Chutikul** *takes a no-nonsense approach to changing the behavior of Thai men: "I ask men why they don't masturbate instead of going to child prostitutes. They nearly die. They think if you do that, your mental ability becomes defective."*

and for many, prostitution is the only way to do this. The worst is poverty plus the greed of the parents or relatives. You send your girl to the brothel because you want a television, a house, or an air conditioner." Chutikul says that in previous years, recruiters took catalogs to parents: "If the parents like a certain house, the agent says, 'If I have your girl for three years, we'll build this house right away. This bigger house, your girl for five years.' "

Recruitment practices, however, are changing since the economic collapse. More girls are voluntarily entering the trade directly from their villages without involving recruiting agents. "Before, the agents had to go to the village and arrange everything," says Sompop Jantraka, a rock star turned social activist who founded the Development and Education Program for Daughters and Communities, in Mae Sai. "Now there are agents who just sit in big cities and a local middleman can pick up a mobile phone and arrange travel and a meeting place. Some girls now travel down to the job alone." Thai women are also more likely to seek out agents who will help them go abroad as sex workers, because they can no longer earn enough money at home.

One of the most alarming trends has been the enormous supply of young girls from Burma, Cambodia, Laos, Vietnam, and China, fleeing civil strife, famine, poverty, and failed development policies. The girls are ripe for exploitation because they don't speak the language and are working without documents. The largest influx is from Burma, and in general, the Burmese girls have less money, education, and access to information than Thai girls. As a result, the local brothels are now filled with undocumented immigrants at risk of finding themselves in slaverylike conditions. "These dismal buildings are often sealed up so tight, the girls never have any fresh air. Loud music goes all the time," says Sanphasit Koompraphant of the Center to Protect Children's Rights, who has led a number of raids to free trapped girls. "Many are forced to live and work in tiny rooms, sometimes 24 hours a day, some even chained to their beds. They often work without enough food to eat. Toilets are crude and clean water is in short supply."

"Trafficking is really a migration issue about girls traveling to whatever jobs are available to them," says Therese Caouette, who compiled a report for Human Rights Watch on sex trafficking from Burma into Thailand. "I've seen people trafficked into construction sites or factories in conditions similar to brothels."

Among the many girls Caouette interviewed was Lin Lin, who was 13 years old when an agent offered her father 16,800 baht ($480) for her. According to Caouette's report, "Lin Lin worked in . . . four different [local] brothels, all but one owned by the same family. . . . Her clients, who often included police,

paid the owner $4 each time. If she refused a client's demands, the owner slapped and threatened her." By the time Thai police raided her brothel, Lin Lin "spent over two years of her young life in compulsory prostitution, and tested positive for the human immunodeficiency virus, or HIV."

HIV infection is a looming threat for the girls in the sex industry. Close to a million Thais are reported to be infected. According to the *New England Journal of Medicine,* by 1993 the number of HIV-positive Thais was roughly equal to the number in the United States, which has a population four times as large and an epidemic that has been in existence twice as long. Researchers don't know precisely how many of the infected are young girls. But they do know that HIV transmission in Thailand is mainly heterosexual, and according to the 1998 UN/AIDS report, female sex workers have the highest risk.

Many customers, both foreign and local, now seek out ever-younger girls in the belief that they are free of the HIV. In fact, the opposite is more likely to be true. Young girls are particularly vulnerable to vaginal and anal wounds that expose them to the deadly infection. Preliminary research also suggests that vaginal mucous may act as a barrier to viral transmission, and that young girls produce less of it than older women. Even a condom is no guarantee of protection: repeated intercourse over a short period of time may cause friction sores that aid HIV transmission. For these reasons, public health experts now fear that HIV is widespread among the young girls in the sex trade.

Thailand's exploding AIDS crisis has played a major role in fanning international and local outrage against the trafficking of girls. Bowing to pressure from activists, the government passed laws in 1996 and 1997 that outlaw child prostitution, ban parents from indenturing their children, reduce a prostitute's punishment from imprisonment to a fine, and increase the penalties for agents and brothel owners who traffic girls or women.

But Therese Caouette doubts whether the anti-child-prostitution law will prove effective in its current form. "Most trafficked girls have no documents," she says. "If asked, they always say they are 18. Without convincing evidence, no one can prosecute anybody, so everyone is off the hook." Caouette says targeting working conditions is a better strategy: "If they're locked in, if there's barbed wire, if there are armed guards, if they're slaves to debt bondage, that should be enough to prosecute, without the need to also prove age."

And stiffer punishments do not necessarily mean a greater number of convictions, because tougher laws cost more to enforce and demand more specific trial evidence and rigorous witness selection. "We still have a problem of identifying who are the trafficking victims and persuading them to bring charges or to testify," says government prosecutor Wanchai Roujanawong. "Thailand has no witness protection, even though the constitution directs us to have one. We lack the know-how, and models such as the U.S. protection program are too expensive for us. And if a child's family is involved, what child is going to testify against her own family?"

"The new laws passed just as our economy collapsed," says Sudarat Sereewat of FACE, who has taken on the daunting challenge of monitoring police raids and court cases nation-wide. " We've seen no big difference yet, because there has been no money for public awareness or seminars to educate the police." In fact, when Sereewat monitored a raid in the beach resort of Pattaya last January, "The police didn't even have a copy of the new law." Enforcement will also require a major effort to get police and judges to bring charges and try cases under the new trafficking law and not the existing prostitution codes, which are much less punitive and treat the sex workers as offenders. "Many law enforcers have no idea about the shift from punishing prostitutes to criminalizing those who exploited the girls," says Saisuree Chutikul. "We're promoting a revolution in law enforcement, telling them to now think of the girls as victims, not criminals."

The question remains whether the government will commit its resources to enforcing the new laws or merely pay them lip service. Human Rights Watch contends that the sex trade could not operate at its current scope without the involvement of government officials, border guards, military personnel, and police who alternately raid brothels and profit from them.

It's also uncertain whether officials are willing to confront the lack of jobs for young people. The vast majority of the thousands of girls who enter the sex industry each year set out from home with little education and few skills or job prospects. Certainly, no other work can offer a comparable salary. The average prostitute in a local brothel earns at least twice as much—and a Bangkok prostitute up to 20 times as much—as a domestic servant or factory worker.

Despite the tremendous challenges, NGOs in Asia have begun pursuing human rights projects over the last decade that confront the widespread poverty, inequality, and discrimination that allow trafficking to thrive. They are cautiously encouraged. In 1993, when Therese Caouette investigated trafficking from Burma, "It was hard to find anyone who believed it was a problem. Now trafficking has become a big issue, talked about in the international arena and in Thailand's government circles. The situation won't change overnight, but it won't ever operate like it used to. I feel certain, slowly, slowly the exploitation of young girls is going to change and they will be protected." Slowly, slowly political pressure and new legal tools promise to shift the balance of payments in this pervasive trade and confront the squandering of girls' lives. But how many girls and women will be sacrificed before this change occurs?

> "IT WON'T CHANGE OVERNIGHT, BUT I FEEL CERTAIN THAT SLOWLY, SLOWLY, the exploitation of young girls is going to change and they will be protected."

Betty Rogers is a writer and radio journalist who has produced documentaries on sex trafficking in Thailand and the former Soviet Union for National Public Radio. This article is excerpted from her book-in-progress on international trafficking.

Is AIDS Forever?

Experts now agree that a vaccine is our only hope of stopping the pandemic. The quest to develop one is gaining momentum.

By Geoffrey Cowley

To most Americans, the story of AIDS is one of scientists racing to develop better treatments, and succeeding. During the past couple of years, potent new drugs have eased AIDS mortality throughout the developed world, and preventive efforts have slowed the spread of HIV. But if you've come to think humanity is winning out over the virus, consider a few numbers. Worldwide, according to a new report from the United Nations' AIDS office (UNAIDS), a staggering 30 million people are now living with HIV. Nearly 6 million contracted the virus last year alone—some 16,000 every day. And because 90 percent of all infected people live in the developing countries of Asia and sub-Saharan Africa, where Band-Aids are a luxury, few will ever see a protease inhibitor. Most will die within a decade, UNAIDS predicts. And most will have no idea they're infected until they've had several years to pass the virus to others.

How can this juggernaut be stopped? Campaigns against needle sharing and unsafe sex can help, but they won't stop the spread of AIDS—not in countries like Zimbabwe and Botswana, where one in four adults is already HIV-positive. Our only real hope, experts now agree, is to create a preventive vaccine. As scientists, activists and health officials gather at the world AIDS conference in Geneva this week, no one is predicting imminent victory. But the goal is beginning to seem feasible. Everyone from Bill Gates to Bill Clinton is pledging support for a research effort on the scale of the Manhattan Project, and scientists are reporting real headway. "There's a lot of cautious optimism," says Dr. Anthony Fauci, director of the National Institute of Allergy and Infectious Disease, "that we'll have a vaccine within the next 10 years."

The goal, of course, is to train the immune system to recognize and ward off HIV. Researchers are pursuing several different strategies, and a number of teams are now testing experimental vaccines in humans. Just last week a California firm called VaxGen launched a trial that will involve 7,000 volunteers in the United States and Thailand. The test subjects—mainly gay men and IV drug users who test negative for HIV—will receive serial injections of either placebo or a formulation called AIDSVax. Researchers will then advise both groups to avoid risky behavior, and follow their subsequent infection rates. AIDSVax consists of tiny fragments of "gp 120," the appendage that HIV uses to bind with target cells. If the vaccine works as intended, it will trigger the production of antibodies—and the antibodies will stick to critical regions of gp 120, preventing HIV from infecting susceptible cells.

Unfortunately, few experts expect that to happen. During the 14 years that compounds like AIDSVax have been knocking around in labs, researchers have learned that gp 120 is

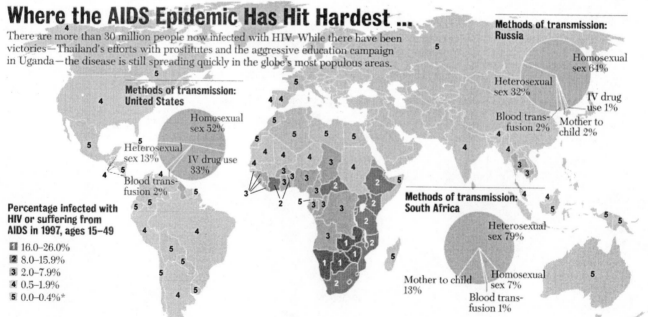

Where the AIDS Epidemic Has Hit Hardest ...

There are more than 30 million people now infected with HIV. While there have been victories—Thailand's efforts with prostitutes and the aggressive education campaign in Uganda—the disease is still spreading quickly in the globe's most populous areas.

Methods of transmission: United States
Homosexual sex 52%
Heterosexual sex 13%
IV drug use 33%
Blood transfusion 2%

Methods of transmission: Russia
Homosexual sex 64%
Heterosexual sex 32%
IV drug use 1%
Blood transfusion 2%
Mother to child 2%

Methods of transmission: South Africa
Heterosexual sex 79%
Mother to child 13%
Homosexual sex 7%
Blood transfusion 1%

Percentage infected with HIV or suffering from AIDS in 1997, ages 15–49
1. 16.0–26.0%
2. 8.0–15.9%
3. 2.0–7.9%
4. 0.5–1.9%
5. 0.0–0.4%*

*DATA NOT AVAILABLE FOR GREENLAND, ICELAND, FR. GUIANA, KASHMIR, TAIWAN, AND WESTERN SAHARA. SOURCE: UNITED NATIONS. RESEARCH BY BILL YOURVOULIAS. GRAPHIC BY DIXON ROHR—NEWSWEEK

the shiftiest part of the virus. It mutates so fast that its structure can differ by 30 percent from one strain of HIV to the next. AIDSVax may elicit antibodies to one or two strains, but it won't cover them all, and its effect will wane as HIV evolves. But that's just part of the problem. Antibodies, by themselves, may not adequately protect us from *any* strain of HIV. They can help subdue free-floating virus, but they can't destroy infected cells. And as Harvard immunologist Norman Letvin observes, HIV often travels via cells, passing directly between them. The immune system can learn to kill those cells, but priming it requires a different kind of vaccine.

Several companies are now racing to develop one. One promising candidate is HGP-30W, an experimental vaccine developed by the Virginia-based Cel-Sci Corp. Cel-Sci's trick was to identify a stable region of HIV—a protein segment from the core of the virus that holds its form while other parts mutate. When a person is injected with that molecule, specialized immune cells cut it up and display pieces of it on their outer surfaces, priming the rest of the immune system to attack any cell that harbors it. The question is whether that's enough to protect people. When Cel-Sci researchers placed blood from immunized humans in 50 lab mice, then injected the animals with various strains of HIV, 78 percent resisted infection. But large-scale clinical trials are still a couple of years off.

While VaxGen and Cel-Sci pursue their disparate strategies, other teams are developing vaccines that combine elements of both.

At the French company Pasteur Merieux Connaught, for example, researchers have engineered a canary-pox virus that carries the genes for three components of HIV: the surface protein used in AIDSVax, the core protein used in HGP-30W and one enzyme. The genetically altered bird virus infects human cells, without causing illness. And it primes the immune system to attack both free-floating virus and HIV-infected cells. If the altered virus can infiltrate the mucosal cells that line the rectum and vagina, the resulting immune response may help the body stop HIV before it even enters the bloodstream.

"A safe vaccine may leave many people unprotected. And an effective vaccine may make some people sick."

All these vaccines appear safe. But can any vaccine based on pieces of HIV provoke strong enough immunity to protect people out in the world? Some experts doubt it. Ronald Desrosiers, a vaccine researcher at Harvard Medical School and the New England Regional Primate Research Center, notes that whole, weakened viruses have been our best weapon against polio and smallpox. And he believes that live HIV is what will ultimately save humankind from AIDS. By deleting certain genes from simian AIDS viruses (the so-called SIVs), Desrosiers has created highly effective monkey vaccines. He's now eager to test the same principle in people. Working with Massachusetts-based Therion Biologics, he has engineered a type of HIV that can infect human cells but lacks three of the real virus's nine genes. Experience suggests this vaccine would outperform the others now in development—and several hundred AIDS experts are so eager to see it tested that they've volunteered to serve as guinea pigs. The concern, shared by Therion, is that the weakened virus might cause AIDS in people with feeble immune systems, or evolve toward more virulent forms once it was in wide use.

How much risk is worth taking? In the not-too-distant future, we may have to choose between safe vaccines that leave many people unprotected, and effective vaccines that make some people sick. Governments may have to decide whether flawed vaccines are better than no vaccines, and manufacturers will face ethical dilemmas about testing and marketing. But with luck, we won't have to watch idly as HIV continues its ghastly world tour.

With MARIAN WESTLEY *and* ERIKA CHECK

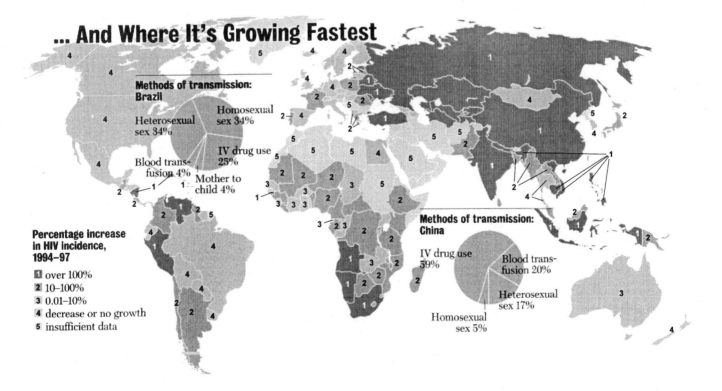

... And Where It's Growing Fastest

Methods of transmission: Brazil
Heterosexual sex 34%
Homosexual sex 34%
IV drug use 25%
Blood transfusion 4%
Mother to child 4%

Percentage increase in HIV incidence, 1994–97
1 over 100%
2 10–100%
3 0.01–10%
4 decrease or no growth
5 insufficient data

Methods of transmission: China
IV drug use 59%
Blood transfusion 20%
Heterosexual sex 17%
Homosexual sex 5%

State Abandons Kidnapped Kids

By Timothy W. Maier

Two State Department reports—yet to be made public but obtained by *Insight*—don't tell true story of the government's failure to help rescue children abducted to foreign countries.

Whitewash, deceit and cover-up are some of the charges levied by parents against the Department of State concerning two draft government reports on the status of international abduction of children. The reports sidestep concerns raised by Senate Foreign Relations Committee Chairman Jesse Helms of North Carolina during hearings last fall. Moreover, the unpublished drafts fail to portray what really happens when children are abducted by estranged spouses to foreign countries that ignore U.S. laws.

Obtained by **Insight** as part of this magazine's continuing investigation into official treatment of aggrieved parents caught in international tugs-of-war, the reports deal with (1) the Hague Convention, an international treaty signed by 54 countries that promises the return of abducted children, and (2) a multiagency task-force analysis of the ongoing problems associated with international child abduction.

The first is a 44-page report to Congress on *Compliance With the Hague Convention on the Civil Aspects of International Child Abduction*. It was written by Mary Ryan, assistant secretary of state for consular affairs, and Barbara Larkin, assistant secretary of state for legislative affairs.

The Hague report is intended to respond to Helms' demands that State produce a list of "all countries" that have failed to return abducted children, a list of all outstanding parental-abduction cases involving European nations, a list of all countries that protect kidnappers and much more. But the authors fail to provide the requested details and, instead, use diplomatic terms and phrases that sources tell **Insight** are designed to skirt issues raised by Helms and the many U.S. parents clamoring for assistance and an end to stonewalling.

The second document—a 47-page report titled *Subcommittee on International Child Abduction of Federal Agency Task Force on Missing and Exploited Children and the Policy Group on International Parental Kidnapping*—was produced under the auspices of Attorney General Janet Reno's office but coordinated and written by the State Department with input from the Justice Department and the National Center for Missing and Exploited Children, or NCMEC. It is to be delivered to Reno by the end of May.

Neither of these draft reports, which are being circulated within the federal government for comment, deal with the fact that most abducted or illegally detained children never return home. Ryan's report fails even to name the countries involved in protecting child abductors in 84 unresolved cases that are at least 18 months old. Arguments that naming the countries and/or the children might harm ongoing and mostly private efforts to rescue and return the children are not relevant, say parents and those involved in recovery efforts, since the names and pictures of the missing kids are provided freely by the NCMEC.

When State does list the five worst offending countries in one section of Ryan's report, the children are not identified. The five cited as failing habitually to honor the treaty are Austria, Honduras, Mauritius, Mexico and Sweden.

But conspicuously missing from this list is Germany. That, no doubt, will be shocking news to Lady Catherine Meyer, whose case involving abduction of her two sons to Germany has received wide media attention. She spent $200,000 in court and legal fees but has failed to get her boys back.

After children abducted by a parent to Germany have lived there for one year, the German courts claim it would harm the child's health to return him or her to the lawful custodial parent in the United States. Joseph Howard, whose 10-year-old daughter Priscilla was abducted by his ex-wife to Germany five years ago, shared with **Insight** some explosive records he obtained from Germany confirming that country habitually violates the Hague treaty. The State Department's own records show that of 243 such cases filed in Germany there were only 40 court-ordered returns, which is 16.4 percent. Germany's report to the European parliament on Hague cases puts returns at a paltry 9 percent. "These records should be available for every parent," says Howard, who spent 21 years in the U.S. Army, including a tour in the Persian Gulf War. "Why is the State Department covering up for Germany's criminal behavior?"

Howard hasn't filed a Hague petition. "Lady Catherine spent $200,000 and, with all the diplomatic connections she has, all she got was 11 hours with her two children," he says. "I'm a poor soldier. I don't even have an address or phone number for my child. I just can't afford to file a Hague petition."

So Howard turned to the Department of Justice seeking an international-fugitive warrant. Justice refused, saying such a warrant would prevent the mother from ever returning to the United States to challenge the U.S. court's custody ruling. It turns out that federal warrants are issued in less than one-tenth of 1 percent of international parental-kidnapping cases. As Howard observes, "Parental kidnapping is therefore an easy, viable way of obtaining custody or changing an American custody order."

Senate sources charge that the "Reno" task-force report champions the process but fails to explain how the system is broken and needs to be fixed. As one government source familiar with this multiagency report says, "The State Department knows that parents have two choices: Write off the child or do a rescue mission." The task-force report even fails to show that foreign countries have little respect for U.S. laws or court orders in, these matters and often lack procedures to enforce access or visitation, the source says. It often paints the crime as victimless and neglects the fact that parents as well as children are victims of this combination of foreign-treaty violations, unenforceable laws, prosecutorial discretion and the unwillingness of the State Department to rock the diplomatic boat, even to protect kidnapped children. And neither report so much as suggests that the NCMEC might deal as effectively with the outgoing cases as it does with the incoming cases where children are abducted from a foreign country and taken to the United States. Here such cases are handled quite effectively, with a 90 percent return rate. "The national center is frozen out of all the outgoing cases," says a senior government insider close to the issue.

Nancy Hammer, director of the NCMEC, says the national center should be involved in these cases, but "I guess we could upset foreign countries and be blamed for destroying relations." The Reno task-force report suggests that might be something to discuss, which infuriates advocates at the NCMEC because nowhere in their charter are they restricted to helping

only parents whose children still are living in the United States.

Questioned generally about the multi-agency report drafted for Reno, Hammer faxed a statement to **Insight** explaining that the NCMEC did not participate in the policy group that authored the task-force report but is familiar with its findings. "This type of interagency communication and cooperation has been needed for a long time," the statement says. "Although we are optimistic about more proactive involvement by individual agencies, actions speak louder than words and the true level of commitment on the part of the government to the victims of international child abduction remains to be seen."

The task-force report often paints the crime as victimless and neglects the unwillingness of State to rock the diplomatic boat, even to protect children.

She elaborates in a telephone interview, characterizing the task-force report as "glorifying the process," which includes federal responses, civil remedies and international treaties. "In reality that's about how one or two cases are handled and it is by no means the majority of cases," she says. Hammer couches her words carefully, perhaps sensitive to the need to maintain a civil working relationship with the State Department, but sources close to the NCMEC tell **Insight** the national center is exasperated by the lack of cooperation from State.

The multiagency task-force report says the State Department has no idea how many international parental abduction cases there have been, but State acknowledges handling 11,000 such cases since the 1970s. Ryan relies on Hague figures to suggest success of the process, failing to note that many of these are incoming cases in which children abducted illegally to the United States are returned. And these numbers leave out the many cases in-

volving abduction to most of the Middle East and other non-Hague countries.

Regardless, Ryan now tells **Insight** that of 1,124 Hague cases processed from May 1997 to March 1999, 52 percent or 580 have been "closed." She does not say how many children were returned to the United States. Parents tell **Insight** they expect Helms to ask that question and get an answer. They think the number is so low as to be appalling.

Helms was unavailable for comment. But sources tell **Insight** the Senate Judiciary Committee is anxious to hold hearings once the multiagency Reno task-force report is released. Says one committee source, "This administration cares more about foreign relations than about American children. It's ludicrous."

Once the hearings begin, the Judiciary Committee may want to find out whether the State Department suborned witnesses in prior testimony to downplay criticism, according to sources who claim this happened during Helms' hearings last fall. The Judiciary Committee also should bring in the General Accounting Office, or GAO, investigators who were tasked to conduct a probe into the matter by House International Relations Committee Chairman Benjamin Gilman of New York. **Insight** has learned the GAO probe, expected to be completed this month, has run into some major roadblocks. Sources in and out of government charge the State Department has been less than cooperative with GAO investigators, and there appears to be some political hardball being played inside the GAO office with senior management officials withholding the resources and manpower necessary to do a thorough job. As one insider says, there is a major split with some investigators wanting to come down hard on the State Department for incompetence and higher ups pushing for a "toned-down" report.

When **Insight** shared some of the findings in these unpublished State Department-led reports with parents who recently attended the 1999 International Parental Abduction Conference in Arlington, Va., most were deeply disappointed. Particularly upsetting was a task-force declaration that these are "private custody disputes" and the general omission of concern that prosecutors refuse to enforce or implement the 1993 International Parental Kidnapping Act, resulting in virtually no convictions. Instead, the Reno task-force draft reaffirms the view of the State Department's Ryan, author of the Hague draft report, who criticized "Kids Held Hostage" (March 8) in a long letter published by this magazine. Ryan's letter and, in particular, the labeling of these kidnappings as "custody disputes" have raised the ire of frustrated parents who carry around briefcases of custody orders, copies of international warrants and receipts showing their expenditures of hundreds of thousands of dollars. Many have bankrupted themselves fighting corrupt foreign courts unwilling to honor international law and a reluctant Justice Department unwilling to file for international criminal-arrest warrants.

When **Insight** showed some of the parents that Ryan's Hague report listed unresolved cases but omitted names, some searched in vain for their cases by reading the descriptions. The State Department just closes cases if it decides there is no chance of ever bringing the child home, parents charge, something senior department officials recently have confirmed to **Insight**.

At the end of their conference the parents gathered outside the White House and held a candlelight vigil in hope of turning their cases into a human-rights crusade. Despite first lady Hillary Rodham Clinton's snub of the Arlington conference, and following **Insight**'s May 10 follow-up story, "Kidnapped Kids Cry Out for Help," comments by the first lady at a separate British Embassy fund-raising event have given hope to these grieving and angry parents that their cause yet may receive official support. Clinton told those gathered at the $500-per-plate dinner, "This is an international issue, and this is a human-rights issue."

But parents wonder if that is mere lip service. A recent internal teletype memo obtained by **Insight** and sent from a U.S. Embassy in Europe to Secretary of State Madeleine Albright suggests Hillary may have spoken out of turn. The teletype cautioned against turning parental-abduction cases into human-rights issues. The U.S. ambassador is hesitant "to have this matter raised in the Human Rights Report until it could be determined that there was a clear pattern of such an abuse."

With parental abductions climbing into the thousands, and more and more studies showing that children are psychologically and sometimes physically harmed by these kidnap-

Stolen child: *The fact is that most abucted or illegally detained children are never returned to the U.S.*

pings, aggrieved parents wonder how many more cases it will take to convince the State Department and the White House to take this matter as seriously as the Justice Department and the Clinton administration take cases of domestic child abduction. "It may never happen," says an inside source. "As soon as the bureaucrats can say this is a custody case and not a human-rights violation or crime, that gets the government out of the problem. So both the State and the Justice departments have a vested interest in labeling it just that—child-custody cases. Then they don't have to monitor anything."

Indeed, the Reno task-force report claims: "The federal government has limited power to respond to international abductions once the abductor and child reach a foreign country." But parents see this as a bold-faced lie, considering such potential remedies as freezing financial assets of kidnappers who continue to do business in the United States, denying visas and passport renewals to kidnappers and their families or even cutting off U.S. assistance to countries such as Egypt that continue to hold American children illegally.

Many victimized parents expect little to result from these two yet-to-be-released reports. While the Reno taskforce report advises greater access to files for parents concerning their cases, internal documents reviewed by **Insight** show the State Department consistently refuses to provide records and has opposed all legislation that would require annual audits or greater openness on this issue. Some records belittled the parents, calling them "mentally unbalanced," or showed that the State Department had been advising the kidnapper about obtaining an attorney.

Tom Sylvester of Ohio knows this all too well. His 13-month-old daughter Carina was abducted by his ex-wife to Austria in 1995. Sylvester can't get the State Department to press Austria to abide by the Hague rules, even though the Austrian courts have granted him custody. Convinced of a cover-up, he filed a Freedom of Information Act request two years ago for all the records concerning his child. Not one response. Parents whose children are caught up in this international shell game say this is a too-familiar pattern.

Index

AE Article Review Form

We encourage you to photocopy and use this page as a tool to assess how the articles in **Annual Editions** expand on the information in your textbook. By reflecting on the articles you will gain enhanced text information. You can also access this useful form on a product's book support Web site at **http://www.dushkin.com/ online/.**

NAME: _____ DATE: _____

TITLE AND NUMBER OF ARTICLE: _____

BRIEFLY STATE THE MAIN IDEA OF THIS ARTICLE: _____

LIST THREE IMPORTANT FACTS THAT THE AUTHOR USES TO SUPPORT THE MAIN IDEA:

WHAT INFORMATION OR IDEAS DISCUSSED IN THIS ARTICLE ARE ALSO DISCUSSED IN YOUR TEXTBOOK OR OTHER READINGS THAT YOU HAVE DONE? LIST THE TEXTBOOK CHAPTERS AND PAGE NUMBERS:

LIST ANY EXAMPLES OF BIAS OR FAULTY REASONING THAT YOU FOUND IN THE ARTICLE:

LIST ANY NEW TERMS/CONCEPTS THAT WERE DISCUSSED IN THE ARTICLE, AND WRITE A SHORT DEFINITION:

ANNUAL EDITIONS revisions depend on two major opinion sources: one is our Advisory Board, listed in the front of this volume, which works with us in scanning the thousands of articles published in the public press each year; the other is you—the person actually using the book. Please help us and the users of the next edition by completing the prepaid article rating form on this page and returning it to us. Thank you for your help!

ANNUAL EDITIONS: Deviant Behavior 00/01

Here is an opportunity for you to have direct input into the next revision of this volume. We would like you to rate each of the 47 articles listed below, using the following scale:

1. Excellent: should definitely be retained
2. Above average: should probably be retained
3. Below average: should probably be deleted
4. Poor: should definitely be deleted

Your ratings will play a vital part in the next revision.
So please mail this prepaid form to us just as soon as you complete it.
Thanks for your help!

We Want Your Advice

RATING

ARTICLE

1. On the Sociology of Deviance
2. Darwin's Truth, Jefferson's Vision: Sociobiology and the Politics of Human Nature
3. Taboo: Don't Even Think about It!
4. Mortality around the World
5. Marks of Mystery
6. Men, Honor and Murder
7. We Are Training Our Kids to Kill
8. Stopping Abuse in Prison
9. Can Hackers Be Stopped?
10. Stolen Identity
11. The Problem with Marriage
12. I'm O.K. You're O.K. So Who Gets the Kids?
13. How Are We Doing with *Loving?* Race, Law & Intermarriage
14. The Perils of Polygamy
15. The Consequences of Violence against Women
16. An American Sweatshop
17. Razing Appalachia
18. It's What's for Dinner
19. What Doctors Don't Know
20. Sex Work: What Are the Rules?
21. Addicted
22. Passion Pills
23. Crank
24. More Reefer Madness
25. Beyond Legalization: New Ideas for Ending the War on Drugs

RATING

ARTICLE

26. Where'd You Learn *That?*
27. The Sex Industry: Giving the Customer What He Wants
28. Who Owns Prostitution—and Why?
29. The Pleasure of the Pain: Why Some People Need S & M
30. Gay No More?
31. Idleness and Lawlessness in the Therapeutic State
32. Social Anxiety
33. Dying to Be Thin
34. The Infection Connection
35. Mental Health Reform: What It Would Really Take
36. Where Bias Begins: The Truth about Stereotypes
37. Corporate Welfare
38. Plucking Workers: Tyson Foods Looks to the Welfare Rolls for a Captive Labor Force
39. Does Silencio = Muerte? Notes on Translating the AIDS Epidemic
40. Hunger in America
41. Q: Should Juries Nullify Laws They Consider Unjust or Excessively Punitive?
42. The Wrong Men on Death Row
43. Crimes of War
44. Yakuza Inc.
45. Bitter Harvest
46. Is AIDS Forever?
47. State Abandons Kidnapped Kids

(Continued on next page)

ANNUAL EDITIONS: DEVIANT BEHAVIOR 00/01

BUSINESS REPLY MAIL
FIRST-CLASS MAIL PERMIT NO. 84 GUILFORD CT

POSTAGE WILL BE PAID BY ADDRESSEE

**Dushkin/McGraw-Hill
Sluice Dock
Guilford, CT 06437-9989**

IIIııııIIııIıııIııIIIıııIIIıIıIıIııIıIıIııIIIıIıI

ABOUT YOU

Name _____ Date _____

Are you a teacher? ☐   A student? ☐
Your school's name _____

Department _____

Address _____ City _____ State ____ Zip ____

School telephone # _____

YOUR COMMENTS ARE IMPORTANT TO US!

Please fill in the following information:
For which course did you use this book?
_____

Did you use a text with this *ANNUAL EDITION*? ☐ yes ☐ no
What was the title of the text?
_____

What are your general reactions to the *Annual Editions* concept?
_____

Have you read any particular articles recently that you think should be included in the next edition?
_____

Are there any articles you feel should be replaced in the next edition? Why?
_____

Are there any World Wide Web sites you feel should be included in the next edition? Please annotate.
_____

May we contact you for editorial input? ☐ yes ☐ no
May we quote your comments? ☐ yes ☐ no